D1715652

THE QUIET EVOLUTION

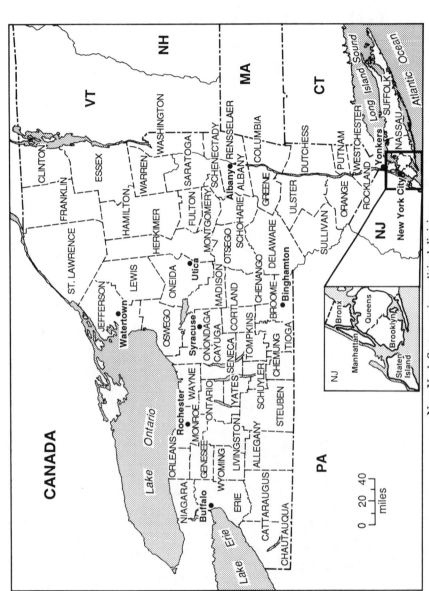

New York State: major political divisions.

THE QUIET EVOLUTION

POWER, PLANNING, AND
PROFITS IN NEW YORK STATE

Michael K. Heiman

PRAEGER

New York
Westport, Connecticut
London

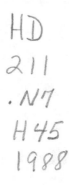

Library of Congress Cataloging-in-Publication Data

Heiman, Michael.
  The quiet evolution.

  Bibliography: p.
  Includes index.
    1. Land use—New York (State)—Planning.   2. Land
use—Government policy—New York (State)   I. Title.
HD211.N7H45   1988   333.73'17'09747   88-5838
ISBN 0-275-92476-9 (alk. paper)

Library of Congress Catalog Card Number: 88-5838
ISBN: 0-275-92476-9

First published in 1988

Praeger Publishers, One Madison Avenue, New York, NY 10010
A division of Greenwood Press, Inc.

Printed in the United States of America

The paper used in this book complies with the
Permanent Paper Standard issued by the National
Information Standards Organization (Z39.48-1984).

10 9 8 7 6 5 4 3 2 1

Contents

Maps

Acknowledgments

The research and observations recorded in the ensuing chapters cover many disciplines, just as land use and planning themselves have physical, economic, political, cultural, and other components. This interdisciplinary breadth is not enigmatic though, particularly for geographers who are trained to recognize spurious divisions in knowledge. The boundaries between disciplines tend to be conservative because they reinforce a division of understanding necessary to train individuals to fit specialized roles in current production systems. Through this differentiation people are robbed of the ability to analyze and grasp the totality of the social systems in which they operate, to penetrate the veil of partial experience to see the underlying forces at work, and, as a result, to effect meaningful change.

I was introduced to the multidisciplinary critical social theory informing my research while a graduate student at University of California Berkeley. There, to my great fortune, I had the honor of working with Allan Pred, Ann Markusen, and Richard Walker, three of the most productive and influential scholars in the social sciences today. Special recognition is due Dick Walker, my principal mentor and a close colleague and friend. His commitment to social justice, critical insight, and uncompromising excellence in scholarship is by now legendary, and he continues to provide a powerful example both for my own work and for that of many other former and future students. No doubt there have been other teachers whose lessons are found between the pages of this book. Among these Pierre Clavel and Richard McNeil from Cornell University, and Carolyn Merchant from Berkeley have been most influential.

As with most projects of such proportion, this book would not have been possible without the generous, enthusiastic, and, yes, even critical commentary and support from numerous individuals. Here at Syracuse University my colleagues John Mercer, John Agnew, Marwyn Samuels, John Western, and Stuart Corbridge reviewed various portions and stages of the text, and Mark

Monmonier provided important insights on graphics and production. Their suggestions and corrections are much appreciated. A special note of thanks is due department chair Robert Jensen for his enduring support for manuscript preparation.

Exceptionally detailed and eloquent reviews of the Hudson Valley material were provided by Jonathan Smith, a doctoral student in our department, and by J. Winthrop Aldrich of the New York State Department of Environmental Conservation. Jonathan's intense cogitation has already distinguished him as one of the brightest young geographers today, while Wint's remarkable tenacity to continue as special assistant to the DEC commissioner while administrators come and go speaks volumes about his service, magnificence, and love for New York State, its landscape, and its history. At the DEC, recognition is also due current and former staff officials Langdon Marsh, Charlie Morrison, Betty Hawkins, and Henry Williams for their inspection of earlier drafts. Added to this list of commentators are Ben Coe of the Tug Hill Commission for his insights on rural planning, Duane Chapman at Cornell on the State Power Authority, David Johnson of the University of Tennessee on the Regional Plan Association, and Jameson Doig of Princeton University for his thorough critique of the chapter on public authorities. Their expert evaluations, and those of other professionals contacted during the course of my research, enabled me to appreciate the gap between literary accounts and administrative practice.

Jim McConnell and Richard Anderson of the Regional Plan Association were both candid and sincere with their opinion on, and correction of, my analysis of their agency. While they may have difficulty recognizing it, the RPA chapter benefited from their forthright review. Additional comments and insights on my work were provided by those indefatigable spirits Victor Jones of UC Berkeley, Frank Popper of Rutgers University, and Nancy Kleniewski of SUNY Geneseo. Their support and enthusiasm were infectious.

Finally, and of greatest consequence for the final product, the detailed and extensive dialogue with Charles Geisler of Cornell was indispensable. It was Chuck who asked the tough questions and introduced me to the literature suggesting a theoretical foundation for my observations on consumption. Moreover, Chuck alone poured through the entire first draft of the manuscript and subsequent revisions thereof. As with his comments and those of the aforementioned scholars and professionals, the observations and criticisms, whether accepted or not, were essential for the sharpening of my argument, even as I bear sole responsibility for the final interpretation.

Turning to institutional support, grateful recognition is given to the journal *Society and Space*, Columbia University Press, and the Regional Plan Association of New York for their generous permission to quote from and reprint passages, maps, and tables to which they hold copyright. At Syracuse University two grants, one through the Senate Research Committee and the other from the Appleby-Mosher Fund, enabled me to visit Berkeley's Institute of Governmental Studies where the finest library on public administration and policy in the country is housed. Under the capable direction of Jack Leister, the talented library staff, and in particular Terry Dean, Ron Heckart, and Marc Levin, were knowledgeable, patient, and ever eager to assist with my numerous information searches. Were it not for the IGS Library and its accessible collection on New York State, I would have had to spend many more months on document retrieval in Albany and New York City.

For map execution I relied upon the very talented staff of Syracuse University's Cartographic Lab under the direction of Michael Kirchoff. Here Margaret Vance, assisted by Tod Logan, prepared all the graphics. Their patience in the face of numerous style requests seemed boundless while their adroit skills speak for themselves in the pages to follow. At Praeger Karen O'Brien is singled out for her enthusiastic direction of manuscript production and senior editor Jim Dunton for his persevering support and encouragement.

My greatest professional debt, and one that can only be acknowledged through our understanding that this book is also her book, belongs to Kay Steinmetz. She took my raw copy and in various guises as typist, copy editor, desktop designer, indexer, and final photocomposer, was responsible for every stage of the manuscript's evolution and appearance. A veritable one-woman publishing house, Kay is easily the most competent, dedicated, and sagacious editor one could hope for. As other authors will attest, most manuscripts would never see the light of day, nor be intelligible, without the major contribution of a handful of dedicated professionals such as Kay.

There are good reasons why most authors recognize their family only at the end of their acknowledgments. These cherished beings form the bedrock upon which all other efforts and aspirations rest. My parents, Martin and Ruth, continue to be a major source of inspiration and encouragement. Born during the gestation of the manuscript, my sons Jonathan and Eric have an enormous influence on my ability to grasp the totality of home and consumption. My wife Paula constantly challenges me to acknowledge that a home is more than just a refuge. Her careful proofing, advice, and unwavering support add immensely to the quality of my work. It is to my family, with love and respect, that this book is dedicated.

Michael K. Heiman
Syracuse, New York

Abbreviations

ALI	American Law Institute
APA	Adirondack Park Agency
CBD	Central Business District
CRPNY	Committee on (the) Regional Plan of New York and Its Environs
DEC	Department of Environmental Conservation (New York State)
DLMA	Downtown-Lower Manhattan Association
EFC	Environmental Facilities Corporation (New York State)
EFCB	Emergency Financial Control Board (New York City)
EIS	Environmental Impact Statement
HFA	Housing Finance Agency (New York State)
HRVC	Hudson River Valley Commission (New York State)
LILCO	Long Island Lighting Company
MAC	Municipal Assistance Corporation (New York City)
MHP	Mid-Hudson Pattern for Progress
MTA	Metropolitan Transportation Authority (New York State)
NAACP	National Association for the Advancement of Colored People
NEPA	National Environmental Policy Act
PASNY	Power Authority of the State of New York
PATH	Port Authority Trans-Hudson (transit line)
RPA	Regional Plan Association (of New York)

RPAA	Regional Planning Association of America
SEQR	State Environmental Quality Review Act (New York State)
SMDA	Syracuse Metropolitan Development Association
SUNY	State University of New York
TBTA	Triborough Bridge and Tunnel Authority (New York City)
UDC	Urban Development Corporation

THE QUIET EVOLUTION

1

Introduction
and Chapter Outlines

A QUIET REVOLUTION IN LAND USE CONTROL?

Property development is a fundamental component of urbanization and the shaping of its spatial dimension. Land use regulation exercised under the police power of the state is, in turn, a basic aspect of property development.[1] Sanctioned through the state planning and zoning enabling acts of the 1920s and 1930s, local control (e.g., city, town, and county control) remains the principal means whereby private land is regulated in the United States. Since the mid-1960s, however, a majority of the states have reassumed a share of the police power originally delegated to municipalities sufficient to address land use issues deemed to be of more than local concern. These include protection of open space and critical environmental areas, energy and industrial facility siting, hazardous and nuclear waste disposal, new town development, and, on a more limited basis, provision for low- and moderate-income housing. First popularized by Fred Bosselman and David Callies in their pivotal 1971 report to the U.S. Council on Environmental Quality, the term "quiet revolution in land use control" has been used to describe this recent state involvement in land use regulation.[2]

Bosselman and Callies' declaration is part of a wide body of literature combining criticism of the existing municipal system of regulation with proposals for reform. This reform literature portrays the thousands of municipal units of government exercising primary land use control as dependent upon property tax for local financing, captive of local business and/or homeowner interests, and technically unable to appreciate regional problems. Hence local governments are depicted as being incapable, by themselves, of effectively dealing with issues of regional, state, and national significance. The suggested reform calls for selective centralization of planning and land use regulations under the aegis of the state sufficient to account for the broader regional interest in land development.[3]

Virtually all of the analyses done by geographers, planners, and social scientists on this so-called quiet revolution of state intervention in local land use control accept too easily the reformist view that a geographic dichotomy exists between parochial economic self-interest, whether expressed in a local progrowth or an antigrowth position, and regional public goals. It is generally assumed that local governments are unwilling or unable to account for the broader environmental and social externalities of their land use decisions. Furthermore, most of the analyses done on state preemption of local regulation accept the reformist categorization of centralized land use regulation as a recent phenomenon, arising primarily out of the environmental movement of the late 1960s and early 1970s and, to a lesser degree, concern with local exclusionary zoning where it blocks regionally beneficial development such as for low- and moderate-income housing or energy projects. Finally, the various attempts at state preemption of local decision making, be they for critical area protection, facility siting, open housing, or any of a variety of goals, are attributed by reformers and planning analysts alike to a single impulse, born of a popular and broad-based recognition that the existing structure of local regulation is somehow inherently unsuited to account for the public's social and environmental interests.

Frank Popper, for example, in a recent book, *The Politics of Land-Use Reform*, traced the origins of the quiet revolution and its move to centralize land use regulation to the late 1960s when a unified environmental movement first realized that local control of planning and zoning was unable to account for the effects of the urban development boom then occurring. In a similar vein Robert Healy's well publicized study for Resources for the Future, *Land Use and the States*, attributed state involvement to growing public knowledge about ecological disruption and concern over the destruction of aesthetic and other natural amenities.[4]

As detailed in the following chapters, these appraisals may prove incomplete, for they fail to acknowledge the political history and complexity of land use regulatory motivations in the United States. While there certainly has been much environmentally motivated legislation in recent years, reform to move the locus of land use decision making to a higher and more centralized unit of government is neither novel nor simply an environmental impulse. Centralization of land use regulation in the United States is a goal that goes back to the last century. Its strongest advocates have included representatives from prodevelopment and large-scale enterprises. Periodically these businesses were concerned that local municipalities were ill prepared or unwilling to accommodate and service their needs. This was most likely to occur when the scale of their operations and resource requirements increased beyond the capacity of local jurisdictions.

Although environmental and social advocates apparently joined the dialogue in large numbers in recent years, evidence suggests that there is no unified public interest exclusively associated with centralized regulation. Rather, social and environmental advocates, as well as business and progrowth supporters, have readily seized upon all levels of government in the federal system to further specific goals, with the favored locus of regulatory control largely a question of political strategy.

Despite the flurry of state legislation in recent years to centralize land use control, the public agenda for reform is neither quiet—as homeowners, developers, and other interest groups continue to battle it out at planning and zoning board meetings and through the ballot box—nor revolutionary in the sense of unprecedented change. Rather, recent state attention to land use is merely the latest manifestation of an ongoing *evolution* in planning and regulation. This occurs as the public sector, or State, at all levels, adjusts to and mediates between competing demands both by pro- and antidevelopment concerns. Moreover, much of the public response to competing demands over land use bypasses democratic participation. To cite a common situation, special authorities and service districts are established with sufficient police power over land use to address particular siting problems without direct recourse to either voter or legislative approval. Whether accountable to the electorate or not, the agenda of public authorities and planning agencies (at all levels) is often prepared by private planning consultants and advocates. These private advocates are themselves accepted by the media and citizenry as serving the public interest. In this manner centralization of land use regulation may proceed in ways that are protected from more animated popular scrutiny and participation. Often overlooked by conventional planning analysts, it is this *quiet evolution* in land use control, born of State response to the changing spatial requirements of capital accumulation as it unfolds in the U.S. political economy, that is the subject of this book.

THE LIBERAL PLANNING REFORM MOVEMENT

The vast bulk of the literature on land use regulatory reform is recognizable by its ideological support for a liberal planning reform movement.[5] The planning reforms advocated are liberal because they promote public intervention to correct deficiencies and address social and environmental problems with a competitive (land) market while still championing the capitalist principles of private property and private ownership of the production process. Regulation thus supplements the market but does not replace it.

Liberal reform movements involve a long process of ideological formation, with problems presented and solutions suggested by a coterie of influential individuals working through policy and planning institutions and at various university-related research centers.[6] Liberal attention to land use reform attains coherence as a movement because already since the 1920s attempts to "reform" local zoning and planning were, and continue to be, led by a small group of influential individuals. Constituting the basis for conventional wisdom on land use reform, their ideas have been uncritically accepted by an entire generation of planners and social scientists. Furthermore, the reformers work out of a handful of private real estate and legal firms, civic organizations, and nonprofit academic or quasi-academic research institutions.[7]

Finally, conventional treatments of the so-called quiet revolution are ideological, indeed participatory advocacy for the most part. They neither acknowledge who promulgates, funds, and benefits from reform, nor do they analyze the economic, cultural, and political context of reform. Concentrating on the geographic scale of regulation as the essence of social conflict rather than on political, economic, or class differences, and examining only the form, structure, and arrangement of the implementation procedure, the liberal reformers overlook the relationship government has to the wider economic and social processes of which it is a part. Moreover, the local versus regional public interest debate ignores divisions between and within class interests over the desired locus and substance of regulatory reform. This has left the field of regional planning analysis without an adequate theory capable of addressing the diverse experiences encountered by local, regional, and state authorities as they attempt various types of land use control reform measures.

Given the rather tight network of leading people and institutions attempting to steer discussion and state experimentation with regulatory reform, we should be suspicious of the populist rhetoric offered by the reform movement. Mainstream liberal planning reform ideology accomplishes the following: (1) it obscures, behind a screen of social harmony and public interest rhetoric, real conflicts of interests, either between different segments of the capitalist class or between prodevelopment interests and the populace; (2) it makes exaggerated claims for the ability of centralized land use control to solve environmental and social problems; and (3) it points a finger at the structure of government, uncoordinated competition among small property developers, and local opposition to regionally desirable growth (i.e., at questions of scale, organization, and parochialism in the immediate sense) as sources of public problems. More specifically, it diverts legitimate popular protest against the social, environmental, and economic impacts of property development into a form useful for prodevelopment interests. This is done by imputing social ills as the sole source of demand for reform and by overlooking changes in the nature, scale, and structure of urban development and capital accumulation actually requiring the more centralized level of planning and regulatory control advocated by the reformers.

TOWARD A FRAMEWORK FOR ANALYSIS

The prevailing liberal interpretation of a quiet revolution in land use control holds that State intervention, representing a centralization of regulation, is in response to the public's recent recognition that local decision making cannot account for environmental protection or for socially desirable development. I propose an alternative interpretation, to wit: the recent move to centralize land use regulation at the state level is merely the latest expression of a historical process of public (or State) intervention, at all levels, in the land development process. This process is framed by recurring struggle between competing social interests, where the favored locus of regulation is largely a question of more immediate political strategy. The presence of this contest may be anticipated from an understanding of inherent contradiction contained within the capitalist mode of production as this contradiction takes a specific spatial form within the U.S. political economy. Liberal land use reform, where it calls for a centralization of regulation, continues as an attempt to steer a clear path through this social protest to re-create a system of land use control conducive to the evolving requirements of capitalist production. Finally, the so-called quiet revolution stage of state intervention, despite appearances, is part of an evolution in land use regulation that is broader, older, and more relentless than commonly recognized.

These assumptions are derived from the following model of the capitalist process of economic development and of the role of public intervention when addressing structural contradiction generated by accumulation as it unfolds in space. Although the terminology and framework for this analysis derive mainly from the writings of Karl Marx and his followers, the Marxist interpretation, by focusing on social contradiction arising from the structure of the *production* process (mode of production), provides insufficient attention to the tenacity of local social movements based upon a defense of residential and other *consumption* interests in the landscape. Thus, the writings of Max Weber and contemporary neo-Weberians will also be called upon, because these scholars recognize the lived experience of individuals and groups whose social identification and alliances derive more from shared consumption characteristics than from any clear recognition of their class positions in the production process.

These two schools of social thought are not mutually exclusive interpretations, the one accounting for class consciousness and State intervention as it derives from the structure of our production system, and the other as it addresses State attention to the goals of local consumption-based social movements. The neo-Weberian analysis accurately describes, but cannot explain, the popular attention to environmental and land use issues that has caught the attention of conventional planning analysts. The Marxist approach suggests an explanation for this social phenomenon and for State action serving production as well as consumption interests but, to date, has not accounted for the specific form and outcome of State action. It lacks sufficient appreciation of human consciousness and agency as divorced from a recognition of production-based class position. Furthermore, for the Marxists specific outcomes are all too often reduced to the "logic of capital," where State action, in all its forms, is too easily taken as functional for the perpetuation of capitalism and capital class interests.[8]

The Capitalist Mode of Production and the Commitment to Growth

All living organisms transform nature, taken as matter and energy, into other forms of matter and energy to survive. So-called higher organisms, including humans, do this not only as individuals, but also as members of social groupings whereby food is procured, shelter built, and, for humans, clothing made. *Mode of production* refers to the social relations we enter into whereby nature is transformed into products necessary and useful for our survival, and the tools we use to transform nature are known as the *means of production*. In addition to hunting implements, tractors, factories, and other tools, the latter include land (used to grow crops and as a container or base for the construction and placement of other tools) and, above all, our own labor power. It is through labor power that all the other means of production are fashioned or used, and it is upon the ownership of labor power by the individual worker (as distinct from ownership of the other means of production that have been fashioned or transformed by labor, e.g., land) that the Marxist commitment to the laborer or proletarian rests.

There are a variety of ways to classify different modes of production. Basic characteristics entail the social structure of the production system as determined by who owns and controls the means of production, and the distribution of goods that are captured, grown, and produced. Thus, in the hunting and gathering mode of production the bows, arrows, slings, and other means of production are widely held, while the products captured and gathered are distributed according to kinship and tribal obligations. Under feudalism, another mode of production, the landlord owns and rents out the land to tenant farmers, peasants, or serfs (if bound to the land). They in turn own most of the other means of production, such as oxen and plows, and they pay a portion of the harvest as rent or tax to the lord. Under feudalism there is a weakly developed town-based market system where goods and services produced beyond subsistence needs may be bartered for, or exchanged through, the medium of money (representing abstract labor value).

In its classic form as described by Marx, capitalism is a mode of production wherein the means of production are owned and controlled by a sector known as the *capitalist class* or *bourgeoisie*, while the majority of the people, *labor* or the *proletariat class*, own only their own labor power in the production process. This they sell to the capitalists for a wage.[9] Capitalism acquires its dynamic quality, some say its "genius," through the presence of a competitive market wherein the goods that are produced through labor power (commodities) are sold or exchanged by many private enterprises for other goods, with money as the medium of exchange. Every commodity has a *use value*, or utility value, to the person or organization using it, as well as an *exchange value*, which is realized when the commodity is sold on the market. Quantitatively and qualitatively the use and exchange values of a commodity can and, usually do, differ. Thus, for example, homeowners live, and have a use value, in their homes, but typically seek the maximum exchange value when they put them on the market.

In the process of commodity sale for exchange value, the private capitalist, or entrepreneur, must reinvest into research, development, market expansion, new technology, etc. a portion of the *surplus value* left after paying for maintenance of the means of production (wages, rent, and interest). This is a requirement of the competitive market, for without reinvestment there exists the risk of losing one's business. Capitalism as a unique mode of production is defined by the presence of a competitive market and the control of the means of production (except for labor) by an elite capitalist class, where the majority sell their labor power for a wage.

Finally, communism, which will not concern us here, in its transitory form toward a classless society, has the State controlling the means of production in the name of the workers. Here State allocation and planning ("from each according to his ability, to each according to his needs") replace free market allocation of commodities.[10]

Conventional economic theory recognizes capital as money, machines, and other fixed investments that can be used or invested in the production process. In Marxist terminology, capital involves more: fixed capital and money require labor to function. Thus capital represents the ability to command (hire) labor and accumulate more wealth through the ownership of wealth.[11] Whichever interpretation is used, both conventional economists and Marxists agree that under capitalism there exists a drive to accumulate capital. This continuous drive is not exclusive to capitalism, and indeed other modes of production, such as communism, may also be growth oriented. Nonetheless, for capitalism accumulation is a basic *structural* (i.e., deriving from the basic structure of the production system) requirement. Capital accumulation, occurring through expansion of the forces of production and, in its spatial form, through urban growth and land development, is both a necessary requirement of the capitalist system and the generator of renewed *contradiction*.

Contradiction is an unavoidable structural defect in a mode of production, the permanent solution to which inevitably requires a change in the basic social structure defining that production system. In brief, two basic forms of contradiction emerge under the capitalist mode of production, characterized as it is by the domination of labor by capitalists and by the existence of a competitive market. On the one hand, class struggle over the size and distribution of surplus value pits labor against capitalists and, within classes, different factions (e.g., finance versus industrial capital, or union versus nonunion labor) against one another. On the other hand, contradiction also emerges from the private appropriation of surplus value in a competitive market, as individual capitalists, acting in their own immediate self-interest, produce aggregate results (for example, production of commodities beyond what the market will optimally bear or wasteful use of common resources such as air and water) adverse to their collective class interest. Taken together, these two basic expressions of contradiction derive from the single contradiction intrinsic to capitalism, that is, the tension between the social nature of production and its private appropriation.

In a system of class conflict (our primary, or social, form of contradiction), a growing economy temporarily encourages social harmony since each segment hopes to share in the larger surplus generated. The "trickle-down" phenomenon, while perhaps more fancy than fact, is nonetheless deeply ingrained as a commonsense notion. This expectation of continued economic growth and prosperity is widespread, promoted by a host of public and private bodies with a stake in social accord and growing profits or, for the State, tax revenues. Furthermore, even though it now takes two incomes to support what was once considered a "middle-class" standard of living, the capitalist production system in the United States has, in the past, succeeded in delivering "the goods" in sufficient quantity and often enough to secure most of the population's allegiance.[12]

In addition to the public and private quest for social harmony, backed by consumer demand for commodities, the private appropriation of surplus value within a competitive market is also a major stimulus for economic expansion. This occurs as entrepreneurs are driven to increase their hold on that market, expand existing markets, and develop new ones, while simultaneously seeking to lower the cost of production through cheaper supplies of raw materials, including labor. Economic growth then is a response to production requirements and to consumer demands, where both practices have a basis in the social structure composing the mode of production.

This constant drive for accumulation, while temporarily contributing to social harmony, generates new expressions of contradiction and crisis. Thus the search for market expansion and supplies of cheaper labor and other resource inputs leads to uneven development, volatile pockets of unemployed or displaced labor, and contamination of the resource base, including worker health and quality of the "natural" environment.[13] Responding to these negative externalities, first private- and, if need be, public-sector planning and regulation are evoked by affected business, labor, environmental, and other interest groups to achieve collective outcomes that individual entrepreneurs could and would not support on their own.

Capital Accumulation and Land Use Control

Local zoning has long been the linchpin of land use control in the United States. Widely adopted in urban areas in the 1920s and 1930s, zoning practice has been based upon the segregation of discordant land uses in order to protect the operating freedom of business, defend residential differentiation along race, class, ethnic, and other lines, and promote property values in general. This ability to define, protect, and enhance local material, ethnic, and class values through the regulation of land use has served as the driving force behind the tremendous surge in suburban incorporations since the 1930s. Local municipal governments have exercised primary jurisdiction in zoning and other forms of development regulation, and they have traditionally made decisions on a case-by-case, parcel-by-parcel basis. Also, local governments, including a large number of special taxing districts and public authorities, have provided basic public services from education to sewage treatment.

This system of local regulation and the provisioning of urban development has been quite favorable to capital accumulation. Overzoning and liberal variances have been the rule, master plans (upon which the zoning was to be based) rarely drawn and little used, and capital investment liberally extended independent of planning and zoning schemes.[14] Behind the progrowth positions of most municipalities lay a local growth coalition consisting of property interests and small businesses. Larger corporations seeking industrial sites and housing for employees generally favored local control but usually did not participate in it directly because, by and large, the existing system, dominated by small businesses and property interests, served them well enough.[15]

The obsolescence of local decision making proclaimed by the liberal planning reform movement is not inherent in the design of zoning or the structure of local government. It can only be explained in terms of changing circumstances and class alliances that render previously useful government arrangements a hindrance to further profit-making activity. Individual capitalists tend to underinvest in infrastructure and services needed for production that may be used by many producers and are too expensive, or the benefits too diffuse, for them to provide and capture on their own. Thus the public sector, or State, is called upon to provide goods and services favoring accumulation that private entrepreneurs would not furnish themselves. There is a long-standing tendency toward the concentration of capital in large corporations and toward an increasing scale of production. Concurrent with the increasing scale in production, public goods and services are required (e.g., highways, mass transit systems, and public education of a trained labor force) on a scale beyond the ability or will of local municipalities to provide. Seeking to optimize their control over public investment and regulation, production interests (be they business concerns, real estate developers, or financial institutions) usually support the lowest level of public intervention commensurate with their needs. They will, however, lobby for metropolitan, regional, and, if need be, state and federal coordination and assistance in the expansion of production forces and of space given to production uses when confronted with local inability or reluctance to accommodate their requirements. In general, the larger the scale of the production concern and the more extensive its requirements for public assistance, the more likely the production concern will push for centralized planning and land use regulation to fulfill these requirements.[16]

Although federal, state, and local governments are pressured by production interests to protect the private investment climate and assist with economic expansion, these governments are simultaneously under pressure from the social and environmental problems generated by economic growth and a growing production system. Hence, the public sector is called upon by social advocates to address social problems, as exemplified by agitation for housing, welfare, and unemployment programs. In addition, the public sector is petitioned by environmental, homeowner, and consumer groups to attend to the environmental disruption caused by production. The latter may be seen, for example, through support for the Federal Clean Air and Clean Water acts, landscape preservation, and ordinances restricting manufacturing to specified zones. To examine the role of government, or the State, as it mediates between economic growth and protection against the negative externalities of economic growth, we must first consider how individuals and groups active in land use regulation come to have an interest in the use of land.

The Derivation and Implications of Class Positions on Production and Consumption

Classes may be defined as groups of individuals sharing the same economic (material) and social status. Individual members of a class tend toward a common *ideological* outlook; that is to say, they share common beliefs and attitudes about the nature and worth of social systems of which they are a part. These beliefs constitute the basis for political and social (class) platforms. In the Marxist tradition, classes are recognized according to the relation they bear to ownership and control of the means of production. The bourgeoisie are postulated to have a fundamentally different ideological position from that of the proletariat, and one that is in conflict over control of the surplus value produced through production. Class distinctions are rooted in the production system. This is a *necessary* categorization for capitalism because without the presence of the proletariat and bourgeoisie as distinct classes, one could not postulate the presence of capitalism as a unique mode of production.

Max Weber and his followers rejected the Marxist concept of class as materially too deterministic, and as overlooking other shared characteristics and ideology stemming from religious and cultural practices, and from patterns of consumption, for example. They focused on individual actors' own accounts of what they were doing and on their own conception of their social position. Weber considered class only as a sociological construct imposed upon reality by the social analyst and as limited to the classification of individuals sharing common "life chances" for possession of goods and income from their participation in labor markets.[17] For Weber the distribution and possession of income, as influenced by these life chances, appeared more important in defining individuals' accounts of their own social position than did their perceived relation to the sphere of production.

Although not deduced as such by Weber, the commonsense concept of a middle, upper, and lower class are merely descriptive categorizations used to distinguish different access to property and income. With respect to the capitalist mode of production, these are *contingent* categories because, unlike the Marxist concept of class, they bear no necessary relation to the production system. They are merely descriptive and are not necessary for the supposition of capitalism. Thorstein Veblen, another eminent sociologist concerned with social classification, provided a descriptive view of class based on status position as determined by consumption. As with Weber, this view of class is contingent on, rather than bearing a necessary relation with, the mode of production.[18]

The strength of the Marxist analysis of class and class-based ideology lies in the demonstration of a necessary relation between these constructs and the existence of a dominant mode of production. Certainly when Marx was active, over a century ago, individual workers were more aware of their class position in the production system because this was the engrossing center of their lives. For many, toiling long hours under wretched conditions, there was precious little time left for family life and for enjoyment of the limited consumption items that their meager wages could purchase. What Marx could not have foreseen in his day was the tremendous expansion, in industrial economies, of the time and space given to consumption activities. Through union and political struggles, laborers won wage concessions and reduced working hours enabling them to devote more income and attention to activities and places removed from their workplace and worktime.

Consumption, in its common usage, refers both to the act of purchasing consumer goods and to the act of using them. In the Marxist framework consumption is derived from its necessary relationship with production. The use value of consumption lies in its necessary association with the formation of the working class. Workers must physically consume goods and services to reproduce their labor power for sale to the capitalist class. Where orthodox Marxist thought looks at the social act of purchasing consumer goods, it recognizes consumption as necessary for the realization of value, because without consumption, there would be no way that capitalists could realize a profit (surplus value) through sale, nor could there be any way for producers to acquire the resources necessary to keep on producing. In fact, consumption and production are inextricably, and even dialectically, linked. Every act of production is also an act of consumption as producers consume resources, including labor power, to produce commodities. In a similar manner, every act of consumption is also an act of production as individuals consume resources and commodities to perpetuate themselves and their labor power.

Consumption occurs in space; and beyond the physical act of consuming, many of the items we consume occupy space. In terms of our relationship with the landscape, we can categorize it as divided into areas given over to the production of commodities (*production space*), and areas set aside for consumption (*consumption space*). The latter include, for example, residential districts, recreational areas, and shopping arcades. This division between consumption and production in the landscape is heuristic, contingent if you will, because it is not necessary for the existence of capitalism and only became identifiable for the working class as capitalism moved out of the cottage industry phase of production and workers were presented with a workplace (factory) spatially separated from their place of consumption. Moreover, as every act of production is also an act of consumption, and vice versa, the same place actually serves both production and consumption purposes. Consider, for example, housing, hospitals, schools, and other elements of the urban landscape where labor consumes services and is also physically and mentally prepared for a productive place in the workforce.

Our personal relationship with a place too can vary, depending upon our social activity at the time. Thus the same highway can carry us to work or to the beach, an active farm may also be valued as open space by nearby residents, and a winery can be popular among imbibing tourists. Although the spatial separation of production from consumption space is largely perceptual and merely contingent under capitalism, it is a common feature of landscape perception in advanced industrial economies and, at least for capitalism, a basic (although not necessary) expression of underlying contradiction contained within that mode of production.

As in Marx's day, class distinctions are still rooted in the production process. However, with increasing frequency, popular recognition of class positions is refracted through the lens of consumption. Consumption, including consumption of residential and leisure goods and services, has actually blurred class consciousness with respect to the production system. In particular, workers have come to accept a small measure of control over their consumption and family (reproduction) activities as a substitute for control and ownership in the workplace. Although the genesis of this ideological reformulation is beyond the scope of this introduction, it does appear that, at least in the United States and in many other advanced economies, consumption characteristics have come to substitute for real (necessary) class distinctions. This is captured through such familiar maxims as "you are what you eat," and "a man's home is his castle."

Arising initially from the social division of labor, class demarcations were reinforced by differential access to residential space, leisure time, education, and other consumption amenities.   However, the separation of work from consumption space also led to a bifurcation in labor's struggle to control the social conditions of its own existence, with conflict occurring both at the workplace and at the place of residence or consumption. With production, or social relations, reflected in property relations and, ultimately, cemented at a given point in time through land development, control over the use of land frequently served as the locus for displaced social struggle from the sphere of production.[19]   Encouraged by a popular culture equating consumption characteristics with social standing, a growing segment of the American labor force since the Second World War turned away from organized struggle in the workplace over wages and control of the production process toward struggle in the consumption sphere to maximize use value in residential location and to protect what was accepted as a middle-class standard of living. In the process of focusing on consumption issues, class consciousness derived from production relations was obscured and new alliances formed, generating social movements that cut across rigid Marxist class categories.

The Spatial Tension between Production and Consumption and Implications for Land Use Reform

As postulated by Weber and other social scientists, human beings also perceive of themselves as grouped along gender, ethnic, religious, national, and other political, biological, and cultural lines transcending Marxist class positions.[20] While these specific groupings may have a partial basis in class distinctions (e.g., the Jewish working-class unions of the early twentieth century), the ethnic, cultural, and political distinctions are not reducible to Marxist class categories. Although these social categories may be necessary for the existence of other social systems of which individuals are a part (e.g., family, church, and political jurisdictions), they are not necessary for the existence of capitalism. Rather they take a specific contingent form in articulation with capitalism. Consumption, on the other hand, bears a necessary relationship to capitalist production (as it does with any mode of production), and consumption, perceived as use value in the landscape, has served as the most important basis for contemporary land-based social movements in the United States. While consumption, as an activity, is necessary, consumption-based social movements may still occur along these nonessential ethnic, religious, gender, and other social divisions.[21]

While a Weberian analysis helps us to recognize the existence of contingent social movements based upon a defense of perceived consumption interests in the landscape, we must return to the Marxist framework to explain the presence of these movements and the ideology they represent. Thus, the basis for social movements committed to land use in advanced capitalist societies lies in the tension between the necessary expansion of production and the necessary realization of surplus value and reproduction of labor power through consumption, as these processes take their contingent spatial forms.

Marx himself did not investigate the social conditions of the reproduction of labor power through consumption, nor did he recognize it as a potential barrier or strength for the expansion of capitalism.[22] All too often Marxist scholars, when they did look at consumption, conceived of it as automatically functional for the perpetuation of capitalism and used this functional value to explain its existence. This teleological argument mistook the results for an explanation. It is only in recent years, and with the rise of mass consumerism and the emergence of a popular consumption-based ideology, that neo-Marxists have come to appreciate the true dialectical relationship that consumption bears with production. Thus the two spheres of human activity require one another, but also exist in tension with one another. This is patently obvious when production and consumption are expressed through contingent forms in the landscape.

As is always the case with structural contradiction within a mode of production, there are no permanent solutions to the defect, though temporary ones may arise. Consumption may be expressed and perceived through the use of land and the built environment (i.e., buildings and other human artifacts in the landscape). In dialectical relationship with production, consumption presents temporary solutions, as well as barriers, for the expansion of the forces of production (capital accumulation). To illustrate, the differentiation of residential space from production space, in practice and ideology, displaces workplace struggle, reproduces a labor force appropriate to the needs of the production system, and stimulates both consumption and investment. The suburban lifestyle, for example, is both capital- and energy-intensive and is a major arena for capital accumulation. However, this "suburban solution," as termed by geographer Richard Walker, is only historically contingent with advanced capitalism as urban development proceeded in the U.S. political economy, rather than the result of some premeditated and necessary strategy.[23] Although the result appears useful for capital accumulation, this outcome cannot explain the presence, form, and specific process of suburban development. Rather (and as shall be explained in greater detail in Chapter 3), individuals, be they capitalists or laborers, homeowners or developers, acting in their own immediate self-interest, tend to replicate the social system(s) by which they are defined and of which they are a part. In this manner the suburban development process, with its numerous participants, unfolds in a manner that, at first glance, appears to perpetuate capitalism. However, what appears as a "solution" also presents barriers to further accumulation. For capital accumulation to continue, new "solutions," or "forced rationalizations," of the urban development process will be required as contradiction reemerges.

In the situation before us, the so-called nogrowth movement taking hold in middle-class suburban areas presents real problems for residential developers and, ultimately, for urban growth forces seeking to expand into these areas. Furthermore, the popular understanding of nature and residential districts as personal consumption space, or as islands of refuge (use value), initially assists production forces through acceptance of the areas outside the "parks," "residences," and "critical environmental zones" as open to development. However, at a future date, this temporary compromise may clash with production requirements as economic forces seek to invade these sanctuaries in search of cheaper resources and new investment opportunities.

This ongoing search by individual capitalists for solutions to the ever-present problems posed by the defense of consumption in its spatial form is amply demonstrated through recent court battles to open up wilderness preserves to oil and mineral exploration, and through the continuing search for sites, not already claimed as consumption space by some social group, where power plants, hazardous waste, and other noxious land uses may be located. In this situation, a successful local defense of consumption amenities and space may encourage production concerns to organize and support a centralization of regulation, thereby preempting or circumventing local intransigence.

The conventional explanation for centralized land use regulation, commonly identified as a "quiet revolution," envisions the states as responding to popular protest over destruction of consumption amenities enjoyed by a broad-based coalition of environmental interests. A more insightful explanation for the current wave of state attention to land regulation, where it specifically addresses consumption, is possible. This would first acknowledge the necessary drive for economic expansion under capitalism. As expansion of the forces of production inevitably compromises the integrity of consumption amenities and space set aside for social reproduction, and popularly accepted as reward for toil in an alienating production system, social protest and political mobilization appear likely. To illustrate, the emergence of a broad-based environmental movement around the Earth Day Teach-In in 1970 derived from public recognition that environmental contamination associated with a large-scale and more mobile production system had spread and was finally invading middle-class residential neighborhoods.

Returning now to pressures on the State, and focusing on consumption, we would anticipate that tenants, homeowners, environmentalists, sports enthusiasts, and other consumption interests would support a neighborhood and local level of regulatory control when it suits their specific needs. On occasion, however, they, like production interests, would also rely upon metropolitan, regional, or state intervention to block local decisions, perhaps by a neighboring community or by their own town or city, threatening their residential and leisure consumption amenities and the consumption space they occupy.

It would appear that the State, at whatever level, is not an autonomous regulator independently setting an agenda guaranteeing the perpetuation of capitalist class relations and system maintenance. Certainly special interests and class factions can capture portions of the State apparatus to pursue more select private agendas. Nonetheless, in practice, where the State pays attention to the demands of production and consumption groupings spawned by the process of capitalist development, it also tends to perpetuate the social system, i.e., capitalism, giving rise to these social demarcations. In this manner, the "captured versus autonomous" debate over the role of the State appears spurious (Chapters 3 and 5 discuss in more detail the role of the capitalist State and the interests served).

From the foregoing model of the accumulation process under capitalism, and aware of the tensions generated through the expansion of production and the defense of consumption amenities, we can theorize that the recent state intervention in local land use decisions is the latest response to a continuing process whereby a more centralized authority is called upon to address these unavoidable, and often conflicting, pressures placed upon the public sector. Although centralized land use regulation has historically furthered production goals, consumption as well as production forces would be expected to lobby for regional or state planning and zoning when the existing local land use controls, or, in many instances, an absence of controls, frustrate the goals sought.

Where production concerns are confronted by a strong local defense of consumption space, they could support a centralization of regulation should it promise to reduce the tension between production expansion and consumption defense in a manner still receptive to urban expansion and transformation. Although portrayed by the liberal planning reform movement as the result of popular demand for defense of consumption amenities and use value in the landscape, centralized land use regulation has been used to provide an environment conducive both to economic expansion and to the protection of social and environmental amenities. The conservation-and-development approach to land use, championed by liberal reformers as in the broader public interest, is actually a direct attempt to steer popular social protest over consumption issues toward reform accommodating the requirements of an expanding production system. This is clearly illustrated through the American Law Institute's Model Land Development Code, Florida's Environmental Land and Water Management Act of 1972, and policy proposals of the National Land Use Policy Act, the (Rockefeller) Task Force on Land Use and Urban Growth, and other important products of the liberal planning reform movement.[24] While centralized land use regulation and the conservation-and-development approach to land use regulation are not necessarily intrinsic to capitalism, liberal planning reform, because it attempts to ameliorate spatial and social expressions of contradiction inherent to the mode of production, is bound to be frustrated. Thus conservation and development will continue to clash, and lasting equilibrium between the forces of production and the defense of consumption would appear unattainable.

THE PREEMINENCE OF NEW YORK STATE
IN THE QUIET EVOLUTION

Tending toward idealistic impulse as the basis for change, most of the planning reform literature fails to examine empirically the material and social conditions generating real practice.   The practice of land use regulation, however, displays a certain rationality were one to attend to the history of capitalist accumulation and to the expression of, and response to, contradiction thereby engendered. As presented in the chapters to follow, this alternative interpretation of land use reform is empirically grounded and historically specific.   It critically evaluates existing reform ideology and reveals its connection to the established social and economic order. Thus, it is hoped, the interpretation proposed may provide greater explanatory power and, ultimately, generate more democratic and socially equitable policy options than what passes for conventional wisdom.

The creation of context-free and unbiased experimental conditions in social science research is problematic because we are trying to replicate open systems where all of the variables are not under our experimental control. In addition, we are biased as researchers by our socialization and its impact on the specific knowledge we seek and acquire. As a consequence, we are never absolutely sure whether our results replicate social reality. Our "test" of theory thus becomes its application to the historic record and its power to predict the future. The former "test" is difficult because it is hard to avoid a teleological functionalism when attempting to explain the presence and outcome of past events. As all ideas, even ones based upon false premises, have material impact if acted upon, our attempt to model the present and use this to predict the future is also problematic. Ultimately, then, the best test of theory in the social sciences is its adequacy to explain social phenomena and its capacity to generate new knowledge about these situations, realizing, of course, that all knowledge about social life is context-dependent, as knowledge itself is socially produced.

Focusing on the specifics of historic practice rather than on the use of abstract models, we can attempt to gain an understanding of planning reform through the case study approach. Case studies are justified because, from a historical point of view, all social situations have unique components. Case studies are required to bridge the gap between the theoretically fertile, but empirically underdeveloped, Marxist critique that the structure of production relations is the dominant force shaping social reality, and the empirically vigorous, but theoretically idealistic, liberal focus on form and description of contingent relations as a substitute for necessary explanation.

Given the breadth of state and regional land use reform across the United States, an adequate analysis of the history of regulatory reform in all 50 states would be an unrealistically monumental task. Comprehensive coverage at the cost of shallow analysis has been the bane of the literature in this area. Of course, the day-to-day land use regulations and the specific programs developed by civic, environmental, and social reformers vary according to the geographically unique circumstances of every region. Nonetheless, these are embedded in the broader influences characteristic of U.S. political and economic systems as they articulate with the dominant mode of production. If we cannot understand the interaction of the general and the particular in one case, we cannot hope to understand the overall situation in 50 states.

So in choosing one state for my case study, I sought three elements. The first was a region that had experimented with all of the major permutations in regulatory reform addressed by the literature, such as critical area protection, coastal zone management, special facility siting, and wetland protection. The requirement to address state intervention to spur both conservation and development led me to focus on those states with well-developed programs in both of these seemingly contradictory areas.

The second requirement was the particular state's importance in the national land use reform movement. California, Vermont, New York, Florida, Hawaii, Oregon, Maine, North Carolina, and several others have attracted the most attention.[25] Some of these states have adopted land use regulations on a "comprehensive" basis (e.g., Vermont, Oregon, Hawaii, and Florida) whereby the entire state was surveyed, with appropriate regulations adopted for critical areas and/or for special facility siting. Others, such as New York and California, have taken a more "incremental" approach, proceeding on a case-by-case basis with specific legislation for the siting of facilities and for critical area protection. Given this incremental approach, New York stands apart because one of its critical areas, the Adirondack Park, is so large, and the regulations adopted there so detailed, that on its own the Adirondack reform structure more closely approximates that found in the comprehensive reform states.

Finally, the state chosen for study needed to have a well-researched power structure network and a complete and readily identifiable record of administrative practice. This is important in identifying all of the relevant actors in the land reform movement, including those operating covertly, out of public view.

Putting all of these factors together, California and New York appear as clear leaders. Political scientists agree that the two states rank among the top three or four as innovators in a wide variety of state initiatives, including attention to land use reform. As a result, administrators in other states are more likely to look to them for leadership and guidance.[26] Moreover, both the conventional planning reformers and their critics recognize that these two states are at the forefront of experimentation on land use regulation.[27] Both states traditionally serve as models in development of the reform ideology and analysis of its impact. Of the two, New York presents the most opportunities to examine the evolution and expression of planning and regulatory reform. It experimented with a wider variety of reform proposals and for a longer period of time than did California. Furthermore, as noted, the scale of regulation in the Adirondacks is such that it has some instructive bearing for comprehensive approaches to land use reform.   Finally, state regulatory reform and the literature associated with it are primarily involved with the planning and zoning of private lands and have little to say about activities on federal lands where state and local governments have no jurisdiction. With approximately 44 percent of its area under federal ownership, California presents a more complex region in which to examine land use regulatory reform.[28]

New York State has been a national leader in adopting innovative regional land use planning and development control programs. While its experience is atypical due to its long record of land use reform and the complexity of the permutations adopted, the state is still instructive, since it has had to face many of the dilemmas addressed in geographically less diverse states, whether committed to a comprehensive or an instrumental approach to land use reform. The state actually pioneered development of statewide regional planning in the 1920s, and was a leader in the provision of home rule powers to local municipalities.[29] From the very start, when cities and villages first received authority to plan and zone under the enabling acts of the 1920s, the state also encouraged cooperative planning efforts to move the locus of decision making to more centralized units of government. The major impetus for regional planning and regulatory reform came through private business-led organizations and foundations such as the Rochester Municipal Research Bureau, the Regional Plan Association of New York, and the Russell Sage Foundation (Chapters 2 and 3).

Under strong pressure from large-scale industrial and financial interests, New York has led the nation in the use of public authorities and corporations to provide the infrastructure and services necessary for continued property development with minimum public discussion and regulatory delay (Chapter 4). New York was the first state to develop an operational "one-stop" power plant siting process. When combined with the politically sheltered public authority provision of nuclear and fossil fuel power generation, the siting process resulted in vociferous struggle in rural communities slated for energy development to service distant metropolitan areas (Chapter 4). Social demarcations have also been evident in the conflict surrounding transportation and housing development, both areas where state preemption of local controls and regulation has been extended through use of public authorities.

More recently the state, already active in protecting the Catskill and Adirondack critical environmental areas, extended state review of local land use regulation into the Hudson Valley and via agricultural districting and environmental quality review legislation (Chapters 4, 5, and 6). The possibility of additional state preemption of local control came through liquefied natural gas and hazardous waste treatment facility siting, with mixed support from both business and environmental groups (Chapter 4). As shall be demonstrated, the tremendous physical, social, and economic diversity of the state itself was a major contributing factor to this outpouring of regulatory reform, even as the purpose and product of reform paralleled efforts and results in other states where the pressures of production confronted the defense of consumption.

CHAPTER OUTLINES AND SUMMARIES

Chapter 2: Private Planning for the Public Sector

With the rise of the modern corporation in the 1890s, the central districts of the larger urban complexes turned increasingly from industrial to office-based control functions necessary for multilocational production, investment, and marketing decisions. Concurrent with the growing specialization of the central city as a place for production management, suburban districts were developed as places of residence for office workers and support personnel. Following on the heels of the wealthier industrial and financial entrepreneurs, midlevel office workers found the suburban environment to be a special place from which the messy forces of production could be banished. There laborers or managers could escape from the vigors of the workplace, to consume the hard-earned amenities of their efforts. The new corporate city, with its suburban residential districts and downtown office and retail centers, required many more public services than the earlier and more compact industrial city. Thus, for example, public provision of improved transportation by trolley, rail, and, later, highway access; port development; provision of utilities; urban redevelopment; and water and sewer service were on the political agenda of downtown business interests.

Early in this century corporate managers, developers, and financiers were already aware that the increasing scale and specialization of production and the need to more boldly provide the infrastructure, housing, and other conditions required for continued urban expansion threatened to overwhelm the capacity of the local municipalities in the metropolis. Business support for regional land use planning and control grew in the New York City metropolitan area, as elsewhere, out of the earlier municipal reform movement of the late nineteenth and early twentieth centuries. Designed ostensibly to stop the graft and corruption associated with ward-based political machines, the municipal reform movement sought economy and efficiency in providing public services and removing as many of these services as possible from the political arena.

Organized into private civic groups (e.g., the Commercial Club of Chicago, the Regional Plan Association of New York, and Pittsburgh's Allegheny Conference on Community Development) and active through private foundations and municipal research bureaus, central-city business interests continued to support regional planning and regulatory reform over the ensuing half century. Proposals were made to increase municipal capability to accommodate large-scale projects through adoption of land use controls and permissive zoning ordinances and, where necessary, through the selective centralization of urban services including transportation, water, and sewer supply. This private planning for the public sector accelerated during the postwar economic boom, and by the mid-1950s almost every major U.S. metropolitan area had its own nonprofit and privately sponsored regional land use planning advocate.

In Chapter 2 this private planning for the public interest is examined and the human and historic links to the earlier municipal reform movement are uncovered. Particular attention is paid to the Regional Plan Association of New York because it is nationally accepted by observers of the planning reform movement as a genuine proponent of the public's interest in environmental protection. As will be demonstrated, regional planning and centralized regulation are not objectives wholly attributable to environmental and consumption forces. In practice, much of the thrust for reform is promulgated by production concerns and represents attempts to circumvent barriers to capital accumulation arising as the scale of development increases and more units of local government adopt land use controls.

Chapter 3:   Regional Planning for Global Accumulation

Classwide capitalist interest in the built environment is not monolithic, and a variety of intraclass tensions can arise along sectoral lines (for example, among industrial, banking, and real estate interests), as well as along geographic boundaries. In the latter instance, local business leaders with property or investments in a specific location may compete with one another for public resources and private investment available in the broader metropolitan setting. In Chapter 3, two other private planning advocates active in the New York metropolitan area are introduced. Although both operate in geographic districts overlapping with the Regional Plan Association's region of concern, these organizations support the objectives of more select segments of capital.

With the postwar ascent of financial capital as the regulatory force in the global expansion of capitalist development, New York City emerged as one of the leading control centers for the worldwide division of labor. In lower Manhattan, banking, securities, insurance, and other services required for global accumulation concentrated. The Downtown-Lower Manhattan Association was established as an advocate for the real estate interests (comprising both use and exchange values) of this geographically centralized and sectorally specific faction of capital. Seeking to secure and enlarge lower Manhattan's preeminence as the heart of global capitalism, the Downtown-Lower Manhattan Association pursued an agenda that, at times, clashed with those of other planning advocates in the metropolis. Although at a broader sectoral scale, the Mid-Hudson Pattern for Progress was also created to lobby for geographically specific interests. In this instance attention focused on the seven-county region north of the city where office, industrial, and residential development was expanding.

Through the introduction of these two other privately sponsored planning advocates, the unavoidable tension within liberal planning reform, where it supports a classwide interest in continued accumulation and where more select sectoral and geographic goals are served, becomes apparent. Lest the analysis lapse into a naive instrumental (self-serving) interpretation of business-led planning activities and their impact upon the role of the State, this chapter introduces a process termed "structuration." Thus, it is acknowledged that individuals and groups acting in their own self-interest tend to perpetuate the overall social systems giving rise to their social demarcations and to the generation of their specific goals.

Chapter 4: Public Authorities and Facility Siting Legislation

The push for town, county, and eventually, state land use powers was spearheaded by progressive "good government" reformers with strong ties to large-scale capital interests. Original efforts focused on improving local ability to site development through adoption of planning and zoning ordinances. However, where local municipalities, with their newly found powers to plan and zone, elected to protect local consumption amenities against what were perceived to be the social and environmental ravages of expanding production systems, stronger measures were called for. This may have occurred when the municipalities refused to accommodate large-scale industrial, energy, or infrastructure projects, or to voluntarily cede authority to a higher regional level of government such as the county or special service district. In New York State, as in many others, the remedy appeared in the form of state-chartered public benefit corporations or authorities.

Often retaining some of the police power over land use necessary to accomplish their mission, free from local property taxes, and financed by tax-exempt obligations, public authorities were in an ideal position to implement massive development projects without direct recourse to the state electorate or to local zoning approval. Over the last half century, and with strong support from industrial and financial interests, New York State led the nation in the use of state-chartered public authorities to circumvent local regulations and to provide the infrastructure and services necessary for continued urban development. Public authorities, including the Port Authority of New York and New Jersey, the Urban Development Corporation, and the Power Authority of the State of New York, proved themselves to be remarkably effective mechanisms. In fact it was not until the early 1970s when environmentalists and other consumption concerns, armed with the new federal and state environmental quality review legislation, began to challenge projects constructed by these heretofore autonomous authorities. Consequently, prodevelopment forces found it necessary to support direct state siting legislation for power plants, transmission lines, hazardous waste disposal sites, and other locally undesired land uses.

The use of public authorities to bypass local opposition to major development projects, while just as surely a part of the quiet revolution as special facility siting legislation, is generally ignored by the planning reform literature. In this chapter the evolution and application of this important mechanism is examined, together with the more familiar state experimentation with facility siting legislation. In New York State, as elsewhere, environmental groups rarely spearhead this push for state preemption of municipal regulation through use of public authorities or, for that matter, via state facility siting legislation. Instead they are, with increasing frequency, siding with local interests in opposition to the development of large-scale projects at variance with expressed local consumption interests.

Chapter 5: Critical Area Protection and the Ideology of Liberal Planning

Designation of "critical" environmental, resource, and development areas, in addition to the use of public authorities and facility siting legislation, is the third element in New York's arsenal of regional land use regulatory mechanisms. Critical areas are those where local governments are unprepared or unwilling to accommodate a wide variety of outside interests, be they for recreation, scenic preservation, and watershed protection (as in the Adirondack and Catskill mountains), or for residential, transportation, and energy development (as in the Hudson Valley and the coastal zone). With extraregional consumption and production demands converging on these areas, the state has been called on to help resolve the conflict between continued economic expansion and protection of cherished consumption amenities, whether expressed at the local or the regional level.

The liberal planning reform literature is quick to point to impressive victories by environmental and landscape protectionists, particularly along the coast and in fragile wetland and mountain areas, as evidence of a broad and popular basis for state intervention in land development. Yet, even here, we find input from production forces.

In the Adirondacks, for example, the pioneering creation of a state forest preserve over a century ago derived from efforts by merchants and industrialists concerned that unsound logging practices were threatening the critical watersheds supplying the Erie Canal and Hudson River navigation corridors. Extraregional consumption concerns, in the form of recreation and vacation pursuits, coexisted amiably enough with the outside production concerns.

Although the contemporary animosity expressed by local residents toward state planning and zoning of private lands in the Adirondack region appears to fit the geographic dichotomy between local parochial and regional public concerns portrayed by the planning reform literature, the situation is more complex. Local development concerns are actually trying to service outside consumption demands, while extraregional production interests continue to recognize the value in maintaining the Adirondacks as a "park," available for the leisure consumption requirements of their workforce. Elsewhere, in the Catskill and Tug Hill regions, the specific form of state attention to critical area protection also articulates with the mix of local and outside consumption and production interests, as alliances are formed and positions are taken, transcending a simple local versus regional bifurcation.

Chapter 6: Landscape Preservation and Social Conflict in the Hudson Valley

The State is under dual pressure in a system where growing productive forces and urban expansion generate social and environmental problems. The first is to protect the private investment climate and to assist with economic development. In addition, the State is called on to address the negative externalities generated by growth. With a rich history of conflict dating back to the colonial era, New York's Hudson River Valley is perhaps the nation's most celebrated battleground between the forces of production and those seeking protection of cherished leisure and residential landscapes. Using attempts to regulate development in the Hudson Valley as a case study, this chapter examines the double role of the capitalist State in protecting environmental (consumption) amenities, while also ensuring that land, infrastructure, and other goods and services required for continued capital accumulation are provided in an expeditious manner.

In practice, the centralization of land use planning and regulatory authority can take many forms and serve diverse purposes. Governor Rockefeller's creation of a Hudson River Valley Commission is an interesting case in point. The conventional liberal explanation focuses on popular consumer demand and is at variance with strict (Marxist) attention to production requirements. However, the commission appears to have been an attempt at placating concerns of the valley's residents in protecting their privileged lifestyle from the ravages of poorly planned urban development, while also ensuring that public investment in transportation, energy, and residential development required for ongoing capital accumulation could continue.

As discussed in this chapter, the Hudson River Valley experience also presents a provocative study for development of a theory of the State. The commission, so closely associated with the governor, did address expressions of the structural contradiction besetting capitalist accumulation in the valley, in this case where a social movement based upon protection of bourgeois consumption interests posited barriers to continued development. However, it did so in a manner bearing the mark of apparent self-enrichment for the Rockefeller family.

Chapter 7: Conclusion

As summarized in the conclusion, an interpretation has been presented that the so-called quiet revolution in land use control proclaimed by the liberal planning reform movement is merely the latest expression of a protracted attempt by regional commissions and state agencies to accommodate the aims of environmental protection and economic expansion through a centralization of land use regulation. Since this goal has itself been defined in response to inherent contradiction contained within the capitalist mode of production, its attainment remains enigmatic despite the wide variety and wide range of attempts to resolve the dilemma. This rendition of the movement to centralize land use control has been tested through its ability to explain the historic record in New York State.

NOTES

1. Standing by itself, independent of geographic identification, state (lowercased) refers to the political subdivision in the U.S. federal system, while State (uppercased) refers here to the public sector, or government in general (at any jurisdictional level).

2. Fred Bosselman and David Callies, *The Quiet Revolution in Land Use Control* (prepared for the U.S. Council on Environmental Quality) (Washington, DC: Government Printing Office, 1971).

3. For representative and widely publicized accounts of the "revolution" in land control: American Law Institute, *A Model Land Development Code* (Washington, DC: American Law Institute, 1975); Richard Babcock, *The Zoning Game* (Madison: University of Wisconsin Press, 1966); Fred Bosselman, *Alternatives to Urban Sprawl: Legal Guidelines for Government Action* (prepared for the National Commission on Urban Problems), Technical Report no. 15 (Washington, DC: Government Printing Office, 1968); Marion Clawson, "Economic and Social Conflicts in Land Use Planning," *Natural Resources Journal* 15 (1975):473-89; Committee for Economic Development, *Guiding Metropolitan Growth* (New York: Committee for Economic Development, 1960); John Delafons, *Land Use Controls in the United States,* 2d ed. (Cambridge, MA: MIT Press, 1969); Fred Bosselman, Duane Feurer, and Charles Siemon, *The Permit Explosion: Coordination of the Proliferation* (Washington DC: Urban Land Institute, 1976); Anthony Downs, *Opening Up the Suburbs* (New Haven, CT: Yale University Press, 1973); Bernard Frieden, *The Environmental Protection Hustle* (Cambridge, MA: MIT Press, 1979); Robert Healy, *Environmentalists and Developers: Can They Agree on Anything?* (Washington, DC: Conservation Foundation, 1977); National Commission on Urban Problems, *Building the American City* (Washington, DC: Government Printing Office, 1968); William Reilly, ed., *The Use of Land: A Citizen's Policy Guide to Urban Growth* (Report by the Task Force on Land Use and Urban Growth, sponsored by the Rockefeller Brothers Fund) (New York: Thomas Y. Crowell, 1973); John Reps, "Requiem for Zoning," in *Taming Megalopolis*, ed. H. W. Eldredge (Garden City, NY: Anchor, 1967), pp. 746-60; Urban Land Institute, *Large-Scale Development: Benefits, Constraints, and State and Local Policy Incentives* (Washington, DC: Urban Land Institute, 1977); and Real Estate Research Corporation, *The Costs of Sprawl* (prepared for the U.S. Council on Environmental Quality, the Department of Housing and Urban Development, and the Environmental Protection Agency), 2 vols. (Washington, DC: Government Printing Office, 1974).

4. Frank Popper, *The Politics of Land-Use Reform* (Madison: University of Wisconsin Press, 1981), pp. 3-7; and Robert Healy, *Land Use and the States* (prepared for Resources for the Future) (Baltimore: Johns Hopkins University Press, 1976), pp. 4-6. See also Rutherford Platt, *Land Use Control: Interface of Law and Geography*, Resource Paper 75-1 (Washington, DC: Association of American Geographers, 1976),

p. 13, for a geographer's perception that recent state-level planning and regulatory reform are "a prestigious effort of the environmental movement."

5. To avoid confusion, the terms "reform" and "liberal reform movement" in this work refer to the mainstream liberal position and not to all ideas about, or changes in, land use controls. The liberal position may be distinguished from a "conservative" one that prefers the guiding hand of the market mechanism independent of all regulation, and from a "popularist" stand favoring broad social participation in regulatory practice, with the level of control remaining close to the affected citizenry.

6. See Richard Walker and Michael Heiman, "Quiet Revolution for Whom?" *Annals of the Association of American Geographers* 71 (March 1981):67-83. The existence of a select group of individuals and institutions directing land use control reform policy accords with the findings of others engaged in research on power structures and policy formations, as well as with historical work on past reform movements. Cf. Roy Lubove, *The Progressives and the Slums* (Pittsburgh: University of Pittsburgh Press, 1962); James Weinstein, *The Corporate Ideal in the Liberal State: 1900-1918* (Boston: Beacon Press, 1968); William Domhoff, *The Powers That Be: Processes of Ruling Class Domination in America* (New York: Random House, 1978); John Mollenkopf, "The Postwar Politics of Urban Development," in *Marxism and the Metropolis*, ed. W. Tabb and W. Sawers (New York: Oxford University Press, 1978), pp. 117-52; Marc Weiss, "The Origins and Legacy of Urban Renewal," in *Urban and Regional Planning in an Age of Austerity*, ed. P. Clavel, J. Forester, and W. Goldsmith (New York: Pergamon Press, 1980), pp. 53-80; and Irvin Alpert and Ann Markusen, "The Professional Production of Policy Ideology and Plans: An Examination of Brookings and Resources for the Future," in *Power Structure Research*, ed. W. Domhoff (Beverly Hills, CA: Sage, 1980), pp. 173-97.

7. Walker and Heiman, "Quiet Revolution for Whom?"; Chapter 2 of this work reviews early expressions of liberal planning reform as it evolved out of the Progressive Era in U.S. urban politics.

In the postwar period several individuals and institutions deserve special recognition for their contribution to liberal planning reform. Richard Babcock, for example, from the Chicago law firm of Ross, Hardies, O'Keefe, Babcock, and Parsons, undertook the initial Ford Foundation-funded research into zoning that, in the late 1960s, led to foundation support for the American Law Institute's (ALI) Model Land Development Code (Richard Babcock, "The Chaos of Zoning Administration: One Solution," *Zoning Digest* 12, no. 1 [1960]:1-4; and idem, *Zoning Game*). Intended to serve as a model for revising original state enabling acts, the ALI code established procedures for states to supersede local authority in regulating developments of regional or state significance and in siting projects in areas of "critical state concern," such as around major public facilities and in critical environmental and natural resource areas (American Law Institute, *Model Land Development Code*).

Fred Bosselman, a member of Babcock's law firm, has been a veritable dynamo in terms of promoting land use reform in print and in practice. He became the associate reporter for the ALI model code and was the chief architect of Florida's Environmental Land and Water Management Act of 1972, modeled in part after the code. Along with David Callies, a member of the same Chicago-based law firm, he wrote *The Quiet Revolution in Land Use Control* for the U.S. Council on Environmental Quality and has authored other pivotal reform manuals for federal, state, and private commissions (Bosselman, *Alternatives to Urban Sprawl*; Fred Bosselman, David Callies, and John Banta, *The Taking Issue* [prepared for the U.S. Council on Environmental Quality] [Washington, DC: Government Printing Office, 1973]; Bosselman, Feurer, and Siemon, *Permit Explosion*).

William Reilly, president of the Conservation Foundation, also deserves mention. As a former staff member of the U.S. Council on Environmental Quality, he assisted Bosselman and Callies in their landmark study and helped prepare the Nixon administration's version of a National Land Use Policy Act. Failing to win congressional approval, the latter was also based upon the ALI model code and would have provided incentives and limited coercive measures encouraging the states to formalize a procedure whereby projects of regional significance and development in critical areas would come under state review (Sidney Plotkin, *Keep Out: The Struggle for Land Use Control* [Berkeley and Los Angeles: University of California Press, 1986]). Reilly's most significant contribution to the liberal planning reform movement came through his directorship of the Rockefeller Brothers Fund-sponsored Task Force on Land Use and Urban Growth (Reilly, *Use of Land*). This report was the most influential reform document of the 1970s because it tried to deal with the environmental and nogrowth movements of the period in a manner still accommodating continued capital investment in urban development. Its themes resurfaced in most of the subsequent publications of the reform movement (Cf. Randall Scott, ed., *Management and Control of Growth*, 3 vols. [Washington, DC: Urban Land Institute, 1975]; Healy, *Environmentalists and Developers*; Lawrence Burrows, *Growth Management: Issues, Techniques and Policy Implications* [New Brunswick, NJ: Center for Urban Policy Research, Rutgers University, 1978]; and John Noble, John Banta, and John Rosenberg, *Groping through the Maze* [Washington, DC: Conservation Foundation, 1977]).

8. For example: James O'Connor, *The Fiscal Crisis of the State* (New York: St. Martin's Press, 1973); Manuel Castells, *The Urban Question* (London: Edward Arnold, 1977); and David Harvey, "The Urban Process under Capitalism," *International Journal of Urban and Regional Research* 2, no. 1 (1978):101-31.

9. Karl Marx, *Capital: A Critique of Political Economy* (1867), vol. 1 (of 3) (Chicago: Charles H. Kerr, 1908).

10. Karl Marx, "Critique of the Gotha Programme" (1875), in *Karl Marx: The First International and After*, ed. D. Fernback (New York: Vintage Books, 1974), p. 347.

11. Marx, *Capital*. As distinguished by Marx, capital includes money and fixed capital goods, but it is more than these because without the element of labor power, mere money and nonhuman means of production cannot accumulate more wealth, thus functioning as capital. Although not owned by capitalists, labor is as much a part of the capitalists' capital as are their factories or money (Matthew Edel, "Capitalism, Accumulation and the Explanation of Urban Phenomena," in *Urbanization and Urban Planning in Capitalist Society*, ed. M. Dear and A. Scott [New York: Methuen, 1981], pp. 19-44). Capital is thus a necessary feature of the capitalist mode of production.

12. Since the late 1950s food and fiber consumption per capita has remained fairly constant in America; the floor space of what was accepted as a "middle-class" family home has decreased; and since the 1970s, real wages for blue-collar and for most service-sector workers have fallen in constant dollars. For many households, however, incomes have been maintained and even enhanced through proliferation of two-income

and childless household units. See Barry Commoner, "The Environmental Costs of Economic Growth," in *Economics of the Environment*, ed. R. Dorfman and N. Dorfman (New York: W. W. Norton, 1972), pp. 261-83.

13. In addition to these social and environmental expressions, contradiction can have an economic expression. Thus, contradiction is manifested through a declining rate of profit per dollar invested, a shortage of capital available for investment, and rising interest rates. This occurs as entrepreneurs, in their quest to avoid social conflict with labor (the social form of contradiction), substitute capital- and energy-intensive production processes for labor-intensive technologies. The individual solution to the social contradiction generates renewed contradiction and problems for society (and for the capitalist class) as a collective whole because it exacerbates unemployment and social tension, contributes to environmental contamination and a depletion of the resource base, and constitutes a further drain on capital available for investment.

14. On the origins and practice of zoning: S. J. Makielski, Jr., *The Politics of Zoning* (New York: Columbia University Press, 1966); and Seymour Toll, *Zoned America* (New York: Grossman, 1969).

15. See Harvey Molotch, "The City as a Growth Machine: Toward a Political Economy of Place," *American Journal of Sociology* 82 (1976):309-22.

16. Historically, industrial enterprises had little interest in landownership for exchange value (i.e., profit making through purchase and resale) and primarily viewed land for its use value in the production process. Under these conditions, corporate concerns were inclined to support regional planning and land use regulation to acquire more secure sources of resource inputs (use value) and reduce costly land speculation by local property owners intent on exchange value in the land. On the history of land use reform as sponsored by large-scale residential developers: Samuel Hays, "Value Premises for Planning and Public Policy: The Historical Context," in *Land in America*, ed. R. Andrews (Lexington, MA: Lexington Books, 1979), pp. 149-66; and Walker and Heiman, "Quiet Revolution for Whom?"; see Samuel Hays, *Conservation and the Gospel of Efficiency* (Cambridge, MA: Harvard University Press, 1959) for the, by now, classic exposition on corporate support for the federal conservation of natural resources.

17. Max Weber, "Class, Status, Party," in *From Max Weber: Essays in Sociology*, ed. H. H. Gerth and C. Wright Mills (New York: Oxford University Press, 1946), pp. 181-83; and idem, *Economy and Society*, 3 vols. (New York: Bedminster Press, 1968), pp. 302-7, 927-30. See also Peter Saunders, *Social Theory and the Urban Question* (New York: Holmes & Meier, 1981), pp. 137-39, 142-45.

18. Thorstein Veblen, *The Theory of the Leisure Class: An Economic Study of Institutions* (New York: Charles Scribner's Sons, 1899). For consumption- and status-based interpretations of class consciousness: Daniel Bell, *The Cultural Contradictions of Capitalism* (New York: Basic Books, 1976); William Tucker, "Environmentalism and the Leisure Class," *Harper's* 255 (December 1977):49-56, 73-80; and David Ley, "Liberal Ideology and the Postindustrial City," *Annals of the Association of American Geographers* 70 (June 1980):238-58.

19. For instructive overviews linking production with consumption as areas for social struggle: Manuel Castells, *The Economic Crisis and American Society* (Princeton, NJ: Princeton University Press, 1980); idem, *The City and the Grassroots* (Berkeley and Los Angeles: University of California Press, 1983); David Harvey,

Social Justice and the City (Baltimore: Johns Hopkins University Press, 1973); idem, "Labor, Capital and Class Struggle around the Built Environment in Advanced Capitalist Societies," in *Urbanization and Conflict in Market Societies*, ed. K. Cox (Chicago: Maaroufa Press, 1978), pp. 9-38; Ernst Mandel, *Late Capitalism* (1972; English ed., London: Verso, 1978); and Richard Walker, "A Theory of Suburbanization: Capitalism and the Construction of Urban Space in the United States," in *Urbanization and Urban Planning in Capitalist Society*, ed. M. Dear and A. Scott (New York: Methuen, 1981), pp. 383-429.

20. Cf. Weber, "Class, Status, Party"; Castells, *The City and the Grassroots*; and David Halle, *America's Working Man: Work, Home, and Politics among Blue-Collar Property Owners* (Chicago: University of Chicago Press, 1984).

21. Castells, *The City and the Grassroots*; Saunders, *Social Theory*; and Ira Katznelson, *City Trenches* (New York: Pantheon, 1981).

22. Frederick Engels applied Marxist analysis to the sphere of consumption and family (labor) reproduction (*The Condition of the Working Class in England* [1844] [London: Basil Blackwell, 1958]). See also Saunders, *Social Theory*, pp. 185-88; and James O'Connor, *Accumulation Crisis* (New York: Basil Blackwell, 1984), pp. 149-50.

23. Walker, "Theory of Suburbanization."

24. See note 7 for reference to, and the significance of, these liberal planning reform products.

25. Cf. Bosselman and Callies, *Quiet Revolution*; Elaine Moss, ed., *Land Use Controls in the United States* (prepared by the Natural Resources Defense Council) (New York: Dial Press, 1977); Robert Healy and John Rosenberg, *Land Use and the States* (prepared for Resources for the Future), 2d ed. (Baltimore: Johns Hopkins University Press, 1979); and Popper, *Politics of Land-Use Reform*.

26. See Jack Walker, "The Diffusion of Innovation among American States," *American Political Science Review* 63 (September 1969):880-99; and Fred Grupp, Jr. and Alan Richards, "Variations in Elite Perceptions of American States as Referents for Public Policy Making," *American Political Science Review* 69 (September 1975):850-58. Walker lists New York, followed by Massachusetts and California, as the leading innovative states based upon adoption of legislation in 88 programs. Drawn from a list of basic subject areas similar to that used by the Council of State Governments, the areas include welfare, health, education, conservation, planning, administrative organization, and civil rights, among others (Walker, "Diffusion of Innovation," pp. 381-83).

27. Cf. Bosselman and Callies, *Quiet Revolution*; Reilly, *Use of Land*; Scott, *Management and Control of Growth*; California Land Use Task Force, *The California Land: Planning for the People* (sponsored by the California Planning and Conservation Foundation) (Los Altos, CA: William Kaufman, 1975); American Institute of Planners, *Survey of Land Use Planning Activity* (prepared for the U.S. Department of Housing and Urban Development) (Washington, DC: Government Printing Office, 1976); Healy, *Land Use and the States*; Walker and Heiman, "Quiet Revolution for Whom?"; and Annmarie Walsh, *The Public's Business: The Politics and Practices of Government Corporations* (Cambridge, MA: MIT Press, 1978).

28. For example, because of the increasing popular rejection of nuclear and hazardous waste facility siting, large-scale energy development, and other noxious types of land use, prodevelopment forces are now turning to federal preemption of state land use regulations (e.g., with nuclear waste disposal and offshore oil and gas

development) and/or the siting of such development on federal land. Southern California Edison's San Onofre nuclear power plant at the U.S. Marine Corps Camp Pendleton in San Diego County is a good example of the latter approach.

29. New York State, Commission of Housing and Regional Planning, *Report of the Commission of Housing and Regional Planning to Governor Alfred E. Smith* (Albany: J. B. Lyon, 1926); and Vincent Moore, "Politics, Planning, and Power in New York State: The Path from Theory to Reality," *Journal of the American Institute of Planners* 37 (March 1971):66-77. By 1967 New York State had granted home rule to more municipal governments than had any other state (New York State, Joint Legislative Committee on Metropolitan and Regional Areas Study, *Governing Urban Areas: Strengthening Local Governments through Regionalism* [annual report of the committee] [Albany: Joint Legislative Committee on Metropolitan and Regional Areas Study, 1968], p. 25).

Private Planning
for the Public Sector:
The Regional Plan Association
of New York

As suggested in the preceding chapter, the capitalist State (embracing the public sector at all levels) is under dual pressures in a production system where economic expansion and growing productive forces generate social and environmental externalities. On the one hand, the State is called on to guarantee private property relations, protect the private investment climate, and assist with the provision of services necessary for continued capital accumulation. On the other, it is pressured to address the social and environmental disruption generated by economic growth. At the local level municipalities holding police power attempt to balance conflicting production and consumption interests through land use regulation. Where localities are perceived as favoring production and/or consumption interests to the detriment or exclusion of competing concerns, homeowners, environmentalists, developers, and other groups with a stake in land use may lobby for a regional centralization of local authority. The locus of regulation thus becomes a critical arena for political reform.

Contrary to the prevalent view that centralization of land use regulation is primarily an environmental and social equity impulse in the public's interest, practice suggests that there are many struggling interests in the process of urban development. Where one stands, as an environmentalist, developer, or social reformer, depends more upon the immediate circumstances and propensity of securing one's goals from a specific level of decision making than upon some ahistoric realization of a higher and more harmonious regional level of public interest. The day-to-day practice of land use reform appears as a confusing struggle among conflicting interests with shifting strategies. Beneath the surface of appearances, however, the actual push for regulatory reform, when examined in its historic context, does display a certain logic and order born of the structure of the capitalist mode of production as it takes a specific form in the U.S. political economy.

Capitalist urban development revolves around the interconnected themes of accumulation and class struggle over the social surplus generated. The requirements of capital accumulation and the contradiction generated within this process support urban and regional planning as a necessary activity.[1] As a case in point, planning is required to coordinate those public expenditures required for continued accumulation that individual entrepreneurs, due to the competitive anarchy of capitalist production, would not provide on their own (e.g., transportation, education, and some aspects of research and development). State planning and provision of services are common where benefits cannot be privately appropriated. In addition, planning is used to correct inefficient free market allocation of urban land uses. In this manner consumption space, such as residential, recreation, and shopping districts, can be separated from production (including business) districts. Although not necessarily planned for such, the separation has material as well as ideological value insofar as land values are protected and economic development furthered, while worker struggles and ideological consciousness are deflected to the demarcated sphere of consumption (Chapter 1). Moreover, and in this case directly addressing class struggle, planning is consciously used to allocate social expenses necessary to maintain social harmony. This latter task is evident through welfare, police control, employment, and other social programs.[2] In summary then, State planning helps resolve the conflict between private and decentralized investment (and consumption) decisions and the need for collective action necessary to guarantee production and social relations. Insofar as it coordinates and guarantees the conditions necessary for capital accumulation, the State's planning and allocative apparatus will be called on by those diverse interests benefiting from accumulation.

Using the New York metropolitan region as a case study, this chapter traces the support offered for regional coordination and, where considered necessary, preemption of existing municipal land use controls. Many contemporary planning analysts focus on recent consumer demand for a pleasing residential and recreation environment as the motivating force behind centralized land use regulations.[3] While consumers and environmentalists have become a major political force in recent years, the historic participation by production and supply factors through their push for accommodation of economic development should not be overlooked. The recent surge in centralized regulation, commonly identified as a "quiet revolution," should not be mistaken as merely a new phenomenon directed by a unified environmental movement intent on protecting consumption amenities and space from the ravage of urban development. Much of the thrust for regional reform stretches back to the turn of the nineteenth century. It represents attempts to circumvent barriers to urban development and capital accumulation that arose as the scale of development increased and more units of local government adopted restrictive land use controls.

In this regard, the liberal planning reform movement emerging during the 1960s and 1970s was heir apparent to the earlier progressive or municipal reform movement of 1890-1920, and to the metropolitan planning movement accompanying municipal reform in its later years (1900-1930).[4] Both of these earlier crusades shared with the contemporary liberal movement a concern that critical land use decisions should be moved to a higher citywide or regional level of control. At first this centralization of planning and regulatory authority was necessary to overcome divisive local competition for growth and harness it for large-scale investments that appeared to be in the collective interest of all regional growth advocates. More recently, when access to land development was blocked by parochial political structures unwilling to finance or provide for urban growth, municipal and regional reform was again suggested by production forces as a lubricant to unplug the growth process.

A human and historic bridge connects the early progressive reform movements and more recent efforts by the liberal reformers to centralize decision making. This is amply demonstrated in this chapter through the continuing activities of the Regional Plan Association of New York and through a host of other business-led regional planning advocates across the nation. With antecedents in earlier municipal research bureaus, civic organizations, and commercial clubs, these groups are major sponsors of contemporary planning reform and are central actors in the quiet evolution in land use control.

THE PROGRESSIVE ERA IN MUNICIPAL REFORM AND METROPOLITAN PLANNING

Liberal planning reform favors a longer range and more comprehensive discussion of land use allocation than is typical of the existing local (village, town, and city) level of planning and regulation. And as befitting its progressive stand, it seeks a centralization of land use control necessary to accomplish this mission. As a consequence, the liberal agenda is of concern to large-scale (corporate) production interests operating across many jurisdictions or requiring public services beyond the local (municipal) response capacity. In addition to industrial concerns, these large-scale production interests include financial institutions and utilities, with major investment in housing, offices, service facilities, and other elements of the built environment.

With the rise of the modern corporation in the 1890s, the central districts of the larger urban complexes turned increasingly from industrial functions, which were already moving out of the city center as the scale of production increased, to office-based command and control functions necessary for multilocational production, investment, and marketing decisions. Central-city industrial relocation was in response to numerous push and pull forces. These included the desire by manufacturers to escape urban unions and avoid stricter environmental (nuisance) regulations, as well as the attraction of cheaper taxes, more plentiful supplies of land appropriate to the larger scale of industrial production, and a more favorable political climate. The latter promised the possibility of controlling newly created suburban units of government that would cater to the manufacturers' needs.

Concurrent with the growing specialization of the central city, a professional-managerial sector of midlevel office workers and support personnel (e.g., lawyers, bankers, planners) arose. As did the wealthier industrial entrepreneurs who could first afford the luxury, these white-collar professionals sought a suburban residence safe and secure from the social conflict and environmental degradation accompanying the decaying central-city production process.[5] In the suburbs, office workers and managers could escape the vigors of the workplace, there to consume the hard-earned fruits of their efforts. From the consumption or use value perspective of the middle and upper classes then, the urban landscape was divided into production (including industrial and business) and consumption (bedroom) districts. In the New York metropolitan area, the industrialized Brooklyn and New Jersey waterfronts and the growing central-city (Manhattan) office districts were representative production zones, while vast expanses in Westchester and Nassau counties, and select enclaves in Queens, such as Forest Hills and Jamaica Estates, were characteristic residential areas. Of course for the lower-income industrial workers such a demarcation did not yet exist. New Jersey's factory workers, for example, often lived in polluted production districts close to the industrial plants since they could ill-afford the commute from, let alone a residence in, the suburban residential enclaves. Other industrial employees, left behind in the central city as industry moved out, were forced to seek new employment, commute, or relocate to the new suburban factory complexes.

The new "corporate" mosaic, with its suburban residential and factory districts and its downtown office and retail centers, required many more public services than the earlier and more compact industrial city. Thus, improved trolley, rail, and highway access; port development; provision of utilities; urban redevelopment; and water and sewer supply were among the items on the political agenda of ascending downtown business interests. These included large-scale real estate, finance, retail, and corporate firms. The business and retail concerns actively sought to facilitate the relocation of industry and residence out of the central business district (CBD) through improved suburban access and services, while the downtown realtors and developers were drawn to lucrative office development and renovation in what were formerly manufacturing and working-class residential neighborhoods. Together with others benefiting from absolute urban growth (such as the construction trade unions, local finance capital, and media interests), the downtown realtors, retailers, and business executives constituted an urban redevelopment and growth coalition.[6]

Early in this century top-level corporate managers, developers, and financiers were already aware that the increasing scale and specialization of production, and the need to more boldly provide the infrastructure, housing, and other conditions required for continued urban expansion, threatened to overwhelm the response capacity of the local municipalities. Business support for metropolitan (or regional) planning and land use coordination grew in the New York metropolitan area, as elsewhere in the United States, out of the municipal reform movement of the late nineteenth and early twentieth centuries. Initially designed to stop the graft and corruption associated with ward-based political machines, the municipal reform movement sought economy and efficiency in the provision of public services, and the removal of as many of these services as possible from a political arena where they were subject to patronage and ward-based politics. In New York the 1898 consolidation of the (then) four counties, with their numerous cities, towns, and villages, into the city of New York, and the establishment of a city charter with responsibility for most municipal services vested in the strong executive office of the mayor were the crowning achievements of this earlier "progressive" or municipal reform era.[7]

Early on municipal research bureaus became popular vehicles through which the reform ideology spread. They were most successful in the larger metropolitan areas (including New York and Philadelphia), where competition for community leadership was fragmented between entrenched competitive (local) and monopoly or corporate (multilocational) capital interests. Representatives from the local branches or headquarters of the national corporate business community relied on the nonpartisan bureaus to lobby for a strong mayor and central-city council form of government. The latter was portrayed as more efficient and responsive to the regional citizenry than the earlier ward-based machines favored by parochial neighborhood businesses and their employees.

Many bureaus promoted the application of Frederick Taylor's principles of scientific management to the quagmire of political patronage and suggested the large corporation itself as the model for bureaucratic reorganization. At the national level the National Municipal League, founded in 1894, and the National Civil Service Reform League were among the most active reform groups, while in New York City the New York Bureau of Municipal Research (incorporated in 1907 and surviving today as the Institute for Public Administration) was a leader and prototype for numerous other metropolitan-based reform organizations.[8] Some of the smaller metropolitan areas with large corporate facilities also had active municipal bureaus. In Rochester, for example, the local bureau was founded by George Eastman in 1915 and the Eastman Kodak Corporation was a major source of funding over the years. Buffalo also had a municipal research bureau active through the 1930s.

Upon the successful reorganization of central-city governments, downtown business interests and reformers turned their attention to the metropolitan area in which they were now operating. They organized groups such as the Merchants' and the Commercial clubs of Chicago, merging as the Commercial Club in 1907; the Citizens Committee on (a) City Plan for Pittsburgh, established in 1918; and the Commonwealth Club of San Francisco. They were also active through private foundations, including the influential Russell Sage Foundation, and through municipal research bureaus. These urban redevelopment and growth coalitions supported metropolitan planning and regulatory reform over the ensuing half century. Proposals were made to increase municipal capability to accommodate large-scale projects through adoption of permissive land use controls and, where necessary, through selective centralization of urban services including transportation, water, and sewer supply. This private planning for the public sector accelerated during the postwar boom. By the mid-1950s almost every major metropolitan area had its own nonprofit and privately sponsored regional land use planning advocate. Prominent examples included San Francisco's Bay Area Council, Detroit's

Metropolitan Fund, Pittsburgh's Allegheny Conference on Community Development (evolving out of the Citizens Committee on [a] City Plan), and the Greater Philadelphia Movement, to name but a few.[9]

In New York State, business-supported municipal research and regional planning occurred in the fastest growing sections, particularly where central-city and large-scale corporate interests felt hemmed in by the growing proliferation and power of suburban enclaves. Beginning during the Progressive Era in New York City, this planning process took hold in Buffalo with the 1920 founding of the Buffalo City Planning Association, itself an outgrowth of the City Planning Committee of the Greater Buffalo Advertising Club.[10] In the postwar period private efforts got underway in many rapidly urbanizing centers of the state, including Syracuse (the Syracuse Metropolitan Development Association, founded in 1959) and the Hudson Valley (the Mid-Hudson Pattern for Progress, founded in 1964). However, it was in the New York City region, the nation's largest and most congested metropolis, where business-led regional planning had its most rigorous expression.

FROM CITY BEAUTIFUL TO CITY FUNCTIONAL: EARLY PLANNING AND ZONING IN THE METROPOLITAN REGION

The eminent landscape architect Frederick Law Olmsted, Sr., designer of Manhattan's Central Park and Brooklyn's Prospect Park, prepared the first comprehensive plan for the New York metropolitan region in 1868. Central to Olmsted's plan was a series of "parkways" linking the major parks and shore areas of New York and Brooklyn (then separate cities) with a bridge across the East River in the vicinity of what became, in 1909, the Queensboro Bridge.[11] Although Olmsted's plan had little impact at the time, the parkway idea influenced Robert Moses. As president of the Long Island State Park Commission (1924-62), the notorious "power broker" (after Caro) strung a series of parkways between his major recreation projects on the island (including Queens and Brooklyn). Olmsted's parkway system also found its way into the 1907 report of the New York City Improvement Commission. Also known as the McClellan Plan (after the mayor at the time), the report in essence was a comprehensive plan for the newly consolidated city. Prepared at the juncture when the earlier emphasis on urban aesthetics, known as the City Beautiful Movement, was giving way to the more pragmatic focus on economic efficiency and scientific management of the Progressive Era, the McClellan Plan was a product of the former but with an eye toward the latter. This was evident through the commission's membership, comprising prominent businessmen, architects, and artists. The plan, in turn, survived as an inspiration for the Committee on (the) Regional Plan of New York and Its Environs, as well as for Moses' own New York City parkway proposals.[12]

In 1909 a plan was published in Chicago that set a national benchmark for metropolitan planning in the two decades to follow. The Plan of Chicago, a private initiative of the Chicago Merchants' Club, was actually released by the

Chicago Commercial Club following merger of the two business groups. The driving force behind the plan was Charles Dyer Norton, a prominent local financier and future secretary to President William Taft. With assistance from railroad president and Merchants' Club secretary Frederic Delano, Norton recruited the eminent urban planner Daniel H. Burnham to prepare the plan.

Burnham's plan was truly monumental for the time. As the first comprehensive plan for an American metropolis, it incorporated both the consumption (residential and recreational) areas and the production (industry and office) districts necessary to service a large metropolitan region with a growing central office center. With Henry Ford's (1907) Model T just appearing on the scene, the forward-looking plan envisioned a highway system stretching up to 60 miles from the downtown loop, together with a major program of street widening and avenue expansion for the city proper. An outer metropolitan system of forest preserves, connected via parkways, complemented recreation space in the inner city, where parks, beaches, and offshore islands were envisioned. Detailed plans for new railroad terminals, harbor development, and civic improvements completed the attention given to the careful demarcation of production from consumption space.[13]

Eager to turn vision into reality, the Commercial Club funded a "citizens'" promotion group, known as the Chicago Plan Commission, to lobby for implementation. In 1911 the commission succeeded in having the Chicago Plan officially adopted as the General Plan of Chicago. Many of the plan's proposals were implemented in the period 1910-30 through a series of municipal bond offerings.[14]

As we shall see, the Chicago planning process had an influence far beyond its regional confines. It emphasizes physical planning to separate what were perceived as production from consumption zones (thereby attempting to moderate the conflict between the two while furthering absolute urban expansion), and it called for the creation of a sophisticated public education advocate. In a reverse migration of influence that no chauvinistic New Yorker would ever recognize, the Chicago process also became the structure upon which regional planning in the New York metropolitan region proceeded. Furthermore, as was to be the case in New York and as befitting its business sponsorship, the Chicago Plan gave primary attention to servicing the office and commercial center of the region while accommodating the consumption interests of central office workers through suburban recreation and residential districts. Scant attention was paid to the needs of lower-income factory workers and to the improvement of the squalid slums in which they still lived. More significantly, the Chicago Plan clearly demonstrated the potential impact of private planning upon the public sector. Coaxed through the private initiative, urban landscapes could be reconstructed by public bodies in a manner benefiting the sponsoring economic interests. Finally, the plan addressed territorial conflict and promoted political reform insofar as the region's citizenry was persuaded that the "scientific rationality" of regional comprehensiveness had more to offer than parochial political pursuits following actual class and territorial interests.

Land use controls were an important component of municipal reform during the early decades of this century. Police power over land use was indispensable to plan implementation where the private market and public investments, by themselves, failed to achieve the desired results. In practice, however, zoning and building regulations often preceded careful planning and were in response to more immediate nuisances threatening established land values or uses.

Support for zoning in New York originated with the Fifth Avenue Association, a group of retail merchants operating the luxury department stores. Having already fled up Fifth Avenue to escape the congestion and social discord swirling around the city's then-burgeoning garment industry, the merchants sought to keep the sweatshops from migrating up the avenue along with their undesirable immigrant garment workers. The garment manufacturers, in turn, sought the midtown location to be nearer the hotel district and rail stations (Penn Central and Grand Central) frequented by the out-of-town buyers.

In 1913 Manhattan borough president George McAneny—a lawyer, journalist, and leading foe of Tammany Hall (the Democratic political machine) —responded to the association's complaint. With assistance from the City Club of New York, an organization of business executives similar to Chicago's Commercial Club, McAneny won approval from the New York City Board of Estimate to create the Committee on City Planning. McAneny's close associate, Edward M. Bassett—a lawyer, former congressman, and, by most accounts, the "father" of zoning in America—served as chair of the committee. Lawson Purdy, the city's chief assessor and president of the National Municipal League, served as vice-chair. This committee, in turn, supported two zoning commissions, both chaired and vice-chaired by Bassett and Purdy respectively. They were drawn from representatives of the Fifth Avenue Association and downtown real estate, financial, and professional (architecture and law) groups. As it evolved under their guidance, zoning became a tool used not only to protect existing property values, and indirectly, social, ethnic, and class differences, but also to promote urban expansion into new territories. As a result of these efforts the city's first zoning ordinance was a landmark in U.S. urban history due to its comprehensiveness, accommodation of continued urban agglomeration, and, ultimately, its impact upon subsequent municipal adoption across the nation.[15]

Entitled the Heights of Buildings Commission, the city's first zoning commission addressed the lack of sunlight and heavy pedestrian burden at street level imposed by the bulky skyscrapers and by the new sweatshop lofts then under construction in Manhattan. The department store merchants and many office landlords and tenants objected to the severe congestion caused by buildings such as the Equitable tower at 120 Broadway. This 42-story "box" concentrated 13,000 workers on a single city block and lowered rental and tax values for neighbors stuck in its long shadow.[16] The commission report adopted a compromise allowing for the tall height and associated prestige of towering skyscrapers in exchange for building setbacks and bulk limits. This resulted in the familiar ziggurat structure dominating building design in Manhattan for the next several decades.

The second commission, known as the Commission on Building Districts and Restrictions, also had a major impact on the city's landscape. Incorporating the report of the first commission, the second commission actually designated the height, bulk, and land use zones of the city. With the entire city divided into four zones (residential, commercial, unrestricted, and undetermined), each containing a variety of height restrictions, Bassett's ordinance slowed the invasion of labor-intensive manufacturing shops and other "nuisance" uses into the sanctioned office and retail areas. The 1916 ordinance limited manufacturing to no more than 25 percent of the space in an area from Third to Seventh avenues and from Thirty-second to Fifty-ninth streets. A new center for the garment industry (under pressure to provide cleaner and safer loft space) was planned for Seventh Avenue between Thirty-fourth and Thirty-ninth streets. The Times Square district, where theater owners were also complaining about congestion and noise accompanying the garment industry, was additionally zoned against manufacturing.[17] As shall be demonstrated, theater owners and retail merchants were later to support the Regional Plan Association in its attempt to rid designated office, retail, and theater districts of garment manufacturing and the congestion accompanying hordes of immigrant workers.

Impatient for the final ordinance and concerned that it did not eject garment manufacturers already established ("grandfathered") in the new nonindustrial zones, the Fifth Avenue Association launched its own campaign. Its Save New York Committee received contributions from large retailers across the nation and took out full-page ads in the New York *Times*. Overt pressure was used. The major banking and insurance institutions aligned with the retailers refused to extend loans to, and retailers threatened a boycott of, offending manufacturers. In this manner, the association managed to rid the theater, retail, and, by now, emerging midtown office districts of most garment production.

Already at this early date, and continuing for over half a century, a split in support for land use controls developed. On the one side, the downtown corporations and the larger financial, professional, and commercial firms serving them supported the regulations; on the other side, the smaller competitive sector of capital and its suppliers opposed the controls. As a case in point, the large Manhattan-based architectural firms and real estate owners favored citywide zoning and building codes while smaller architectural firms, located in the outer boroughs and working in local neighborhoods, joined with local developers in opposition to these comprehensive regulations.[18]

The major life insurance, real estate, banking, business, and commercial associations in the city were virtually unanimous in support for the 1916 ordinance once convinced that it would protect and improve the value of their investments. These larger capital interests crushed the opposition mounted by the small-scale real estate speculators and unorganized local property owners.[19] Objections from social reformers (including Lawrence Veiller, a member of the second zoning commission), who supported slum clearance and decongestion of the city's tenement districts but found the ordinance too accommodating to business interests, went largely unheeded.

Having secured the zoning ordinance, McAneny, Bassett, and the other progressive reformers turned their attention to urban planning. Although after the fact for the city center, planning ideally would precede zoning in the region's other municipalities, thus bolstering the claim that zoning laws were not arbitrary and capricious. Moreover, with the fragmented political system already in place at the metropolitan level, reformers in New York, as elsewhere, realized that local jurisdictions had to implement home rule powers prior to any coordination of these regulations for the regional good. Finally, the reformers realized that planning would have to be coordinated on a regional level to prevent parochial municipal ordinances from thwarting metropolitan needs, such as for highways, garbage dumps, and low-rent worker housing. Thus, in a sense, the regional vision and coordination continuing today as the liberal "quiet revolution in land use control" emerged at the very dawn of municipal land use control.

THE COMMITTEE ON (THE) REGIONAL PLAN OF NEW YORK AND ITS ENVIRONS

Regional planning in the New York metropolis arose out of the existing progressive concern with economy and efficiency in municipal administration and with provision of public services necessary for continued economic development. It was the brainchild of Charles Norton, the guiding light behind Chicago's 1909 regional plan. Coming to New York in 1911 as the new vice-president of the First National Bank of New York, Norton formed a close association with George McAneny, then borough president of Manhattan. In 1914 McAneny appointed Norton chair of the advisory committee to his Committee on City Planning. In that capacity Norton had some input into the 1916 zoning ordinance. Aware of the need for a much broader and more comprehensive approach to urban land regulation than could be offered through the preparation of a local zoning ordinance, Norton sought private business support for a planning effort that would embrace the entire metropolitan area. In a memorandum to his committee, Norton observed that

> no plan of New York will command recognition unless it includes all the areas in which all New Yorkers earn their livelihood and make their homes. . . . From the City Hall a circle must be swung which will include the Atlantic Highlands and Princeton; the lovely Jersey hills back of Morristown and Tuxedo; the incomparable Hudson as far as Newburgh; the Westchester lakes and ridges, to Bridgeport and beyond; and all of Long Island.[20]

Norton's grand vision of the New York "region" centered on production space in New York City together with the consumption districts occupied or utilized by the city's workers and commuters. The scale envisioned appealed to

McAneny, Bassett, and other zoning leaders who recognized a need for regional planning to coordinate what would otherwise be individual parochial efforts. In 1918 Norton accepted the invitation of Robert DeForest to sit on the foundation's board of trustees. Deforest was president of the Russell Sage Foundation and, in his own right, a wealthy philanthropist, and railroad, insurance, and bank director. With DeForest's blessing, Norton persuaded the foundation to support a survey for a regional plan to be modeled after his earlier work for the Chicago Commercial Club.

In 1921 the Russell Sage Foundation made the first of many contributions to Norton's effort.[21] The Committee on (the) Regional Plan of New York and Its Environs (hereafter also CRPNY) was formed among several trustees of the foundation. The committee included Norton and DeForest, together with John Glenn (the foundation's secretary), Dwight Morrow (a partner in J. P. Morgan and Co.), and Frederic Delano (Norton's colleague from his Chicago days, vice-governor of the Federal Reserve Bank, and an uncle of the governor and future president of the United States, FDR). With little public support and no media notification until the survey work was well underway, the committee decided to increase its membership and establish an independent status from the sponsoring foundation. This was accomplished through the addition of several "prestigious" members of the financial, publishing, and planning communities. They included (1) John Finley, an associate editor of the New York *Times*, former editor of *Harper's Weekly*, and a past president of the City College of New York; (2) Henry James, a trustee of the Carnegie Corporation and manager of the Rockefeller Institute for Medical Research; (3) George McAneny, by then executive manager of the New York *Times* and chair of the New York State Transit Commission; (4) Frank Polk, an attorney, acting secretary of state in the Wilson administration, and a director of half a dozen insurance, banking, and railroad firms; (5) Frederick Pratt, a Brooklyn real estate developer and founder of Pratt Institute (a leading architecture school in the city); and (6) Lawson Purdy, the past president of the New York City Department of Taxes and Assessments and a chief architect of the 1916 zoning ordinance.

For his staff to work on the survey Norton went on to recruit the stars of the then-budding urban planning profession. Prominent personnel included Thomas Adams, founder and first president of Britain's Town Planning Institute; Edward H. Bennett, Daniel Burnham's chief assistant on the Chicago Plan; George Ford and Harland Bartholomew, two of the most active planning consultants in the nation; and Frederick Law Olmsted, Jr., son of the famous landscape architect and, by this time, a leading planner in his own right.[22] Additional primary consultants to the committee included zoning expert Edward Bassett; housing reformer Lawrence Veiller; former chief engineer to the city's Board of Estimate Nelson Lewis; and transportation expert Ernest Goodrich.

While all of the CRPNY luminaries were either recruited from or had strong ties to the business community through professional contacts, it would be a mistake to attribute their motives to a crude search for an ideal plan optimizing the value of their sponsors' real estate and business holdings. On the other hand, the self-serving characterization of the committee by its public relations staff as "a citizens' committee, representing a disinterested movement for improving the collective home of all the people of the New York Region" is also suspect.[23] Rather, the committee and the plan eventually prepared were products of a progressive ideology impatient with an inefficient laissez-faire market allocation of land use. Regional intervention was necessary to demarcate and service production and consumption landscapes from which certain undesirable elements had to be removed for the greater good of the whole. This regional goal was accepted as the accommodation of continued urban expansion. As we shall see, the progressives were not unlike their liberal counterparts today. Both groups sought a physical landscape that was conducive to the reproduction of the social structure of capitalist production. However, while benefiting capitalists as a class, State intervention to further capitalist accumulation was bound to favor certain factions more than others at the municipal and regional levels. Thus, individual capitalists (and their corporations) supported these efforts only insofar as their particular needs were served.

The committee's survey of the region appeared in eight volumes between 1924 and 1929. The survey, in turn, supported Volumes 1 (*The Graphic Regional Plan*) and 2 (*The Building of the City*) of the regional plan, appearing in 1929 and 1931 respectively.[24] The pivotal 1929 volume was the product of a monumental effort. Also known as the 1929 Plan, it covered hundreds of jurisdictions and some 5,000 square miles containing almost one-tenth of the nation's population. At its core the plan was primarily concerned with setting up a circulation system that would encourage and service an idealized urban landscape. This would entail a reconcentration and expansion of office employment in the central city (Manhattan), with industry relocated to industrial parks along major suburban transportation arteries. Residential development was to be spread throughout the metropolis in rather compact neighborhoods, leaving a lot of land left over for open space and for the recreation amenities so vital to attracting talented white-collar professionals to the region. In this respect the plan basically took then-current trends and projected them as normative goals for the future. Although industry and residential development was proposed for areas where manufacturing and office, as well as industrial, workers were already moving, the plan went much further by actively encouraging an acceleration of these trends through a massive program of public infrastructure investment.

The 1929 Plan proposed an astonishing 2,527 miles of new highways for the region which, in 1928, had only three and one-half miles of limited access roadway.[25] In addition to the highways, parkways, and accompanying tunnels and bridges, the plan suggested new suburban railroad links and other services geared to increasing the mobility of the newly emerging middle class, elements of which were now moving out of the central city into the suburbs. The rail and roadway links also supported the decentralization of manufacturing, and, where workers could afford it, a decentralization of central-city working-class residents to new suburban enclaves.

The 22-county region covered by the plan encompassed major portions of northern New Jersey and western Connecticut (Map 2.1). Centered on Manhattan, the area defined as "New York and its environs" covered 436 units of government and approximately 10 million people in 1929, of whom 6 million lived in New York City.[26] Although the committee was vague on the justification for boundary determination, a certain logic did emerge. This was born of attention to production interests in New York City and to the social reproduction of the city's workforce. According to the committee:

> The boundaries were determined largely on four grounds, namely: (1) they embraced the area within which the population can and does travel in reasonable time from home to place of work—that is, the commuting area; (2) they included the large outlying recreational areas within easy reach of the metropolitan center; (3) they followed the boundaries of cities and counties at the periphery of these areas, so as to relate the plans to the areas of administration; and (4) they had regard to the physical characteristics, such as watersheds and waterways.[27]

It thus appears that the geographic area covered by the plan, once adjusted for political boundaries, encompassed the labor pool working in New York City *and* the immediate surrounding urban centers such as White Plains, Yonkers, Newark, and Jersey City, *if* there was any overlap. This was taken together with sufficient area to encompass the immediate locus of consumption—primarily residential and recreation space. As a result, the whole of Long Island (with its many fine beaches and extensive farmland ripe for residential development) was included, as were important recreation districts in the nearby Ramapo Mountains and along the Hudson Valley.

THE REGIONAL PLAN ASSOCIATION OF NEW YORK AND THE IDEOLOGY OF PROFESSIONAL PLANNING

In 1929 the Committee on (the) Regional Plan inaugurated a separate Regional Plan Association (hereafter also RPA) to promote adoption of the 1929 Plan. Formally known as the Regional Plan Association of New York, the RPA was, and continues to be, the most influential and successful regional planning advocate in New York State, if not also the nation. Over the past 50 years the RPA sought to coordinate regional planning in the tristate New York metropolitan region. Other organizations might lay claim to intellectual influence (such as the Regional Planning Association of America—active in the 1920s and 1930s) or may have greater influence over the local political process (e.g., Pittsburgh's Allegheny Conference on Community Development) than the RPA. None, however, approach the RPA in breadth of concern (the largest metropolis in the nation, embracing almost one-tenth of its population) *and* influence (at least as measured by public and private investment consistent with the goals and plans advocated by the organization).[28]

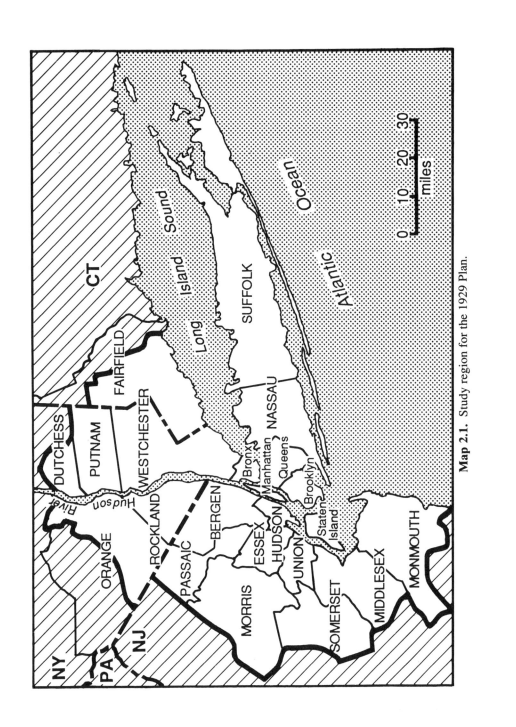

Map 2.1. Study region for the 1929 Plan.

While membership in the RPA was nominally open to the public, recruitment was primarily from the region's financial and business community. During its formative years (1929-40) the board of directors was limited to prominent business leaders and to urban professionals so vital to the preparation of the surveys and plans. CRPNY members formed the initial core of the RPA, with George McAneny serving as president until 1940. The Russell Sage Foundation provided the major funding for the association up until the Second World War, after which membership fees, research grants, and private donations became dominant.[29]

The RPA was portrayed in a sanctioned biography as a means whereby corporate leaders could discharge "some of the civic participation and philanthropic obligations attendant to high status."[30] It was McAneny's contention that ". . . official planning in the Region [could not], for some years at least, be truly effective without the support, assistance and criticism of this private citizens' organization, which, aloof from politics and sectional interests, [was] free to approve or disapprove planning proposals, or allied public measures, with an eye single to the common good.[31] As such, the RPA promised to pursue the public's interest in an objective and nonpartisan manner by excluding public officials from its ranks and by hiring what became the largest and most technically competent regional planning staff in the metropolis.

The RPA's fascination with the application of "rational" business practice to the political quagmire of urban administration was a legacy of the progressive reform ideology of its founders. As expressed in the first survey volume leading to the 1929 Plan:

> The metropolis, in one of its aspects, is essentially a piece of productive machinery competing with other metropolitan machines. It will prosper or decline as compared with other metropolises roughly in proportion to the relative efficiency with which it can do economic work—that is, produce economic goods and services. The area of New York and its environs may be likened to the floor space of a factory. Regional planning designates the best use of this floor space—"the proper adjustment of areas to uses."[32]

Efficiency and economy in urban development would be promoted through public intervention where individual market decisions threatened existing investments or diminished aggregate urban expansion:

> This, then, is the type of control needed: that which will ensure the fullest use of the space facilities available consistent with the proper functioning and future development of the entire area, which will allocate to each activity its real costs, and will prevent the parasitic encroachment of lower functions upon the facilities of the higher functions. Planning consists not merely of beautiful pictures of civic centers or interesting projects for pleasure boulevards. It includes also the designation of the uses of areas and the equipment of those areas with means of access. It seeks to achieve its ends by both voluntary cooperation and legal compulsion.[33]

The central strategy called for municipal adoption of land use and capital improvement plans, with zoning regulations implementing the plans. For its part, the RPA would help spread the planning gospel and assist local communities in coordinating their efforts with the regional plan.

The recruitment of business-led, unofficial planning committees to prepare and promulgate what amounted to a massive and far-reaching plan for public investment was warranted, according to the 1929 Plan, because the region under study covered parts of three states and hundreds of jurisdictions—a situation frustrating collective public action. With local home rule powers jealously guarded and interstate competition for investment a regional fact of life, a private, nonprofit organization could possibly fill the vacuum where the local politicians feared to tread:

> In view of the facts as they are, it appears that unified government in the New York region as a whole is out of the question. It is because of this that regional planning is the more necessary, for in an important sense regional planning may be a substitute for centralization of government. If sufficient co-operation between the communities in a region can be obtained so that they will agree on the broad outline of a plan for all their areas together, and if they collaborate to carry out such a plan, they can go far toward attaining the ideal which would be possible under a united government.[34]

The self-characterization of the RPA's motives did not rest unchallenged. Lewis Mumford of the Regional Planning Association of America (RPAA) was the foremost critic of the sponsorship, intent, and possible impact of the RPA's effort. He concluded that the RPA and its product merely accommodated then-current trends into the future without any recognition of the self-fulfilling social and political consequences of a physical plan. Thus portrayed, the plan served the private and public interests responsible for, as well as benefiting from, existing patterns of urban development.[35]

The survey volume on population trends in the metropolis must have given Mumford pause for thought. Predicting that "the remarkable growth of population in the Region is not likely to suffer any serious retardation until twice the present number has been reached," the authors of this volume observed that "it is wise for regional planners to accept maximum estimates [of future growth], because no serious mistake in planning can be made if they provide for a larger increase than actually comes about."[36]

Rather than accepting the existing speculative land market as a given, Mumford and his Regional Planning Association of America argued for a more forceful shaping of urban development to serve social needs. In his words:

> To assume that growth within an arbitrary metropolitan area will continue automatically in the future under the same conditions that prevailed in the past, is to beg the whole question: it is to place a premium on inertia and routine and to register a vote against those possibilities of social control which a plan, by its very nature, must conjure up.[37]

The urban historian was particularly critical of the RPA's proposal to use extensive public investment in roads and infrastructure to accelerate the drifting toward centralization of office functions and suburban diffusion of residence and factories. These trends, Mumford projected, would eventually lock the central city in massive congestion while threatening it with bankruptcy.

Three decades later Forbes Hays, the RPA's sanctioned biographer, responded to some of the criticisms raised by Mumford and others. He stressed that the plan was certainly not the result of a business conspiracy since there was widespread confidence in the "technical expertise" and "inherent rationality" of a "well-developed plan." Furthermore, the RPA's precarious financial condition at the time, and over the intervening years, "casts doubt on the suggestion of elite bias." In practice, according to Hays, the "RPA's commitment was simply to recruit as distinguished and as committed a group of 'public-spirited citizens' from throughout the region as possible," since the RPA itself "has always been perceived as an appropriate instrument for fulfilling civic responsibilities by most of its board members."[38]

Hays's interpretation is, however, incomplete. The claims of low financial support from special interests and a nonpartisan "rational" and "professional" outlook are characteristic of private nonprofit policy-forming organizations. These positions strengthen the public interest rhetoric of such groups. To be sure, the concentration of corporate leadership within the RPA's board of directors (nonvoting membership was open to the public) is striking. Of the 144 directors serving with the RPA from 1929 to 1963 (the era during which the first regional plan held sway), 58 were company presidents or board chairs of either business or financial corporations and an additional 35 were vice-presidents or midlevel executives. Seventeen more were attorneys—usually professional associates of the corporate members—and of the remainder, the majority were planning, architecture, or engineering professionals—again with close ties to the corporate sector through grants or contracts.[39]

As was common among other business-led regional planning groups (see note 9), the RPA board membership was concentrated in two major sectors. These included representatives from (1) large-scale (monopoly capital, multilocational) organizations with plants, headquarters, or major real estate holdings in the region (e.g., Western Electric, General Motors, American Telephone and Telegraph, and Johnson & Johnson); and (2) the spatially circumscribed and locally monopolistic or oligopolistic enterprises including (a) large-scale utilities (e.g., NY Edison, NY Telephone, NJ Telephone, and the Long Island Lighting Company); (b) private transit companies (e.g., the Pennsylvania, New York Central, and Long Island railroads); (c) insurance and financial institutions (e.g., Williamsburg Savings Bank, NY Life Insurance, First Federal Savings and Loan Association, and Metropolitan Life Insurance); (d) the media (e.g., the New York *Times*); and (e) the largest downtown department stores (as, for example, Bloomingdale Bros. and R. H. Macy and Co.). Representation from small-scale competitive and labor-intensive manufacturers, including the very significant garment, food processing, and printing industries, as well as from retail and trade businesses operating in only one or two locales within the metropolis, was conspicuously absent. During this period the only labor official serving on the board of directors was Harry Van Arsdale, Jr., the powerful leader of the New York Central Labor Council (incorporating 550 different locals with most in the construction trades or having close ties to them).[40]

Hays's claim of civic responsibility notwithstanding, the discriminating concentration of specific factions of the business and professional communities among the RPA's leadership may be explained through an examination of the 1929 Plan and the programs it supported. Geographically the RPA and its plan were clearly geared to preparing the central business district (CBD)—defined in the plan as Manhattan south of Fifty-ninth Street—as the center for the then-expanding office industry (Map 3.2). Labor-intensive manufacturing, together with the working-class tenants, would be encouraged to relocate out of this prime district. This spatial rearrangement naturally attracted support from the large-scale corporate and financial firms seeking headquarters and real estate investment in the city. In addition to rearrangement of the center, the RPA furthered absolute urban expansion throughout the region. While urban expansion may not appear to be a well-defined goal of the corporate groups (to be sure, they sought to avoid the accompanying congestion and sprawl) they did, however, benefit from burgeoning suburban residential districts providing shelter for their office personnel. They also favored the relocation of wholesale and manufacturing functions. The manufacturing interests represented on the RPA board were usually those that already had suburban or exurban plant locations (for example, Johnson & Johnson, Otis Elevator, and Pitney Bowes) or were involved in downtown office and headquarter development (such as Socony Mobil Oil, Radio Corporation of America, and General Motors).[41]

As occurred within the RPA, the corporate concerns aligned with the larger-scale regionally circumscribed interests such as NY Edison, R. H. Macy and Co., and the Pennsylvania Railroad. This alliance between national, or international, conglomerates and local service sectors may not seem unusual if one considers the extent of control and ownership by national concerns in the local sector. Originating with national financial investment in the utilities, and continuing with development of national newspaper chains and television station affiliations, this phenomenon spread to financial services. With the recent push toward deregulation, even local savings and loan institutions are finally coming under conglomerate control.[42]

While the contemporary tendency toward interlocking directorship and diversified ownership may be reducing barriers between national and local capital, we must still account for the earlier participation, as separate entities, of the local service sector in the RPA. These interests, through monopoly or oligopolistic control over their immediate service area, did directly benefit from the RPA's commitment to urban growth. Turning to support for CBD vitality, however, another pattern emerges. Concern by the region's leading corporate and financial institutions for regional planning to further office expansion and urban renewal is fairly easy to theorize and document. Nevertheless, the heavy representation by newspaper publishers, utilities, and department stores in the

RPA's efforts at CBD renewal requires further clarification. Certainly the newspapers (e.g., the New York *Times*) and department stores (e.g., Macy's, Bloomingdale's) represented on the RPA's board were those utilized by the office workers and their dependents, with suburban branches appearing later. We must, however, also consider the geographic locus of these enterprises and their subsequent desire for an urban landscape catering to their needs. The urban geographer James Vance provides a clue, since the region-serving newspapers typify what he would call "local-consumption manufacturers." These generally locate in the central core of an urban region to centralize news assembly and minimize distribution costs. Department stores offer many lines of "narrow-appeal" goods under one roof and, relying on a diverse and crowded level of patronage, are also dependent upon a central location.[43] Moreover, the regional media and those department stores still tied to a CBD location during the 1920s could be expected to rally against the labor-intensive garment industry and existing retail, manufacturing, and low-income residential developments contributing to intense core congestion. They would also be expected to support an improved transportation network to the CBD for their suburban patrons. Finally, the utilities—major beneficiaries of absolute urban growth—also had a stake in energy-intensive central-city development with its office towers and electrically generated heating and cooling systems.

Turning to the urban professionals on the board of directors, the link between vocation and advocation is clear. Most of the architects, planners, and engineers were respected leaders in their fields with strong professional links to urban redevelopment and expansion projects. Finally, Harry Van Arsdale, Jr., the sole labor representative on the board of directors and a major regional power broker, represented an amalgamation of construction trade unions whose members stood to benefit from an aggressive program of office and public works construction. With his large following among the construction trades, Van Arsdale became the darling of the urban growth coalition and of the political machine it supported.[44]

Repeatedly the RPA characterized the economic vitality of New York City and its CBD as essential to the welfare of the region as a whole.[45] As might be expected, this led to some suspicion of the RPA outside New York City, not only among those competitive capital interests concerned about local growth and development, but also among monopoly service (utilities, newspapers, etc.) and finance sectors tied to the older urban centers in the region including Newark, White Plains, Yonkers, and Paterson. State boundaries exacerbated this situation by restricting the service area of regulated industries, such as banks and public utilities. Despite a concerted effort to achieve a broader regional balance, central-city business continued to dominate on the RPA's board of directors through the 1960s.

Forbes Hays comments favorably on the RPA's efforts to broaden board membership:

Although many of those residing outside New York City had primary business interests in the central city, RPA has usually assumed that place of residence is a sufficient basis for achieving geographic balance on the board. . . . [In this manner the] . . . RPA's commitment to create a board of leading citizens of the region has been at least partially implemented.[46]

This apparent confusion of consumption with production interests is striking. With local expression of the former frequently presenting a barrier to regional expansion of the latter, the very essence of liberal land use reform calls for regional intervention to balance the two (Chapter 1). In this effort liberal reform advocates typically fail to adequately identify either production or consumption concerns, or to link them together in the overall structure of accumulation. After all, recognition of competing interests might undermine the crucial claim to the public interest when, in practice, there are many publics and even more claims to them.

In summary then, the RPA's plan was an attempt by select capital interests with a broader vision to attain a consensus on necessary public actions and private investment decisions required for continued accumulation. The association's appeal came about through the well-worn liberal dictum of planning in the public interest. The public interest, in turn, was defined as seeking an efficient and equitable distribution of goods and services through a decentralization of the labor-intensive industry and accompanying working-class tenement districts still concentrated in the CBD, and a centralization of office functions and support services in the vacated center.

The plan would emerge through the application of location "science" where the free market failed to provide for an optimum spatial arrangement:

". . . One of the most stupendous dreams of the social control of civilization concerns the remaking of cities. . . . It is proposed to decentralize them deliberately. By removing obstacles, or interposing deflecting factors, the decentralization which is actually going on may be guided, accelerated and focussed. This is the meaning of modern city planning. In the process of deliberate decentralization, science is ultimately to decide what elements in the present city ought to remain and what ought to go."

When the city planners speak of decentralization, they usually have prominently in mind the decentralization of factories. Manufacturing seems to many of them one thing which certainly does not "belong" in the center of the metropolis.[47]

The focus on efficient, equitable, and aesthetically pleasing growth required a coordination and consolidation of authority for public investment and regulation. As a result, a regional framework for continued accumulation on a larger scale was supported.[48]

Clearing the Central Business District
for Office and Retail Development

The uneven spatial and temporal advance of capitalist development under competitive conditions has split capitalist enterprises into different sectors (e.g., industrial, financial, and real estate) and scales (i.e., large and small scale—see Chapter 1). In terms of scale and market domination, James O'Connor has distinguished between a small-scale, labor-intensive, competitive sector, usually operating in one locale or region and, at the other extreme, a large-scale, energy- and capital-intensive sector typically operating in many locations and often under monopoly or oligopoly market conditions.[49] O'Connor's simple dichotomy applies best, if at all, to the manufacturing sector. Variations from this bisection do exist elsewhere. For example, the monopoly utility and service sectors are usually spatially circumscribed while many multilocational firms maintain labor-intensive branch offices. Nevertheless, once we acknowledge the variations from O'Connor's theoretical extremes, his matrix based upon scale and market domination is useful as a first attempt to organize the different factions competing for space in the urban landscape.

I have intimated that the RPA's 1929 Plan upholds the economic (or material) concerns of select business interests supporting the association. These are addressed through an overarching liberal reform process supportive of capital as a class. It is now incumbent to demonstrate how the plan actually attempted this feat. While a complete demarcation of all social sectors (both capitalist and labor) and their relation to the plan are beyond the scope of this survey, a case study can illuminate how the formation and implementation of a regional plan could move ideals toward reality. For this I turn to the plan and its treatment of the garment industry.

In 1910 the residential population of Manhattan peaked at approximately 2,331,000—more than 900,000 above the level in 1980. According to the 1910 census, 1.25 million residents were crammed into the 9.5-mile-square CBD south of Fifty-ninth Street, one of the highest densities known in the world.[50]

The teeming mass of humanity, when taken together with the additional thousands of people who streamed into the borough to work in its labor-intensive sweatshops, already presented a serious barrier to the pedestrian and traffic circulation necessary to service the CBD as an office, retail, and cultural center. The situation, in turn, prompted the Fifth Avenue Association (including the B. Altman, Bonwit Teller, Gimbel Brothers, R. H. Macy, Saks, Stern Brothers, and Franklin Simon department stores) to threaten a boycott of any garment manufacturer moving into their commercial-retail district. By 1924 the CBD was already receiving nearly 2 million daily commuters and generating a typical weekday population of approximately 3 million.[51]

At the time during which the regional survey was prepared, the New York region was the nation's dominant manufacturing center. It led in production of a wide variety of goods such as tobacco products (cigars and cigarettes), wood-working (pianos, pencils, umbrella handles, etc.), textiles, garments, printing, fine jewelry, food processing (including baking and sugar refining), petroleum refining, and chemical production (from cosmetics to armament manufacturing). While most of the capital- and energy-intensive production lines with bulky products and massive plants located near the rail terminals and ports in New Jersey and east of Manhattan along the Brooklyn waterfront, much of the small-scale, labor-intensive competitive sector was concentrated in Manhattan's CBD close to the dense tenement districts of the workers. Here, in 1922, the survey found nearly 420,000 workers employed in factories, an increase of 44.8 percent over 1900 (Table 2.1).[52]

During this same period (1900-1922) retail, financial, and professional activities were also expanding south of Fifty-ninth Street. Accounting showed a particularly sharp increase from 43 firms in 1900 to 726 by 1922. Similarly, the number of lawyers in the CBD more than doubled to 12,769, while the floor space occupied by large department stores (in excess of 25,000 square feet) increased 73 percent to over 7 million square feet.[53] A showdown between the corporate office and affiliated service expansion on the one side, and the still vibrant competitive manufacturing sectors on the other, was inevitable.

The regional survey was particularly critical of the huge and then-expanding clothing industry. Concentrated in Manhattan's CBD, it was occupying land needed for office and commercial expansion, while contributing to urban congestion and decay hindering office, retail, and leisure (theater access) functions:

> New York is an immigrant city; the clothing trades use almost no other labor. Italians number about 400,000 in New York and Jews have come to be over 1,600,000. The idiosyncrasies of these newly arrived people are expressed by the clothing trades at almost every point. Their untiring ambition, their intense individualism, their willingness to engage in cut-throat competition, their readiness to embark themselves among the risks of unstandardized and speculative enterprises, have all been thoroughly exploited. Slums and ghettos, obsolete and unsanitary working places, congested selling districts, have been among the building materials with which the immense local structure of the clothing trades has been reared....
>   ... There have already been complaints that the workers in the new Garment Center district jam the Times Square subway station at just the time that matinee crowds are going home from the theater.[54]

> Obviously, the clothing industry should not be permitted to spoil the character of the choice shopping district by flooding the shopping streets with throngs of non-buying pedestrians. Again, it should not be permitted to block the avenues leading to the shopping district with vehicles which prevent the flow of merchandise and shoppers into the shopping center. Further, it should not be permitted to pre-empt the transit facilities to the detriment of the shoppers and the employes of merchandising establishments.[55]

Table 2.1

EMPLOYES OF INSPECTED FACTORIES CLASSIFIED BY INDUSTRIES AND BY ZONES IN NEW
YORK AND ITS ENVIRONS IN 1900, 1912, 1917, AND 1922, WITH PER CENT OF INCREASE OR
DECREASE, 1922 OVER 1900

| Industry | Number of employes | | | | Per cent increase, 1922 over 1900 |
	1900	1912	1917	1922	
Zone I—Manhattan south of 59th Street					
Chemicals	5,400	6,262	7,775	7,523	39.4
Men's clothing	35,471	63,189	70,119	52,670	48.5
Women's clothing	59,181	112,756	128,108	114,061	92.7
Metals	37,623	44,940	42,870	42,065	11.8
Printing	35,946	50,648	52,868	53,873	49.9
Food	22,361	25,393	27,457	24,197	8.2
Textiles	9,774	11,437	10,325	11,417	16.8
Wood	21,701	20,774	17,058	14,872	−31.5
Tobacco	10,515	11,740	6,658	5,423	−48.4
All others	51,931	62,996	97,225	93,683	80.4
Total	289,903	410,135	460,463	419,784	44.8
Zone II—Twenty-mile industrial zone					
Chemicals	21,336	36,560	38,914	56,882	166.6
Men's clothing	10,045	37,024	36,516	43,110	329.2
Women's clothing	6,911	20,510	26,364	28,210	308.2
Metals	89,200	147,973	164,161	182,814	104.9
Printing	5,374	9,871	13,233	16,601	208.9
Food	23,201[a]	39,553	38,516	53,177	129.2[a]
Textiles	55,255	87,520	82,940	96,420	74.5
Wood	18,804	40,731	31,280	36,393	93.5
Tobacco	12,319	17,595	13,147	19,946	61.9
All others	59,301	106,255	94,488	128,407	116.5
Total	301,746	543,592	539,559	661,960	119.4
Zone III—Outlying area					
Chemicals	1,284	2,185	15,722	6,096	374.8
Men's clothing	4,580	7,015	8,545	12,119	164.6
Women's clothing	4,220	3,931	7,662	7,924	87.8
Metals	23,638	36,177	63,881	44,200	87.0
Printing	983	1,738	2,132	2,870	191.4
Food	2,760[a]	2,586	3,899	5,098	84.7[a]
Textiles	8,380	11,672	12,944	15,924	90.0
Wood	2,494	2,469	2,773	4,298	72.3
Tobacco	1,005	1,010	1,486	1,126	12.0
All others	15,994	35,737	24,593	24,724	54.6
Total	65,338	104,520	143,637	124,379	90.3

Source: Committee on Regional Plan of New York and Its Environs, *Major Economic Factors in Metropolitan Growth and Arrangement*, Regional Survey of New York and Its Environs, 8 vols. (New York: Regional Plan of New York and Its Environs, 1927), 1:34.

[a] A comparison of the factory inspection figures for New Jersey in 1900 with fragmentary figures from the census indicates that perhaps as many as 2,000 workers in food plants were omitted from Zone 2, and as many as 600 from Zone 3.

While 27 percent of all U.S. employees in the men's clothing industry worked in New York City, the women's garment industry was the leading employer and object of concern. Employing over one-sixth (126,700) of all workers engaged in manufacturing in New York City in 1919, the production of women's apparel was a heavily unionized and predominantly female occupation. By 1921, 74 percent of total U.S. production occurred in the city and, of that, the vast majority concentrated in Manhattan south of Fifty-ninth Street.[56] The Committee on (the) Regional Plan was clearly worried over the recent and rapid emergence of an industry "which was relatively insignificant before 1900":

> These figures indicate the magnitude of this industry's contribution to the city's transit congestion and to the complexity of its problems as a central market for the country's needs. An industry which daily draws 126,700 people to its factories is a considerable factor in the crowding of subways, elevated trains and sidewalks. And an industry which produces clothing to a value of nearly a billion dollars is responsible for a noticeable share in the jamming of the streets with trucks, in the crowding of hotels and terminals by those coming to buy its product, and in the erection of buildings wherein its varied products are made and sold.[57]

Whereas in 1900 the women's apparel industry was located almost exclusively on the Lower East Side, south of Fourteenth Street and east of Fifth Avenue, by 1912 the northern spread of the rapidly expanding enterprise was well underway. This was prompted by worker demands for better sanitary conditions, and by a competitive desire for convenient access to buyers stationed near the midtown passenger rail terminals and hotels. According to the survey, by 1922 almost two-thirds of the industry was centered on 4 percent of Manhattan's land, from Fourteenth to Thirty-eight streets and from Fourth to Eighth avenues (Maps 2.2 and 2.3). Here it competed with office development "and all the leading department stores" for land on which the rent was bid up by virtue of its low space requirements considering the number of employees hired in the sweatshops.[58] Under such circumstances, the rental market could not be relied on to help clear the district for retail and office development: "No one interviewed in the course of this study was of the opinion that high rental was an important enough factor in production cost to influence garment manufacturers to move from the center of Manhattan to the outlying sections of the city or of the region."[59]

At the time, the committee was resigned to a conclusion that the women's garment industry was going to remain small scale, competitive, labor intensive, and unionized. This was by virtue of rapidly changing fashion trends supporting a "chaotic" spot market in New York City and, moreover, by the "psychological peculiarities of the predominant racial group which has provided both wage-earners and manufacturers." These characteristics, in turn, worked against decentralization:

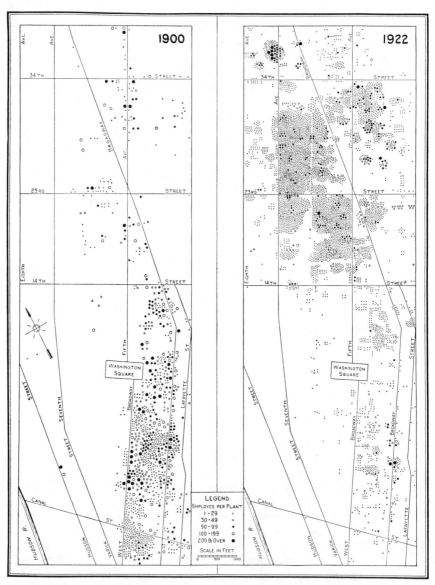

Maps 2.2 and 2.3. Location of plants in the women's garment industry in area of greatest concentration in Manhattan in 1900 and 1922.

Source: Committee on Regional Plan of New York and Its Environs, *Major Economic Factors in Metropolitan Growth and Arrangement*, Regional Survey of New York and Its Environs, 8 vols. (New York: Regional Plan of New York and Its Environs, 1927), 1:86.

[I]t is possible to say broadly that the power of reconciling the clothing industries to frequent and sudden changes of style and fashion, the value of convenient access to an immense market which demands quick delivery, and the presence of a volume of immigrant labor with special peculiarities adaptable to the needs of a fickle and exacting market, have all been of great importance to the local development of these industries.[60]

The committee lamented a lack of standardization in the industry encouraging larger-scale production and possibly suburban or extraregional plant relocation. Aware of the link between transportation access and industrial location, the committee did hope, however, that "development of belt lines of rapid transit passenger transportation may accelerate a trend toward fabrication in the periphery rather than the center of the region." The committee also speculated on the possibility of continuing the concentration to the new garment district provided for by the 1916 zoning ordinance. In this manner the congestion would be moved over to the West Side where, theoretically, it could be housed in "eight city blocks" of "modern loft buildings." Finally, the committee anticipated a day when the recent change in immigration policy (the quota system was established in 1921) would help to cut off the flow of Jews and Italians to New York, and hence, "small contractors may thus be gradually eliminated and large factories maintaining steady work throughout the year may be established in increasing proportions."[61]

This treatment of the garment industry by the committee and the RPA is quite informative, for it clearly demonstrates that capitalists, as a class, are not united on the specifics of urban policy. There are different factions split by sector (industrial, utility, retail, financial, and real estate) as well as by scale (small competitive and large monopoly), superimposed one on the other. Ultimately this splintering emerges through support for land use regulations. In the case before us, the monopoly or large-scale industrial and financial sectors united with affiliated financial, retail, utility, and real estate interests in support of a plan that would rid the CBD of the small-scale, competitive industrial sector.

Factional competition can take many forms, however, and need not be limited to competition over urban space. Carrying O'Connor's analysis of the general dichotomy between competitive and monopoly sectors a bit further, we can detect competition occurring not only over demands placed on the State, or over market control, but also over access to supplies of labor.[62] While the committee was aware that "American white girls in New York have a prejudice against factory work . . . and prefer clerical work at low wages to the high wages of the needle trades," it was also concerned that "compared with almost any other of the large women-employing industries, such as candy, tobacco, and paper boxes, the garment trades far outbid them in wages. . . . In a short labor market they therefore will crowd their competitors for woman labor."[63] As was the case in New York, this form of competition may also surface in the specifics of a land use plan.

The dual goal of planned urban expansion and transformation of the CBD into a center for office control was evident in the 1929 Plan. The proposed extensive transportation network addressed the rail and highway commute needs of a growing sector of midlevel office and service workers required to staff the emerging national center for corporate control.[64] The plan virtually ignored any improvement in the rapid transportation system (referring here to elevated rail lines and subways) still used by millions of urban industrial workers and their dependents—a position quite in line with the desire to rid the CBD of its numerous small-scale, labor-intensive manufacturing shops.[65] As we shall see, this conscious neglect of any public or private improvement in mass transit to the CBD was a serious omission that the RPA, some 40 years later, would have to address as the thousands of garment workers were replaced by subway-dependent clerical workers and secretaries.

Proposed suburban rail and highway routes reached all the way into the CBD, eliminating dependence on the city's own rapid transit system for suburban commuters, while necessitating extensive urban renewal in the industrial and low-income residential neighborhoods through which these arteries would run.[66] The relocation of industry would serve a dual purpose, making way for more productive and aesthetically pleasing urban development, while helping manufacturers escape the power of the militant and well-organized urban unions. This last factor may have accounted for the absence of significant opposition to the RPA's plan from the largest garment, printing, and other competitive manufacturing concerns, since there were cost advantages to be gained from moving large-scale standardized processes to low-wage and nonunionized rural areas:

> In some lines of activity in New York City there is much complaint regarding the competitive disadvantages suffered because of the "extractions" of trade unions. The clothing manufacturer who announced to an investigator his intention to move his plant from New York to some town where he could "tell those damned Bolsheviks to go to hell" undoubtedly voiced the sentiment of many exasperated fellow-employers. In the printing industry, also, this circumstance is of great moment, occupying an important place in the arguments of both employers and unions in the wage negotiations of recent years.[67]

While O'Connor downplayed the power of organized labor in the decentralized competitive sector of manufacturing capital, one should remember that labor in portions of this sector—including the women's apparel, construction, and printing industries—was, on a local level (as in New York), well organized and, at times, very militant. To avoid the higher costs of a union shop, the committee went so far as to choose a nonunionized Philadelphia firm (W. F. Fell) to print the regional plan, even as it praised the strength of New York City's own printing industry.[68]

Servicing the Consumption Landscape

The regional survey and plan were conservative on public provision of low-income housing, preferring to let market forces reign where higher-income residences were already displacing low-income and working-class neighborhoods. As was the case in numerous other metropolitan areas, many urban professionals already lived in the suburbs. New York, however, presented a "peculiar" case due to its size and attendant congestion. These gave rise to an "increased tendency" for high-class residential development in the CBD. According to the committee, all housing development should yield "a fair return on investment," with direct public funding limited to parks, playgrounds, and street widening in low-income neighborhoods.[69] Such a program would support redevelopment of the business district for office, retail, and nearby upper-income residence functions while pushing laborers toward the suburban or extraregional districts where manufacturers were encouraged to relocate.

For the Lower East Side, still the primary residence for thousands of workers in the garment and other competitive trades, the plan proposed wholesale tenement replacement with "club-like" apartment complexes for Wall Street executives. These projects would be on the order of Sutton Place and Tudor City, fashionable developments on the edge of the midtown office district. According to the survey:

> At present the Wall Street banker or broker has no way of reaching his office—if his home is on Manhattan—except by a tedious and time-wasting trip by motor or the still more unpleasant channel of the congested subway. He needs as never before a way of living closer to his work. . . .
>
> Among those to whom the scheme would appeal are men of the financial district who have come to value the quality of the moments in which their lives are passed, who are sensitive to the intolerable waste of nervous energy involved in the hours, and half- and quarter-hours, daily spent in automobile trips through crowded city streets. . . .
>
> Occupants of a club apartment, if it were situated in the lower East Side, could reach the financial district in a ten-minute ride; and evenings, they could enjoy a club, a hotel, a library, a gymnasium or swimming pool, and perhaps a play, without any motor-car hazard at all—simply a descent in an elevator and a short walk through a carpeted corridor or a tessellated arcade. Likewise, wives could call on friends, attend society meetings or musicals, and arrange entertainments without leaving the club. . . .[70]

Redevelopment would displace the existing tenants but this process was, after all, part of "the natural course of events" and might even be in the best interests of current residents. As expressed by John H. Finley, CRPNY member and editor of the New York *Times*:

One has but to visit the Lower East Side on a summer's evening to realize that, as Mr. Brogan, of the East Side Chamber of Commerce, has said, it is "essentially a neighborhood of children and mothers." What with groups of women guarding baby carriages inside the curb, or huddled on stoops or on doorsteps, little ones toddling about and older children racing and darting in and out, pedestrians have difficulty in making their way. Everywhere there is such squalidness, such ugliness of surroundings, such turmoil, that one wonders how life can be endurable there.[71]

Although ultimately this dense tenement district should give way to "superior residential improvements" some assistance was necessary for the process of gentrification to occur (whereby more expensive residential districts replace lower-income neighborhoods):

Where land has a value based on a more profitable use than low cost housing, such as business, or expensive residence, it should not be used for such housing. Where this value is based on the use of land for congested housing, the city should endeavor to lessen the congestion and thereby reduce what is fundamentally a false value.[72]

According to the plan, decongestion could be accomplished through the condemnation of unsanitary tenements and a major program of street widening and park development. Along the East River "a park of 75 acres, which would be large enough to attract good residences to the neighborhood," was suggested.[73]

The committee did not totally abandon industrial workers. The key to encouraging workers to leave the city was to first relocate their factories. For those able to follow employment to the new suburban industrial zones new communities were suggested. These would be on the order of Radburn in New Jersey, then under construction as a model industrial city.[74] However, no serious attempt was proposed to underwrite lower-income housing or prevent suburban municipalities from zoning out the higher-density development that displaced central-city families might afford. This was unfortunate for the workers and, in due time, for the manufacturers, for whom worker housing, with the exception of company towns, was yet to be an issue.

With Radburn as an interesting, but limited, experiment, the survey and plan gave only passing reference to several lower-income housing projects in Harlem, and in Sunnyside and Jackson Heights Queens. The housing community model receiving most attention in the final plan was Forest Hills Gardens in Queens. This was a planned development built by a subsidiary of the Russell Sage Foundation as an "investment for social betterment." Surviving today as one of the most exclusive enclaves in the city, Forest Hills was developed as an "urban neighborhood" for mid- to upper-income urban professionals who could hop on the adjacent Long Island Rail Road for the quick trip to midtown.[75]

In summary then, the committee, where it did address urban housing, preferred limited public assistance for the requirements of mid- and upper-level office workers, with the clublike complexes for those too harried to commute, and a more spacious country club setting for the serious commuters. The unemployed and blue-collar workers would have to fend for themselves and hope that jobs and a receptive housing market would await them in the new suburban industrial belts.

Turning to Long Island, Westchester, and the other suburban landscapes surrounding the city, a different pattern emerged. Here the automobile reigned supreme. By 1926 the 22-county region covered in the plan already contained 1.3 million registered motor vehicles (including trucks) with the majority belonging to suburban residents. With the typical suburban family already owning an automobile (5.2 persons per automobile in the suburbs versus 10.8 for the city), the accompanying congestion during commute hours and on weekends, when thousands drove to the mountains or shore, rivaled that of the city itself. Anticipating a regional fleet of over 3 million vehicles by 1935, the plan extensively promoted existing highway and parkway proposals while recommending additional routes to meet future demand.[76]

Fundamental to the committee's commitment to improved automobile access from suburban residential districts to the city and to outlying recreation areas was a recognition that for most of the region's inhabitants, the trend toward separate working and consumption (or residential) districts would continue: "The most striking feature in the growth of the New York region in the past 20 years, as has been emphasized in the regional survey, is the extent of separation and the increasing tendency towards wider separation, between the places of residence and the places of work."[77] While the committee did encourage highway beltlines at the periphery to facilitate industrial relocation and, in turn, labor migration, it also accepted as inevitable this separation of occupation from residence for most of the city's office workers. In response to, as well as abetting, this spatial division, radial and circumferential highway and railroad lines would be necessary.

Open space and recreation were portrayed by the committee as the principal regional drawing cards:

> New York has probably lost hundreds of thousands of comparatively wealthy residents because of inadequacy of open spaces. People submit to crowded travelling to and from the suburbs because of their desire to live more in contact with nature than is possible in a city so sparsely provided with open space as New York City.[78]

The plan extensively promoted an immense and comprehensive system of public beaches and regional parks. As was the case with the provision of highways and rail lines, parks would function to attract and guide residential development to outlying regions away from the congested core. Toward this purpose a unique highway, known as the "parkway," evolved. First envisioned in the 1868 Olmsted plan for New York City, the parkway was a limited-access highway running through abutting park lands. With RPA encouragement the parkway became the dominant highway form in suburban New York (especially on Long Island and in Westchester), and the region far outpaced the rest of the nation in use of this road system. Exclusively reserved for passenger cars, the limited-access parkway became the guiding influence whereby residential zones could be separated from commercial and industrial zones. The latter were forced to concentrate nearer the boulevards and expressways accessible to trucks and shoppers seeking roadside establishments.[79] Moreover, as we shall see, parkway planning served to set in stone the racial and class demarcations occurring on the suburban landscape.

Individual Interests and Class Welfare

The most significant and durable contribution of the RPA and its plan was the recognition that the physical use of land directly influenced the urban political economy. Certain barriers to capital accumulation, be they unproductive real estate (i.e., fixed investment in the built environment that was no longer economically viable), a militant labor force, physical congestion accompanying development, or the high reproductive cost of managerial labor, could be temporarily swept under the rug via massive public investment encouraging the rearrangement of urban land use. Although members of the RPA and similar business-led planning groups individually may not have been conscious of their collective class interest in the reforms proposed, they generally supported the reform process, entrusting a trained professional staff to delineate areas of common concern.

Among contemporary Marxist theories, there is a standing debate on the relative autonomy of the State. The structuralists view State intervention as independent from the interests of particular class factions and, moreover, consider this relative autonomy as functionally necessary to reproduce capitalism per se. The instrumentalists, on the other hand, recognize ruling elites and powerful interest groups as capturing the State apparatus to pursue private agendas.[80] The RPA and its plan, by way of example, underscore the need to avoid either of these generalizations about the role of the capitalist State in the absence of detailed empirical analysis (also covered in Chapters 5 and 6). Certainly a common class interest in accumulation may be identified, with the RPA serving as an independent agent to arbitrate among competing interests in the formation of State policy. Nevertheless, classes are not one-dimensional and divisions occur along sectoral, size, and territorial lines. In the case of the New York region, large-scale corporate and financial sectors, together with regionally dominant retail, utility, and media interests, privately supported solutions to problems besetting capitalist accumulation that were not upheld by all capitalists. Furthermore, while capitalists are powerful, they are not hegemonic in all instances. The local State apparatus also can be captured by working-class interests as, for example, in the ward-based urban political arena of the last century. Whatever their class origins, homeowners, environmentalists, and other groups defending consumption space are another challenge to capitalist class hegemony.

Although a divergence of interests in land use planning in the New York CBD was clear (for example, between the retail and office-seeking corporate sectors, on the one hand, and the labor-intensive garment industries, on the other), we can detect still further divisions within identified sectors. Ultimately for the capitalist class this fragmentation arises from the structure of the production process itself where individual capitalists operate in a competitive market. As such, factional antagonism is another manifestation of the basic contradiction between the social nature of production and its private appropriation (Chapter 1).

Classes are composed of individuals, and although these individuals may band together in defense of mutual goals, such as urban expansion, consensus is not automatic, and individual dissent is common. This was the case, for example, with the RPA's promotion of urban decongestion through setbacks and bulk limits on the office buildings that would be rented or owned by some of its members.[81] Moreover, intrasectoral conflict can occur over pursuit of production and consumption goals by the same parties (Chapter 6), with individual defense of the latter thwarting urban expansion and accumulation. These intraclass divisions became visible through implementation of the plan, a topic to which I now turn.

IMPLEMENTING THE REGIONAL PLAN

Many analysts underestimate the impact that a private planning effort, such as that of the RPA, may have upon the urban landscape. Influence, however, is often gained through popular acceptance of the self-professed nonpartisan public interest claims of the private organization. Its proposals, thus legitimated in the public eye, may in turn be implemented by other public and private enterprises. John Friedmann and Clyde Weaver in their 1980 book *Territory and Function*, to cite an example, claim that the 1929 Plan was never implemented; whereas Robert Caro, in his Pulitzer Prize-winning biography of Robert Moses, *The Power Broker*, appears to accept Moses' own boast that the enormous transportation and park systems built by his public authorities in the metropolitan region were solely the manifestation of his own fertile vision.[82]

The RPA itself had no doubts about the influence of its plan. In a fiftieth year review of the plan's unveiling, the RPA laid claim to nearly all of the major parks of the region or substantial additions to them, the location of all four of the region's major airports, the vast majority of the highway and parkway network built, the idea and location of Lincoln Center, and numerous other urban renewal projects.[83] With Frederic Delano, former chair of the CRPNY, moving on to join the National Planning Board under FDR, the New Deal gave a major boost to implementation of the RPA's plan. According to a 1942 progress report on the plan, over 54 percent of the vast 2,500-mile highway network first proposed was either built or under adoption, with the Lincoln and Queens-Midtown tunnels opening in 1939 and 1940 respectively. The Brooklyn-Battery Tunnel (built over the objections of Moses who favored a bridge at the site), the Bronx-Whitestone Bridge, the Triborough Bridge, and New Jersey's Garden State Parkway were several other notable projects proposed in the 1929 Plan (or earlier drafts) that were carried out during the New Deal administration. In the 1960s the Verrazano-Narrows Bridge, connecting Staten Island with Brooklyn, was completed along an alignment proposed some 40 years earlier in the original plan.[84]

Between 1923 and 1932 alone the number of planning commissions in the region increased from 10 to 108, and the number of zoned communities more than quadrupled from 59 to 237. In many instances CRPNY (and later RPA) members and staff directly initiated the process, with the regional survey and 1929 Plan serving as a basis for the preparation of local plans and ordinances. By 1942 most of the outlying towns and villages in the 22-county region had, with CRPNY and RPA encouragement and assistance, established planning commissions and adopted zoning ordinances necessary to implement local portions of the plan. In New York City Lawrence Orton, general secretary and staff director of the RPA, served as project director for Mayor LaGuardia's Committee on City Planning. With RPA staff assistance he organized and directed the basic studies leading to the 1938 establishment of the city's Planning Commission and Department of Planning.[85]

Accepting political reality, the RPA had to rely on local implementation of its plan. It was aware from the beginning, however, that independent assertion of home rule could thwart regional planning. Viewing with some alarm the proliferation of political subunits (as on Long Island), the RPA promoted county-level planning as the primary coordinating mechanism. At the state level it helped draft or strengthen county planning enabling legislation for New York, New Jersey, and Connecticut while, at the local level, RPA members formed county and local committees to lobby for local adoption of elements of the 1929 Plan. Where planning legislation required citizens' advisory committees, the association suggested that its locally sponsored committees "constitute themselves delegates, or appoint delegates, to a county planning council for the purpose of giving requisite citizen cooperation to the county authorities in planning matters."[86] By 1936 all of the region's counties had planning boards with the majority initiated through RPA efforts. Furthermore, in the absence of local expertise, the RPA staff was ready and willing to assist with plan preparation and implementation.

Technical assistance went hand-in-hand with the stimulation of planning sentiment. The association was keenly aware that the thousands of speculators, developers, and local lending institutions dominating suburban political life would view planning and zoning as hostile governmental interference in the workings of an unbridled real estate market. To counter the antiplanning forces, a coalition of business, civic, and sympathetic public leaders, backed, where possible, by informed public sentiment, would have to stand in defense of rational urban management. Toward this end, the RPA not only helped initiate planning and land use regulation throughout the metropolis, but also diligently strove to deliver the necessary support for these fledgling efforts:

When planning becomes official, it inevitably becomes, in a sense, political, and its importance as an instrument of public service depends primarily upon the attitude of changing administrations, which may or may not reflect an informed public opinion. It will always be one of our functions, not only to create and maintain popular sentiment for planning, but to see to it, so far as we can, that government is responsive to that sentiment.[87]

To be accepted as a delegate in the public's interest the RPA had to convey an aura of nonpartisan, objective rationality. Recognition was forthcoming. By the mid-1930s the association had been appointed publicity director for the official planning bodies in New York State, New Jersey, and New York City. In the two states alone over 250 newspapers ran a regular series of planning articles written or edited by RPA staff.[88]

It was through this advice and behind-the-scenes lobbying that the RPA was to have its greatest influence. As RPA president George McAneny put it:

We have helped to secure the necessary enabling legislation; influenced local authorities to take advantage of it by setting up the necessary planning machinery; and advised and aided these local planning bodies in their work. . . .

. . . It is no exaggeration to say that . . . organizing the counties for the promotion of planning projects, helping them to qualify for Federal aid, and so establishing planning as an integral part of the county government, was the most important single activity of the Association. . . .

There are few, if any, major planning projects promulgated in the Region regarding which our engineering staff is not consulted. A striking illustration of our usefulness to others was found in a letter from the Chairman of the Queens-Midtown [Tunnel] Authority who advised us that in making its request for a Federal loan and grant of $58,000,000 the Authority submitted the tunnel proposal of the Regional Plan for the reason that it represented studies far beyond the ability of the Authority to make within any reasonable period, and conclusions that were accepted as sound.[89]

Often content to let others take credit for the idea and programs it initiated, one would be hard pressed to exaggerate the RPA's impact during FDR's New Deal administration. This was the period when the plan formed the basis for many of the public works constructed in the region. In New York State the RPA helped organize the State Planning Board with McAneny appointed chair of its Works Committee. The National Resources Board designated the association's chief engineer, Harold M. Lewis, primary consultant to the State Planning Board. Here he would coordinate New York's application to the Public Works Administration in Washington, DC.[90]

Although the RPA had considerable success in securing those aspects of the plan that required public action to implement (i.e., highway, bridge, tunnel, open space, and park development, together with the initiation of local and county planning efforts), those portions of the plan relying upon private sector action did not go very far. This was particularly true with suburban rail development. At the time, all of the region's major rail lines were under private ownership. Over the next 40 years the once-profitable railroads were to see their power and resources slip away, as they were pushed toward bankruptcy (e.g., the Susquehanna Railroad), merger (e.g., the Pennsylvania and New York Central railroads), and public takeover (e.g., the Long Island Rail Road). Although the success of the massive public highway program—which directly competed with the private rail lines for suburban riders—was a major factor in this demise, the railroads also suffered from poor financial management, speculative real estate ventures, and rapidly rising labor costs. Moreover the railroads, without public subsidy, could not profitably cash in on the growing commuter market, since the extra machines, labor, and rail ties necessary to service the few hours of peak performance a day would lie idle most of the time.

ROBERT MOSES: THE MAN AND THE PLAN

Although fragmentation of civil authority has been shown to frustrate public regional planning, it remains to be demonstrated how a private effort can have more success. The RPA, while boldly proclaiming successful implementation of its physical plan, was also quite modest in explaining just how influence was exerted. In his thoughtful study of the 1929 Plan, David Johnson provides a clue. He observes that the RPA, "lacking authority and power of its own . . . was designed to achieve influence by appealing to those who possessed influence."[91] Chief among these individuals, in the public sector, was Robert Moses, "czar" of construction in New York City and throughout New York State by virtue of his highway, bridge, tunnel, and park authorities (Chapter 4).

We have already seen how the CRPNY and the RPA initially defined and filled a vacuum in regional leadership through advice and guidance when the need for regional coordination became apparent to community leaders (both public and private) during the 1920s. By the 1930s Moses appeared as a serious competitor in the quest for regional leadership. Was he, however, the independent power broker of Caro's masterpiece? Did the region represent a biographical landscape "authored" by Moses, as geographer Marwyn Samuels suggests?[92] To answer these questions we must turn to the ideas and plans existing when Moses arrived on the scene to assume his most important posts as president of the Long Island State Park Commission in 1924 and as head of New York City's Park Department and Triborough Bridge Authority in 1934.

Comparing initial survey proposals, the 1929 Plan, and landscapes subsequently constructed by Moses and his public authorities, we realize that while it may not have been as simple a matter as Moses having to "pour concrete on the dotted lines" (after Fitch), ideas, nonetheless, were certainly in the air. The RPA helped create a climate of opinion among the business and political leadership, which both supported and steered Moses and his staff toward projects favored by the RPA. Clearly what we have here was a two-way flow of influence. In some instances, as with the Long Island parkways and the

Triborough Bridge alignment, the RPA adopted the projects, prepared site plans, and lobbied for routes already laid out by Moses or commissions preceding him (e.g., New York City's 1907 McClellan Plan). Elsewhere the association first suggested or promoted projects that Moses was later to complete and claim as his own. Examples of the latter include the Cross-Island Parkway, the Cross-Bronx and the Brooklyn-Queens expressways, and the Bronx-Whitestone and the Verrazano-Narrows bridges.[93] Over all projects, whether Moses-initiated or otherwise, the RPA and its plan drew the connections between heretofore separate transit and recreation efforts. Furthermore, the association anticipated the impact of Moses' numerous activities on industrial, office, and residential development for a region even wider than that over which Moses had official jurisdiction.

In a penetrating analysis of the RPA and its impact, Robert Fitch portrays Moses as a pawn of the organization and its real estate and financial sponsors. He thus finds fault with Robert Caro's abstract empiricism. This empiricism isolates Moses—"the great man"—and the political climate in which he operated from the overall capitalist environment (with its cycles of accumulation and crisis) and from private-sector coordination of the growth ensemble.[94] Although the RPA and Moses may have shared a common ideology it would, however, be a mistake to gloss over their significant dissimilarities. Each had a unique and distinct power base as well as a vision of what significant barriers stood in the way of progress.

In addition to the more familiar conflict between the needs of production and the practice of consumption (Chapters 5 and 6), clashes can occur within the spheres of production and consumption. The RPA's often stormy relationship with Moses paralleled dissent both within and between these realms, and the created landscapes reflected these conflicts. Moses built his power base among a newly emerging middle class to whose transportation and recreation needs he catered. While the construction of a built environment for the consumption by, and reproduction of, this segment of the labor force served corporate production interests, it also, at times, clashed with actual consumption by individual members of the upper class. As a consequence, Moses developed a reputation for standing up to the wealthy and pushing his highways and parks through their estates, often deriding their defense of privileged consumption.

With direct ties to corporate interests, the RPA, on the other hand, was more cautious when attacking the production or consumption practices of its members (either as firms or as individuals), even when these presented barriers to what might be considered a collective class interest (as in opening up the suburbs for worker housing). The Committee on (the) Regional Plan (and later the RPA), for example, successfully opposed Moses' alignment for the Northern State Parkway on Long Island. Taken ostensibly for "aesthetic and cultural preservation," this position more practically sought to steer the parkway away from the large estates of the corporate and financial barons then residing on Long Island's northern "Gold Coast":

> This hilly land in the north of Long Island is peculiarly adaptable for large
> residential properties forming what are practically private parks. . . .
>   . . . If wealthy citizens incline to use their money in developing and
> preserving the natural landscape, they are creating for the Region and for
> the nation something that may be as valuable from a cultural point of view
> as any collection of works of art.[95]

Caro is clear where Moses' personality and quest for power got in the way of a collective capitalist class interest in continued development. Unable to gain control of the authority created to build the Queens-Midtown Tunnel first proposed in the RPA plan, Moses went to great lengths to block funding for—and thus (unsuccessfully) destroy—the authority.[96] In a similar, and not uncharacteristic, power play, he held up construction of a tunnel from the downtown financial district to Brooklyn because he favored a bridge at that site. In this instance he directly clashed with Wall Street corporate, financial, and real estate interests. They saw the bridge, with its massive buttress, as utilizing too much of the valuable land in the area and, furthermore, as blocking the view of and from their high-rise office buildings. Although primarily committed to the tunnel, the RPA sought an accommodation between aesthetic sensibilities and the economic benefits of improved access to the financial district. In this instance the RPA supported a major reconstruction of the existing Brooklyn Bridge, tripling its vehicular carrying capacity, and later threw its weight behind the tunnel. Having squared off over the bridge, the (tacit) relationship between Moses and the RPA rapidly deteriorated after this incident and, by implication, slowed official adoption of remaining portions of the 1929 Plan.[97]

The intense opposition by Moses to minority and lower-income use of his parks and parkways is instructive. As an agent of the State, his actions further emphasize the unavoidable conflict between production expansion and what is defended as consumption space, while further obscuring the boundary between a structural and an instrumental interpretation of urban history. Residential segregation according to income helps to protect and stimulate private consumption, while racial segregation can divide working-class unity. A structuralist interpretation of income and racial segregation as functional for capital accumulation should be eschewed, however, because segregation can also raise the cost of labor and, in turn, the cost of production. This is especially discernible when solutions in one era become dysfunctional in a new cycle of property development and capital accumulation. Hence, for example, Moses literally froze racial and income class demarcations into stone by insisting on curved overpasses for his parkways of such height that mass transit buses could not pass under them.[98] This position, when coupled with his intense opposition to any mass transit, not only added to the eventual automobile congestion (and commute time) in the region, but also slowed the spread of the working class into suburban neighborhoods. The eventual outcome was a higher cost for this labor power, both for suburban manufacturers and for CBD firms drawing on the suburban labor market.

The RPA and its members may not have anticipated this potential threat to their collective class interest in 1929, and in some cases probably applauded the reservation of Westchester and Long Island for car-owning middle- and upper-income families. By the 1940s, however, with the suburban rail lines in disarray and the highways clogged, improved mass transit to the outer boroughs and suburbs had become an imperative. The initial indifference to urban mass transit—that is, subways for the city and buses for the suburbs—may have stemmed as much from the private concerns of RPA members, many of whom lived in suburban enclaves, as from any miscalculation of the future requirements of the region's labor market, or from a notion that the mass transit system was only fit for sweaty garment and other industrial workers. In any case, the silence on working-class transit needs was a situation that the RPA was forced to address some 30 years later in its Second Regional Plan (see below). By then the oversuccess of its first plan, which helped flood the city with cars, had become painfully obvious.

With the 1929 Plan mined for about as many projects as it could yield, the RPA found itself in the postwar period with the need for a new mission. By now it was evident that the extensive highway network was a mixed blessing. On the one hand, it permitted the centralization of office-based control functions to the point of an overcongested traffic grid, while, on the other, it furthered the phenomenal spread of large-tract suburban housing development and amplified the waste in time and energy associated with the grueling commute. Moreover, core congestion, exclusionary zoning in suburban enclaves, and the overextended "spread city" were increasing production costs (including labor), thus encouraging firms to move their manufacturing and, later, their routine information-processing activities to suburban and, eventually, to extraregional locations. A new planning effort was called for, one that could still further central district corporate, retail, and professional service development by promoting the efficient decentralization of residence, manufacturing, and, by now, routine office functions first called for in the 1929 Plan. Once again the RPA attempted to rally and coordinate individual members to support a regional solution to problems of overcongestion threatening the economic health of the core, while circumventing the barriers to efficient urban expansion now thrown up by suburban municipalities.

THE NEW YORK METROPOLITAN REGION STUDY

By 1945 much of the first regional plan had been implemented. The cooling of relations between the RPA and the Moses-led public authorities, the end of New Deal support for public works, and a reduction in Russell Sage patronage contributed to a period of retrenchment, and the RPA's acknowledged leadership in regional planning slackened. During the ensuing decade the association largely survived on research and technical studies for public and private clients. The return to a regionwide focus came in 1956. Under the presidency of Harold Osborne, chief engineer with AT&T, and through the directorship of Henry Fagin, the organization successfully negotiated support from the Rockefeller Brothers Fund and later from the Ford Foundation for the major New York Metropolitan Region Study. The aim was to generate a large databank on demographic and economic conditions in the region with projections to the year 1985.

Public acceptance of this privately sponsored activity appears to have been a prominent concern. On insistence of the Rockefeller Brothers Fund the project was subcontracted to the Harvard Graduate School of Public Administration with the RPA providing staff and support services.[99] A "broader-based," "prestigious group" of "prominent citizens" was also set up as an overview committee to monitor the project. According to the RPA's biographer:

> The committee was carefully chosen and well balanced. It included a newspaper executive, two bankers, two railroad presidents, a department store president, two economists, a real estate executive, a university chancellor, the city administrator of New York City, the chairman of the Port of New York Authority, New Jersey's Commissioner of Conservation and Economic Development, the president of the Government Affairs Foundation, and a labor union official (RPA's first contact with organized labor) in addition to the four RPA board members.[100]

This group was later enlarged to 33 members (including chief executives from American Airlines, Bankers Trust, AT&T, Chase Manhattan Bank, Mobil Oil, CBS, Chemical Bank of New York, and the Bowery Savings Bank). It was recruited by the RPA from those "groups within the metropolitan area that are most likely to be the users of the final product and others most competent to advise on various aspects of the project."[101]

The research was published as a series of reports by Harvard University in 1959-60. In a summary volume, project director Raymond Vernon stressed the significance of New York City's office industry to the overall well-being of the region, picking up the slack as manufacturing enterprises began to leave the area in search of lower labor costs. While smaller manufacturing firms remained in the CBD, standardization in product lines, the wide availability of trucks for easy access to markets from lower-wage production areas, and the decline of cheaper immigrant labor in the central city following the end of liberal immigration policies contributed to the push and pull away from the core for the larger-scale garment, printing, and similar labor-intensive manufacturing enterprises.[102]

The concentration of corporate head office and supporting professional services (e.g., financial, legal, accounting, and advertising) in the CBD was impressive. As identified in the Harvard study, the need for "face-to-face" communication, agglomeration of business services, presence of skilled office labor, prestige of a New York address, and ease of air transport to other urban centers were major location factors contributing to the concentration of control functions in the CBD.[103] By 1956, 31 percent of the *Fortune* 500 companies had their headquarter offices in the New York metropolitan region (predominantly in the CBD), including 44.2 percent of those having $750 million or more in assets. The Manhattan CBD (defined here as south of Sixty-first Street) held 4 percent of the region's population in 1956 and 37 percent of its employment.[104] This density of employment was much higher than that found in the nation's other metropolitan centers, where key employment sectors (e.g., aircraft in Los Angeles, automobile production in Detroit, and food processing in Chicago) were still industrial and tended to be more dispersed locally. As the RPA was to repeat in subsequent publications, the situation in Manhattan emphasized the significance of the CBD to the economic welfare of the entire New York metropolitan area. At the same time, the Harvard report and the RPA warned against those trends threatening the future well-being of "grey" areas surrounding the core, such as obsolete housing, inadequate transit facilities, and crime.[105]

Robert Wood's *1400 Governments* was the most influential report in the Harvard series. Subtitled *The Political Economy of the New York Metropolitan Region*, Wood's study was among the first in the nation to attack political fragmentation as a threat to regional interest in metropolitan expansion. By this time, most of suburban New York was already zoned to the teeth, and barriers to further urban development were emerging in the form of exclusionary zoning and nogrowth platforms.[106] As a harbinger of the liberal planning reform agenda during the 1960s, Wood anticipated the later critique of local land use regulation offered by Richard Babcock, Fred Bosselman, the Rockefeller Task Force on Land Use and Urban Growth, the Urban Land Institute, and the National Commission on Urban Problems (Chapter 1, note 7). Claiming that current political boundaries contributed to a "municipal mercantilism" stifling regional economic growth, Wood anticipated a future "revolution" in the nature of land use regulations. This could lead to "transformations in political habits and major new government arrangements—not marginal changes but changes of the character not seen since the boroughs of New York City formed a more perfect union or the Port of New York Authority was established."[107]

According to Wood, many of the smaller municipalities could not effectively allocate public resources or administer land use controls necessary for economic development:

> They are neither in a position to establish and enforce public criteria for appropriate conditions of growth nor to provide public services which the private sector requires on a Regionwide basis. . . .
> . . . [R]olling with the punch of urbanization, their responses have been found to be mainly defensive, unpremeditated, and parochial, and their influence upon the private sector must be considered haphazard and localized.[108]

Acknowledging "the cherished democratic tradition of home rule," Wood nevertheless recognized that it can be "hopelessly unsuited to the realities of modern metropolitan life." The solution proposed was a classic expression of liberal pragmatism when faced with obstreperous local opposition to regional growth. It recommended a bifurcation in government, with those services necessary for urban economic development allocated to a regional authority and the rest (presenting no barrier to expansion) remaining local. Thus, transportation, utilities, and urban redevelopment should be addressed by "regional enterprises," such as the more effective and efficient Port Authority and other public authorities, while control of police, fire, welfare, and education services should remain under local regulation. Finally, some type of regional government responsible to a broader electorate was recommended for those services requiring police power and rejected by the public authorities as unprofitable ventures, such as the acquisition of land for recreation development and the subsidization of commuter transportation.[109]

In sum, the New York Metropolitan Region Study, while not providing the detailed graphic plan of the 1929 effort, did rely, as did its predecessor, on projections of existing conditions as a guide for future expectations. When used as a database for project planning, it also tended to accommodate, rather than challenge, those forces already shaping the New York metropolitan area into a center for corporate control of the global circulation of capital. The primary concern appeared to be the production of a built environment for continued capital accumulation, while addressing barriers to accumulation, such as obsolete housing, inadequate core access, and congestion caused by labor-intensive activities, as they arose.

Seeking Public Support for Continued Agglomeration in the CBD

In 1960 the RPA initiated work on a second regional plan. This would translate the findings of the Harvard study into a physical projection of what the metropolis would be like in 1985 with and without appropriate action. In 1962 an influential interim report, *Spread City*, was published. It blamed suburban zoning for the housing shortage, long commute to the CBD, and inefficient urban expansion. With over half of the region's jobs located within five miles of Times Square, *Spread City* predicted that office employment would continue to concentrate at the center and suggested that provision be made to accommodate this trend.[110]

Sensitive to criticism that its 1929 Plan was prepared without public input, the association now sought to broaden participation. "Regional leaders" were targeted. These could be expected to support the effort when informed about the growth projections of the Metropolitan Region Study and the options available to accommodate and guide unavoidable expansion. Under a Ford Foundation grant, the RPA set up a program to develop supportive participation. This began with a series of conferences held in 1961 and 1962 for business executives.

The Arden House Conferences, as they came to be known, exemplified the manner whereby civic and reform groups may coalesce individual interests around collective goals. Attendance concentrated among the same participants traditionally supporting the RPA's efforts (e.g., utilities, national corporate concerns, local dailies, department stores, financial institutions). Agreement was reached that core congestion, transportation to the CBD, urban blight, political fragmentation, and large-lot zoning in the suburbs (contributing to urban sprawl and raising housing costs for workers) were common concerns. Regional "guidance" was accepted as necessary to prevent "spread city." The situation, unless checked by a reconcentration of housing development nearer the CBD, would lead to an intolerable commute and, in turn, higher wage demands.[111]

The Arden House Conferences were followed by a more ambitious project to develop planning "within the framework of democratic processes."[112] Apparently the RPA considered it sufficient to solicit public response to a plan that it was going to prepare without public input. In a pilot project, the RPA organized 5,600 participants, arranged in hundreds of small study groups, to comment on its program. These response groups were to be given enough information so that they could react usefully.

The attempt to canvass commentary from a large number of participants was, at the time, innovative for a privately sponsored civic planning organization. Nevertheless, the entire gesture was carefully orchestrated to sanction the RPA as the appropriate forum for the development of regional goals and policies to be implemented by the public sector. In response to a self-raised question of whether its role was "legitimate," the association concluded that as "a citizen group without direct responsibility to anyone *but* our Board of Directors . . . [the] Regional Plan can [still] contribute to development decisions *in as democratic a fashion as a government agency* as long as we make clear the assumptions on which our recommendations are based and try to keep the debate on value questions in the public arena."[113]

Among the participants, 96.3 percent were white, with 59.9 percent having a college degree or beyond (compared to a regional average of only 9.5 percent college graduates). While admitting the sample bias, the RPA accepted the group as a legitimate representation of the public interest. This was portrayed as proper because the assembly comprised those individuals most interested in regional issues anyway and, moreover, represented a bias in favor of the next generation:

> That generation will have higher incomes than today's average and longer education and more skilled jobs, and probably a smaller percentage will have been born in another country or Puerto Rico. In fact, the 1963 sample had an income distribution not too different from that projected by Regional Plan economists for the Region as a whole for the year 2000—if present economic trends continue.[114]

Alert to a possibility that it may be charged with "brainwashing" the participants, the RPA concluded that "since three-quarters had been to college and nearly half were professionals or executives, it seems far too flattering to the Regional Plan staff to assert that many respondents were unduly swayed by false argument."[115]

From this survey the association concluded that "at least the educated activists of the Region were ready for fairly sharp changes in the current development trend, even though they were, on the whole, highly satisfied with the present."[116] With primary attention given to the organization of metropolitan leadership, the RPA did not "rely too heavily on public education by itself but [instead sought] to influence a few key decisions that [would] result in a re-structuring of the choices presented to local governments and key individuals."[117] Toward that goal the RPA set up the Committee on the Second Regional Plan composed of 125 community leaders who would be sympathetic to the RPA's goals. Participation on the committee was concentrated among the traditional business constituency for the RPA's activities, the professional groups serving these interests, private foundations, the local media, university personnel (particularly from Columbia University), and several representatives of minority and labor interests (e.g., National Urban League, NAACP, United Auto Workers, and AFL-CIO).[118]

The Second Regional Plan and Housing

Released in 1968 as a draft for discussion, the Second Regional Plan was a call to tame "the metropolitan explosion" of the postwar period. It reflected goals "much the same as those identified in the 1920s." These were steering investment and policy to support construction of a landscape accommodating efficient urban expansion, with office agglomeration at the core and manufacturing relegated to discreet suburban sites.[119] Now the RPA focused on the externalities of uncoordinated public and private decisions presenting barriers to continued accumulation. Chief among these were misguided local attempts to curb necessary growth, aggravating rather than slowing the problem of inefficient suburban sprawl. Responding to a then-emerging nogrowth critique offered by environmentalists and suburban homeowners, the report suggested remedial measures whereby the projected 60 percent increase in the region's population could be accommodated by the year 2000. With reference to unsuccessful attempts to curb metropolitan expansion in Europe and Japan, the RPA concluded that growth was not only inevitable, due to the natural increase in population, but also could be reconciled:

> In sum, the policies proposed are: . . . Accept the Study Area's prospective share of the nation's projected population growth to the end of the century (about 11 million more people) and make the most of having them while protecting open space and organizing metropolitan communities within the urban corridor.[120]

Building upon the optimism of *Spread City*, the Second Regional Plan suggested an absolute increase of over 400,000 additional jobs in the CBD by the year 2000 (to be accompanied by a net gain of 500,000 office and 125,000 service-sector jobs and a net loss of 200,000 manufacturing and wholesaling jobs). This prediction and others of the RPA during the 1960s appealed to selected interests with fixed investments in the core by helping to fuel the speculative fever surrounding the office boom then under way. Between 1970 and 1976, however, New York City actually suffered a net loss of 542,000 jobs, with many of these in the office sector, as firms moved routine office functions, and even headquarters, out of the core area. The hyperactive construction boom was still in full swing from 1968 to 1972, during which an estimated 8 million square feet of office space were vacated in Manhattan due to corporate relocation out of the CBD.[121]

The Second Regional Plan also addressed the mismatch of employment and residential districts. In brief, suburban segregation had "been turning the Region inside out geographically for decades, making it difficult for workers to relate their residence to their place of employment." For inner-city, blue-collar workers, this necessitated a costly "reverse commute" because it required use of an automobile to scattered industrial sites not serviced by regularly scheduled public transportation.[122] Mid- and upper-level office personnel, on the other hand, had to contend with congested highways and a dilapidated rail system as they commuted from the suburban enclaves to the city each working day.

While worker housing was of concern to employers, the RPA's attention to the residential landscape requires further explanation. In a 1972 report (financed by the Carnegie Corporation) to the National Committee Against Discrimination in Housing, the RPA observed that exclusionary suburban zoning practices were a major factor raising the price of labor for suburban manufacturers. By this time many RPA affiliates, while continuing to maintain CBD office locations, were engaged in suburban construction or had established suburban manufacturing, publishing, and service plants. Of even greater concern to the RPA, however, and as benefiting its central city-based sponsorship, was the growing number of CBD white-collar jobs that were unfilled due to a dwindling supply of skilled clerical workers in the central city.[123]

The RPA presumed that office sector wages were insufficient to attract the suburban (female) labor force that would have to commute to these jobs. In addition to a job-training program for racial minorities to fill these higher-level white-collar positions, the RPA suggested increased provision for the residential needs of upper- and middle-income families nearer the CBD. This proposal emerged in a massive development plan under preparation by David Rockefeller's Downtown-Lower Manhattan Association to provide housing for over 100,000 people (Chapter 3).[124] By the early 1970s, however, the corporations were already moving routine office functions to the suburbs to utilize the less expensive female labor force and lower rent costs, while remaining CBD office tasks were attracting unmarried adults financially able to live in the city. As a consequence, the RPA's proposals had little additional impact. With a deepening fiscal crisis in New York, the association became more concerned about absolute job loss from the CBD than about increasing housing opportunities for those who might work and live there. Following the 1975 collapse of efforts by the Urban Development Corporation (UDC) to build low-income housing in the suburbs (Chapter 4), suburban integration for minority industrial and office workers was also relegated to a back burner.

The RPA and Postwar Transportation Policy

By the 1960s it was clear that the planned deconcentration of residence into the suburbs promoted by the earlier 1929 Plan also supported wholesale (routine as well as headquarter) office relocation. The push and pull factors behind the corporate exodus from the CBD were complex. Certainly a desire to tap the suburban female labor pool, while locating nearer the homes of mid- and upper-level management, was significant. The resulting sprawl of employment and residential functions across the metropolis attracted local nogrowth critics.

Responding to inefficient urban growth and alarmed by a local reaction threatening to stifle future growth, the RPA promoted reconcentration of employment in Manhattan's CBD. Robert Fitch, in his insightful analysis of the RPA, correctly characterized the Second Regional Plan as addressing the unanticipated boom in suburban office development, with a policy suggesting a recentralization in the CBD. He overemphasized, however, the actual attainment of consensus on the need to preserve Manhattan's real estate values.[125] While the Second Regional Plan, as the first, was concerned with fixed investment in the CBD, it was more concerned with servicing this area as a corporate control center for its use value than it was with preserving its exchange (market) value. One result of the emphasis on use value rather than on exchange value was the provision for "borough downtowns," as in Jamaica Queens, Fordam Road in the Bronx, and downtown Brooklyn. Here routine office and service functions could be located closer to Manhattan's core at the nexus of suburban rail and urban subway access. This would stem some of the desire for central offices to leave the city altogether, as their support services would be close at hand. Moreover, in a concession to its corporate members, who individually were moving routine office (if not also headquarter) functions out of Manhattan, the RPA and its plan assented to limited office development in suburban centers. In the end, some two dozen additional "metropolitan centers" of 30,000 to 100,000 population each were suggested for the region's other existing urban areas. Accommodating the primary locus of residence and leisure for what were now accepted as over-lapping labor pools (e.g., New York City, White Plains, Paterson and New Brunswick in New Jersey, and Stamford in Connecticut), the RPA expanded its official region of concern (Map 2.4). This now encompassed 12,570 square miles spread out over 31 counties (including the boroughs of New York City).[126]

Overall, the Second Regional Plan projected an incredible 87.5 percent increase in office employment in the region by the year 2000, with 35 percent of this increase going to Manhattan's CBD. To supply the transit needs of the projected surge in office employment the RPA supported several controversial highway projects. These included the ill-fated Lower Manhattan Expressway (first proposed in the 1929 Plan), and the rebuilding of the Westside Highway.[127] Both of these proposals resulted in strong and well-organized community resistance from residents and commercial shopowners whose homes and businesses were near, or in the path of, the proposed development (Chapter 3).

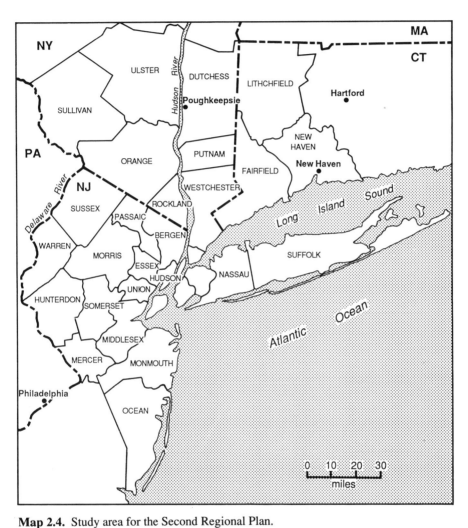

Map 2.4. Study area for the Second Regional Plan.

Source: Boundaries drawn from information provided in Regional Plan Association of New York, *The Second Regional Plan: A Draft for Discussion*, Bulletin no. 110 (New York: Regional Plan Association of New York, 1968).

Together with the Downtown-Lower Manhattan Association, the RPA led the push to complete redevelopment of the Westside Highway. At an estimated cost (in 1984) of well over $2 billion, the 4.2-mile, six-lane highway would have linked the Brooklyn-Battery and Lincoln tunnels, requiring 196 acres of new landfill along the Hudson. As first proposed in 1971 by the Urban Development Corporation, and subsequently modified, the project would have replaced the rotting piers of the once-thriving Manhattan shipping district with some 93 acres of new park land (out to the old pier line) and several thousand new apartment units, leaving the residual for the sunken roadway and adjacent office and commercial projects (Map 3.2).

The strongest opposition to the highway came from existing West Side residents in neighborhoods adjacent to the proposed route who perceived their own consumption space as threatened. They countered that the highway, in effect a redevelopment scheme for the entire west side of lower Manhattan, would only benefit downtown real estate interests and the small number of executives commuting by car, while 87 percent of lower Manhattan's office workers would still have to rely upon mass transit. As a countermeasure, they preferred that the federal funds allocated for the designated interstate highway instead be used for mass transit via a trade-in provision permitted under federal law. In September 1985, following more than a decade in litigation, Westway was finally defeated when the environmental impact statement was revoked on procedural grounds and the deadline grew near for the federal trade-in-allowance.[128]

The 1929 Plan severely underestimated the importance of mass transit (subway) to the expanding office sector. The Second Regional Plan and subsequent RPA efforts sought to rectify the damage. Support for Westway notwithstanding, the RPA in the postwar period was a leader in attempts to strengthen the region's decaying rapid transit system. Central-city business and retail interests had become proponents of urban fixed rail (subway and railroad) construction. Spreading radially from the CBD, the original railroad and subway systems encouraged employers and retailers to centrally locate as they could draw upon regional labor and consumer markets. Following the postwar collapse of the private railroad system, however, actual development of a bistate compact between New York and New Jersey necessary to unify and publicly support the decaying passenger rail service during the 1950s was frustrated by Jersey fears that a regional rail system would exacerbate the loss of retail customers and office tenants to Manhattan. With 75 percent of all subway and railroad rides within the region originating in, or going to, Manhattan's CBD (in 1977), the RPA's focus on rail transit in the Second Regional Plan was clearly in line with proposals to strengthen the economic viability of Manhattan's office district.[129]

Transportation policy became a primary justification for federal support of regional planning in the 1960s. In 1960 the RPA was commissioned by the Senate Committee on Interstate and Foreign Commerce to prepare a pilot study on commuter transportation in the New York metropolitan region. This project, in turn, led to the first federal aid for public transportation, the provision of which was to be in accordance with a comprehensive metropolitan transportation plan. In 1964, again in large part due to the RPA's pioneering efforts, the Federal Highway Act mandated comprehensive regional planning as a prerequisite for federal aid.[130]

The suburban rail commute to the CBD was long a major focus of RPA attention. With the 1929 proposals for the ten privately owned rail lines collapsing in the 1930s along with the rail companies, the RPA was at the forefront urging public acquisition of the bankrupt lines. The RPA successfully lobbied for inclusion of New York State's suburban rail lines together with New York City's bus and subway system when the Metropolitan Transportation Authority (MTA) was formed in 1967 (Chapter 4). Through the MTA the suburban rail lines (and in particular the Long Island Rail Road) became the most heavily subsidized section per ride offered.[131]

BUSINESS COORDINATION OF NEW YORK CITY'S FISCAL CRISIS

At the onset of the fiscal crisis gripping New York City in the early and mid-1970s, the RPA focused attention on measures to strengthen the regional economy. Under a grant from the Andrew W. Mellon Foundation it completed a series of studies on the region's economy, linking it to national and international trends. The *Regional Accounts Study* supported a shift in state and federal policy toward revitalization of the Manhattan CBD and maintenance of existing urban centers in the surrounding region. It suggested programs to reverse the move toward suburban office locations, and it stressed the stake suburban residents had in the Manhattan office district.[132]

From the 1940s until this period the RPA had received most of its funding from private foundations and occasional federal and state grants. The corporate community, when it supported the RPA, often preferred the less visible avenue of foundation support. Direct corporate funding, other than membership fees, was only sporadically provided. The RPA, despite a lack of financial support, attained influence among public and private actors largely at the idea inception and propagation level, due in large measure to the absence of other competing actors at this level.[133]

In 1975 William Ellinghaus, then president of NY Telephone (and by 1976, vice-chair of AT&T), became chair of the RPA board of directors. Under his guidance the RPA successfully revitalized its ties with the corporate business community. By the late 1970s direct business contributions had overtaken grants from private foundations as the RPA's chief means of support. Whereas business support for the RPA was formerly concentrated among regional large-scale "service" capital (the utilities, newspapers, and savings banks), direct contributions from the larger commercial banks, life insurance companies, and the national corporations with headquarters in the region now became dominant. The new interest by the national firms was promoted, in part, by Ellinghaus's success in shifting RPA emphasis away from documenting the effects of urban sprawl, to a project-oriented focus on transit and urban development in the region's existing cities.[134]

Concurrent with rising corporate influence in the RPA, the large national and international financial and corporate sectors of capital were completing their dominance over New York City's public affairs. Between 1947 and 1980 Manhattan experienced one of the most prolonged office booms in capitalist history, with over 145 million square feet constructed.[135] Much of this represented fixed investment by industrial and finance capital for headquarter or control functions. The wholesaling and labor-intensive industrial activities once dominant in the CBD were successfully displaced with generous assistance through the city's zoning and renewal schemes. While the roots of the city's fiscal crisis in the mid-1970s are complex, they may be traced, in large measure, to the costly public welfare program required to address the social demands of unemployed and displaced labor during this period of disinvestment by older manufacturing sectors in the local economy.[136] Whatever the origins, the crisis presented corporate capital with an ideal opportunity to discipline the city and its unruly public unions, while making sure that the public services it required would continue to be funded. If necessary, this would come at the expense of those social investments not directly benefiting corporate investment in the region (education, health, mass transportation, etc.).

Concentrating on visible debate and on formal political participation by competing interest groups, many analysts overlook the oblique role of the corporate sector in public decisions (see below). Professionally staffed civic and "citizen" groups, such as the RPA, are important to this process, helping to set an agenda that might be implemented by others, such as Robert Moses. In New York City's case, corporate control became virtually absolute during the fiscal crisis. Set up to put the city's economic house of cards in order and guarantee renewed access to the bond market, the Municipal Assistance Corporation (MAC) and the Emergency Financial Control Board (EFCB) were composed of eminent financial and corporate leaders. Ellinghaus, for example, besides being chair of the RPA, a trustee of Union Dime Savings Bank, president of NY Telephone, and a director of Bankers Trust Corporation, was also a board member and later chair of the MAC and one of the three public members on the EFCB.[137]

As described by columnists Jack Newfield and Paul DuBrul, the business leaders succeeded in setting up a "permanent government." With members recruited from the business community, the permanent government included public authorities, municipal corporations, and semipublic advisory boards that were appointed rather than directly responsible to the electorate. Eight of the nine original members of the MAC and all three of the "public" members on the EFCB were private corporate or financial executives.[138] Together, the bipartisan MAC and the EFCB had virtual control over the city's budget for several years with power, if necessary, to override existing municipal union contracts. They succeeded in ending free tuition at the city's public university and colleges, securing a massive reduction in property taxes on corporate-held real estate, freezing municipal wages, and forcing higher transit fares and major service cuts in the city's low- and middle-income residential neighborhoods.

These austere measures contributed to the desired outcome. The city was not only saved from declaring bankruptcy but, by 1981, was able for the first time in nearly a decade to float $100 million of its own bonds in a tight municipal bond market. Corporate office construction, moreover, was again on the rise. The new building boom was fueled by a weak housing market and a continuing search by venture capital for profitable investment (exchange value) in the built environment, together with the historic play of forces leading to concentration and centralization of control functions (use value) as capitalist production and consumption expanded globally.[139]

With the fiscal crisis leaving management of the city's economic affairs in the hands of a select and concentrated group of business leaders and state officials, a crisis in public confidence arose and various proposals were studied whereby some semblance of democratic control could be resurrected. The political ascendancy of neighborhood planning boards was of particular concern. These groups, upon receiving formal recognition from the city's planning commission, became a focal point for public resistance to the large-scale redevelopment and infrastructure projects advocated by the city's business leadership.

In 1972 a study prepared by the Bar Association of the City of New York, and funded by the Ford and Rockefeller foundations, was released. Favoring a bifurcation in governance first proposed by Robert Wood over a decade earlier, the report suggested creation of a two-tier system of representation. Thirty to forty new district units, each headed by a chief executive and legislative council, would be responsible for education, social services, criminal justice, and housing policy. Apparently this was the maximum amount of devolution tolerated. Tax assessment and business, building, and land use regulations were to be kept centralized under control of a reinforced central-city administration.[140] In particular, community control of environmental policy was to be avoided, since it could be used to block economic and industrial development benefiting a wider area.

While this proposal came to nought, there has been a diminution in the power of existing community planning boards, with limits placed on their ability to delay major projects. The RPA, long an advocate of informed public participation rather than full democratic participation in planning decisions, initiated and mobilized several "citizens committees" to support favored projects under attack by neighborhood planning boards. The most prominent example was New York Citizens for Balanced Transportation, the chief lobbyist for Westway. Concurrently the RPA broadened membership on its board of directors to include representatives from several suburban fair housing and neighborhood redevelopment groups, though the traditional corporate, financial, and service sectors clearly continued to dominate.[141]

CONCLUSION: THE RPA AND THE PUBLIC INTEREST

The RPA has been the subject of numerous research reports and figures prominently in almost every history of regional planning in New York State. Most of these accounts uncritically accept the reform ideology offered by the RPA as rational and as representing the public interest. Rarely do they examine the narrow class basis of its directorship or the disparity in who actually benefits from proposed reforms, nor do they critically examine the substance of these reforms cognizant of the pressures placed upon the capitalist State by virtue of the structure of the mode of production that it represents (Chapter 1). One might expect uncritical analyses from those reports sponsored by the RPA or by other research foundations (such as the Ford and Rockefeller foundations) with close ties to large-scale capital interests. However, the overall paucity of meaningful explanation for the motives and actions taken by the RPA and similar "civic-minded" reform organizations underscores the pervasion and virtual hegemony that the liberal ideology holds over questions of land use reform and regional planning.[142]

The success of liberal reform depends, in part, on the generation and control of information that may be of use to the public sector. Wherever possible this effort is made to appear as objective and in the public interest. The ideological assumption of neutrality is bolstered by a claim to technical competence, which is contrasted with uninformed partisan conflict in the political arena. Yet the ways whereby researchers bend to the winds of power are legion. Despite claims to objective and value-free inquiry, most research staff represent the interests of those employing them. In the past liberal reform was directly supported by civic organizations created on an ad hoc basis by business and civic leaders to deal with particular issues, a situation reminiscent of the Commercial Club of Chicago and its 1909 plan. Today the process is more institutionalized, with private foundations and research institutes often taking the lead, a process actually pioneered by the Russell Sage Foundation through its support for the first regional plan. Foundations and institutes (e.g., the Ford, Rockefeller, and Carnegie foundations, Resources for the Future, and the Brookings Institute) can be used, in a sense, to launder corporate financial support for liberal reform. Foundation support, in turn, flows to university personnel and research centers such as the MIT-Harvard Joint Center for Urban Studies and the Center for Urban Policy Research at Rutgers University. These become important agents of legitimation through the ideological claim to neutrality.

Often retaining a large in-house technical staff of their own, and relying on these outside foundations and university research centers for financial support or data acquisition, nonprofit civic or "citizen" groups, such as the RPA, share public confidence. As a consequence, their policy proposals are also accepted as in the public interest. Rarely do public decision makers and policy analysts question who actually *initiates* the agenda for reform, *hires* the professional-managerial staff, and, in the long run, actually *benefits* from reform implementation. Whether staff research actually coincides with broader interests or not, it is ludicrous to isolate as value-free and apolitical a professional-managerial staff recruited by private interests and hired to research and formulate reforms according to a specific and controlled agenda.

Over the years the RPA was so successful in presenting itself as an impartial regional planning advocate that it even managed, in 1975, to capture the federal contract to audit the A-95 review process of the Tri-State Regional Planning Commission. Although designated by the U.S. Department of Housing and Urban Development as the region's official Council of Governments (with responsibility, through A-95, for coordinating federal grants and projects through comprehensive regional planning), the Tri-State Regional Planning Commission was unable to convince enough local governments that its services were worth their continued support, and it folded in 1983.[143] For the time being this leaves the RPA as the principal comprehensive regional planning talent in the tristate metropolis (with the much larger planning staff of Port of New York Authority focusing on economic and infrastructure development for the New York-New Jersey waterfront—Chapter 4). The RPA's reports now carry more weight among public and private decision makers than at any time since the 1930s.

The RPA continues today in its quest to unite various factions of capital to support a collective class interest in providing the services and infrastructure necessary to further capital accumulation on a regional and, by implication, national and global scale. Where possible the class and sectoral goals are identified with a common public interest. Certainly business objectives and the environmental, or social, goals of a wider constituency need not clash. When defined as favoring recreation amenities, a pleasing residential or office environment, lower housing costs, and efficient mass transit, the public interest may also, for example, lower the cost of labor, reduce worker alienation on the job, and open new areas for commodity production (such as the recreation industry). In practice, however, a common platform is frustrated because there are many "publics" whose interests rarely coincide or are identical with those of the business sector. This leads liberal planning reformers and their business sponsors toward proposals and solutions challenging local home rule where it represents more parochial concerns that stand in opposition to capital accumulation. In the New York metropolitan area, for example, the RPA and many other business-led reform groups supported the creation of public authorities. These, in turn, implemented the bulk of the 1929 Plan. As they were not directly accountable to the general electorate or to the legislative bodies establishing them, the authorities were very effective in overcoming the strong objections in neighborhoods slated for urban renewal, transit development, and expansion (Chapter 4).

Within the RPA itself class alliance across the region is frustrated by the inherent anarchy arising from private appropriation of profit. Dividing forces include, and are not limited to, market competition, political boundaries, and the varying regulations imposed upon individual enterprises. As a consequence, retail and business leaders in the established cities of Connecticut and New Jersey, such as Stamford, Bridgeport, Newark, and Jersey City, frequently challenge the RPA position that the New York region comprises a unified social and economic unit with Manhattan at its core.[144] This lack of regional identity dilutes the RPA's impact. Although the association favors recentralization of office development in the CBD and acquiesces to office location in a limited number of regional centers, it avoids direct criticism of member activities. Thus it was silent on the massive New Jersey suburban office expansion by AT&T occurring in the 1970s, a time when Ellinghaus was also chair of the RPA. The association was quiet as well on headquarter relocations from Manhattan (American Can, AVCO, Cheeseborough Pond, etc.) to Greenwich, Connecticut, scattered some miles from the closest designated regional center at Stamford, Connecticut.

In all likelihood the RPA's local dominance cannot match that exerted in less complex urban centers, contained within one state, where a more centralized and less diversified business sector exerts more direct influence. Detroit's Metropolitan Fund, Pittsburgh's Allegheny Conference on Community Development, the San Francisco Bay Area Council, and the Greater Hartford Process provide some examples of the latter situation. Nevertheless, although capital unity across product, scale, and geographic lines has not been attained in the New York region, the RPA seeks and commands a higher visibility in the public eye and among environmental and professional planning groups than most privately sponsored advocates in other regions. Failing to penetrate the veil of liberal ideology, public officials, research foundations, and many academics and practitioners (including the RPA's own staff) accept RPA participation as an environmental or public interest advocate in the urban dialogue, refusing to recognize the coalition of more select interests behind it.[145]

The RPA's private planning for the public sector continues precisely because large-scale and regionally dominant office and service sectors can recognize a common agenda in urban development and can coalesce around a reform process addressing these concerns. In the land use arena, these interests typically support limitations on local expression of police power when it threatens urban expansion. They also favor provision of roads, bridges, sewers, worker housing, and other services furthering economic development that the private sector cannot or will not provide on its own. Insofar as the RPA additionally sponsors a regional perspective and centralization of regulatory authority, individual businesses will support the association when it furthers the coordination and guidance of those separate investment and production decisions that, exercised on their own, might reduce overall regional growth potential or threaten existing investment. With direct collective self-regulation unlikely due to conflicting private interests (and possibly illegal under antitrust law), public regulation, coordination, and assistance—under private (RPA) guidance if possible—is accepted as the best alternative.

The emergence of business-led regional planning groups in virtually every major metropolitan area of the United States is a measure of the success of this approach, whereby corporate interests guide the State, or public sector, in the provision of infrastructure and services supporting and ultimately coordinating the activities of individual firms. While other metropolitan regions typically have one recognized planning advocate among the business community, the New York region, by virtue of its size and complexity, has several. Within New York State alone we find two other active groups. These geographically represent more circumscribed sections of the region than the RPA. In the next chapter these potential contenders for community leadership will be examined. In doing so I hope to uncover the mechanism, if any, for organizational coordination. Moreover, through comparison with the RPA, we can address the question of whether these more spatially focused planning advocates have a better chance of program implementation given their narrower objectives.

NOTES

1. David Harvey, "The Urban Process under Capitalism," *International Journal of Urban and Regional Research* 2, no.1 (1978):101. See Chapter 1 on the contradictions generated by capitalist development. On planning as a social response: David Harvey, "Labor, Capital and Class Struggle around the Built Environment in Advanced Capitalist Societies," in *Urbanization and Conflict in Market Societies*, ed. K. Cox (Chicago: Maaroufa Press, 1978), pp. 9-38; Allan Scott and Shoukry Roweis, "Urban Planning in Theory and Practice" (Paper delivered at the Seventeenth European Conference of the Regional Planning Association, Krakow, Poland, August 1977) (Toronto: Department of Geography, University of Toronto, 1977); Richard Walker, "The Transformation of Urban Structure in the 19th Century United States and the Beginnings of Suburbanization," in *Urbanization and Conflict in Market Societies*, ed. K. Cox (Chicago: Maaroufa Press, 1978), pp. 165-213; idem, "A Theory of Suburbanization: Capitalism and the Construction of Urban Space in the United States," in *Urbanization and Urban Planning in Capitalist Society*, ed. M. Dear and A. Scott (New York: Methuen, 1981), pp. 383-429; and Richard Walker and Michael Heiman, "Quiet Revolution for Whom?" *Annals of the Association of American Geographers* 71 (March 1981):67-83.

2. Cf. James O'Connor, *The Fiscal Crisis of the State* (New York: St. Martin's Press, 1973); Harvey, "Urban Process"; Scott and Roweis, "Urban Planning."

3. E.g., Frank Popper, *The Politics of Land-Use Reform* (Madison: University of Wisconsin Press, 1981); Michael Danielson and Jameson Doig, *New York: The Politics of Urban Regional Development* (Berkeley and Los Angeles: University of California Press, 1982).

4. The occurrence of political reform movements in capitalist history and their ideological origins have been the subject of critical investigation: William Domhoff, *Who Really Rules?* (Santa Monica, CA: Goodyear Publishing, 1978); idem, *The Powers That Be: Processes of Ruling Class Domination in America* (New York: Random House, 1978); Samuel Hays, "The Politics of Reform in Municipal Government in the Progressive Era," *Pacific Northwest Quarterly* 55, no. 4 (1964):157-69; Roy Lubove, *The Progressives and the Slums* (Pittsburgh: University of Pittsburgh Press, 1962); idem, *Twentieth-Century Pittsburgh: Government, Business and Environmental Change* (New York: John Wiley, 1969); Harvey Molotch, "The City as a Growth Machine: Toward a Political Economy of Place," *American Journal of*

Sociology 82 (1976):309-22; John Mollenkopf, "The Postwar Politics of Urban Development," in *Marxism and the Metropolis*, ed. W. Tabb and L. Sawers (New York: Oxford University Press, 1978), pp. 117-52; James Weinstein, *The Corporate Ideal in the Liberal State: 1900-1918* (Boston: Beacon Press, 1968); and Marc Weiss, "The Origins and Legacy of Urban Renewal," in *Urban and Regional Planning in an Age of Austerity*, ed. P. Clavel, J. Forester, and W. Goldsmith (New York: Pergamon Press, 1980), pp. 53-80.

5. Patrick Ashton, "Urbanization and the Dynamics of Suburban Development under Capitalism," in *Marxism and the Metropolis*, 2d ed., ed. W. Tabb and L. Sawers (New York: Oxford University Press, 1984), pp. 54-81; Ann Markusen, "Class and Urban Social Expenditure: A Marxist Theory of Metropolitan Government," in *Marxism and the Metropolis,* 2d ed., ed. W. Tabb and L. Sawers (New York: Oxford University Press, 1984), pp. 82-100; Walker, "Transformation of Urban Structure."

6. See David Gordon, "Capitalist Development and the History of American Cities," in *Marxism and the Metropolis*, 2d ed., ed. W. Tabb and L. Sawers (New York: Oxford University Press, 1984), pp. 21-53; Molotch, "City as a Growth Machine"; Hays, "Politics of Reform"; John Mollenkopf, "The Post-War Politics of Urban Development," *Politics and Society* 5 (1975):247-95.

7. On the Progressive Era in New York City: David Hammack, *Power and Society: Greater New York at the Turn of the Century* (New York: Russell Sage Foundation, 1982); S. J. Makielski, Jr., *The Politics of Zoning* (New York: Columbia University Press, 1966); Henry Cohen, "Planning Rationally for the City," in *Governing the City: Challenges and Options for New York*, ed. R. Connery and D. Caraley (New York: Praeger, 1969), pp. 179-92; Jane Dahlberg, *The New York Bureau of Municipal Research: Pioneer in Government and Administration* (New York: New York University Press, 1966); and Wallace Sayre and Herbert Kaufman, *Governing New York City* (New York: Russell Sage Foundation, 1960). On the very active progressive movement in Pittsburgh: Hays, "Politics of Reform"; and Lubove, *Twentieth-Century Pittsburgh*.

The Bronx was already annexed to Manhattan (New York City) in two pieces in 1874 and in 1895. It became a separate borough (county) in 1914.

8. On the New York Bureau of Municipal Research: Cohen, "Planning Rationally"; Dahlberg, *New York Bureau of Municipal Research*; Sayre and Kaufman, *Governing New York City*; and Martin Schiesl, *The Politics of Efficiency: Municipal Administration and Reform in America 1800-1920* (Berkeley and Los Angeles: University of California Press, 1977). The bureau was a major proving ground for many of the city's public servants, including Robert Moses (Chapter 4).

9. See Judith Getzels, Peter Elliot, and Frank Beal, *Private Planning for the Public Interest: A Study of Approaches to Urban Problem Solving by Nonprofit Organizations* (Chicago: American Society of Planning Officials, 1975); Hays, "Politics of Reform"; and Lubove, *Twentieth-Century Pittsburgh*.

Pittsburgh's experience was prototypic and served as an inspiration elsewhere. Established in 1918 by Charles Armstrong, W. L. Mellon, Howard Heinz, and other industrial leaders with major regional investments, Citizens Committee on (a) City Plan for Pittsburgh was the major vehicle whereby corporate and large-scale capital concerns attempted to modify the physical environment in what was, at the time, the nation's fourth largest city. As indicated by the 1920 census, however, Pittsburgh was already a declining industrial center, falling behind Detroit and Cleveland in population. Concerned that insufficient and unsanitary housing was a primary barrier to industrial expansion, as well as to development of a white-collar service sector, local business leaders acting through the Citizens Committee became strong advocates of planning and zoning to improve the city's housing stock, build mass transit, provide recreation sites, and, subsequently, lower the cost of labor. Supported by the Pittsburgh Chamber of Commerce, the Civic Club, and the local press, the Citizens Committee's plan for Pittsburgh was opposed by local real estate boards, smaller savings and loan banks, and other representatives of the local small-scale, or competitive, sector of capital (Lubove, *Twentieth-Century Pittsburgh*, pp. 90-100).. This split between the competitive and the large-scale monopoly (or oligopoly) sectors of capital over support for comprehensive planning and zoning was replicated in many other urban centers. To this day, it is a ubiquitous characteristic of business support for liberal planning reform.

10. Buffalo City Planning Association, *Annual Report* (Buffalo: Buffalo City Planning Association, 1947), p. 11.

11. David Johnson, "Seventy-five Years of Metropolitan Planning in the N.Y.-N.J.-Connecticut Urban Region: A Retrospective Assessment" (Paper delivered at the Twenty-sixth Annual Meeting of the Association of Collegiate Schools of Planning, New York City, October 19, 1984), pp. 4-5.

12. Cf. New York City, Improvement Commission, *Report of the New York City Improvement Commission to the Honorable George B. McClellan* (New York: Kalkhoff, 1907); and Robert Caro, *The Power Broker* (New York: Vintage Books, 1975). On the plan's context and influence: David Johnson, "The Emergence of Metropolitan Regionalism: An Analysis of the 1929 Regional Plan of New York and Its Environs" (Ph.D. diss., Cornell University, 1974); and Johnson, "Metropolitan Planning in the N.Y. Urban Region." As was characteristic, Moses never acknowledged the debt (Robert Moses, *Public Works: A Dangerous Trade* [New York: McGraw-Hill, 1970]).

13. On the Plan of Chicago: Robert L. Wrigley, Jr., "The Plan of Chicago," in *Introduction to Planning History in the United States*, ed. D. Krueckeberg (New Brunswick, NJ: Center for Urban Policy Research, Rutgers University, 1983), pp. 58-72; Mel Scott, *American City Planning since 1890* (Berkeley and Los Angeles: University of California Press, 1971), pp. 100-109; and Johnson, "Emergence of Metropolitan Regionalism," pp. 96-112.

14. Wrigley, "Plan of Chicago," pp. 69-70.

15. On the birth of zoning in New York: Makielski, *Politics of Zoning*; Seymour Toll, *Zoned America* (New York: Grossman, 1969); William Wilson, "Moles and Skylarks," in *Introduction to Planning History in the United States*, ed. D. Krueckeberg (New Brunswick, NJ: Center for Urban Policy Research, Rutgers University, 1983), pp. 88-121; and Johnson, "Emergence of Metropolitan Regionalism," pp. 76-84. On the history of zoning in the United States: Lubove, *Progressives and Slums*; and Robert Nelson, *Zoning and Property Rights: An Analysis of the American System of Land-Use Regulation* (Cambridge, MA: MIT Press, 1977). Critical review of the origins and purposes of zoning and associated land use controls are provided by Robert Fitch, "Planning New York," in *The Fiscal Crisis of American Cities: Essays on the Political Economy of Urban America with Special Reference to New York*, ed. R. Alcaly and D.

Mermelstein (New York: Vintage Books, 1977), pp. 246-84; Mark Gottdeiner, *Planned Sprawl* (Beverly Hills, CA: Sage, 1977); Markusen, "Class and Urban Social Expenditure"; David Noble, *America by Design* (New York: Alfred A. Knopf, 1977); and John Reps, "Requiem for Zoning," in *Taming Megalopolis*, ed. H. W. Eldredge (Garden City, NY: Anchor Books, 1967), pp. 746-60.

Although Los Angeles already had regulations dividing the city into residential and industrial districts by this period, New York's 1916 ordinance was more comprehensive (e.g., including bulk with use regulations, and detailing district locations on maps). It became the prototype copied elsewhere (Scott, *American City Planning*; and Nelson, *Zoning and Property Rights*, pp. 8-10). As secretary of commerce, Herbert Hoover was so impressed with Bassett's achievement that he appointed the New York attorney head of the federal commission drafting the 1924 Standard State Zoning Enabling Act.

16. Wilson, "Moles and Skylarks," p. 91.

17. Committee on (the) Regional Plan of New York and Its Environs (hereafter Committee on Regional Plan), "The Clothing and Textile Industries," in *Food, Clothing and Textile Industries Wholesale Markets and Retail Shopping and Financial Districts* (originally monograph nos. 7, 8, and 9 of Economic Series), Regional Survey of New York and Its Environs, 8 vols. (New York: Regional Plan of New York and Its Environs [hereafter Regional Plan of New York], 1928), 1B:76.

18. Makielski, *Politics of Zoning*, pp. 33, 136-42.

19. Lubove, *Progressives and Slums*, pp. 240-43; Scott, *American City Planning*, p. 155; and Makielski, *Politics of Zoning*.

Representing the city's larger business and manufacturing interests, the New York Chamber of Commerce was also a strong supporter of zoning and planning. On the other side, numerous organizations representing small-scale and competitive capital generally opposed such controls.

20. Charles Norton in a letter to Frederic Delano on November 24, 1921, as quoted in Forbes Hays, *Community Leadership: The Regional Plan Association of New York* (New York: Columbia University Press, 1965), p. 9; and in Johnson, "Emergence of Metropolitan Regionalism," pp. 117-18. As expressed in this later letter, the vision was originally stated in a committee memorandum of November 27, 1915 (Harvey Kantor, "Charles Dyer Norton and the Origins of the Regional Plan of New York," *Journal of the American Institute of Planners* 39 [January 1973]:36).

21. Hays, *Community Leadership*, pp. 11-18; and Kantor, "Charles Dyer Norton."

A Russell Sage Foundation grant also helped initiate Pittsburgh's first regional planning effort in 1907. Here the "cosmopolitans," led by the Pittsburgh Chamber of Commerce, were losing the battle for city annexation of Allegheny County and its autonomous surrounding communities (Lubove, *Twentieth-Century Pittsburgh*, pp. 7, 23-28). In time regional planning for select metropolitan functions, such as transportation, housing, and flood control, became a surrogate for politically unacceptable annexation.

22. On the formation of the CRPNY and of its planning staff: Hays, *Community Leadership*, pp. 11-16; Fitch, "Planning New York," pp. 252-55; Kantor, "Charles Dyer Norton"; and Scott, *American City Planning*, pp. 198-203.

23. R. L. Duffus, *Mastering the Metropolis* (New York: Harper and Brothers, 1930), p. 125. This quote appears in a book commissioned by the committee to popularize its final plan. The opposing instrumental (self-serving) position appears in John Fitch's otherwise discerning examination of the origins and purpose of the committee and of its successor, the Regional Plan Association ("Planning New York").

24. Committee on Regional Plan, *The Graphic Regional Plan*, Regional Plan of New York and Its Environs, vol. 1 (of 2) (New York: Regional Plan of New York, 1929); idem, *The Building of the City*, Regional Plan of New York and Its Environs, vol. 2 (of 2) (New York: Regional Plan of New York, 1931). The first eight volumes of the plan were collectively known as *The Regional Survey of New York and Its Environs*.

25. Committee on Regional Plan, *Graphic Regional Plan*; and Johnson, "Emergence of Metropolitan Regionalism," pp. 489-90.

26. Committee on Regional Plan, *Graphic Regional Plan*, pp. 126-27.

27. Ibid., p. 133.

28. Cf. Hays, *Community Leadership*; Johnson, "Emergence of Metropolitan Regionalism"; Robert Lichtenberg, *One-Tenth of a Nation* (Cambridge, MA: Harvard University Press, 1960); and Regional Plan Association of New York (hereafter Regional Plan Association), *A Fiftieth Year Review* (Annual Report for 1978-79), *Regional Plan News*, no. 106 (1979). On the lost vision of the Regional Planning Association of America: John Friedmann and Clyde Weaver, *Territory and Function* (Berkeley and Los Angeles: University of California Press, 1980), pp. 29-35; and Carl Sussman, ed., *Planning the Fourth Migration: The Neglected Vision of the Regional Planning Association of America* (Cambridge, MA: MIT Press, 1976). On the Allegheny Conference on Community Development: Lubove, *Twentieth-Century Pittsburgh*.

29. Hays, *Community Leadership*, pp. 21-23.

30. Ibid., p. 39. Preferring to focus on the capabilities and goals of the staff preparing the regional plan, Scott *(American City Planning*, pp. 261-65) downplays the link between the staff of the CRPNY (and later of the RPA) and its corporate sponsors. This position of staff independence is repeated in the study done for the American Society of Planning Officials (Getzels, Elliot, and Beal, *Private Planning for the Public Interest*, pp. 66-69).

31. George McAneny, *The Ninth Annual Report of the Regional Plan Association* (presented at the Annual Meeting of the Regional Plan Association, New York City, December 1, 1938) (New York: Regional Plan Association, 1938), p. 3.

32. Committee on Regional Plan, *Major Economic Factors in Metropolitan Growth and Arrangement*, Regional Survey of New York and Its Environs, 8 vols. (New York: Regional Plan of New York, 1927), 1:18.

33. Ibid., p. 44.

34. Committee on Regional Plan, *Population, Land Values and Government*, Regional Survey of New York and Its Environs, 8 vols. (New York: Regional Plan of New York, 1929), 2:199. See also idem, *Graphic Regional Plan*, p. 158.

35. Lewis Mumford, "The Plan of New York 1," *The New Republic*, June 15, 1932, pp. 121-26; idem, "The Plan of New York 2," *The New Republic*, June 22, 1932, pp. 146-54. On the RPAA and on its criticisms of the RPA: Lubove, *Progressives and*

Slums; Friedmann and Weaver, *Territory and Function*; and Sussman, *Planning the Fourth Migration*.

36. Committee on Regional Plan, *Population, Land Values and Government*, pp. 26, 34.

37. Mumford, "Plan of New York 1," p. 122.

38. Hays, *Community Leadership*, pp. 37-38, 40.

39. Ibid., pp. 45-51.

40. Ibid. See also Caro, *Power Broker*, pp. 735-38.

41. Hays, *Community Leadership*, pp. 45-51, 105. This situation was replicated in many business-led planning organizations (e.g., Pittsburgh's Allegheny Conference on Community Development, Detroit's Metropolitan Fund, and San Francisco's Bay Area Council). Cf. Lubove, *Twentieth-Century Pittsburgh*; and Getzels, Elliot, and Beal, *Private Planning for the Public Interest*.

42. See David Kotz, *Bank Control of Large Corporations in the United States* (Berkeley and Los Angeles: University of California Press, 1978).

43. James Vance, Jr., *This Scene of Man* (New York: Harper's College Press, 1977), pp. 389-410. See also Committee on Regional Plan, *Major Economic Factors*, pp. 40, 103.

44. Jason Epstein observes that New York's huge construction industry "was a uniquely cohesive unit, politically and ethnically, dominated by a handful of politically connected contractors and their captive unions. Its links to the city's financial and political leadership were evident at a hundred Waldorf banquets" (Epstein, "The Last Days of New York," in *The Fiscal Crisis of American Cities: Essays on the Political Economy of Urban America with Special Reference to New York*, ed. R. Alcaly and D. Mermelstein [New York: Vintage Books, 1977], p. 65).

45. Committee on Regional Plan, *Graphic Regional Plan*, p. 173; idem, *Building of the City*, pp. 126-27; Regional Plan Association, *Spread City*, Bulletin no. 100 (New York: Regional Plan Association, 1962), pp. 17-20; idem, *The Region's Growth*, Bulletin no. 105 (New York: Regional Plan Association, 1967), pp. 114-15; idem, *The State of the Region, 1977, Regional Plan News*, no. 101 (1977):11-12. See also Lichtenberg, *One-Tenth of a Nation*, pp. 20-27, 154; and Raymond Vernon, *Metropolis 1985* (Cambridge, MA: Harvard University Press, 1960), p. 102.

46. Hays, *Community Leadership*, p. 44.

47. Committee on Regional Plan, *Major Economic Factors*, pp. 31-33. The section quoted in the report is from Harlan P. Douglass, *The Suburban Trend* (New York: Century, 1925), pp. 272-74.

48. On the aesthetics of growth: Committee on Regional Plan, *Building of the City*; and on the need for a regional perspective: idem, *Population, Land Values and Government*, pp. 194ff.

49. O'Connor, *Fiscal Crisis of the State*, pp. 13-16.

50. Committee on Regional Plan, *Population, Land Values and Government*, pp. 34, 71.

51. Committee on Regional Plan, *Graphic Regional Plan*, p. 127. This average density actually diminished over the next 40 years. By 1965 the workday CBD population was down to 2.12 million people, of which only 557,000 were residents (Regina Armstrong, *The Office Industry* (prepared for Regional Plan Association of New York) (Cambridge, MA: MIT Press, 1972), p. 133.

52. Committee on Regional Plan, *Major Economic Factors*, p. 34; and Duffus, *Mastering the Metropolis*, pp. 34-62.

53. Committee on Regional Plan, *Major Economic Factors*, p. 35.

54. Committee on Regional Plan, "Clothing and Textile Industries," pp. 15, 60.

55. Committee on Regional Plan, *Major Economic Factors*, pp. 43-44.

56. Committee on Regional Plan, "Clothing and Textile Industries," pp. 16,17,58.

57. Ibid., p. 17.

58. Ibid., pp. 19, 59-60, 76.

According to Robert Fitch, maximization of urban real estate values was the primary rationale behind the RPA and its plan ("Planning New York," pp. 262-63). Correctly sensing the competition between industrial and financial capital for urban space, he nonetheless appears to accept as the dominant RPA position the narrow views of its real estate members. In practice, real estate interests within the business community favor higher rents, while corporate and retail tenants typically oppose rent increases. This situation underscores the inevitable split occurring between different sectors of capital that groups such as the RPA are actually designed to help mend. Moreover, the RPA had a larger agenda than mere optimization of real estate values in the city.

59. Committee on Regional Plan, "Clothing and Textile Industries," p. 62.

60. Ibid., pp. 18-19.

Although the committee referred to the Jews as a "racial group" with "peculiar characteristics" and "idiosyncrasies" (a common ethnic portrayal at the time) one would be hard pressed to prove anti-Semitism as a motivating factor in the committee's deliberations. Elsewhere the committee praised the immigrants as the embodiment of the American dream in their "ambitious" search to improve their economic conditions (ibid., pp. 19, 21). Rather, what we have here is a conscious effort to rid the CBD of competing land uses as well as of a highly paid, unionized, and foreign-speaking (Yiddish) labor force that was of limited use to the office and retail sectors trying to expand in the city.

61. Committee on Regional Plan, "Clothing and Textile Industries," pp. 19, 20, 23, 61.

62. O'Connor, *Fiscal Crisis of the State*. See Richard Barnett and Ronald Müller, *Global Reach* (New York: Simon and Schuster, 1974), pp. 228-31, 267-70, on competition over market control.

63 Committee on Regional Plan, "Clothing and Textile Industries," pp. 24, 58.

64. According to the popular version of the plan prepared for public consumption:

> At the present time most of the commuter traffic is fed into the urban rapid-transit systems, adding to a burden which is already so great as to have passed the limits not only of comfort, but of decency. . . .
>
> Our Plan will relieve both of these situations by establishing an almost entirely new system of suburban rapid transit. It will try to carry the commuter without change, or with a minimum necessity for change, from his home station to within walking distance of his job. . . .
>
> . . . As commuting is expensive and not necessarily a pleasure, the commuting haul should be as short as possible. At the same time the commuter should live where living conditions are best and work where

working conditions are best. His children should be able to reach their schools easily, his wife get to her favorite shopping district, and the whole family find its regular and occasional recreation with the minimum of trouble and effort. (Duffus, *Mastering the Metropolis*, pp. 149-51)

65. Despite the survey's recognition of deplorable crowding on existing subway lines, the 1929 Plan recommended no improvement or additions to the facilities. Renovation would only further congestion by attracting more workers to the CBD and, in particular, advantage the garment industry by allowing its workers to commute from lower-rent outer boroughs:

A total of nearly 70,000 persons must come to a small central section of the city where most of the women's garments for the entire country are made. Translated into terms of subway trains, it would take about 41 ten-car trains, packed to rush-hour capacity, to bring to this manufacturing center the 70,000 workers who have found it necessary to live at a considerable distance from their work.

The effect of the distance at which the majority of garment workers live from their work on the transit facilities of the city is a matter of common knowledge to those who travel daily on the subways and certain of the surface lines. (Committee on Regional Plan, "Clothing and Textile Industries," p. 59)

See also idem, *Transit and Transportation*, Regional Survey of New York and Its Environs, 8 vols. (New York: Regional Plan of New York, 1928), 4:23-27, 40-57, on the transit problem; and idem, *Graphic Regional Plan*, pp. 143-48, 169-71, for recognition that provision of more facilities may only further congestion in the center.

Connecting Queens to the CBD, the municipally owned Independent Subway System, then under construction, received no mention in the plan (Johnson, "Emergence of Metropolitan Regionalism," p. 306).

66. Committee on Regional Plan, *Graphic Regional Plan*, pp. 192, 194; and Duffus, *Mastering the Metropolis*, p. 149. See Committee on Regional Plan, *Graphic Regional Plan*, p. 198, on the "ultimate" suburban rapid transit plan; and pp. 228-29, on a lower Manhattan expressway that would have sliced through the Lower East Side. In congested areas, where new rail lines were not feasible, the committee initially supported plans to allow suburban trains to run on existing subway tracks. The city administration ultimately rejected this vision (Johnson, "Emergence of Metropolitan Regionalism," pp. 300-308).

67. Committee on Regional Plan, *Major Economic Factors*, p. 25; see also pp. 33-34, 61; and idem, "Clothing and Textile Industries," pp. 23-25. According to the survey on garment manufacturing, "The incentive toward movement out of town has admittedly been very largely a desire to escape union domination, and the things which go with union control—chiefly high wages and short hours" (ibid., p. 77).

68. Committee on Regional Plan, "The Printing Industry," in *Chemical, Metal, Wood, Tobacco and Printing Industries* (originally monograph no. 6 of Economic Series) Regional Survey of New York and Its Environs, 8 vols. (New York: Regional Plan of New York, 1928), 1A:13; and Johnson, "Emergence of Metropolitan Regionalism," p. 562. See also O'Connor, *Fiscal Crisis of the State*.

69. Committee on Regional Plan, *Neighborhood and Community Planning*, Regional Survey of New York and Its Environs, 8 vols. (New York: Regional Plan of New York, 1929), 7:107; and idem, *Building of the City*, p. 202. See also Scott, *American City Planning*, p. 293, on the RPA's housing policy. Johnson ("Emergence of Metropolitan Regionalism," p. 561) observed that committee member Frederic Delano went so far as to propose demolition of Harlem in the 1920s at precisely the period when it was emerging as the nation's preeminent center of black culture.

Lewis Mumford attributed the "indefensible" housing position of the committee to the "conservatism" of Thomas Adams, the survey's executive planning director (Mumford, "Plan of New York 2," p. 149). However, mindful of the plan's sponsors and their class interests, one might question whether the RPA's position can be explained by the staff's values without first examining the process of ideology formation and the socialization of the staff.

70. Committee on Regional Plan, *Neighborhood and Community Planning*, pp. 107, 110.

71. John Finley as quoted in Committee on Regional Plan, *Building of the City*, p. 406. Also Committee on Regional Plan, *Neighborhood and Community Planning*, p. 111.

72. Committee on Regional Plan, *Building of the City*, p. 202.

73. Ibid., p. 402. See pp. 398-405 about the Lower East Side proposal as a prototype for urban renewal.

74. Committee on Regional Plan, *Building of the City*, p. 568; and idem, *Neighborhood and Community Planning*, pp. 264-69; also Scott, *American City Planning*, p. 264.

75. Scott, *American City Planning*, p. 90. See also Committee on Regional Plan, *Neighborhood and Community Planning*, pp. 90-100; and idem, *Building of the City*, pp. 195-219.

76. Committee on Regional Plan, *Highway Traffic*, Regional Survey of New York and Its Environs, 8 vols. (New York: Regional Plan of New York, 1927), 3:49.

77. Committee on Regional Plan, *Graphic Regional Plan*, pp. 332-33.

78. Committee on Regional Plan, *Public Recreation*, Regional Survey of New York and Its Environs, 8 vols. (New York: Regional Plan of New York, 1928), 5:21.

79. See Committee on Regional Plan, *Graphic Regional Plan*, pp. 141-43, 269-85, for the plan's visionary parkway proposals.

80. On the structuralist vs. instrumentalist debate on the role of the State: Nicos Poulantzas, *Political Power and Social Classes* (London: New Left Books, 1973); and compare Scott and Roweis, "Urban Planning"; Ralph Miliband, *The State in Capitalist Society* (New York: Basic Books, 1969); and Domhoff, *Who Really Rules?;* idem, *Powers That Be.*

81. See Committee on Regional Plan, *Population, Land Values and Government*, pp. 156-60; idem, *Building of the City*, pp. 180-90.

Indirectly, skyscrapers also helped to maintain industry in the city by preserving "untouched a quantity of obsolete business buildings in which industries that could not pay Manhattan rentals in modern structures [would] still [persist] at the center of the Region" (Committee on Regional Plan, *Population, Land Values and Government*, p. 63).

82. Cf. Friedmann and Weaver, *Territory and Function*; Caro, *Power Broker*; and Moses, *Public Works*.

83. Regional Plan Association, *Fiftieth Year Review*, p. 3. See also idem, *From Plan to Reality: Progress Report. Vol. 1* (New York: Regional Plan Association, 1933); idem, *From Plan to Reality: Progress Report. Vol. 2* (New York: Regional Plan Association, 1938); and idem, *From Plan to Reality: Progress Report. Vol. 3* (New York: Regional Plan Association, 1942).

84. Regional Plan Association, *Progress Report 3*, pp. III-1–III-10. See also Hays, *Community Leadership*, pp. 56-59; Johnson, "Emergence of Metropolitan Regionalism," pp. 492-540; Regional Plan Association, *A Closer Look at the Regional Plan of New York and Its Environs* (New York: Regional Plan Association, 1929); idem, *Progress Report 1* and *Progress Report 2*; and Caro, *Power Broker*, pp. 56-59.

85. See Regional Plan Association, *Organized Support for Planning Develops throughout New York Region and Elsewhere*, Information Bulletin no. 9 (New York: Regional Plan Association, 1932), p. 11; and idem, *Progress Report 3*, p. V-2; McAneny, *The Sixth Annual Report of the Regional Plan Association* (presented at the Annual Meeting of the RPA, New York City, June 6, 1935) (New York: Regional Plan Association, 1935), p. 5; idem, *The Eighth Annual Report of the Regional Plan Association* (presented at the Annual Meeting of the RPA, New York City, December 2, 1937) (New York: Regional Plan Association, 1937), pp. 2-3.

86. George McAneny, *The Second Annual Report of the Regional Plan Association* (presented at the Annual Meeting of the RPA, New York City, May 31, 1931 (New York: Regional Plan Association, 1931), p. 13. See also Regional Plan Association, *Progress Report 3*, pp. VI-4–VI-6.

87. McAneny, *Ninth Annual Report*, p. 2.

88. George McAneny, *The Seventh Annual Report of the Regional Plan Association* (presented at the Annual Meeting of the RPA, New York City, May 28, 1936) (New York: Regional Plan Association, 1936), p. 21.

89. Ibid., pp. 2, 4.

90. McAneny, *Sixth Annual Report*, p. 2. As Governor Lehman noted: "While the suggestion emanated from the National Resources Board in Washington, I leaned heavily upon the advice and assistance of the Regional Plan Association in actually organizing it for work and am pleased with results to date" (Lehman as quoted in ibid., p. 4).

91. Johnson, "Emergence of Metropolitan Regionalism," p. 557.

92. Caro, *Power Broker*; and Marwyn Samuels, "The Biography of Landscape," in *The Interpretation of Ordinary Landscapes*, ed. D. Meinig (New York: Oxford University Press, 1979), pp. 66-67.

93. Fitch, "Planning New York," p. 282; Johnson, "Emergence of Metropolitan Regionalism," pp. 481, 542-43; and Charles Asher, "Comment on Robert Moses," *New York Planning Review* (New York Metropolitan Chapter of the American Institute of Planners) 17 (Spring 1975):A11-13. Cf. Committee on Regional Plan, *Graphic Regional Plan;* and "Landscape by Moses" in Caro, *Power Broker*, pp. ii-v, 5-6. For a description of public authorities and on Moses' role in these institutions: Caro, *Power Broker*; Annmarie Walsh, *The Public's Business: The Politics and Practices of Government Corporations* (Cambridge, MA: MIT Press, 1978); and Chapter 4 (of this volume).

94. Cf. Fitch, "Planning New York"; and Caro, *Power Broker*. See also Marshall Berman, *All That Is Solid Melts into Air* (New York: Simon and Schuster,

1982), pp. 290-312, for an analysis that balances Moses' quest for power with a recognition that power is a social relation.

95. Committee on Regional Plan, *Graphic Regional Plan*, pp. 377, 379. Cf. ibid., pp. 281-82, 377-80; and Caro, *Power Broker*, pp. 149-51, 277-79, 300-304.

96. Caro, *Power Broker*, p. 609.

97. Ibid., pp. 639-78.

98. Ibid., pp. 951-54.

99. Hays, *Community Leadership*, pp. 70-75, 99, 100, 102. See also Dennis Rondinelli, "The Structure of Planning in the New York Metropolitan Region" (Department of City and Regional Planning, Cornell University, Ithaca, NY, 1966, Mimeographed), pp. 26-30. Technical studies and a population projection prepared under contract to the Long Island Lighting Company developed into a comprehensive economic forecasting service (Hays, *Community Leadership*, pp. 97-99).

100. Hays, *Community Leadership*, p. 101.

101. Regional Plan Association, *Project Management Committee Report to the Rockefeller Brothers Fund*, December 22, 1955, p. 5 (quoted in Hays, *Community Leadership*, pp. 105, 119-20).

102. Vernon, *Metropolis 1985*, pp. 30, 35-37, 44-45; and Edgar Hoover and Raymond Vernon, *Anatomy of a Metropolis* (Cambridge, MA: Harvard University Press, 1959), pp. 52-54, 62-77. On the impact of labor costs on industrial location in the metropolitan area: Martin Segal, *Wages in the Metropolis* (Cambridge, MA: Harvard University Press, 1960); and Lichtenberg, *One-Tenth of a Nation*. Segal characterizes the relocation of industrial production in standardized items as a "peeling off" of the region's "wage-oriented" nonunionized labor force. On the other hand, the manufacture of items in rapid product-change lines tended to resist standardization (e.g., women's fashion garments as contrasted with house dresses, and advertising and legal printing services as compared with book printing). These ephemeral enterprises tended to remain in, or in close proximity to, the central city (Segal, *Wages in the Metropolis*, pp. 146-49).

103. Vernon, *Metropolis 1985*, pp. 81-85; and Lichtenberg, *One-Tenth of a Nation*, pp. 144-77. See Allan Pred, *City-Systems in Advanced Economies* (New York: John Wiley, 1977), for an overview of the process of city-system growth and on the strength of various location factors in the siting of nonroutine office functions.

104. Lichtenberg, *One-Tenth of a Nation*, pp. 154-55; and Hoover and Vernon, *Anatomy of a Metropolis*, pp. 8-10.

105. Cf. Regional Plan Association, *Region's Growth*, pp. 114-15; idem, *Fiftieth Year Review*, p. 8; and Vernon, *Metropolis 1985*, pp. 121-22, 133-34.

106. Robert Wood, *1400 Governments: The Political Economy of the New York Metropolitan Region* (Cambridge, MA: Harvard University Press, 1961), pp. 76-79, 93-104.

107. Ibid., pp. 113, 175-76. For the subsequent genesis of this critique of parochial local land use regulation: Richard Babcock, *The Zoning Game* (Madison: University of Wisconsin Press, 1966); Fred Bosselman, *Alternatives to Urban Sprawl: Legal Guidelines for Governmental Action* (prepared for the National Commission on Urban Problems), Technical Report no. 15 (Washington, DC: Government Printing Office, 1968); Committee for Economic Development, *Guiding Metropolitan Growth* (New York: Committee for Economic Development, 1960); idem, *Modernizing Local*

Government (New York: Committee for Economic Development, 1966); Reps, "Requiem for Zoning"; William Reilly, ed., *The Use of Land: A Citizen's Policy Guide to Urban Growth* (Report by the Task Force on Land Use and Urban Growth, sponsored by the Rockefeller Brothers Fund) (New York: Thomas Y. Crowell, 1973); and Randall Scott, ed., *Management and Control of Growth*, 3 vols. (Washington, DC: Urban Land Institute, 1975).

108.   Wood, *1400 Governments*, pp. 113-14.

109.   Ibid., pp. 2, 115-16, 192.

110.   Regional Plan Association, *Spread City*, p. 9. See also Armstrong, *Office Industry*, pp. 129-33.

111.   Regional Plan Association, *The Spreading Metropolis: A Burden to Business?* (Report on the Arden House Conference, Harriman, NY, February 11-14, 1962), pamphlet (New York: Regional Plan Association, 1962), p. 30. See also idem, *Metropolis 1985. Its Meaning to Business* (Report on the Arden House Conference, Harriman, NY, March 3, 1961), pamphlet (New York: Regional Plan Association, 1961).

112.   Hays, *Community Leadership*, p. 165; and John Keith and William Shore, *Public Participation in Regional Planning* (Report of the Second Regional Plan) (New York: Regional Plan Association, 1967), pp. 13, 23. See also Regional Plan Association, *Goals for the Regional Project: Background Booklets nos. 1-5* (New York: Regional Plan Association, 1963).

113.   Regional Plan Association, *Carrying Forward the Second Regional Plan* (New York: Regional Plan Association, 1967), pp. 30-31 (emphasis added).

114.   Keith and Shore, *Public Participation*, p. 28; also pp. 24-28.

115.   Ibid., p. 28.

116.   Ibid., p. 29. Seventy percent of the respondents, after being questioned on the problems caused by local zoning regulations in the neighborhood, favored the relocation of zoning powers to a higher (metropolitan) level of government. A similar plurality favored mandatory construction of affordable housing for suburban factory workers (ibid., pp. 29-30).

117.   Hays, *Community Leadership*, p. 165.

118.   This pioneering public participation process is described in Hays, *Community Leadership*; Keith and Shore, *Public Participation*; and Regional Plan Association, *Progress Report on the Second Regional Plan* (includes insert: Committee on the Second Regional Plan) (New York: Regional Plan Association, 1966). It was supported by grants from the Avalon, Old Dominion, Taconic, and Twentieth Century funds, with major additional input from the Ford Foundation and the Rockefeller Brothers Fund (Keith and Shore, *Public Participation*).

119.   Regional Plan Association, *News Release No. 1356: Regional Plan Association Celebrates Fiftieth Anniversary* (New York: Regional Plan Association, 1979), p. 14; idem, *The Second Regional Plan: A Draft for Discussion*, Bulletin no. 110 (New York: Regional Plan Association, 1968).

From as early as 1950 the RPA was calling for a metropolitan coordination of local land use controls, regional provision of public services and facilities, and "New Town Development Corporations" to build some 50 "intelligently planned and developed centers throughout the Region" (Regional Plan Association, *Second Regional Plan*, pp. 11-12). The RPA proposals anticipated public attention to these issues by more than 15 years. See Chapter 4; and Walker and Heiman, "Quiet Revolution for Whom?"

120. Regional Plan Association, *Second Regional Plan*, p. 34; also pp. 9, 27.

121. Cf. Regional Plan Association, *Spread City*, p. 38; idem, *Second Regional Plan*, p. 49; and idem, *State of the Region, 1977*, p. 7. See also Wolfgang Quante, *The Exodus of Corporate Headquarters from New York City* (New York: Praeger, 1976), p. xv. Between 1968 and 1974, 40 of the city's *Fortune* "500" firms moved their headquarters out of the core, usually to suburban locations and, on occasion, out of the region altogether. During this same period there were eight arrivals in the city (Quante, *Exodus of Corporate Headquarters*, pp. 43-47).

122. Regional Plan Association, *Second Regional Plan*, p. 20; also pp. 8, 11.

123. Regional Plan Association, *Linking Skills, Jobs and Housing in the New York Urban Region* (New York: Regional Plan Association, 1972).

124. Regional Plan Association, *The Lower Hudson*, Bulletin no. 104 (New York: Regional Plan Association, 1966), p. 67.

125. Fitch, "Planning New York," p. 280.

126. Regional Plan Association, *Second Regional Plan*, p. 11.

127. Regional Plan Association, *Second Regional Plan*, pp. 11, 20, 35. Compare also idem, *Lower Hudson*, pp. 5-6; and Committee on Regional Plan, *Graphic Regional Plan*, pp. 227-29, 266.

128. Cf. William Woodside, "Why Westway Is Right," New York *Times*, August 1, 1983, p. A15; Sidney Schanberg, "Westway's Sleaze Factor," New York *Times*, October 9, 1984, p. A33; Sam Roberts, "Battle of Westway: Bitter 10-Year Saga of a Vision on Hold," New York *Times*, June 4, 1984, pp. B1, 4; and New York *Times*, "Death of a Highway," Editorial, September 27, 1985, p. A30. At the time, William Woodside was chair and chief executive officer of the American Can Company as well as of the RPA.

129. Regional Plan Association, *State of the Region, 1977*, pp. 11-12; and Jameson Doig, *Metropolitan Transportation Politics in the New York Region* (New York: Columbia University Press, 1966). See also Boris Pushkarev and Jeffrey Zupan, *Public Transportation and Land Use Policy* (prepared for the Regional Plan Association) (Bloomington: Indiana University Press, 1977).

130. Hays, *Community Leadership*, pp. 154-55; and Regional Plan Association, *Fiftieth Year Review*, p. 9.

131. In 1981 the average MTA suburban commuter rail ride brought in approximately one-half its cost in fares, while the much more intensively used city bus and subway system averaged a 68 percent return rate (Regional Plan Association, *Financing the Metropolitan Transportation Authority*, *The Region's Agenda* 10 [May 1981]).

132. Regional Plan Association, *The Region's Money Flows. Vol. 1. The Government Accounts* (New York: Regional Plan Association, 1977); idem, *Fiftieth Year Review*, p. 20; idem, *The Region's Money Flows. Vol. 2. Business Accounts* (New York: Regional Plan Association, 1979); and idem, *Regional Accounts: Structure and Performance of the New York Region's Economy in the Seventies* (Bloomington: Indiana University Press, 1980).

133. This was suggested by David Johnson, personal communication, 1985 (Graduate School of Planning, University of Tennessee).

134.   Regional Plan Association, *Annual Report for 1981-1982*, *Regional Plan News*, no. 112 (1982):11-14. See idem, *Annual Report for 1983-1984*, *Regional Plan News*, no. 118 (1984):13-15, for the affiliation of major contributors and board members.

135.   Danielson and Doig, *Politics of Urban Regional Development*, p. 46.

136.   On the origins of the New York fiscal crisis and on attempts to resolve it in a manner benefiting the city's dominant corporate and financial interests: Roger Alcaly and David Mermelstein, eds., *The Fiscal Crisis of American Cities: Essays on the Political Economy of Urban America with Special Reference to New York* (New York: Vintage Books, 1977); Jack Newfield and Paul DuBrul, *The Abuse of Power: The Permanent Government and the Fall of New York* (New York: Viking Press, 1977); and William Tabb, "The New York City Fiscal Crisis," in *Marxism and the Metropolis*, ed. W. Tabb and L. Sawers (New York: Oxford University Press, 1978), pp. 241-66.

137.   Newfield and DuBrul, *Abuse of Power*, p. 181.

138.   Ibid., pp. 179-82.

139.   *World* (Journal of Peat, Marwick, Mitchell and Co.), "The City that Came Back," no. 4 (1981):18-22. On the spatial arrangement of capitalist control functions: R. B. Cohen, "The New International Division of Labor: Multinational Corporations and the Urban Hierarchy," in *Urbanization and Urban Planning in Capitalist Society*, ed. M. Dear and A. Scott (New York: Methuen, 1981), pp. 287-315; and Harvey, "Urban Process."

140.   Cf. Walter Farr, Jr., Lance Liebman, and Jeffrey Wood, *Decentralizing City Government: A Practical Study of a Radical Proposal for New York City* (New York: Praeger, 1972), pp. 90-91, 99, 185, 191; and Wood, *1400 Governments*, pp. 115-16, 192. On the functional separation of political power as it might be applied in the tristate region: Edward Costikyan and Maxwell Lehman, *New Strategies for Regional Cooperation: A Model for the Tri-State New York-New Jersey-Connecticut Area* (New York: Praeger, 1973).

141.   Regional Plan Association, *Annual Report 1981-1982*, p. 14; idem, *Annual Report 1983-1984*, pp. 14-15.

142.   Major studies addressing RPA activities that were either sponsored by the RPA or foundations supporting RPA efforts at the time include Thomas Adams, *Planning the New York Region* (New York: Committee on Regional Plan, 1927); Duffus, *Mastering the Metropolis*; Wood, *1400 Governments*; and Hays, *Community Leadership*.

143.   See Regional Plan Association, *Implementing Regional Planning in the Tri-State New York Region: A Report to the Federal Regional Council and the Tri-State Regional Planning Commission* (New York: Regional Plan Association, 1975). In her review for the U.S. Advisory Commission on Intergovernmental Relations, Joan Aron concluded that in the absence of innovative leadership by the Tri-State Regional Planning Commission, the RPA "appears to serve as the most visible generator of new ideas for guiding the region's growth and development" (Aron, "The New York Interstate Metropolis," in *Regional Governance: Promise and Performance. Volume 2: Case Studies*, Advisory Commission on Intergovernmental Relations, 8 vols. [Washington, DC: Government Printing Office, 1973], p. 207).

144.   Doig, *Metropolitan Transportation Politics*, pp. 146-48; and Danielson and Doig, *Politics of Urban Regional Development*, pp. 147-51.

145. The eminent urban geographer Peter Hall provides a striking example of allegiance to the self-professed aims of the organization. Liberally drawing from the Second Regional Plan for his study on metropolitan trends in the New York area, and uncritically defining this metropolitan region along the same political boundaries used by the RPA, he accepts the association as "the only body, official or unofficial, taking a serious and continuous look at the New York Region as a whole" (Hall, *The World Cities*, 2d ed. [New York: McGraw-Hill, 1977], p. 178).

See also Danielson and Doig, *Politics of Urban Regional Development*, pp. 4, 34-35, and 82ff., for another important study liberally drawing upon RPA data and photographs with inadequate recognition of the actual sponsorship of the RPA and how this might influence their definition of the region and their interpretation of the data available.

3

Regional Planning
for Global Accumulation:
Servicing New York's Production
and Consumption Landscapes

The New York metropolitan region has several other business-led civic organizations with a primary interest in land use planning and regulation. Within New York State, the Mid-Hudson Pattern for Progress (MHP) and the Downtown-Lower Manhattan Association (DLMA) have had the greatest impact. Focusing on Manhattan south of Canal Street, the DLMA has identified a territory of geographic concern within that of the Regional Plan Association (RPA); the locus of MHP attention, seven counties along the Hudson north of New York City, overlaps with the RPA's region (Map 3.1). In this chapter the agendas of these two other privately sponsored planning advocates are introduced. In so doing, the unavoidable tension within business-sponsored regional land use reform, where it supports a classwide collective interest and where more select geographic and sectoral goals are served, becomes evident.

In its dynamic and expanding form, capitalist real estate development during one period of accumulation generates a built environment that is ill suited for the next stage. An example would be the expansion of lofts for manufacturing, or construction of adjacent worker tenements, on property that will be later used for office development. In this process collective action and centralized planning help to coordinate the forced adjustments, such as the urban renewal, infrastructure provision, and dissolution of militant working-class neighborhoods, required for the new cycle of accumulation and real estate development. However, while this holds for the overall process of capital accumulation, immediate capital interest in the built environment is not monolithic. As a result, a variety of intraclass tensions may arise, as, for example, between the labor-intensive competitive sector and the large-scale corporate sector over CBD location in the early part of this century, or when office landlords confront corporate tenants over rent. These class factions can divide along sectoral as well as geographic divisions. The RPA, DLMA, and MHP represent reform groups that form in support of the objectives of these more select segments of capital rather than all capital.

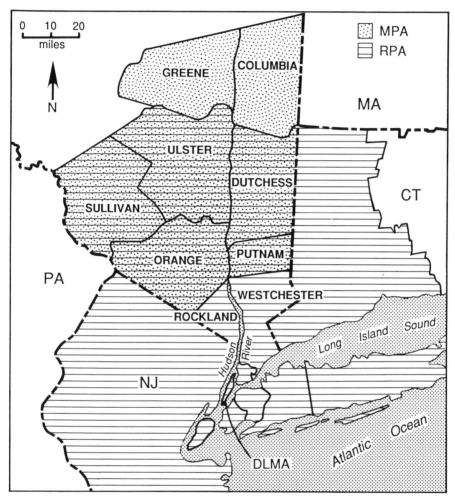

Map 3.1. Overlapping areas of concern for the Regional Plan Association, the Mid-Hudson Pattern for Progress, and the Downtown-Lower Manhattan Association.

To avoid a naive instrumental interpretation in my rejection of crass structuralism (class preservation) as a motive for business-led planning activities and public-sector planning, I also acknowledge in this chapter a process known as "structuration." Thus, when individuals and groups are striving to further their own or members' self-interests, such as planning advocates, they also tend to perpetuate the overall social system (capitalism) giving rise to their social demarcation and goals. As shall be discussed, an understanding of this process is important for an explanation of the role of the State in land use reform, and for an appreciation of its relative autonomy from private interests.

Outside of New York City, the region's other urban centers also have active business and civic organizations with a more local orientation than that of the RPA. These groups often define "regionalism" as a cooperative effort between their own central city and the immediate surrounding suburbs. Accordingly, they may take exception to RPA activities supporting a regional identity when they perceive their own centers as relegated to a peripheral suburban position.[1] Such is not the case, however, with the DLMA and the MHP. Contained within Manhattan's CBD, the DLMA cooperates with the RPA on projects maintaining and strengthening the region's core. The MHP also cooperates with the RPA and accepts the association's classification of the mid-Hudson area as an important residential district for Manhattan's workforce and for workers in the area's own industrial parks.

THE DOWNTOWN-LOWER MANHATTAN ASSOCIATION

The DLMA stands out as one of the most spatially concentrated expressions of capital interest in urban development found in this nation. The RPA and the MHP, by contrast, are concerned with a larger urbanizing region. The DLMA's membership is recruited primarily from the large-scale financial sector operating in the international arena (including commercial and investment banking, insurance, securities exchange, and support services such as finance law and accounting). Hence, the association cannot be understood without first examining the global spread of the capitalist economy and the importance of New York City as a control center in this process.

The Ascent of Finance Capital as a Regulatory Force in Advanced Economies

The expansion of capitalist production on an international scale entails a new global division of labor and the emergence of an international market for the commodities produced. This scale of production requires centralized financial and administrative coordination. Toward this end, London, Tokyo, New York, Zurich, Hong Kong, Singapore, Los Angeles, and a few other cities emerge as global control centers in the world economy. Their corporate structure is composed largely of multinational conglomerates (e.g., Gulf and Western, ITT), together with financial and accounting services necessary to propel the rapid mergers, acquisitions, and disinvestments characteristic of international production and trade. In the United States this composite is quite different from the business structure of the older centers of "national" capital, such as Detroit, Pittsburgh, and St. Louis. Here predominantly U.S.-based corporations (e.g., General Motors and, until recently, U.S. Steel) concentrated on expanding production and markets in existing product lines rather than branching out via merger and acquisition into new areas of production.

The role of finance capital as a regulatory force in the international expansion of capital increased with the changing corporate structure. In this financial sector administration became centered in a few leading institutions. To cite an example, during the lending expansion of the late 1960s and early 1970s, the eight largest accounting firms in the nation held 94 percent of the *Fortune* 500 firms as clients, and the three leading U.S. banks (Citibank, Bank of America, and Chase Manhattan) financed a majority of foreign investment by U.S.-based corporations.[2] Fiscal regulation was solidified by the industrial sector of corporate capital through increasing reliance on the external financing of the corporate bond market. Investment banks under the control of J. P. Morgan and John D. Rockefeller, Sr. played a major role in the first industrial merger movement of 1889-1903. Banks lost much of their power during the Great Depression, and many industries returned to internally generated investment funds; but with the postwar rise in corporate mergers and accumulation on a global scale, outside funding again gained in importance.

In addition to influence via loans and services, the financial sector directly controls many industrial production decisions. These links are forged through the leading commercial and investment banks that directly own portfolio stock or act as trustees for pensions, foundations, and other major stockholders. Although industrial stock ownership may be widely distributed among many investors, the actual control over board directorship often remains concentrated among a few financial institutions. In 1974 the trust departments of commercial banks held 26.9 percent of all outstanding commercial stock, and this amount was in addition to their own considerable portfolio investment.[3] With controlling, or at least significant voting, interest beginning at a very low percentage in major publicly held corporations (the figures 5 to 10 percent are commonly cited), the leading institutional investors may wield considerable power over industrial policy. Using data obtained through an unprecedented 1968 congressional probe of commercial banking, David Kotz estimated that at least 34.5 percent of the leading 200 U.S.-based nonfinancial corporations (by assets) were under financial control in 1969, with an additional 21.5 percent under internal (owner) control.[4]

New York City rises as the preeminent "global city" in this advanced stage of capitalism. By 1980 firms headquartered in the city accounted for approximately 40 percent of all foreign sales by the *Fortune* 500, while city-based banks held 54 percent of all foreign bank deposits in the United States.[5] Furthermore, among the 200 largest nonfinancial corporations, of the 69 identified as under financial control, 46 were controlled by a New York-based financial institution. Kotz identified Chase Manhattan Bank as the most influential, with controlling interest during the late 1960s in 16 of the top 200 firms.[6]

The Twin Office Centers of New York

New York's financial district arose around the port district of lower Manhattan. Financial preeminence was secured by the 1830s as the city came to lead the nation in manufacturing, wholesaling, and export trade. Manufacturing centered on the processing of bulky raw materials, such as sugar into rum, ore into metal, and cotton into textiles. Trading, in turn, attracted commodity brokers, insurance underwriters (for the ships and their cargos), and commercial bankers. Moreover, with the founding of the New York Stock Exchange in 1792, the Wall Street district began its dominance of securities trading for the nation's largest corporations.

By the late nineteenth century the city was also securing its dominance as the nation's largest life insurance center. The insurance firms were themselves active participants in securities trading. More important, the city was emerging as the leading center for corporate headquarter and office development. The industrial firms chose the New York location for the city's superior business services (insurance, legal, and accounting), and for its banking establishment directing the, by then, furious pace of merger and acquisition.

While the securities brokers and major commercial banks remained downtown in close proximity to the securities markets, the flow of insurance and corporate control activity to the midtown area accelerated after the opening of Grand Central Station in 1871 and Penn Central Station in 1910. Here the main attraction for office development was the availability of sturdy (bedrock) building sites outside the congested lower core on land close by the region's primary commuter rail terminals and the affiliated nexus of mass transportation arteries.

Thus it came to pass that New York City, rather than having a single unified office center (as was the case in Detroit, Philadelphia, Pittsburgh, and Chicago), actually developed two major office centers in the area south of Fifty-ninth Street, defined by the RPA as the central business district. These were the Wall Street area (or lower Manhattan) south of Canal Street and midtown Manhattan from Thirty-second to Sixtieth streets (Map 3.2). As a result of this bifurcation local business leaders with property or interests in either location competed for public services and private investment. The largest business concerns could coalesce around organizations and programs addressing urban development on a macroregional scale, as exemplified by the RPA, the New York Chamber of Commerce, the City Club of New York, and the Economic Development Council (which "loans" executives to help manage city departments).[7] However, they also had a more parochial interest in servicing their own immediate needs and enhancing the value and prestige of their real

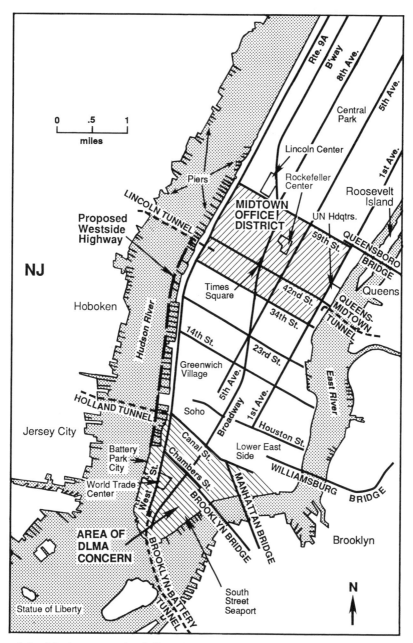

Map 3.2. Manhattan south of Central Park, showing the midtown and Wall Street office districts, and the area of concern for the Downtown-Lower Manhattan Association.

estate commitments. Nowhere was this more rigorously expressed than in lower Manhattan, the historic heart of the nation's financial community.

Rockefeller Power and New York Real Estate

In the 1950s, during the postwar boom in midtown office development, the older lower Manhattan or Wall Street center was threatened by a major exodus of the accounting, legal, and financial institutions, and of the securities markets forming its foundation. David Rockefeller, the youngest of the five Rockefeller brothers, led the effort to stem the tide.

The Rockefeller family already had a long and active interest in Manhattan's development. Its influence was most noticeable through various philanthropic and nonprofit centers it set up in the city, and through the surrounding urban redevelopment accompanying these projects. Philanthropic redevelopment was defined broadly enough to permit the family to "clean up" the area around many charitable projects through construction of privately owned offices and housing. In the process, police power was used to condemn existing land use. To cite an example, Lincoln Center for the Performing Arts, with John D. Rockefeller III as its first president, not only replaced a slum near midtown's Rockefeller Center and the then-expanding West Side office development (Gulf and Western, Exxon, McGraw-Hill, etc.), but also served as the nucleus for construction of 4,200 luxury apartments and a 43-story office tower on land from which 2,000 low-income families were displaced. On the Upper West Side the Rockefeller family-supported Riverside Church and Columbia University spurred development of Morningside Gardens. Begun in 1947 by David Rockefeller, this middle-income housing project displaced 3,000 lower-income residents and set up a buffer zone between the university and Harlem.[8] Rockefeller Center, constructed in the 1930s at the height of an office glut in the city, was itself built on land bequeathed to Columbia University. This helped lower the tax assessment and secured power of condemnation. The $1.6 billion (1985 value) development project was then leased long-term to Rockefeller Center Inc., which, in turn, was owned by a family trust.[9]

The family also had (and continues to have) a controlling interest in the Chase Manhattan Bank, through which it wielded considerable influence over regional property development. Until overtaken by the First National City Bank in the 1960s (since renamed Citibank), Chase Manhattan was the most powerful and wealthiest bank in the New York area. Still considered a leader in real estate investment, it served as the primary administrator of municipal and state bonds, and of debentures offered by private utilities and by public authorities during the 1960s and 1970s (Chapter 4).

The Redevelopment of Lower Manhattan

David, the family's chief representative at Chase, became president of the bank in 1962 and chair in 1969. There he staked out a domain in large-scale real estate development. Rockefeller's leadership at Chase coincided with a period of increasing national control over the older industrial sector by the financial sector of capital. As fiscal control over corporate as well as municipal bond markets was now concentrated in a handful of institutions, many of which were located in lower Manhattan, conditions were ripe for the emergence of an elite group of financial executives who could effectively steer property investment toward more select and geographically concentrated interests.

In 1958 the Downtown-Lower Manhattan Association was formed under David Rockefeller's leadership to secure lower Manhattan as the "dominant center of finance, world trade and shipping." With directorship limited to the area's leading business executives, such as the presidents of Morgan Guaranty Trust, AT&T, and the Guardian Life Insurance Company, the DLMA portrayed itself as "citizens dedicated to the interests and welfare of lower Manhattan."[10] Unveiled in 1958, the DLMA's $6 billion plan for lower Manhattan called for massive private investment in new office structures, extensive demolition and relocation of the area's wholesale produce markets, major improvement in commuter transportation facilities (e.g., heliports, highways, parking structures, and an additional subway extension), and replacement of thousands of low-income tenements with high-quality housing geared to the needs of downtown office personnel.[11]

With an area of concern barely covering one square mile, the DLMA, unlike the RPA, did not have to balance powerful competing interest groups across a broad region (Map 3.2). This central geographic focus enabled the DLMA to mobilize private investment to a much greater degree than could the RPA. In addition to influence through private-sector planning power, the DLMA employed an approach pioneered by the RPA, achieving additional power through influence over public-sector planning and investment. In 1966 the New York City Planning Commission released its *Lower Manhattan Plan*. With major portions of it subsequently implemented, the plan closely paralleled that prepared by the DLMA eight years earlier.[12]

The DLMA's success was phenomenal. Although public outcry prevented destruction of the famed Fulton Fish Market, the relocation of the West Side Produce Market to new facilities at Hunts Point in the Bronx freed an additional 24 acres for development. During 1956, just prior to the DLMA proposal, 110,000 out of the 143,000 truckloads (including rail transfers) of fresh fruit and vegetables entering New York City were handled by the West Side Market.[13] With demand for space surging during the 1960s, the principal concern was to service and, where possible, to attract office construction to lower Manhattan. Together with the construction of a 60-story office tower for Chase Manhattan Bank (making it the largest bank building in the world) and extensive redevelopment of the plaza surrounding it, new offices covering 42 million square feet were constructed in lower Manhattan between 1958 and 1972.[14] This boom was capped by the 9 million-square-foot World Trade Center, built by the Port Authority of New York and New Jersey (Chapter 4).

The DLMA claimed credit for the idea of a world trade center and the proposal that it be constructed by the Port Authority. New Jersey accepted the project only after securing agreement from the authority to take over the bankrupt Hudson and Manhattan rail lines (PATH) and to move the construction site from the east to the west (Hudson River) side of Manhattan (Chapter 4). The center was constructed as the largest office complex in the world. The twin 110-story towers and accompanying hotel, transit, and commercial development were built on a 13-acre site considered a slum by David Rockefeller. This displaced over 300 hi-fi and radio stores composing what was once the city's commercial electronics center. Erected at a cost of over $900 million (1974 value), the World Trade Center precipitated an office glut, undermining the financial security of many of the older buildings in the area. It was saved from a similar fate by the very low fee ($6.5 million in 1974 in lieu of $28 million in property taxes) paid to the city, and by a 40-year lease taken on 60 floors of one tower by the state of New York. Under Governor Nelson Rockefeller's direction (David's brother), the state consolidated many of its city-based activities in the center.[15]

To be sure, midtown Manhattan also underwent a prolonged postwar office boom, and competition between midtown and downtown business leaders for investment continued. Despite a cyclical downturn during the fiscal crisis of the 1970s, Manhattan's real estate market was once again on a roll in the 1980s. With New York banks financing one-third of the nation's foreign trade and all funds transferred in the "Eurodollar market" actually cleared through New York, Manhattan experienced a tremendous expansion in financial activity over the past decade.[16]

Although most of the recent banking activity is concentrated in midtown (from Forty-second to Fifty-seventh streets and between Fifth and Lexington avenues) and some of the older Wall Street legal, accounting, and service firms are moving uptown, vacated offices in lower Manhattan are being renovated and new buildings constructed. The principal tenants are international banking and insurance companies (e. g., Barclays and National Westminster banks) and stock brokerages expanding into banklike activities (e.g., Merrill Lynch, Dean Witter Reynolds, Goldman Sachs, and Shearson of American Express). Between 1983 and 1987 an additional 18.5 million square feet of new office space has been added or was under construction in lower Manhattan.[17] This frenzy of activity cements lower Manhattan as the financial capital of the world, the insurance capital of the country, and the nation's third, and most concentrated, commercial office center (after midtown Manhattan and Chicago).

From its inception the DLMA was concerned about commuter access to the enlarged downtown office center. As such it became the major proponent of the proposed Lower Manhattan Expressway during the late 1950s. Connecting the Williamsburg and Manhattan bridges with the Holland Tunnel, the expressway would have sliced across the densely settled Italian, Jewish, and Chinese neighborhoods of the Lower East Side and the then-emerging studio art center south of Greenwich Village on the West Side (SoHo). The push for automobile access and a major expansion in parking facilities for congested lower Manhattan is informative, since the DLMA itself estimated that 97 percent of the area's labor force relied on public transportation for their commute.[18]

Although public outcry was sufficient to defeat the Lower Manhattan Expressway proposal, planning continued on the equally controversial Westway redevelopment project. Together with the RPA, the DLMA championed the highway, which was designed to speed access from New Jersey and Westchester and provide acres of new developable land in the Hudson River (Chapter 2). The DLMA's concern with improved access for upper-level management was assuredly a major concern.

Construction of the World Trade Center generated 92 acres of adjacent fill in the Hudson. Here the DLMA persuaded Nelson Rockefeller and the state legislature to set up the Battery Park City Authority (since 1979 a subsidiary of the Urban Development Corporation—Chapter 4). Although initially opposed by the city of New York and by local community groups, the authority, exercising power to override local planning and zoning controls, eventually began constructing rental apartments for affluent office workers. Today Battery Park City ranks as the most expensive real estate development ever undertaken in the city (more than twice the size of Rockefeller Center, and eventually to exceed the World Trade Center in size). At Battery Park City the Canadian firm of Olympic and York is building 8 million square feet of office space, in four towers, to include headquarter offices for Merrill Lynch, Dow Jones, Home Life Insurance, and American Express. Adjacent to the office development Lefrak Inc., one of the city's largest landlords, is the lead developer of 5,700 units of upper middle-income housing, with 8,300 additional units approved for later construction. As a state project the land under the Battery Park City complex is exempt from local property taxes. Although the state and developers make payments in lieu of taxes, the development still enjoys substantial tax advantages over private real estate.[19]

On the east side of lower Manhattan the venerable Fulton Fish Market has been enveloped by the South Street Seaport redevelopment, a trendy commercial venture sponsored by the Rouse Corporation. Fast becoming one of the city's leading tourist attractions, the seaport development has, in turn, attracted several million square feet of new office construction, including the new headquarters building for the Continental Insurance Company and national headquarters for Britain's Lloyds Bank and the National Westminster Bank.

With the postwar solidification of New York City as a global city for the international expansion of capitalism, there is a need to turn the CBD over to financial, accounting, and other support services. The DLMA emerges as a leading proponent of regional planning and, if necessary, state intervention to serve this geographically focused interest. While its influence is hard to measure due to its closed membership and the concealed avenues through which its members individually and collectively wield power, the physical manifestation of its goals in transportation, residential, and office development is evident.

At a national level business interests in other metropolitan regions must also cope with structural transformation in the economy as industrial manufacturing decentralizes and the service economy expands. Groups such as the DLMA in New York City, Detroit Renaissance, Pittsburgh's Allegheny Conference on Community Development, and the San Francisco Planning and Urban Renewal Association will arise as the collective voice of those business interests attempting to adapt public policy to support a transformation at the core of the metropolis.[20] As is the relationship between the DLMA and the RPA, these CBD groups often have interests (and members) overlapping with broader-based regional planning advocates, where the latter still see the region as supporting a central business district. In addition to the RPA, examples include the San Francisco Bay Area Council and the Detroit Metropolitan Fund. Alliances can occur when the regional groups work at a scale large enough to encompass the suburban consumption landscapes, such as residential and recreational areas, supporting the productivity of workers and management at the core.

THE MID-HUDSON PATTERN FOR PROGRESS

Like the RPA, the Mid-Hudson Pattern for Progress is a private regional planning advocate concerned with the orderly development of a wide area composing what are perceived and used as production as well as consumption landscapes. Characterizing itself as a "broadly based citizens' regional planning and development corporation," the MHP was founded in 1964 by local business leaders to address urban development in seven rural and urbanizing counties north of New York City and Westchester along the Hudson. With five of its counties also contained within the RPA's (expanded) planning area for the Second Regional Plan, the MHP maintains close ties with the larger organization through joint planning studies and overlapping membership (Map 3.1). Despite an increasing tendency toward open enrollment, the MHP directors are still heavily concentrated among local industrial, financial, and utility interests, many of whom also participate as the mid-Hudson's local monopoly service sector in RPA deliberations (Chapter 1).[21]

The MHP was most active during the late 1960s and early 1970s. The primary aim of the organization during this period was the mobilization of a private-public partnership to direct the huge influx of population and employment then anticipated for the region. This would be accomplished via comprehensive land use planning and guided public investment. Reflecting the optimistic projections of its members, many of whom benefited from population growth (e.g., the utility and banking concerns), these estimates were supported by New York State's Office of Planning Coordination, the RPA, the Urban Development Corporation (UDC), and other groups cooperating with the MHP on publicly and privately funded studies.[22]

MHP offices were originally located in the administration building of the State University College at New Paltz. According to the MHP, this campus location was desirable "neutral ground" central to the region, and its association with the university (several campus administrators sat on its board) helped the organization project a more "objective" image.[23] The tactic paid off. During the late 1960s and early 1970s the Rockefeller administration and private firms were concerned that local governments were unable to meet the planning and zoning obligations required to accommodate anticipated public and private investment in the region. Although the Tri-State Transportation Committee (later called the Tri-State Regional Planning Commission) was the official federal A-95 (regional) review agency for the mid-Hudson, Nelson Rockefeller's Office of Planning Coordination and the UDC often bypassed the federally sanctioned interstate group and preferred to subcontract directly with the MHP for planning studies. As the region's de facto comprehensive planning agency, the MHP also provided support staff for the Mid-Hudson Inter-County Council, a group composed of the seven county executives and their planning directors.

With an overlapping area of geographic focus, the MHP often shared project responsibility with the RPA. In 1969, for example, Governor Rockefeller commissioned the RPA and the MHP to prepare a regional development guide serving as a basis for state investment in housing, education, and transportation. Although downgrading many of the earlier population growth projections of the 1960s, this major planning effort still envisioned mechanisms whereby an expected boom in central-city (New York) and suburban (e.g., Yonkers, White Plains, Newburgh, Poughkeepsie) office employment could be accommodated. Closely paralleling the policy advocated by the RPA (the major data source for the project), the final report condemned suburban sprawl as inefficient and advocated major improvements in public transportation and highway development necessary to link suburban industrial, center, and subcenter office jobs with the labor force. The suburban "housing gap" was a leading target of concern, and UDC cooperation was suggested for the construction of 10 to 15 new towns, which would be tied to existing urban centers.[24] These proposals appealed to various local interests. The clustering of commercial, office, and housing construction in or near existing urban centers would not only address environmental and nogrowth concerns, but would also satisfy local capital interests profiting from additional growth close to contemporaneous centers of capital investment.

By the mid-1970s the MHP's thinly veiled commitment to urban boosterism had clouded its professional judgment, and the organization's projections were clearly out of step with the economic reality then facing the state and region. Working directly with the New York State Atomic and Space Development Authority and the Temporary State Commission to Study the Catskills, the MHP took the lead in regional energy planning and facility siting (Chapter 5). In a 1974 report on energy production prepared for the Catskill Study Commission, environmental considerations were relegated to the aesthetics of plant design. Accepting the utilities' wildly exaggerated projections for power demand as "reasonable," and despite a condemning critique of these estimates by other public agencies and environmental groups, the MHP concluded that the major issue was not whether the power plants were needed, but rather how best to site them.[25]

Ten new plants were suggested by the MHP for a six-county Catskill region (partially overlapping with the mid-Hudson region). This would boost the 1990 projected power generation in the Catskill area from 1,137 megawatts (Mw) in 1974 to 10,000 Mw. With a majority of this power slated for the downstate New York metropolis and with local resistance to power plant siting already vociferous, five of the proposed plants were to be nuclear. According to the MHP, these could offer "more possibilities for an aesthetically pleasing plant design" and should be more acceptable because they would be well guarded by federal as well as state regulation.[26]

SECTORAL GOALS AND SOCIAL REPRODUCTION: STRUCTURATION AS EXPRESSED IN URBAN REFORM

Temporarily renamed Mid-Hudson Pattern Inc. during the 1970s, the "Progress" then being dropped to better secure bonds with environmental groups, the MHP joins the RPA, DLMA, and other business-led planning advocates as examples of business support for centralized regulation to further continued accumulation. This centralization of development authority, public finance, and land use regulation is portrayed by the liberal planning reform movement and its corporate sponsors as a recent phenomenon serving a public interest where parochial municipalities (or, in the case of New York City, neighborhood associations) can no longer accommodate modern production and consumption demands (Chapter 1). There are, however, many "publics" in the process of urban development and even more claims to them. The requirements of the capitalist production system constantly take new forms as accumulation proceeds temporarily and spatially. Centralized intervention, far from being a new phenomenon, has a long history dating from the emergence of large-scale industrial enterprise and the conceptual separation of work, or production, from residential and leisure (consumption) space (Chapters 1 and 2). Today, as in the past, it is called on to address social, environmental, and economic expressions of the fundamental contradiction intrinsic to capitalist production, that is, between its social nature and its private appropriation (Chapter 1). In this manner regional planning and coordination can be used to overcome private resistance to growth and change in neighborhoods set aside as residential or recreation districts during an earlier stage of urban development. Centralized planning and regulation can also spread the expense of public investment over a wider constituency, thus lowering opposition from local tax- or ratepayers. Moreover, with the aggregate of individual production and investment decisions in a competitive market rarely generating collective outcomes of optimal benefit, regional planning can unite individual entrepreneurs to support projects of mutual benefit. This latter task becomes more important as capitalism proceeds on a wider geographic scale, spawning local resistance and greater fragmentation in capitalist class unity.

As we have seen in the New York metropolitan area, the centralization of land use regulations may assist in the transformation and expansion of the forces of capitalist production. It comes as no surprise that the nurturing of public, or State, decisions to further economic transformation and expansion is the most common agenda for private, business-led planning reform. Economic expansion, in turn, helps reproduce, perpetuate, and internally transform the social relations (i.e., affect intraclass divisions) defining the capitalist mode of production. As a result, State assistance, through centralized regulation if need be, in expanding the forces of production benefits capital as a class.

A simple view of the capitalist State as merely perpetuating capitalist class relations, and thereby serving collective class interests, would have to recognize the State as an autonomous agent, not captive of any one faction, be it from the capitalist or the working class. In practice, however, State activities need not be collectively rational with regard to reproduction and expansion of capitalism. With various factions of capital and labor competing in the urban market, the State apparatus can be captured to pursue more select private goals, be they production or consumption oriented. In the case of business-led regional planning, while the scope and locus of geographic concern varies among the privately sponsored planning reform organizations, the associations are inclined toward a coalition of dominant local elites, rather than toward a broad representation from all sectors of capital. This coalition typically consists of representatives from the large (national or international) corporate sector with administrative and/or production functions in the region, as well as participants from the local, but regionally dominant, service sector (including utilities, savings banks, and the local media). The corporate sector, comprising large-scale industrial and financial enterprises, generally favors regional planning to facilitate the urban transformation required for its economic expansion and use value in the landscape. For example, attention to housing, transportation, education, recreation, and other services required by an evolving labor force (including corporate executives) is a principal concern. The local monopoly service sector, on the other hand, joins the dialogue because it anticipates exchange value in the landscape and hopes to benefit from growth in the immediate market area accompanying the changing urban structure. In this manner utilities and local media would benefit from expanding service areas, while local banks and savings and loan institutions with a fixed investment in the built environment would support the property appreciation accompanying growth.

As demonstrated in New York State and elsewhere, the business-led regional planning organizations emerging over the past half century appear to vacillate between policies benefiting their individual membership and those promoting solutions to problems in the overall process of economic development concerning a much wider class constituency. Early RPA attention to zoning changes in the CBD is an example of the former situation, while more recent support for open housing in the suburbs and for mass transit reflects the latter.

Both pluralists and structural Marxists recognize the variety of special interests active in the urban public arena, battling it out for State attention to their goals. Where the two approaches differ, however, is in their conception of how these divisions are determined, the relative influence exerted by the different groups, and the eventual impact on, and outcome from, State response. Pluralists see various business groups coalescing around any of a number of issues. These business groups participate much like any other interest group in the democratic political process—support for political parties, media campaigns, and so on. Moreover, the specific interests of individual actors, as they are at odds with one another, preclude any classwide consensus or resolution. Marxists, on the other hand, proceed from the necessary class division rather than from the myriad of contingent social groupings perceived by pluralists. Marxists consider further intraclass divisions among capitalists as indicative of the basic contradiction inherent in capitalist production when individual entrepreneurs, each pursuing their own self-interests in a competitive market, generate an anarchy threatening collective class interests (Chapter 1). Here the State is seen as necessary for capitalist production because it is the guarantor of those conditions that are essential for the continuation of capital accumulation, and that capitalists could, or would, not address on their own. Examples include maintenance of a money supply, control of militant working-class movements, public education of labor, and support of a welfare system.

The pluralist interpretation fails in its limited view of business participation as just any other interest group in a political process where power and influence can also be covertly exercised, and in its inability to distinguish contingent from necessary social relations and groups (Chapter 1). The structural Marxist view is also unsatisfactory because it confuses the result, in this case State intervention benefiting continued capitalist class relations, for an explanation.

In the area of agreement between Marxists and pluralists that special interest groups attempt to influence the State's urban (development) agenda, Marxists are left with the challenge of explaining how it is that State attention to private goals can further collective (capitalist) class interests without retreating to a naive and teleological functionalism. Moreover, how can the State perpetuate conditions of collective classwide concern when the State appears captive, over and over again, by powerful special interests, as, for example, the planning department of New York City's appearance with respect to the DLMA's agenda?

In practice, attendance to private or special interest concerns, both by private actors and by the State, need not deny concern with collective class interests, nor is complete State autonomy a prerequisite for it to serve classwide interests. Through a process labeled "structuration," the properties of any social system are expressed through the everyday practice of the individuals constituting that system. Practice, in turn (dialectically), generates and reproduces the social system in which it is sanctioned. Thus for any social grouping, be it class, religion, gender, or some other necessary classification (Chapter 1), when individuals of that group act in their own self-interest, they tend to perpetuate the production (social) system giving rise to their social demarcation.[27]

In the case before us, the business leaders supporting RPA activities actually seek to reshape the city for the next stage of accumulation in which they would be dominant participants. Insofar as the RPA does not challenge private property and market relations in the pursuit of private interests, it does help accommodate and reproduce social conditions, such as private property and wage labor, necessary for capital as a class to continue. Furthermore, the individual actors or "agents" in this process of structuration may or may not consciously articulate an agenda for social reform specifically benefiting a collective class interest. To a certain extent groups such as the RPA and the DLMA exist precisely to formulate such a collective class agenda although, as already discussed, it becomes problematic when a distinction is forced between more select goals of benefit to a regionally based faction of capitalists and the social requirements of the class as a whole.

The process of structuration applies to other social groups spawned by the working of the production system. These would include labor (or the prole-tariat) as it works "through the system" to secure class benefits in the workplace, as well as consumption-based movements, such as environmental and nogrowth advocates. The presence of labor as a social group is necessary for capitalism to occur. As such, labor bears a necessary relation to the capitalist mode of production. Turning to consumption we see that while the process of consump-tion is itself necessary to realize production and to reproduce labor power, the specific social movements generated by attention to consumption amenities bear a contingent, rather than a necessary, relation to the mode of production. Capitalism does not depend upon the presence of any one specific form of consumption. Consumption groups come and go as the public periodically seizes upon the defense of specific amenities (e.g., better housing, open space, leisure time, and environmental quality) as social causes.

In both cases—that is, with the necessary presence of the proletariat and with the ephemeral expression of consumption-based movements—participants act on the basis of their understanding of the social system of which they are a part. Since knowledge is itself a socially produced artifact, actions, consciously or not, tend to reproduce the prevailing social system(s) giving rise to knowledge. Now, revolutionary consciousness is a possibility and indeed has been anticipated for the proletariat by Marxists. However, the knowledge necessary for radical transformation of the social structure must come from existing practice or from information obtained outside the norms of social discourse sanctioned by the prevailing social system (Chapter 7). Land use reform promulgated by the DLMA, the RPA, and the MHP, insofar as it eschews radical proposals such as State ownership and worker control of land and the other necessary means of production, furthers capital accumulation and sanctions existing social relations of mutual benefit to all (capitalists), even when these groups lobby for agendas of more select (intraclass) interests.

In summary then, capitalist practice by individual agents tends to reproduce the prevailing social system, together with its inherent contradiction. In addition, challenges to the prevailing social structure, whether from the proletariat or from consumption-based movements, are tempered by capitalist control of the organs of social discourse and by a widely accepted (liberal) reform process designed to ameliorate crisis and further accumulation. In the long run, however, contradiction will continue to spawn negative economic, social, and environmental externalities. Liberal reform can only address these problems on a case-by-case basis because it cannot challenge and amend the basic social structure responsible for contradiction and its manifestations.

LIBERAL REFORM AND THE "LIVEABLE CITY": SOLUTION OR BARRIER FOR CAPITAL ACCUMULATION?

Insofar as the liberal social policies advocated by the RPA, MHP, DLMA, and other business-led planning groups frequently address popular consumption issues, such as affordable housing and open space, they are usually accepted as expressions of the public's will. The inability of social scientists, planning analysts, and the general public to penetrate the conventional wisdom promulgated by liberal business coalitions has already been alluded to. What remains is an examination of how liberal policies, where they are actually sponsored by broad-based political movements independent of conscious or active business support, still articulate with the requirements of the business community.

While capitalist ideology appears hegemonic in everyday social life, capitalists do not consciously, or even actively, control the sphere of consumption in all of its facets (Chapter 7). Certainly the avenues toward the realization of consumption are constrained by the overarching presence of legal, legislative, police, and other components of a State system committed to the preservation of the social relations making up the dominant mode of production (e.g., private ownership of the means of production in a competitive market). Nevertheless, the very act of consumption presents both solutions and problems for the perpetuation and expansion of the forces of production. Furthermore, as mentioned earlier, the State apparatus in all its forms may be captured by more select interest groups or class factions to support goals that challenge a collective and classwide capitalist interest in continued accumulation.

The tendency for U.S. workers, whether industrial or service sector, unionized or nonunionized, to define themselves according to their consumption activities and goals, rather than through their class position in the workforce, has fascinated social scientists since the pioneering work of Thorstein Veblen and Max Weber (Chapters 1 and 6).[28] Social struggle around the sphere of consumption, although considered by orthodox Marxists to be a false division that is fostered by capitalists to split the workers' consciousness so as to reduce workplace militancy, cannot be readily dismissed as a naive expression of false consciousness, or false ideology. Workers are not just passive receptors of capitalist ideology (Chapter 7). Furthermore, ideas, false or otherwise, still have material impact and thereby, when acted upon, tend to generate the actual social conditions, consciousness, and practice that they profess to. On the other hand, it would be a mistake to isolate contingent social divisions, as defined in the case before us, by attention to consumption activity and consciousness divorced from the necessary social relations constituting the mode of production. Were we to do this, we would only be able to recognize and describe, rather than explain, the presence of urban-based social movements founded, in this instance, upon attention to consumption.

Proceeding from the work of Weber and Veblen, sociologist Daniel Bell has outlined the essential elements of a liberal conception of consumption-based urban movements. For Bell, the chief "contradiction" facing capitalism is in the realm of self-realization, or hedonism, in its extreme form.[29] This drive for self-realization is portrayed as a part of Western culture. Culture, in turn, is just one of three realms of social structure, the other two being the economic, where the drive is for efficiency, and the political, where the drive is for equality. More precisely, it is in the realm of culture and in the quest for self-realization through art, literature, and, more generally, through lifestyle and consumption activities that most individuals in advanced economies wish to be identified. It is through realization of these aspirations that the basic threat to, or "contradiction" (in Bell's use of the term) in, bourgeois society (capitalism) emerges. For Bell the contradiction is between the fundamental economic (bourgeois) principles of economizing, efficiency, saving, and frugality on the one hand, and, on the other, the cultural drive for hedonism, whereby satisfaction of unlimited wants and desires is sought.

A basic dilemma here derives from Bell's acceptance of the three realms of social structure and activity (the cultural, economic, and political) as having evolved toward separate, autonomous structures in advanced social systems; rather, the three, while commonly perceived as divorced, are still linked as they were in the past. They take their specific form only in articulation with a dominant mode of production, not divorced from it. In this manner, the earlier bourgeois commitment to radical individualism and "autonomous man," which today has evolved toward the hedonistic individualism perceived by Bell, cannot be explained apart from the requirements of a production system where labor must still, of necessity, be free to sell its power to capitalists. Furthermore, the "atomistic" or individualized consumption of contemporary consumers that is expressed, for example, through the single-family home, the private automobile, and the vast array of clothing styles announcing one's individualism cannot be understood separate from the pressure on producers (or suppliers) in a competitive market where collective forms of consumption and standardized models are not as profitable. After all, mass consumerism, individually realized, is the major way whereby production has expanded. Even the avant-garde artist, portrayed by Bell as the leading edge of social change, while perhaps less directly sponsored by private capitalists than in the last century, must still sell a product to survive and, thereby, is as much conditioned by the market as conditioning it.[30]

In the political realm, the capitalist State's commitment to equality cannot be explained independent from the necessity, under capitalism, for the operation of a free labor market without the indebted servitude, bondage, and slavery of earlier modes of production, nor from the pressure to maintain social harmony in a system where the potential for class conflict still exists. Finally, Bell is right on target with his understanding of self-realization through consumption (of art, homes, leisure, etc.) as presenting a problem for capitalist production. He misses, however, the dialectical relation between production and consumption, whereby economic expansion still requires consumption for its realization but is also threatened through a popular defense of these consumption amenities.

Applying Bell's provocative interpretation to urban social movements, Canadian geographer David Ley provides the most complete and interesting analysis of the ideology of liberal planning reform as it seeks to create a landscape in its image. With evidence from Vancouver, British Columbia, Ley discerns a "new" liberal ideological challenge to the older commitment to urban growth at all costs. The new platform is an outgrowth of the political ascendancy of professional, technical, and administrative workers during the 1970s. This white-collar managerial sector is dominant in Vancouver and several other "postindustrial" cities such as San Francisco and London. According to Ley, "urban structure seemed to be passing from an emphasis on growth to a concern with the quality of life; the new liberalism was to be recognized less by its production schedules than by its consumption styles."[31]

Ley thus implies that protection of consumption amenities is somehow antagonistic to production or business concerns. This is the view first popularized by social economist Thorstein Veblen in his 1899 opus *The Theory of the Leisure Class*, and later expanded by Bell and others.[32] As appears to be the case in Vancouver and in several other Canadian cities, the political ascendancy of a "cultural counteroffensive" seeking protection of consumption amenities may indeed present temporary barriers to capital accumulation and the older urban progrowth coalition. Ley, however, goes further and actually separates the processes of production and consumption, setting one against the other. In so doing he accepts liberal urban reform itself as a new and isolated defense of consumption values. Now, this may appear to be the case in Vancouver where liberal reform was sponsored by a political movement comprising, in Ley's characterization, middle- and upper middle-income professionals concerned with cultural values and consumption amenities. What is missing, however, is any recognition of a connection between production interests and the provision of consumption services, in particular by meeting the needs of the labor force that is staffing the new emerging centers of corporate and financial control.

As Richard Walker and Douglas Greenberg observe, the new "liveable city" movement, wittingly or unwittingly, "acted as a political midwife in a historic transition in urban form and social structure."[33] As noted earlier, this was due to the tendency for social groups, pursuing their own self-interests, to perpetuate the social system giving rise to their social identity (structuration). In this specific case, the lawyers, accountants, and other urban professionals of Vancouver furthered the conversion of the central city from an older industrial landscape to a new center for corporate and financial services.

While business elites in Vancouver and other emerging Canadian office centers may, as yet, be disorganized and perhaps content to let their managers and workers fight their own consumption battles for better housing, an end to industrial pollution, and improved mass transit, such is rarely the case in the United States. Here, urban-based consumption issues are a long-standing concern of downtown business interests. As practiced in the United States, urban reform attempts to mediate the tension between a political defense of consumption space (as occurred in Vancouver) and the requirements of an expanding and evolving production system. Insofar as the compromise reached in Vancouver, New York, and other urban growth centers still accepts continued capital development (as long as it is aesthetically pleasing to artists, critics, and the other avant-garde captains of taste, as considered by Bell and Ley), the proposed reforms favor, rather than challenge, those production forces benefiting from urban redevelopment and expansion. This is also true insofar as the compromise actually provides for the consumption needs of corporate office and professional service personnel.

Ley's description of a transformation from the progrowth reform ideology of the Progressive Era, led by central-city business interests, to the postindustrial goals of environmental quality and aesthetically pleasing development, is mirrored in the 60-year planning legacy of the RPA. Here, instead of a sharp break with the past led by an independent class of white-collar professionals, the new ideology emerging actually represents the contemporary outcome of enlightened corporate-sponsored reform. In the RPA's particular case we can discern a move away from strict attention to physical planning for direct business use of the CBD in an earlier age (the 1920s and 1930s) to a more advanced recognition of the need to also respond to, and even to provide for, the consumption requirements of midlevel office personnel. Ley's "liveable city," with its extensive redevelopment for inner-city white-collar housing, employment, and public transportation, bears striking resemblance to goals advocated by the RPA, the DLMA, and similar business-sponsored civic organizations in the New York metropolitan region and other major metropolitan areas.

To cite an example: Ley describes the False Creek Redevelopment Project—a large-scale, mixed-income housing project built in a decaying industrial section of Vancouver—as a prime example of the transition "from an ethic of growth and the production of goods to an ethic of amenity and the consumption of services."[34] When we substitute the Battery Park City project in New York, the Forest Hills development in Queens, and early RPA plans for the Lower East Side (Chapter 2)—all entailing projects accepted or promoted by local business elites—we can appreciate developments such as False Creek as a response to new residential requirements emerging within a process of continuing capital accumulation and urban transformation. On occasion these consumption requirements will constitute a political agenda for the office and professional workers themselves. As Ley has documented, this appeared to be the case in Vancouver. More frequently, as in the United States, capital interests will assist in the sponsorship of these developments.[35] In a similar manner, selective downzoning in Vancouver and New York City (in the latter case actually permitting higher skyscraper development in exchange for bulk limitations), the relocation of retail shops and polluting industry to suburban locations, the promotion of a clean office environment, and the surrounding uplifting of residential districts all represent a more advanced stage in accommodating changing production relations rather than a sharp break with a past commitment to growth.

Finally, the demarcation of culture by postindustrial theorists as some emergent social trait that can be isolated from historic expression during different stages in accumulation leaves them in a precarious position. Ley's characterization of a "West Coast culture realm," where a "cultural" offensive by professional workers is evident, appears to consign the battles waged by the working class in older Midwest and East Coast cities—as, for example, in the Poletown section of Detroit against construction of a General Motors plant, or in New York City to stop the closing of public hospitals in Harlem or the construction of the Lower Manhattan Expressway—as something less than a "cultured" defense of one's consumption needs and space.[36] Without reference to the structure of production, the separation of an independent class of technicians, professionals, and other service-sector workers on the basis of consumption characteristics remains a recognizable but, ultimately, an arbitrary category. As has been discussed, while consumption itself is necessary to realize production, specific social movements based upon consumption characteristics are merely contingent classifications. Resting upon subjective definitions of modes of consumption, the postindustrial concept of a class, as in Veblen's "leisure class," bears no necessary relation to the overall structure of production or of economic development and capital accumulation. Had the observed modes of consumption been linked with the necessary practice of consumption and the latter, in turn, related to capitalist production, a more precise concept of class would emerge.

As for the liberal reform agenda, it matters little whether the reform administration in Vancouver portrayed itself as an antibusiness group. The fact remains that the liberal style of planning, whether sponsored by production or by consumption forces, occurs within a context defined by the historic evolution of capitalist production relations. As a consequence, the reform suggested tends to accommodate and facilitate the process of capital accumulation and urban transformation. Although liberal political movements oppose the destruction of consumption amenities, they are susceptible to co-optation over time by capitalist-led liberal reform. This tendency rises precisely because liberal debate on the role of the State is limited to what is possible within the existing class-stratified social and economic system.

Liberal planning reform occurs within a commonly accepted set of production and social relations. As a consequence, it is deflected from radical propositions. There are, however, many groups competing in the process of urban development. The specific form of planning and land use control is more complex than that which can be deduced from the collective interest of the hegemonic faction or class. To be sure, the corporate reform groups have enjoyed remarkable success in shaping the urban environment to suit their requirements. Nevertheless, as the RPA's failures (e.g., with Westway and the earlier attempt to coordinate the privately owned rail lines) demonstrate, business-sponsored programs do not always prevail. Certainly other factions of capital can capture the State apparatus to further a process of accumulation more in keeping with their own parochial interests. Furthermore, defense of consumption space by social movements, even if it does not challenge the social relations of production, can still present significant local barriers to urban expansion. In the arena of land use, physical solutions to problems besetting the advance of capitalist production that were implemented during one stage of accumulation often become dysfunctional in the next, generating social protest and new barriers to accumulation. Thus, to cite an example, young urban professionals (or "yuppies") settling in the high-rise residential projects along Manhattan's West Side provide a convenient labor pool for the downtown business concerns while also serving as the nucleus for social protest over the construction of Westway and the further redevelopment of lower Manhattan.

In the following chapters the connection between private interests and public control of land use will be expanded. In so doing we move away from an earlier emphasis on private planning for the public sector toward the actual process of public planning and land use regulation. For this we must broaden the geographic area of inquiry to encompass the whole of New York State. The new boundary is logical because police power over land use in our federal system is held by the states, with discretionary delegation to localities. Furthermore, public innovation emanates from, or at least is sanctioned by, state legislatures. Finally, the new tools of the so-called quiet revolution of state intervention in local land use control are usually applied across the entire state as need and prevailing local social and physical conditions permit.

As the evidence described in succeeding chapters indicates, the actual process of social change is not exclusively directed by the capitalist class, despite near hegemonic control over the planning reform dialogue. In practice, a large portion of the land use regulations actually installed in New York State over the past three decades, particularly at the local level, represents temporary success by social movements to protect local consumption amenities. The liberal planning reform actually sponsored by production interests continues to seek a balance between the requirements of a dynamic production process and the defense of consumption amenities by that system's members. In so doing, liberal planning reform must recognize the dialectical relationship between production and consumption. It cannot ignore consumption for fear of undermining production, even though attention to the former will, eventually, generate new crises for expansion of the latter.

NOTES

1. Michael Danielson and Jameson Doig, *New York: The Politics of Urban Regional Development* (Berkeley and Los Angeles: University of California Press, 1982), pp. 142-51.
2. R. B. Cohen, "The New International Division of Labor: Multinational Corporations and the Urban Hierarchy," in *Urbanization and Urban Planning in Capitalist Society*, ed. M. Dear and A. Scott (New York: Methuen, 1981), p. 299.

3. David Kotz, *Bank Control of Large Corporations in the United States* (Berkeley and Los Angeles: University of California Press, 1978), p. 68.

4. Ibid., pp. 97-98. See also Maurice Zeitlin, "Corporate Ownership and Control: The Large Corporations and the Capitalist Class," *American Journal of Sociology* 79 (March 1974):1086-87; and Richard Barnett and Ronald Müller, *Global Reach* (New York: Simon and Schuster, 1974), pp. 233-34. "Control" as defined by Kotz comprises the retention of power to determine the broad policies guiding a firm. Together, financial- and owner-controlled firms constitute a majority of corporate power structures among the top 200 industrial firms.

5. Cohen, "New International Division of Labor," p. 300. See also Regina Armstrong, *The Office Industry* (prepared for the Regional Plan Association of New York) (Cambridge, MA: MIT Press, 1972), pp. 36-57. On the West Coast San Francisco, with 18 percent of all foreign bank deposits, is the second U.S. global city (a position that is being lost to Los Angeles) (Cohen, "New International Division of Labor," p. 300); see also Barnett and Müller, *Global Reach*, p. 270.

6. Kotz, *Bank Control of Large Corporations*, pp. 110-12.

7. The Economic Development Council was founded in 1965 by George Champion, then chair of the Chase Manhattan Bank. Membership is restricted to the largest corporations and banks with offices in the city (such as Citibank, Manufacturers Hanover Trust, Exxon, Mobil, General Motors, etc.). The council's primary goal is to reverse the business exodus from New York by furthering the social and physical conditions amenable to corporate office location. Among the more immediate goals are measures designed to reduce the militancy of the city's municipal employee unions, limit the property tax burden on business, and reduce the high cost of social services (see David Rogers, *Can Business Management Save the Cities? The Case of New York* [New York: Free Press, 1978], p. 37.)

8. Percival Goodman, "Lincoln Center, Emporium of the Arts," in *Urban Renewal: People, Politics, and Planning*, ed. J. Bellush and M. Hausknecht (Garden City, NY: Anchor Books, 1967), pp. 406-14; Myer Kutz, *Rockefeller Power* (New York: Simon and Schuster, 1974), pp. 48-49; and Peter Collier and David Horowitz, *The Rockefellers: An American Dynasty* (New York: Holt, Rinehart and Winston, 1976), pp. 314-15. See also Alvin Moscow, *The Rockefeller Inheritance* (Garden City, NY: Doubleday, 1977), pp. 221-24, for a sympathetic view of Rockefeller involvement, with David's Morningside Heights renovation attributed to the family's innate generosity.

9. Kutz, *Rockefeller Power*; and Randall Smith, "Rockefeller Center May Refinance or Sell a Part-Interest in the Original Buildings," *Wall Street Journal*, February 4, 1982, p. 44. In 1985 preparations began on the biggest real estate deal ever offered to the public. Rockefeller Center Properties Inc., landlord of the original 6.2 million-square-foot Rockefeller Center, filed an initial $600 million real estate investment trust offering with the Securities & Exchange Commission to have 30 million shares listed on the New York Stock Exchange (*Business Week*, "The Selling of Rockefeller Center," August 12, 1985, p. 65). Rockefeller Center Properties, still owned as a family trust, also constructed a new 41-story corporate headquarters for Continental Insurance and a 23-story operations center for the Irving Trust Co. in lower Manhattan; an office complex in Phoenix; two towers at Detroit's Renaissance

Center; and the 48-story Wells Fargo building in Los Angeles (Smith, "Rockefeller Center").

10. Downtown-Lower Manhattan Association, *Recommended Land Use, Redevelopment Areas, Traffic Improvements* (New York: Downtown-Lower Manhattan Association, 1958), p. 3; idem, *Major Improvements: Land Use, Transportation, Traffic—Lower Manhattan* (New York: Downtown-Lower Manhattan Association, 1963), pp. 3-4. The association was actually forged by David Rockefeller through a consolidation of the older Downtown Manhattan Association (founded in 1937) and his own Committee on Lower Manhattan Inc. (founded in 1957).

11. Downtown-Lower Manhattan Association, *Recommended Land Use.* As outlined, the

> Association believes that eventual business occupancy of the greater part of lower Manhattan will represent the most logical and economically sound use of land in the area. . . . [and] . . . provision should be made for as high a proportion of residential occupancy as is consistent with this principle. (ibid., p. 5)

12. Cf. New York City, Planning Commission, *The Lower Manhattan Plan* (New York: Planning Commission, 1966); and Downtown-Lower Manhattan Association, *Recommended Land Use*; idem, *Major Improvements.*

13. Downtown-Lower Manhattan Association, *Recommended Land Use*, p. 28. A four-lane highway, 12,000 parking spaces, and a new office and residential center were proposed for the Fulton Fish Market area (ibid., pp. 30ff.).

14. Kutz, *Rockefeller Power*, p. 98; and Leonard Ruchelman, *The World Trade Center: Politics and Policies of Skyscraper Development* (Syracuse, NY: Syracuse University Press, 1977). In 1968 Chase Manhattan completed a second 50-story (2.2 million-square-foot) office building at the tip of Manhattan (Armstrong, *Office Industry*, p. 139).

15. Downtown-Lower Manhattan Association, *World Trade Center: A Proposal for the Port of New York* (New York: Downtown-Lower Manhattan Association, 1960); idem, *Major Improvements*, p. 4; Ruchelman, *World Trade Center*, pp. 20, 25, 29; Collier and Horowitz, *Rockefellers*, p. 456; and Kutz, *Rockefeller Power*, pp. 98-109.

16. Martin Mayer, "A Commercial Renaissance," in *New York New York '82* (special advertising section, prepared by the Real Estate Board of New York), New York *Times*, October 31, 1982, p. 8. Recent federal deregulation permitting U.S. banks to operate international banking facilities where permitted to do so by state law has also been a stimulus for New York. The state passed the first authorization for this purpose in the nation (ibid.). On the global preeminence of the Wall Street bond and securities markets: James Sterngold, "New Rivals Aside, Wall St. Still Calls the Tune," New York *Times,* October 9, 1986, pp. D1, 8.

17. Justin Murphy, "Presidential Address Delivered at the Twenty-eighth Annual Meeting of the Downtown-Lower Manhattan Association" (New York City, March 5, 1985, Mimeographed), p. 1.

18. Downtown-Lower Manhattan Association, *Recommended Land Use*, pp. 5-11. Today less than 5 percent of the district's commuters arrive by car, limousine, taxi, or commuter van (Murphy, "Presidential Address," p. 7).

19.   Albert Scardino, "Big Battery Park City Dreams," New York *Times*, December 1, 1986, pp. D1, 10.   See also Jack Newfield and Paul DuBrul, *The Abuse of Power: The Permanent Government and the Fall of New York* (New York: Viking Press, 1977), p. 92; Mayer, "Commercial Renaissance," p. 8; and *Business Week*, "The New York Market Settles Down to a Steady Boil," August 12, 1985, pp. 64-65.   Flush with enthusiasm, the current Battery Park City president envisions a near doubling of the project through a 68-acre extension north to Canal Street (Scardino, "Big Battery Park City Dreams").   In an unusual agreement between the state, the city, and the authority, permitting attention to high-revenue office development at Battery Park City, the authority has pledged payments in lieu of taxes and most revenues in excess of operating expenses to construction of low- and moderate-income housing elsewhere in the city.   Through 1998 an estimated $1 billion will be released for this purpose (Jeffrey Schmalz, "New York City Reaches Agreement on Housing," New York *Times*, December 27, 1987, Section 1, p. 6).

20.   On these organizations: Judith Getzels, Peter Elliot, and Frank Beal, *Private Planning for the Public Interest: A Study of Approaches to Urban Problem Solving by Nonprofit Organizations* (Chicago: American Society of Planning Officials, 1975).

21.   Mid-Hudson Pattern for Progress, *Closing the Gap* (Annual Report for 1968) (Poughkeepsie, NY: Mid-Hudson Pattern for Progress, 1969), p. 43; idem, *New Directions for the '70s* (Annual Report for 1969) (Poughkeepsie, NY: Mid-Hudson Pattern for Progress, 1970), p. 8; and idem, *Crisis to Opportunity* (Annual Report for 1973-74) (Poughkeepsie, NY: Mid-Hudson Pattern for Progress, 1974).   Although the regional boundaries for MHP studies have shifted according to specific requirements, the MHP's board of directors is still composed of representatives from the seven-county area depicted in Map 3.1 (idem, *Mid-Hudson Pattern for Progress, Inc.,* introductory brochure [Poughkeepsie, NY, c. 1986]).

In 1974, at the height of its influence, the 46-member MHP board of directors included executives from the area's leading commercial and savings banks (approximately one-fourth of the membership), utilities, and insurance companies. Additional representation came through several local manufacturers and one member each from the Sierra Club and the Catskill Center for Conservation (idem, *Crisis to Opportunity*, p. 13).   Though limited, this participation by environmental organizations was significant because it enabled the MHP to claim representation from and for environmental concerns.

22.   See Mid-Hudson Pattern for Progress, and Regional Plan Association, *The Mid-Hudson: A Development Guide* (Poughkeepsie, NY: Mid-Hudson Pattern for Progress, 1973); Mid-Hudson Pattern for Progress; New York State, Urban Development Corporation; and Regional Plan Association of New York, *Mid-Hudson Regional Development Program: A Partnership for Progress*, pamphlet (Poughkeepsie, NY: Mid-Hudson Pattern for Progress, 1969); and New York State, Office of Planning Coordination, *New York State Development Plan-1* (Albany: Office of Planning Coordination, 1971).   See Chapter 4 on New York State's Urban Development Corporation.

23.   Mid-Hudson Pattern for Progress, *Closing the Gap*, p. 46.

The MHP favored expansion of the region's higher education system for the economic growth generated as well as for the information supplied to the public and private sectors.   Proclaiming the deficiency in educational services as a "regional problem," the MHP cited the example of IBM (Poughkeepsie) executives having to travel to Manhattan for advanced coursework (ibid, p. 3).

24. Mid-Hudson Pattern for Progress, and Regional Plan Association, *Mid-Hudson Development Guide*, p. 39.

25. Mid-Hudson Pattern for Progress, *Electrical Energy and the Catskill Region* (prepared for the New York State, Temporary State Commission to Study the Catskills) (Poughkeepsie, NY: Mid-Hudson Pattern for Progress, 1974), pp. 38-39.

26. Ibid., pp. 4, 6, 73-74. See Chapter 4 on New York State's electric power facility siting process and Chapter 5 on regional planning for the Catskill area.

27. See Roy Bhaskar, *The Possibility of Naturalism: A Philosophical Critique of the Contemporary Human Sciences* (Sussex, UK: Harvester Press, 1979); Anthony Giddens, *Central Problems in Social Theory: Action, Structure and Contradiction in Social Analysis* (Berkeley and Los Angeles: University of California Press, 1979); idem, *A Contemporary Critique of Historical Materialism* (Berkeley and Los Angeles: University of California Press, 1981); and Allan Pred, "Structuration and Place: On the Becoming of Sense of Place and Structure of Feeling," *Journal for the Theory of Social Behavior* 13 (1983):45-68.

28. Thorstein Veblen, *The Theory of the Leisure Class: An Economic Study of Institutions* (New York: Charles Scribner's Sons, 1899); and Max Weber, "Class, Status, Party," in *From Max Weber: Essays in Sociology*, ed. H. H. Gerth and C. Wright Mills (New York: Oxford University Press, 1946), pp. 180-95.

29. Cf. Veblen, *Theory of the Leisure Class*; Weber, "Class, Status, Party"; and Daniel Bell, *The Cultural Contradictions of Capitalism* (New York: Basic Books, 1976).

30. See Bell, *Cultural Contradictions,* pp. 38-55. Andy Warhol, perhaps this nation's most famous avant-garde artist, began his career as a commercial artist. Still acutely aware of his clients, Warhol had been a leading force behind the commercialization of the avant-garde as fed back to the public through advertising, and of advertising as an inspiration for the avant-garde.

31. David Ley, "Liberal Ideology and the Postindustrial City," *Annals of the Association of American Geographers* 70 (June 1980):239. Richard Walker and Douglas Greenberg ("Post-Industrialism and Political Reform in the City: A Critique," *Antipode* 14, no. 1 [1982]:17-32) provide a penetrating critique of the superficial "post-industrial" characterization of contemporary capitalist social relations and of the liberal ideology supporting this view. See Daniel Bell, *The Coming of Post-Industrial Society* (New York: Basic Books, 1973), on a "post-industrial" society that may be identified according to consumption characteristics, rather than through contemporary expression of the necessary social relations constituting the mode of production.

32. On consumption as a basis for social demarcations (and movements): Veblen, *Theory of the Leisure Class*; Weber, "Class, Status, Party"; Bell, *Cultural Contradictions*; William Tucker, "Environmentalism and the Leisure Class," *Harper's* 255 (December 1977):49-56, 73-80; and Chapter 6. On the "quality of life" issue in geographic thought: cf. Ley, "Liberal Ideology and the Postindustrial City"; Nicholas Helburn, "Geography and the Quality of Life," *Annals of the Association of American Geographers* 72 (December 1982):445-56; and Andrew Sayer, "Epistemology and Conceptions of People and Nature in Geography," *Geoforum* 10 (1979):19-43. By and large, Ley views popular concern with quality of life as a new phenomenon and as a

direct threat to existing production concerns; Helburn understands consumer demands and ideology as, at times, coming under corporate influence, while still holding out the possibility of direct conflict between production and consumption interests; and Sayer provides an explanation of how production interests not only attempt to dominate the dialogue, but actually define the commonsense notion of "quality of life."

33. Walker and Greenberg, "Post-Industrialism: A Critique," p. 28.

34. Ley, "Liberal Ideology and the Postindustrial City," p. 252.

35. This cross-national difference is not unexpected as the specifics of political economy differ across national boundaries, even where the dominant mode of production remains the same.

36. See Ley, "Liberal Ideology and the Postindustrial City," p. 245.

Getting the Job Done:
Public Authorities and
Facility Siting Legislation

Early in this century industrialists, developers, and financiers were already aware that the increasing scale in industrial production and the accompanying need to provide the infrastructure, housing, and other conditions required for continued capital accumulation threatened to overwhelm the response capacity of the local municipalities. These capital interests funded municipal research bureaus, private foundations, and other liberal reform organizations such as the Regional Plan Association of New York (RPA). The reformers, in turn, sought to increase the ability of local governments to accommodate large-scale projects through coordinated local land use regulation and the centralization of select urban services.

Under state enabling acts many jurisdictions in New York State, as elsewhere, adopted local zoning ordinances during the 1920s and 1930s. Organized through Chicago's Commercial Club, the RPA, the Citizens Committee on (a) City Plan for Pittsburgh, and a host of other civic organizations, business interests promoted zoning in rapidly growing metropolitan areas (Chapter 2). Local regulation of land use in New York and across the nation was quite favorable to the accommodation of urban growth. Overzoning and liberal variances were the rule, master plans were rarely drawn up and little used, and capital investment was generously extended by public and private sources independent of planning schemes.[1] However, where local municipalities, with their newly found powers to plan and zone, elected to protect local consumption amenities, such as residential and recreation space, against what they perceived to be the social and environmental ravages of expanding production systems, strong measures were called for. This may have occurred when the municipalities refused to accept large-scale industrial, energy, and infrastructure projects, or to voluntarily cede authority to a higher regional level of government, such as the county or special service district.

With local land use regulations in place, one possible remedy to this impasse was creation of comprehensive regional land use agencies with regulatory authority for those projects deemed to be of more than local concern.

Although business interests and developers sporadically supported comprehensive regional planning, they generally did not accept comprehensive override of local regulations (Chapters 2 and 3). Individually they preferred instead to keep their own options open on a case-by-case basis. Consequently, capital concerns promoted circumvention of local approval only for those select projects that the municipal governments were unlikely to accept, or for those projects requiring a multitude of permits from numerous jurisdictions. In New York State, as in many others, the more acceptable alternative prescription to the ills of local intransigence first appeared in the form of state-chartered public benefit corporations or authorities.

Often retaining some portion of the state police power over land use necessary to accomplish their mission, free from local property taxes, and financed by tax-exempt obligations, public authorities were in a position to implement massive development projects without direct recourse either to the state electorate or to local zoning approval. Over the last half century New York State led the nation in the use of state-chartered authorities to gather private institutional and financial support for provision of the infrastructure and services required for continued urban expansion. Shielded from public participation and municipal influence, authorities could more directly respond to the large-scale financial and corporate interests dominating on their boards of directors and directing their agenda of activity. In the New York metropolitan area, for example, the business-led RPA relied upon public authorities to implement the bulk of its 1929 Plan. This public authority approach to infrastructure development was quite effective in overcoming the strong objections from neighborhoods slated for urban renewal or expansion.

Environmentalists, armed with the new federal and state environmental quality review legislation, began to challenge those projects constructed by the heretofore relatively autonomous public authorities. Thus, in practice it was not until the early 1970s that prodevelopment interests were forced to support the more familiar state facility siting legislation for power plants, transmission lines, hazardous waste disposal sites, and so forth.

With the major exception of the Urban Development Corporation (UDC—itself a unique extension of the public authority concept), the use of state-chartered public authorities to bypass local discussion and opposition to major development projects, while just as surely a component of the quiet revolution as state facility siting legislation, is ignored by most planning and urban land use analysts.[2] The oversight, whether conscious or not, helps steer public attention away from the real quiet evolution occurring in the scale of property development and in the day-to-day accommodation of development through the activities of public authorities and, to a lesser extent, through the use of state siting legislation.

PUBLIC AUTHORITIES AS AGENTS OF THE QUIET EVOLUTION IN LAND USE CONTROL

Often referred to as the "fourth branch of government," public authorities (also known as public benefit corporations) are created to build and operate large-scale public works, provide essential urban services, clear land for private redevelopment, and perform a host of other functions required for urban development. In the past they enjoyed widespread support from a public seduced by the belief that the efficiency and administrative methods applied in the private business sector can best define and address public responsibilities. Created by legislation defining their areas of activity, public authorities generally raise capital from private investors on the bond market to invest in revenue-producing activities. The authorities do not levy taxes but instead retain their own user-fee earnings. As in New York State, they are usually exempt from property and corporate taxes levied by federal, state, and local governments. Although they operate as agents of the state and are not independent governments (with taxing power), the authorities enjoy a high degree of autonomy once established. This includes freedom from most of the administrative requirements placed on other state agencies, such as civil service and pay scale regulations and detailed audit procedures. Moreover, they have an independent corporate status with the right to own property, sue, and be sued, and they do not rely on the services of the attorney general's office. Above all, authorities have the financial independence to invest their earnings as they see fit, subject to broad generic limitations. Unless in fiscal difficulty, authorities are independent of legislative appropriations. As described by Annmarie Walsh, one of the nation's foremost experts on public authorities, they are, in a sense, "corporations without stockholders [and] political jurisdictions without voters or taxpayers."[3]

The use of public authorities to construct and operate urban infrastructure dates back to the seventeenth century when they were first used in England to build turnpikes and harbors. During the late eighteenth and early nineteenth centuries federal- and state-chartered corporations in the United States were active in turnpike and canal construction, operating in a manner akin to modern authorities. Following the 1837 economic depression, when many such public-private partnerships failed, and with the rise of the modern private corporation, a new laissez-faire attitude arose. At the state level this attitude supported a complete separation of public from private investment in development projects and supported constitutional debt limits, with voter approval necessary, before bonds backed by the "full faith and credit" (i.e., the taxing power) of the state could be issued.[4]

In 1907 the National Civic Federation, whose members were closely aligned with large-scale industrial concerns, completed a study that demonstrated the inefficiency of small-scale municipal and privately owned electric power companies, and that supported the eventual public authorization and regulation of monopoly ownership in the utility industry.[5] Although concerned here only with public regulation in exchange for monopoly franchise, this major reform of the

Progressive Era furthered an ideology supporting public intervention in, and, if necessary, provision of, those facilities and services required for continued economic development that the private sector could no longer profitably provide on its own.

Created through a 1921 bistate compact to provide for the orderly development of the transportation facilities of New York Harbor, the Port of New York Authority (hereafter also the Port Authority) was modeled after the Port of London Authority (formed in 1908). As the first major "modern" authority created in the United States, the Port Authority in turn furnished an administrative structure and organizational objective used by hundreds of subsequent authorities set up in its image.

Clearly the greatest attraction of public authorities arose from their ability to generate investment for physical infrastructure without recourse to legislative appropriations or to the voter approval required for general obligation bonds. This was accomplished through revenue bonds backed by user fees and rents, a more equitable allocation of costs than that backed by general obligation bonds. During the New Deal administration President Roosevelt promoted local and state use of public authorities and revenue bond financing as innovations to circumvent the collapsed municipal and state bond markets.[6]

Although access to financing in a tight bond market may head the list of desirable characteristics, public authorities have other attributes often overlooked by policy analysts. Chief among these in the political arena of land use is the ability to site and construct major facilities with a minimum of public discussion and regulatory delay. Already in the 1920s and 1930s as administrative centralization for many types of urban services (e.g., transportation, water and sewer development) proceeded, public authorities became a much-lauded vehicle to bypass local resistance to municipal consolidation. The latter was also designed to centralize public functions and provide a broader base for financing but, following the burst of consolidation during the Progressive Era, it met with only limited success. In the postwar period public resistance to urban consolidation heightened and was registered in unyielding and restrictive local land use controls designed to protect local consumption amenities from further development. More recently, a growing taxpayers' revolt contributed to constitutional and statutory debt limits on municipal borrowing via general obligation bonds. Public authorities, however, managed to maintain their popular support because most of the populace was convinced that the authorities were financed independent of public assistance. Moreover, the public preferred the authorities' tolls and charges to the higher taxes resulting from municipal operation of services and structures. With this acceptance, public authorities became the only type of independent public institution still increasing in numbers since 1960.[7]

Today there are over 6,000 local and regional authorities operating in the United States and some 1,000 state and interstate authorities. In some states public authorities can be independently chartered by cities, towns, and counties, as in California and Pennsylvania. Elsewhere the state legislature must approve all authorities, as in New York.[8] In New York the governor usually appoints members of statewide and regional authorities, on occasion with the advice and consent of the senate or local leaders. Some authority members are appointed ex officio by virtue of holding other public offices, over which New York's governor also wields considerable power.

In most states, the "special district" or "special purpose agency" performs many functions similar to New York State's public authorities (e.g., the San Francisco Bay Area Rapid Transit District; the East Bay Municipal Utility District; and the Golden Gate Bridge, Highway, and Transportation District). Although lumped together with "public authorities" as a "special purpose (local) government" by the U.S. Bureau of the Census, special districts should be considered independent from public authorities. While all gradations exist between the public authority and the special district, the latter can be generically distinguished as a genuine "limited purpose government," elected by local property owners or citizens, and frequently with power to assess property and sales taxes in addition to collecting user fees and service charges.[9] In New York State special districts for education (school and community college districts), health care, agricultural preservation, and fire control are common, while revenue-producing activities are usually left to public authorities.

Providing the major avenue whereby urban development could proceed without direct recourse to either public finance or municipal approval, public authorities enjoyed enthusiastic support from prodevelopment and financial interests. In addition to the more traditional bridge, tunnel, and highway development, public authorities, as evident in New York State, were used to build colleges, convention centers, sports stadiums, hospitals, and industrial parks. In recent years and with increasing frequency, they also have been used to construct offices, factories, hotels, pollution control facilities, transmission lines, and power plants, with sale or lease-back provisions for the private operators.

With easy access to financing, the nation's local and state authorities became the largest borrowers on the tax-exempt municipal bond market. In New York, following aggressive expansion during Nelson Rockefeller's reign as governor, the state public authority system generated an outstanding debt in 1971 of more than two and one-half times that of the full faith and credit of the state. One authority alone, the Housing Finance Agency, had an outstanding obligation greater than that of the state itself![10]

In 1968 Congress and the Internal Revenue Service attempted to limit the tax-exempt status of general obligation and revenue bonds principally aiding private interests. However, partially in response to a deepening recession, industrial development bonds used for transportation development, parking facilities, power plant construction, housing, land development, and other services were largely exempt from this action. The tax loophole became a chasm. Of the $41 billion in tax-exempt municipal and authority bonds nationally issued in 1981, only $10 billion went to traditional public purposes such as water, sewer, school, and mass transportation development. The remainder, according to *Business Week*, went to "areas not crucial to local governments' basic mission—for example, construction for private industry, financing for single-family housing and building power plants for the private sector." The use of tax-exempt authority bonds to purchase pollution control equipment for low-cost lease to private industry became especially popular following the passage of the Federal Clean Air and Clean Water acts. By 1981 the sale of industrial pollution control bonds had mushroomed to account for one-quarter of all long-term municipal bond financing.[11]

THE SEPARATION OF SOCIAL PRODUCTION FROM SOCIAL CONTROL

Although already active in the nineteenth century, the use of public authorities greatly expanded during the twentieth century. Today they are a ubiquitous feature of the capitalist State. Through tax breaks, use of police power, and other measures denied the private sector, they help support the general rate of profit throughout the economy by attracting private funds to projects and enterprises required for continued accumulation that the private sector would or could not provide on its own (e.g., education, housing, and transportation).[12] In most instances the projects undertaken require large investments beyond the capacity of any one private corporation and are rarely profitable in the short run. Within this general arena for State intervention there is a need for those developments accelerating private investment to be constructed in an expeditious manner with minimum public debate and delay. Public authorities play a useful role in this process through the separation of social production from social control.

Public authorities harness private capital for social expenditures through a revenue-backed, tax-exempt, bond market. They thus provide a relatively secure outlet for accumulated industrial, insurance, financial, and personal (household) funds. In the postwar period there have been few defaults among public authorities; notable exceptions are the Chesapeake Bay Bridge and Tunnel Authority, the Chicago Transit Authority, and, more recently, the ailing Washington Public Power Supply System.[13] As a consequence, the larger state- or city-sponsored authorities usually receive much higher bond ratings (from Moody's, Standard and Poor's, etc.) than general obligations of municipal and state governments, often squeezing the latter out of the bond market during periods of tight money. In this process the big investment and commercial banks with municipal bond departments also benefit as bond underwriters and trustees. This activity is highly concentrated with a few New York City-based banks and brokerage houses, such as Goldman Sachs; Chemical Bank; Manufacturers Hanover Trust; and Morgan Guaranty Trust, leading the pack.

The crucial separation of social production from social control must first be accounted for and then reviewed to understand the role of public authorities as agents of the quiet evolution in land use control. Financial independence is promoted by the authorities and accepted by the public as sufficient justification for freedom from political accountability. As such, public authorities strive to generate enough revenue to service their debt obligations. Thus they are most visible in the profitable fields of middle-class housing, transportation, and industrial development. Authorities rely on federal and state grants when they do undertake projects of more limited revenue-producing ability, such as mass transit and low-income housing construction.

These efforts at fiscal freedom notwithstanding, most public authorities rely upon "first instance appropriations" from state legislatures to begin operations. In recent years a disturbing number of authorities have failed to pay off these loans whether due to poor fiscal management, a declining market for their services, or some other miscalculation of revenue flow. As of 1981, New York State had "loaned" some $750 million to 17 authorities, with millions more written off as additional advances and first instance appropriations never to be collected. The biggest culprit was the UDC, beneficiary of a $397 million interest-free loan, the vast majority of which is unlikely to be repaid.[14]

Undoubtedly some of the toll-collecting transportation authorities, including the Triborough Bridge and Tunnel Authority, the Port Authority, and the New York State Thruway Authority, grew enormously wealthy, surely the model of efficient corporate management warranting political independence. We must realize, however, that in practice these authorities actually removed from municipal control those projects offering the greatest promise of producing surplus revenue. As described by Walsh, "the authority solution to regional problems tends to amputate from local governments only the revenue-producing services, isolating revenues from heavily burdened city budgets and leaving cities with the expensive services."[15] Many of the bridges and tunnels constructed by the Port Authority and Robert Moses' Triborough Bridge and Tunnel Authority (TBTA) in the New York metropolitan area have, in the past, generated substantial revenues and provided a high rate of return for their bond investors. With massive surpluses available, the authorities invested in projects of more select service to their corporate supporters, such as the World Trade Center (constructed by the Port Authority) and the New York Coliseum (a large convention center and office tower built by the TBTA). New York City and surrounding communities were often left holding or completing nonrevenue-producing local transportation arteries and widening existing streets to the toll plazas. To illustrate, New York City's decrepit Manhattan Bridge and the connecting Canal Street became the main funnel from Brooklyn across Manhattan to the Port Authority's Holland Tunnel toll plaza. With this situation in mind, comparison between the efficient and effective public authorities and inept municipal provision of services and infrastructure appears superficial (e.g., "there's not a pothole on the George Washington Bridge" while the authorities' "bridges and buildings rise on schedule—and seldom fall down").[16]

Finally, the balance sheet must be interpreted realizing that these authorities operate under publicly protected monopoly franchises. Hence they are, in a sense, not unlike their corporate cousins, the investor-owned private utilities. The latter accepted public regulation and the scrutiny of public service commissions years ago in exchange for lucrative monopoly franchises and an unofficial guaranteed rate of return on investment. While maintaining most of the franchise benefits, the authorities, on the other hand, have even escaped the detailed public audit required of the investor-owned utilities. This freedom derives from their professed commitment to the public interest, with profits reinvested to pursue some common goal, as well as from a widely accepted, but controvertible, notion that proven economic efficiency should not be tampered with.

When examining so-called public authorities, care must be taken to distinguish between *ownership* and *control* of public resources. In most authorities, private control is assured through governing board selection. With the public succumbing to the ideological claim that revenue-producing enterprises should be managed by business and free from political and social influence, most people accept the domination of authority directorship by representatives from financial and, to a lesser extent, industrial enterprises. As characterized through a Dun & Bradstreet review of the Port Authority, "emphasis on service to the community rather than on financial compensation gives membership on the board special distinction, facilitates the selection of prominent citizens who would not ordinarily be interested in seeking public office, and tends to increase public confidence in the objectives of the organization."[17]

In addition to direct board member control, major public authorities, such as the Port Authority and the UDC, are heavily influenced by investors. With direct ties to board members through business affiliations, social connections, and common class origins, investors frequently rely upon covenants to limit popular political influence over the authorities' activities. Consequently, many large authorities with members recruited from business interests tend to be more responsive to their investors than to the public they are supposed to serve. The Port of New York Authority (since 1972 known as the Port Authority of New York and New Jersey) and Robert Moses' Triborough Bridge and Tunnel Authority provide examples.

The Port Authority was the nation's first modern authority by virtue of its multitude of activities. Until the Port Authority's inception, public authorities were specifically created to construct and operate only one project, which usually reverted to municipal control and ceased charging fees or tolls once the principal and interest were paid off. In 1935 the Port Authority became the first to issue a general purpose bond backed by a revolving fund from revenues derived through its numerous activities. Robert Moses was the innovator of this revolving fund financing. Reneging on the tradition of relinquishing the project to municipal control once paid for, he gathered the surplus revenues to finance more ambitious projects. His Triborough Bridge Authority (originally set up in 1933 and eventually consolidating as the Triborough Bridge and Tunnel Authority) became involved in highway construction and park development, and even had its own police force. Unprofitable auxiliary ventures were subsidized by direct federal and state grants.[18]

Representation on the original board of the Port Authority was contested between progressive liberal reformers, led by the New York Chamber of Commerce, and the old, ward-based, machine. The reformers won and local public participation was excluded. The chamber actually drafted the bistate compact setting up the authority, and its president served as the authority's first chair. With six members appointed by the governors of the states bordering the harbor (New York and New Jersey), the Port Authority board has been dominated by financial, real estate, and corporate interests since its 1921 founding. Representation from labor, women, and organized community and minority interests was absent. Over the years compact provisions and a tradition of reappointment led to a high degree of autonomy, with authority officials frequently having longer tenure than their appointing governors.[19] In 1987 the Port Authority had three senior bankers and three corporate chairs on its board. Accounting for one vacancy, the remaining members included four corporate attorneys and William Ronan—a businessman and key associate of the Rockefeller family.[20]

In summary, it appears that public authorities, once characterized by President Eisenhower as "creeping socialism," have actually enlarged the avenues available for profitable tax-exempt private investment, while limiting popular discussion and control of urban development.[21] In the New York metropolitan region, for example, the location of most of the bridges and tunnels constructed by the Port Authority (with a monopoly over Hudson River crossings) and Moses' TBTA was determined on the basis of where the largest revenues could be generated. Little attention was given to the resulting displacement of lower-income neighborhoods abutting the crossings and their approaches.[22] In addition to direct investment considerations, these automobile-oriented projects were designed to ease the commute by suburban office workers to Manhattan's central business district (Chapter 3). As a consequence, they lowered the cost of labor for those same interests (the commercial banks and insurance companies) already benefiting from high bond rates and tax advantages.

As we shall see in the next section, the neglect of inner-city social needs and the continuing disregard for local consumption space (primarily residential) where it stood in the way of infrastructure expansion eventually produced a backlash against the authorities. In the 1960s, as urban social unrest surfaced, the authorities were forced to attend to moderate- and lower-income transportation and housing needs. Concurrently, as the central-city business community (particularly in New York City) came to appreciate the need for mass transit for central business district (CBD) office workers, the public authorities were also pressured to support these transportation requirements (Chapter 3). Finally, in the decade to follow, the authorities came under the new state and federal environmental quality review legislation providing for formal public participation in development review.

THE BATTLE OVER MASS TRANSIT

Regional public authorities (such as New York's Metropolitan Transportation Authority and the Rochester-Genesee Regional Transportation Authority) that are active in areas embracing two or more municipalities help reduce competition between and among public and private suppliers of goods and services. The Port Authority was originally established to coordinate the counterproductive competition between New York- and New Jersey-based railroads. Its jurisdiction extended for approximately 25 miles from the Statue of Liberty. One of its first actions was to set up a uniform fare schedule. Although the Port Authority had only limited success in getting the highly competitive railroads to agree on integrated freight and terminal plans (in retrospect a situation contributing to duplication of services, inefficient capital development, and eventual bankruptcy for many lines), it did reduce intermunicipal competition over harbor and, later, airport expansion. In the intervening years since its first brush with unbridled competition and unprofitable fixed rail transit, the Port Authority successfully concentrated on low-risk and high-return projects.[23]

Today the Port Authority is the nation's wealthiest public authority, with over 8,000 employees and an annual operating budget approaching $1 billion on revenues of $1.2 billion. It has responsibility of operating all three of the major airports in the New York metropolitan area, eight marine terminals, four bridges, the two Hudson tunnels (Holland and Lincoln), two bus terminals, several truck terminals and heliports, and the World Trade Center. Consistently enjoying the highest bond ratings (with aggregate earnings in 1985 more than twice its debt service), the Port Authority is eyed as a likely candidate to support the region's deteriorating mass transit system.[24]

As executive director from 1942 until 1972, Austin Tobin frequently rallied the authority's lenders as his constituency in battles with the state legislatures over attempts to use surplus revenues to fund mass transit. Covenants prepared under his direction limited Port Authority investment to profitable projects. In 1962, however, the New Jersey legislature finally forced the authority to take over and rehabilitate the bankrupt Hudson and Manhattan Railroad (PATH) as a condition for approving construction of the World Trade Center. Vigorously promoted by David Rockefeller's Downtown-Lower Manhattan Association, the center itself served as an outlet for commitment of the Port Authority's conspicuously large surplus funds (Chapter 3). A subsequent covenant, enacted to effectively prohibit the authority from assuming responsibility for any other unprofitable public rail operations, was decisive in Tobin's successful attempt to ward off pressure to develop mass transit links to the Kennedy and Newark airports. In 1974, at the height of the energy crisis, and faced with mounting public, as well as corporate, pressure for improved mass transit, both states repealed the covenant. This action, however, was struck down by the U.S. Supreme Court.[25]

In the meantime, Robert Moses lost a long struggle to prevent his numerous authorities from funding mass transit, the deterioration of which had reached crisis proportions. In 1967 he was forced to merge the very profitable TBTA into Nelson Rockefeller's new Metropolitan Transportation Authority (MTA). The latter had responsibility for mass transit in New York City and for the financially ailing suburban rail lines on Long Island and in southern New York State.[26] Under William Ronan's initial guidance, the MTA unsuccessfully attempted several projects championed by the governor and local business leaders. The first of these was a six and one-half-mile bridge and causeway spanning Long Island Sound from Oyster Bay to Rye, New York. The forces of consumption rallied. Vigorous opposition from local residents and from environmental groups eventually blocked construction. In a successful ploy, the Long Island terminus was actually declared a national wildlife refuge following a donation for that purpose by the Town of Oyster Bay.[27]

In 1970 the federal government quietly transferred inactive Stewart Air Force Base, 65 miles north of Manhattan, to the MTA. Under Ronan's supervision the MTA began extending the existing runway to accommodate commercial flights and condemned an additional 8,650 acres. This was accomplished without any prior consultation with municipal governments. When word finally leaked that the MTA was preparing to construct a commercial jetport eventually exceeding the size of Kennedy Airport, nearby land prices sharply increased. Local residents and public officials opposed to the project joined environmentalists and demonstrated against the clandestine manner whereby the MTA, initiating the project solely with state funds under executive control, managed to avoid the usual federal environmental impact statement (under the National Environmental Policy Act of 1970) required for projects of this magnitude. With its internal finances in shambles from poor fiscal management and a decline in anticipated demand for a fourth regional jetport, the MTA was forced to abandon the project. The state assembly subsequently passed legislation forcing the MTA to release information before acting on projected plans.[28]

The Port Authority's existing airport operations have also been under attack by nearby homeowners and environmentalists. First organized in the late 1970s to protest environmental contamination and to protect property values, Queens Citizens Committee Organization has grown to include thousands of families across a broad socioeconomic range and racial mix. To date, the committee has succeeded in forcing the authority to renegotiate operating licenses that are more favorable to the city, while setting aside funds to mitigate community impacts accompanying airport expansion.[29]

The struggle by the MTA and the Port Authority to push large-scale projects past a hostile local constituency is an informative demonstration of the use of public authorities as agents in what liberal planning reformers have identified as a quiet revolution. In effect, the transportation authorities attempted the same goals championed by the liberal planning reform movement through the latter's support for state override of those local land use regulations that blocked regionally beneficial development. The fact that the authorities could not successfully shield their projects from local challenge was indicative of a changing political climate. The older system of representative democracy, one which the public authorities were designed to evade, was being replaced by one of participatory democracy. In this new arena consumption interests were organized into environmental and homeowner associations such as the Hudson River Valley Council (for the Stewart battle) and Citizens for Social Planning (one of several groups contesting plans for the Sound crossing). They successfully used the new forums for public participation and court challenge afforded by recently enacted state and federal environmental quality review legislation. The shift from representative to participatory democracy diminished but did not completely thwart the public authorities' ability to detour around local defense of consumption space.

The campaign to have the metropolitan area's public authorities assume some of the burden for mass transit is illuminating also because it accentuates the inevitable struggle within the capitalist class. This tension arises as the private quest for profit generates outcomes at variance with a collective class interest in further urban expansion and in capital accumulation. In the case of mass transit, the individual concerns of the authorities' bondholders and sponsors were at odds with a broader (class) interest in lowering the cost of labor power through improved commuter transportation. While the restrictive covenants between the Port Authority and its bondholders, arising out of the 1962 PATH compromise, held up in court, Governors Rockefeller and Carey of New York and Cahill and Bryne of New Jersey, continued to push for a stronger commitment to suburban mass transit. In this they had the blessing of the region's business leadership. Threatening to veto future projects, toll increases, and bond offerings, the governors forced the recalcitrant authority to upgrade bus facilities at Manhattan's Forty-second Street Port Authority Bus Terminal and to purchase a new fleet of commuter express buses. These were leased to the two states with guarantees to the Port Authority against purchase, operating, and maintenance losses.[30]

In the wake of the $440 million transit commitment, the Port Authority's surplus revenues have been harnessed for other ventures benefiting the region's economic growth. Today the authority is involved in industrial park planning and development. It is also preparing a major telecommunications center to coordinate the flow of information between central-city headquarters and their suburban "back" offices. A Regional Development Bank for infrastructure repair, mass transit needs, and job creation in the private sector will be partially funded through the higher rents the authority charges private tenants on space vacated by the state of New York in the authority's World Trade Center. The state's move back to decentralized regional offices freed up approximately 2.5 million square feet of office space on which it had been paying less than one-third the going rental rate. In this manner, the state's taxpayers, having bailed out the World Trade Center when first constructed during a depressed office rental market (Chapter 3) and, as a result, now the beneficiary of low rental rates in a hot market, are once again footing the bill. In the meantime, the authority manages to protect its high revenue flow.[31]

The Triborough Bridge and Tunnel Authority did not fare as well. With an aging Robert Moses succumbing to Rockefeller's unfulfilled assurance that Moses would still have a major role in regional transportation decisions, the TBTA was taken from Moses to be a cash cow for the MTA. Backed by an additional 1967 voter-approved $2.5 billion transportation bond issue, the MTA also incorporated the New York City Transit Authority (buses and subways) and suburban bus and rail lines on Long Island and in Westchester, Rockland, Dutchess, and Putnam counties.

Formation of the super authority was unsuccessfully challenged by Chase Manhattan Bank on behalf of the TBTA bondholders. This suit was quietly dropped following a closed-door meeting between Nelson and David Rockefeller (the latter then chair at Chase), with the TBTA bondholders receiving an additional one-quarter percentage point on outstanding bonds.[32]

In the intervening years since its inception, the MTA proved a useful device for bailing out New York State's bankrupt rail lines. The most prominent was the notorious Long Island Rail Road, long the bane of affluent suburban commuters. Early in 1983, with the New York City subway system in a state of near collapse, the MTA was additionally burdened with direct responsibility for operating the Westchester rail lines when Conrail (the federal freight system) stopped local passenger service. With cash flow remaining problematic, the authority put the TBTA's New York Coliseum up for sale in 1985. The four-acre parcel was the largest commercial site made available in midtown Manhattan since Rockefeller Center was first established.[33]

For the most part, city and state administrations acquiesced to the strong-arm tactics of Austin Tobin and Robert Moses. The authority chairs were allowed to accumulate and reinvest surplus revenues as they saw fit, subject to very broad generic guidelines. With Nelson Rockefeller, however, a new era began.

Nelson, the most politically astute and aggressive of the five Rockefeller brothers, was elected to the second most powerful executive position in the nation. Free from the financial temptation of graft and consumption, and assured by brother David of support from the financial community, Nelson took personal control of the state's authorities. Under his guidance they became the primary vehicles with which he demonstrated his ability to tackle the nation's pressing housing, energy, and transportation problems in his relentless quest to assume the top executive position in the White House.

AUTHORITY EXPANSION DURING THE ROCKEFELLER ADMINISTRATION AND IMPLICATIONS FOR A THEORY OF THE STATE

Under Nelson Rockefeller's administration (1959-73) public authorities became the dominant sector in public finance. Whereas New York had only 26 state authorities at the onset, by the time he left office to assume duties as vice-president in the Ford administration, the number had ballooned to 42. Along with the unrivaled construction boom, Rockefeller left a legacy of debt lasting well into the next century. By 1978 the state and its political subdivisions accounted for over one-third of all revenue-backed bonds issued nationally.[34]

Arthur Levitt, state comptroller during much of the Rockefeller administration, criticized the governor's lavish building and spending schemes. He labeled the authorities "the fourth branch of government."[35] However, in practice, the authorities, at least as they operated during the Rockefeller administration, could more appropriately be considered an extension of the executive branch. In this capacity they were used by the governor as powerful agents of the real quiet evolution in property development and in its day-to-day accommodation in the face of local resistance to growth.

Rockefeller found the authorities to be an extremely useful means whereby constitutional debt limits, state budget appropriations, open bidding on public works construction, and civil service requirements could be avoided. These powers would prove useful when implementing the multibillion-dollar construction programs in housing, education, transportation, and energy development designed to showcase his ability to get the job done. Requiring only the advice and consent of the senate, a body he politically dominated, the governor's direct control over authority board appointments was a major legacy of the strong executive dominance characteristic of New York's political structure.[36] Under his guidance new state authorities were created for atomic development—the Atomic Research and Development Authority (today known as the Energy Research and Development Authority); residential, commercial, civic, and industrial development—the Housing Finance Agency, UDC, and Battery Park City Authority; transportation—the Capital District Transportation Authority and Metropolitan Transportation Authority; university construction— the State University Construction Fund; private sector job development—the Job Development Authority; and pollution control—the Pure Waters Authority and Environmental Facilities Corporation. According to reliable estimates, Rocke- feller-backed authorities spent more than $30 billion on construction during his administration. The outstanding debt of state authorities mushroomed almost tenfold from $129 million in 1962 to an incredible $12 billion by 1974. This latter amount was four times the voter-approved general obligation debt of the state itself.[37]

Rockefeller vastly increased the authorities' borrowing power through use of the so-called moral obligation bonds. These were backed by a "moral" obligation rather than the full faith and credit of the state, a necessary procedure if voter approval for general indebtedness was to be avoided. Moral obligation financing was fashioned by John Mitchell (of Watergate fame) in 1960 when, as a Wall Street bond attorney, he assisted Rockefeller in setting up the Housing Finance Agency (HFA). By this time Rockefeller had found it nearly impossible to acquire voter approval for full faith and credit bonds to support construction of moderate-income housing. With the legislature succumbing to his claim that these bonds would be self-liquidating through revenues and federal subsidies, and the financial community convinced that if push came to shove the state would have to step in with appropriations to cover principal and interest to maintain its credit rating, the bonds took off. They were used for many financially risky projects where the legislature was reluctant to raise taxes for financing and the governor did not want to go to the voters for approval. By the end of the 1970s, some 30 states had followed New York's innovative approach to financing politically untenable projects through the use of moral obligation bonds.[38]

Through moral obligation financing "the buck could be passed," at least for the time being. From 1960 until 1973 the legislature obediently increased the nonguaranteed debt limit for the state's public authorities at the governor's request. The financial community went along for the ride, satisfied with the slightly higher interest carried by the bonds. For many large-scale public projects moral obligation financing was actually preferred by financiers. After all, finicky voters could always turn off the tap on full faith and credit financing.

Under Rockefeller's tutorage, the state's own nonguaranteed agency and authority construction bond debt grew to $7.4 billion by 1974. This constituted almost one-quarter of the entire nonguaranteed state debt in the nation.[39] The HFA was the worst offender. Created primarily as a financing agency for housing and, in time, for a wide variety of public and private nonprofit facilities, including hospitals, day care centers, nursing homes, and senior citizen centers, the authority became the nation's leading issuer of tax-exempt securities backed by moral rather than guaranteed obligations. Moral obligations were also pivotal in the multibillion dollar (over)expansion of the 73-campus state university system, considered by many to be Rockefeller's most ambitious and successful project, and in the shaky funding of the UDC.

Rockefeller also pioneered use of lease-purchase agreements. Here the project bonds were issued by a local municipality with the state leasing the facility at rental rates equal to principal and interest payments. This technique circumvented voter as well as legislative debt limit approval, and relied only on executive order and local ratification for its execution. Its most notable application came through a new $2 billion (including debt interest) capitol complex designed to house most of the state offices in Albany.

Financed through bonds issued by Albany County, the 98-acre Albany South Mall included 11 office buildings and the highest building in the state outside New York City. Conceived at an initial estimated cost of $250 million, repeated delays and cost overruns (the entire edifice is faced with white Vermont and Georgia marble) made the public project the most expensive in the state's history. The complex was actually a massive redevelopment project for the city of Albany. Anticipating that the city itself would not support the mall, the governor condemned the land without public disclosure and invited county participation. The mall itself displaced an embarrassing slum located adjacent to the state capitol building and replaced it with a visually stunning urban center worthy of a would-be president or "frustrated builder" (as his admirers were prone to refer to Rockefeller). The impetus for the project came to Rockefeller following a visit by Queen Juliana of The Netherlands. As the governor was to reminisce later: "I could see the way the city was running down and what this lady might think. . . . Here was a great Dutch city built in the New World, and then she came to look at it, never having seen it before. My God!"[40] Ironically, earlier plans to relocate the 9,000 low- and moderate-income residents displaced by the mall were shelved as too costly.[41]

Rockefeller's deployment of public authorities presents an interesting enigma for the development of a theory of the capitalist State. On the one hand, Rockefeller's activities may be viewed as a response, albeit individualistic and somewhat unique, to problems besetting capitalist development. These included, and are not limited to, local resistance in residential neighborhoods to infrastructure construction required for administrative functions and economic expansion, a longer commute, exclusionary zoning, and rising housing prices. All of these are problems emanating from the spatial separation and perceptual reification of consumption space as distinct from production space. The solution to these problems would (structurally) benefit capital as a class (Chapters 1 and 3). On the other hand, Rockefeller's program did not merely address specific needs for housing, transportation, and educational development, but apparently did so in a manner instrumentally benefiting family interests.

The Rockefeller family became the most famous and powerful kinship group in the nation. Family connections, in turn, were used to perpetuate ruling-class power over public affairs, thereby enriching family fortunes.[42] The redevelopment of lower Manhattan, an area of heavy Rockefeller family investment, provides an example. Certainly the multibillion-dollar series of public and private projects guided by brother David's Downtown-Lower Manhattan Association could not have been possible without the close participation of the state's public authorities under Governor Rockefeller's enthusiastic direction. The Port Authority was responsible for construction of the World Trade Center and the renovation of docks, commuter rail lines (PATH), and a heliport in the area; the UDC and the Battery Park City Authority were engaged in urban renewal with residential, office, and commercial construction; and the MTA worked on subway expansion (along Second Avenue) to the downtown area.

With controlling involvement in Chase Manhattan and several allied bond investment firms, and major real estate investments in the area, the Rockefeller family materially gained from downtown urban renewal and office expansion.[43] A methodological problem arises, however, when interpreting these connections. Although financial gain is a necessary explanation for an instrumental interpretation of the governor's actions, it is not sufficient. The Rockefeller family controls such vast financial resources that direct self-benefit seems incomplete as an explanation (see also Chapter 6). This tremendous wealth, in turn, is used to bolster the popular view that the governor was beyond petty personal self-enrichment. On occasion, as is plausible with the incorporation of the TBTA into the MTA and his acquiescence to the Port Authority's forced involvement in public transportation, the governor's program may have clashed with the more pragmatic economic concerns of David Rockefeller.

Although instrumentalists are pressed to demonstrate significant and direct financial gain to Nelson Rockefeller through the activities of his authorities, he nonetheless benefited from them in other ways. The public authorities provided the perennial presidential candidate with a means whereby he could demonstrate his resourcefulness and ability to get the job done while also endearing himself to the state's powerful construction unions and progrowth advocates. Several of the authorities established during his administration were in response to immediate crises confronting his leadership, such as the Medical Care Facilities Agency (created after deplorable conditions in state health care institutions were publicized) and an authority to plan for new prisons (after the Attica uprising). Other authorities, including the HFA, the UDC, the Battery Park City Authority, and the MTA, were created in anticipation that voters would not approve the massive expenditures required for agendas showcasing the governor's resolve to tackle national housing and transportation problems.[44]

Although instrumental ruling-class hegemony over the process of capitalist development requires domination of the public arena, the governor's quest for political power through the use of public authorities still has a structuralist (class-preserving) component that cannot be ignored.[45] Regardless of whether he was motivated by personal financial gain, political power, altruistic sentiment, or public responsibility, in public life Nelson Rockefeller helped perpetuate a social system directly benefiting his common class origins. Thus, personal attention to the provision of services and infrastructure required for continued accumulation helped further economic development of collective interest, even if it also increased the governor's personal power and influence. As discussed in the following section, the governor's involvement in housing, industrial, and energy development provides the clearest example of ventures addressing problems besetting capital accumulation in general, which were carried out in a manner designed to bolster the governor's prestige and quest for the presidency. These major arenas for State intervention are highlighted to demonstrate the use of public authorities as agents of the quiet evolution, a situation bypassed by the liberal quiet revolution propagandists, as well as to develop a theory of the State transcending the confining instrumentalist versus structuralist debate.

THE URBAN DEVELOPMENT CORPORATION

Postwar Housing Policy

Housing is a major arena for intervention by the capitalist State. This stems from a high consumption demand for homes, as well as from the ideological and material requirements of the capitalist social structure.[46] Homeownership strengthens conservative allegiance to the status quo as workers fear loss of their "sweat" equity during times of social unrest. Homeownership also helps to shift the locus of ideological identity away from one's relationship with the mode of production toward a less threatening identity defined according to the quality and quantity of consumption. It is not surprising that increasing homeownership among the working class in the postwar period is accompanied by a tendency toward a local politics based upon defense of consumption space at the expense of production-based class alliances.

Housing construction also has an important countercyclical role in the economy, providing an outlet for overaccumulated capital from the primary industrial production circuit while priming the pump during economic recessions. State subsidy creating conditions favoring homeownership and profitable investment in housing occurs through loan guarantees, tax benefits, creation of secondary mortgage instruments to facilitate capital investment, provision of infrastructure and services to new developments, and a host of other assistance programs. State aid is essential because the private sector, on its own, is incapable of providing housing of the type and quantity needed to promote social stability and economic growth. When labor is in a position of being able to link wage demands to the cost of living, as occurred during the 1960s and early 1970s, and with housing a major component of this index, capitalists have a further interest in rationalizing the production and servicing of the built environment used for the reproduction of labor power. These trends, in turn, have led large-scale corporate and financial concerns to join together with developers and real estate interests in support of the modification of local and state regulations, building codes, and other statutes tending to raise the cost of housing.[47]

Acting on the recommendations of neoclassical macroeconomists, state and federal governments became actively involved in housing policy during the New Deal administration, with New York State as a leader. Following a 1938 amendment to the state constitution permitting direct state assistance for subsidized housing, New York created programs to assist private developers in urban renewal and the construction of low- and middle-income housing. Although housing was constructed at a feverish pace in the postwar period, it was not necessarily situated in a location and of sufficient density to service the central-city white-collar labor market or the suburban manufacturing complexes. Insufficient supply compounded by the practice of local exclusionary zoning had led to a costly mismatch between the locus of employment and the locus of consumption. This separation was in excess of any reasonable partitioning to support a social identity based upon access to the sanctuary of consumption. By the 1960s the Regional Plan Association and similar corporate-funded regional planning advocates in Rochester, Syracuse, and Buffalo were arguing for new devices to prevent inefficient urban sprawl and to site low- and moderate-income housing nearer the locus of employment (Chapters 2 and 3).[48]

The Housing Finance Agency

Already prior to becoming governor, Rockefeller privately funded a Conference on Metropolitan Area Problems. The organization published an influential newsletter promoting a regional approach to "metropolitan problems" like inadequate low- and moderate-income housing, transportation access, and antiquated and parochial land use regulations.[49] Soon after assuming official duties in 1959, Rockefeller commissioned a report calling for the creation of a housing finance agency to float tax-exempt bonds for the construction of middle-income housing. The task force was chaired by Otto Nelson, then vice-president of the RPA and also of the New York Life Insurance Company (at the time a major developer of middle-income housing across the nation). The recommendation that the bonds carry less than the full faith and credit of the state was made in anticipation that the voters would not approve a general bond for this purpose.[50]

Upon release of the report Rockefeller moved quickly. In 1960 he created the Housing Finance Agency as the first state-supported housing assistance agency in the nation. Over the next 13 years of his administration the HFA raised more than $10 billion on the tax-exempt bond market. This came about largely through pioneering use of the moral obligation bond. Abandoning construction of unprofitable low-income housing to federal and municipal agencies (e.g., the New York City Housing Development Corporation), the HFA became the state's largest financier of privately developed middle- and upper middle-income housing. During the 1960s income eligibility ceilings on HFA-financed housing quickly escalated from $10,000 to $35,000.[51] By the early 1970s the HFA had easier access to the bond market than either the state or New York City, and it had branched out into a multifocus conglomerate with subsidiaries responsible for the financing of health care, university, nursing home, and other types of facilities. Many of its projects were constructed for private nonprofit owners stymied by financing difficulties and local development regulations.

Creation of the Urban Development Corporation

Following a long postwar period of sustained urban expansion, widespread popular disenchantment with the existing development process surfaced by the early 1960s. Discontent emerged first in the central cities where housing discrimination by realtors and insufficient attention to the needs of low-income residents became a contributing factor to the civil rights movement and, ultimately, to the urban riots of 1965-68. In the suburban areas dissatisfaction with urban sprawl, grueling commute trips, loss of amenities, and concern with property values took the form of a "nogrowth" movement. This was portrayed by advocates and opponents alike as one facet of a broader environmental movement.

By the mid-1960s suburban flight by middle-class whites from the inner cities was well underway, partially in response to a lack of affordable housing in the cities. At the same time, much of the low- and moderate-income housing stock that was left behind was unfit for human habitation. The resulting spatial arrangement of development entailed a mismatch between housing and employment opportunities. This led to an increase in the cost for suburban manufacturing labor (where employees had to travel long distances to work in areas where housing was not affordable), an impoverished public service-dependent inner-city population that was excluded from suburban housing markets, and other noxious externalities. The prescribed solution to these urban ills seemed clear. The time had come for state and federal intervention in the local control of land use sufficient to site socially beneficial development.

During the Johnson administration the nation's housing policy became a major focus for social reform. Several prominent professional and federally appointed advisory commissions tied the issue of social inequality and environmental degradation to uncoordinated parochial control of suburban growth. Much of this debate came to the fore in 1968: the (Kerner) National Advisory Commission on Civil Disorders attacked exclusionary zoning in the suburbs as a cause of inner-city ghettos; the (Kaiser) President's Committee on

Urban Housing recommended policies for overcoming restrictions on the availability of land, such as through public land assembly; and the (Douglas) National Commission on Urban Problems undertook a full review of land use controls, arguing for a complete overhaul of the old system through state intervention to encourage large-scale residential development in the form of new communities.[52]

With the nation's most ambitious public program for residential development already established, Nelson Rockefeller rose to the challenge. He began assembling the components of a state program to assist private developers in large-scale, mixed-income community development. David Rockefeller was the first to suggest the idea and gather investor support for creation of a public corporation that would attract private funds to urban construction through use of lucrative tax breaks, state seed money, loan guarantees, and the promise of state override of obstructive local zoning and building codes.[53]

A three-year study on measures to attract major industrial corporations to community development also had an impact on policy development in New York State. It was prepared by the General Electric Corporation, itself a major land developer, for the Kaiser Committee. "Unrealistic zoning" and "archaic building codes" were highlighted as regulations preventing the introduction of more efficient, larger-scale, manufactured and prefabricated housing. The report was also critical of high wages in the unionized building trades and of problems with land cost and assembly. The suggested remedy called for establishment of a well-funded state development corporation to assist the private sector in meeting public needs.[54]

Between 1962 and 1968 New York's voters overwhelmingly rejected five of Rockefeller's housing bond proposals addressing these issues. The HFA itself would not accept responsibility for risky inner-city projects where the revenues could not meet debt obligations. As a result, a new authority was required that had enough power to attract private financing for credit-worthy projects while commanding access to the new federal loan guarantees and assistance programs for subsidized housing available through the housing acts of 1966 and 1968. In 1968, a year after voters defeated a constitutional package that included broad state authority to override local home rule powers for urban renewal, housing, and new community development, the governor pushed his Urban Development Corporation Act through a reluctant legislature.[55]

The UDC had unprecedented authority as a public benefit corporation. This included the power to condemn property, override local zoning ordinances and building codes, and issue over $1 billion in general purpose moral obligation bonds. It could act as a lender, builder, planner, and developer of almost any aspect of urban development, including provision of low-, middle-, and upper middle-income housing, as well as commercial, industrial, and civic facilities for sale or lease to public and private parties. Eligible for federal and state grants for subsidized housing, the UDC became a participant in the federal New Communities Program, through which it received assistance in the development of several upstate projects. The authority also took full advantage of the Section 236 federal subsidy available under the 1968 Federal Housing Act, capturing over 50 percent of all federal funds for this program paid to state agencies.[56] Easy access to federal assistance and its extraordinary powers enabled the UDC to move quickly. By December 1970, just one and one-half years after inception, the UDC had 7,500 housing units and $68 million in commercial development under construction in two dozen cities. In addition, some 45,000 housing units, including three major new communities, were under consideration.[57]

The UDC maintained close ties with the large commercial banks administering and investing in its bonds. Additional support came through the liberal planning reform movement and from the private developers with whom the UDC subcontracted. Through the enabling legislation a special exception was made that allowed individuals to serve on the UDC's board of directors despite conflicts of interest. Appointed by Rockefeller, the nine-member board was chaired by George Woods, a former president of the World Bank and a senior director and former chair of the First Boston Corporation. Woods accepted the position on the condition that his bank be designated the senior managing underwriter for all UDC offerings.[58] In addition to heavy participation from development and financial interests, the board included Rockefeller-appointed ex officio agency and department heads (i.e., the commissioner of the Department of Commerce, the director of the Office of Planning Services, and the superintendent of Banking and Insurance). A business council set up to assist the UDC involved David Rockefeller, Robert Tishman (a leading real estate developer), Harry Van Arsdale (head of the powerful New York Central Labor Council), and others with a vested interest in construction and in urban renewal.[59]

Rockefeller turned to Edward Logue as executive director, a nationally recognized construction administrator with a reputation from New Haven and Boston for erecting major urban renewal projects without being stalled by neighborhood political resistance. It was Logue who demanded that the UDC have the power to override local zoning and building codes, while being allowed to meet its debt obligations from a pool of revenues rather than on a more conservative project-by-project basis (as was the practice of the HFA).[60]

The financial community responded enthusiastically to the UDC's initial bond offering, convinced that Rockefeller could dominate the legislature to support the UDC should the need arise. Chase Manhattan Bank, Citibank, Morgan Guaranty Trust, Bank of America, and Security Pacific National Bank were the major bond trustees. UDC credit was liberally extended. By the summer of 1972 the governor had cajoled the legislature into raising the authority's debt authorization to $2 billion.[61] As events would prove, the overly optimistic faith by both the legislature and the financiers in the UDC resulted in slipshod control and an almost criminal neglect of UDC management.

An essential ingredient for private investment in the UDC was its ability to form profit-seeking subsidiaries on a project-by-project basis. These were entitled to all of the legal privileges of the parent corporation, including exemption from local property taxes on value added after acquisition, power to issue tax-exempt bonds, and ability to override local land use controls. As long as the UDC held at least one-half of the voting shares in the subsidiaries, the latter could have private, profit-seeking participants. In this manner, the constitutional prohibition against state assistance to private corporations could be avoided. In addition to private concerns, subsidiaries could include public and nonprofit investors and sponsors such as religious institutions and housing agencies.

With a UDC project ultimately capable of being leased or sold to private occupants, this public-private amalgamation vastly increased the leverage available for private development. Vincent Moore, a one-time planning director for the UDC, viewed creation of local subsidiaries as "a partial answer to the problem of reshaping home rule on a more coherent basis." As he observed, "the state is 'withdrawing' some aspects of power it has delegated to municipalities (such as zoning veto) and is redistributing it to a new public-private coalition with an areawide interest."[62] The attack on municipal home rule was unmistakable.

Many social advocates initially welcomed the UDC as a means to open the suburbs to lower-income residents. In addition, they viewed the authority as a legitimate response to mounting criticism that urban renewal, as carried out during the 1960s under the aegis of corrupt local development agencies, was primarily concerned with the replacement of slum dwellings by profitable upper-income housing and office development.[63] From a more pragmatic perspective, however, and with a view toward project profitability, the UDC's policy was to build 70 percent of the housing on a particular site for middle-income families, with 20 percent given to housing for low-income families and the remainder for the elderly.

In Syracuse, Rochester, Buffalo, and other upstate urban areas, the UDC established subsidiaries with the cooperation of religious, civic, business, and civil rights organizations. Despite widespread and rigorous opposition by local constituencies, the UDC managed to locate several thousand units of subsidized low- and moderate-income housing in the tightly zoned suburbs surrounding these major cities. Success was most pronounced in Rochester. Here the large industrial corporations, concerned about obstructive zoning and inadequate housing for their workers, persuaded local municipalities to accept UDC projects as a condition for plant expansion.[64]

Syracuse was another upstate locale for UDC investment. The Syracuse Metropolitan Development Association (SMDA), one of the postwar, privately sponsored regional planning advocates (Chapter 2), was the local UDC contact. Formed in 1959 by the region's dominant manufacturers and allied utility and service industries, the SMDA was an early proponent of state intervention to promote transportation and housing development. The UDC hired a nonprofit SMDA-sponsored subsidiary to manage its projects in the area. Faced with mounting opposition from surrounding communities to a large mixed-income new town under construction north of the city, the UDC launched a public relations campaign. Business control over provision of housing amid the unreceptive communities was virtually assured when the SMDA itself was designated by the UDC as the public's representative with responsibility for assembling the UDC's (required) community advisory committee.[65]

New York State's New Community Program

In addition to numerous inner-city housing and commercial projects, the UDC made a major commitment to new communities. At the time privately sponsored new communities, mixing residential, commercial, and industrial functions, and sited through the state power of eminent domain, were promoted by liberal planning reformers as the most rational manner to site production and residential development with minimum local opposition and regulatory delay.[66] The UDC went further, however, and actually championed state-initiated new communities as the proper antidote for the social and environmental problems resulting from local control of the development process. Responding to the recommendation of the Douglas Commission report, a major UDC policy statement suggested that two-thirds of *all* new housing in the state be constructed in UDC-initiated new communities by the 1990s.[67]

The UDC launched three new communities. These included a 5,000-unit town-in-town on Manhattan's Welfare Island in the East River (since renamed Roosevelt Island), the Radisson project north of Syracuse (originally planned for 5,000 units together with a major industrial park), and the new town of Audubon (where 9,000 units were envisioned in conjunction with construction of a new $1 billion campus for the state university at Buffalo).[68]

New York has four state university centers: Buffalo, Albany, Binghamton, and Stony Brook. Each underwent major expansion during the Rockefeller administration. At Buffalo, campus development was tied to a broader program of urban development. The integrated project was designed to showcase Rockefeller's commitment to bold new approaches in community development. Strongly supported by local business interests and developers, the new campus was expected to be a major growth pole for the northeast suburban section of the city, generating 24,000 new jobs and a demand for 42,000 additional housing units in a three and one-half-mile corridor between downtown Buffalo and the new campus. Overall the corridor would gain 92,000 jobs and require 70,000 new housing units by 1985, with the UDC responsible for most of the development.[69] However, as was the case with many other state economic and demographic projections during the Rockefeller administration, the UDC's projections turned out to be wildly optimistic. With the regional economy in decline during the 1970s, and the new campus years behind schedule and still under construction as of 1987, a chastened UDC was forced toward more modest commercial projects with greater revenue-producing potential.

The Radisson project also failed to live up to original expectations. Surrounding communities feared that the development would become a low-income housing project. Thwarted by a local lawsuit and financing difficulties, construction at the site proceeded at a snail's pace. Following the UDC default in 1975, emphasis was placed on self-sufficiency. With over $22 million already invested (representing direct federal and state grants, not UDC loans), local fears were alleviated when the project moved toward a more conventional suburban housing formula. Strict zoning requirements, detailing every aspect of construction and design down to house color, trash can placement, and the location of mail boxes, attracted a wealthy clientele seeking firm protection of their consumption space. The lack of adequate public transportation reinforced this exclusion.[70]

Today Radisson's lots and homes sell in one of the region's most expensive real estate markets. With a new health center, golf course, and plans for a major marina underway, Radisson has strayed far from the original UDC intent to open the suburbs to minority and lower-income workers.

The Roosevelt Island project is the most advanced of the UDC's three communities. The development has four sections: one for upper-class families, one for "financially deprived" families, and the other two for middle-class families. Built in partnership with the city of New York, the island was reportedly given to the UDC in return for development of low-income housing in other parts of the city. A 1980 state audit estimated that the project primarily benefits a "relatively affluent" population while, in the end, it will cost taxpayers an additional $236 million in subsidies over the next 40 years.[71]

Local Resistance to UDC Programs

From its inception, the most controversial aspect of the UDC was its authority to override local zoning and building regulations and condemn land, if necessary, through eminent domain. New York City's Mayor John Lindsay denounced the UDC as an intolerable infringement on home rule powers. He also expressed concern over the tax-exempt status of the authority and its subsidiaries. At the other end of the state, negotiations between local officials and the UDC over the new community of Audubon broke down in 1971 when the town of Amherst (site of the project) sought a court order to halt development on environmental and fiscal grounds. Development only resumed following formal UDC assurance that the new community would not damage the local tax base.[72]

In Manhattan's Harlem, residents were particularly incensed over destruction of 300 apartments and 90 businesses to make way for a state office building. The confrontation reached a zenith in the summer of 1969 when community activists, convinced that the office building was the leading edge for white penetration into the cultural capital of Black America, staged a three-month sit-in at the site. Rockefeller had to call upon the politically insulated UDC to sponsor the project after he had the squatters ejected from the site. Elsewhere in Harlem over 1,000 UDC units were completed along the typical income allocation formula, and while this generated more housing for moderate-income families, it also forced the eviction of hundreds of low-income tenants from the condemned construction sites.[73] Harlem Negotiating Committee, the local subsidiary set up by the UDC to contract and manage the project, was drawn from, and supported by, black representatives of the community's business, religious, and construction leadership, all individuals likely to benefit from urban renewal.

Municipal suspicion of the UDC ran highest in the suburbs, the very heartland of Rockefeller's Republican support. Efforts to open up these communities to low- and moderate-income housing came to a head in 1972. All hell broke loose when the UDC released a modest proposal to locate several hundred subsidized units in nine affluent Westchester towns. The local outcry was sufficient to force the governor and legislature to strip the UDC of much of its override powers, including the ability to circumvent town and village zoning and building codes.[74] Legislation accepted by the governor in 1973 allowed suburban towns to exercise final approval over residential construction by the UDC. The authority retained override powers for industrial and commercial projects and, in the cities, for residential construction as well.

Westchester County was notoriously deficient in affordable housing. Its own lower-income minorities and elderly were experiencing difficulty living there. In response, the UDC proposal would have given top priority to the county's then-current residents. Be that as it may, no powerful constituency for subsidized housing appeared in the county. Curiously, despite a major boom in suburban office location, with IBM, General Foods, Pepsico, Nestlé, AMF, and other multinational conglomerates locating headquarter and routine office functions in the county, the Westchester business community did not rally behind the UDC proposal.[75]

Noting the sharp contrast with Rochester, where hundreds of low-income units were located with help from the local business community, several analysts attributed the lack of project sponsors in Westchester to a weak level of corporate-led civic leadership.[76] While this may be the case, particularly for individual suburban firms where local political domination lessened the need for civic coordination, we should also consider the nature of the labor force employed. In Rochester the large corporations, such as Eastman Kodak and Xerox, were relocating manufacturing plants to the suburbs. Here industrial workers were having difficulty finding affordable housing in the immediate vicinity. In Westchester, however, most of the expansion and relocation involved office functions. Here an increasing reliance upon the immediate secondary female labor force for routine office tasks diminished corporate concern with finding adequate housing for primary wage earners.

Furthermore, business concerns in Westchester, when they did consider housing opportunities, appeared more attentive to their own top-level management and frequently located near high-income suburban communities. While demonstrating the inextricable link between production and con-sumption—in this case attention to the latter lowering the cost of the former—new problems invariably arose. Here, as elsewhere, production threats to this sanctified landscape, whether in the form of moderate-income housing for industrial workers, power facilities, hazardous waste treatment facilities, or highways, were met by a local defense of consumption space that presented political barriers to urban development. Today wealthy suburban communities disenchanted with the accompanying traffic congestion and other growing pains are even rejecting the office parks, retail centers, and research campuses once eagerly sought after as a boon to the local tax and employment base.[77]

The Collapse and Resurrection of the UDC

In 1970 the UDC confidently suggested that within 20 years some two-thirds of all new housing starts in the state would occur within UDC-sponsored new communities. Some four years later the UDC's financial house of moral obligation cards fell apart. The well-publicized default and subsequent bailout were expected to cost the state an additional $650 million for debt service through 1988.[78] There was more than enough blame to go around. At the federal level the Nixon administration suspended Section 236, the subsidy for low-income units, in January 1973. While Rockefeller managed to maintain support for projects already underway, the cutoff shook confidence in the UDC's future since fully 90 percent of its residential units had, up to that time, received some form of federal aid. Changing federal tax laws limiting the exemption on industrial and commercial development further contributed to declining investor interest.[79] The strident suburban opposition to the UDC's exercise of police power and the legislature's subsequent curtailment of this power were warning signs of faltering political support. Furthermore, the internal management of the authority was in shambles. Construction commitments for financially risky housing projects were allowed to accumulate far in excess of the authority's ability to raise capital on the bond market. For its part, the financial community aggressively promoted and marketed UDC obligations, even as the bond offerings listed previous shortcomings and warned of uncertainties yet to come.

By mid-1973 the UDC was having a serious problem with cash flow and the operating deficit was approaching $1 million a day. With inflation wreaking havoc on the bond market and a national recession setting in, the UDC's moral obligation bond had become an unattractive investment. Nelson Rockefeller resigned as governor that fall to prepare for his presidential bid. With the authority's strongest supporter now gone, the financial community began a sobering and long-overdue reevaluation of the UDC. In October Moody's Investors Service lowered the UDC credit rating from A to Baa-1. The following spring, Morgan Guaranty Trust, a lead underwriter of UDC bonds, withdrew from the sponsoring consortium.[80] Throughout 1974 the authority was forced to offer much higher interest rates. As recourse to direct state subsidies increased, the stage was set for a major overhaul of the authority's mission and structure. In February 1975, with Rockefeller no longer available to rally financial and political support, the banks made their move. Refusing to roll over short-term obligations into long-term bonds, the banks technically forced the UDC to default on a $104 million bond anticipation note.[81]

Despite additional loans totaling hundreds of millions of dollars made in 1973 and 1974 to take advantage of the higher interest rates then offered, bondholders took no loss on their gamble. The UDC's difficulties, however, had a disastrous impact on the public sector left holding the bill. Although bound by only a nebulous "moral obligation," the state, under threat of blocked access to the credit market, was forced to rescue the UDC through legislative appropriations and a high interest on the bonds issued by the temporary agency created to take over UDC financing. Beyond the UDC's tab, there was an even greater price to pay. The UDC's brief (two-month) staged default forced the state and its municipalities to pay much higher rates on general obligation and revenue-backed bonds. Subsequently this situation became a contributing factor to the "fiscal crisis" faced by New York City and the state in 1974-76.[82]

Rather than bearing some responsibility for its enthusiastic support and misguided control of UDC activities, the financial community managed to protect its investment, shift the burden for the rescue onto the public sector, and in the process narrow the UDC focus to projects of even more direct benefit to private interests.[83] In testimony before the state assembly Frank Smeal, executive vice-president of Morgan Guaranty Trust, summarized the bankers' prognosis: "Social goals are funded one way in this country and economic goals another way."[84]

Upon taking office in 1975 Governor Hugh Carey took this message to heart and he appointed Richard Ravitch, head of one of the nation's largest construction firms, to replace Logue as executive director of the UDC. Under Ravitch's guidance the authority was restructured to focus less on consumption expenditures, such as housing and health care facilities, and more on production investments directly increasing private profit.[85]

The UDC is portrayed today as one of New York's primary tools in the interregional battle for private investment to stimulate job development. Most of its projects are designed to assist private capital. Notable examples include the $180 million expansion of a Chrysler plant near Syracuse, the $80 million conversion of New York City's Commodore Hotel for the Hyatt Corporation, and the major redevelopment of Times Square as an office and shopping district. The UDC also assisted the Rouse Corporation in the $120 million redevelopment of New York City's South Street Seaport and constructed the $375 million Jacob K. Javits Exposition and Convention Center. Elsewhere across the state, the emphasis is shifting to assistance for high-technology entrepreneurs in computers and information processing.[86]

The UDC and the Quiet Evolution

Although much of its override authority for residential development was clipped in 1973, the UDC is still exempt from local land use and building codes for other types of development. As such, it is a powerful tool in the quiet evolution to site industrial, commercial, correctional, and office projects that municipalities will not, or are politically afraid to, site on their own. In New York City, for example, UDC participation, with the city's blessing, permits condemnation and project approval where direct city sponsorship and use of eminent domain to clear and acquire a site would be subject to a lengthy community review and regulatory process. Furthermore, the UDC constructs projects that, when leased instead of sold for private use, permit lower payments in lieu of property taxes. The Albany Hilton, New York City's Grand Hyatt, and other existing and planned projects stand on land that has been or will have to be condemned by the authority for lease back to a developer.

At Times Square plans for the four office towers, merchandise markets, a hotel, and "legitimate" theaters intended to flood the area with well-heeled office workers and tourists are facing intense opposition. Community activists are concerned about the plight of the area's transient and homeless persons, while nearby merchants and tenants fear a displacement of the Times Square "problem" into their neighborhoods.[87] Here UDC participation promises to short-circuit the elaborate rights of participation in zoning decisions won by the city's neighborhood advocates in recent years.

In summary, it appears that the UDC has shifted attention away from a concern with social investments lowering the cost of labor, as through a subsidized housing program, to concentrate more directly on support for private production where it stimulates employment. This shift from consumption to production investment occurred during the fiscal crises gripping New York City and New York State during the mid-1970s. In the course of these difficult times large-scale capital interests tightened their grip on many organs of the State apparatus, intent on using them to provide for immediate production and investment needs.[88] The change in the UDC's mission, then, is a measured response to this pressure as well as to diminished social protest over inadequate housing and other consumption needs, as public attention, during the recession, turned to more pressing employment and production concerns.

The UDC of the 1980s thus reemerges as a powerful conglomerate capable of providing assistance for almost any aspect of private accumulation. By and large, the recommendations of the Moreland Commission, set up in the wake of the UDC's near collapse to investigate the corporation's management and the overall regulation of other authorities in the state, have been ignored. Even the minimal legislative overview normally occurring during an authority's enabling authorization has been undercut in the case of the UDC through its continuing ability to spin off subsidiaries without legislative approval, as has been done for Battery Park City, Times Square, the Javits Convention Center, and other controversial projects.[89] In those few areas where the UDC is not authorized to enter, such as for provision of transportation and energy services, other existing or newly created state agencies and authorities have picked up the slack. It is to the Power Authority of the State of New York, one of the most important statewide authorities servicing urban development, that I now turn.

THE POWER AUTHORITY OF THE STATE OF NEW YORK

Public Regulation in Exchange for Monopoly Franchise

The provision of utilities is a prerequisite for urban development. Private gas and electric companies were eager to meet this need in high-density service areas where profits were assured. Over time the utilities became a leading front in the push for urbanization. This came about because the search for larger markets and resulting urban sprawl could be subsidized by existing consumers, with the utilities allowed to provide power throughout their service area at the average cost of service for the area. In addition, long-term bond financing was essential to this process. Through the debt obligations and pricing structure, the private utilities (and later public utilities) were locked into a system forcing them to become progrowth advocates. This was evident through their early and continued participation in the business-led metropolitan reform and regional planning movements (Chapter 2).

By the turn of the century energetic competition had given way to monopoly ownership in most urban centers. In New York City, for example, Consolidated Gas, the parent company of Consolidated Edison (Con Ed), began its rise to dominance at the end of the nineteenth century, eventually absorbing all of the 296 separate electric- and gas-generating distribution systems serving the city in 1900.[90] Public outcry over high rates, however, led to a threat of municipal provision of power resources as an alternative designed to force rates down. Publicly owned utilities could, and usually did, undersell private power by virtue of an ability to finance projects through tax-exempt bonds, easier access to power of condemnation, and freedom from property taxation and from a need to siphon off profits for shareholders. Under guidance from liberal corporate and enlightened business reformers, compromise was reached during the Progressive Era (1890-1920). In return for public regulation—which was both a concession to, and an aid for (via exclusive franchise), monopoly provision of utilities—privately owned conglomerates were allowed to absorb most of the municipal and smaller private gas and electric companies.

During the Progressive Era public service commissions were established to regulate the rate structure charged by these "natural" monopolies. The commissions were promoted, in part, by the National Civic Federation, an important organ of business-led reform. Speaking for the collective class interest of its industrial-based membership, the federation sought to lower utility rates and held out the threat of public competition should regulation of investor-owned utilities fail. By 1932 every state in the nation, except Delaware, had a public service commission.[91]

Public provision of power continued in several regions as a "yardstick" used to influence private rates. Public power was also enlisted to provide low-cost energy in rural areas where the private sector refused to go. In response to a national commitment to rural electrification, public utilities enjoyed a re-surgence during the 1920s and 1930s. At times they clashed with private utility companies when reaching out to areas that might be profitably serviced or when linking up to federal and state hydroelectric projects constructed during the New Deal administration.[92]

By the 1940s the progressive challenge of public power development was compromised through the realities of a class-dominated production system and an accompanying ideology demanding that the State cease direct competition with the private sector and limit itself to the creation of a climate conducive to private accumulation. This process was clearly demonstrated through the history of the Power Authority of the State of New York (PASNY, and since 1985 known as the New York Power Authority), the pioneering public power agency in the East.

The "Birch Rod in the Cupboard"

Under Governor Franklin D. Roosevelt's guidance, PASNY was established in 1931 to harness the hydroelectric potential of the St. Lawrence River. It became a model for his National Power Policy and Tennessee Valley Authority programs. Through these, public power was envisioned as the "birch rod in the cupboard," encouraging the private sector to lower rates and extend service to the rural hinterland.

Restrictions on the allocation and pricing of authority-generated power were incorporated into the 1931 State Power Authority Act. Through the enabling legislation, PASNY was to sell St. Lawrence power "for the benefit of the people of the state as a whole and particularly the domestic and rural consumers to whom the power can economically be made available." Moreover, "sale to and use by industry [was to] be a secondary purpose, to be utilized principally to secure a sufficiently high load factor and revenue returns which will permit domestic and rural use at the lowest possible rates and in such manner as to encourage increased domestic and rural use of electricity."[93] Clearly intending that PASNY be free to stimulate lower rates, Roosevelt exempted it from Public Service Commission rate regulation and management audits because the commission, at the time, was seen as unduly influenced by the regulated industry.[94]

During the 1930s PASNY lobbied for lower rates to stimulate employment and increase household demand for electric appliances in the depression-ravaged economy. It actually encouraged importation of cheap Canadian hydropower and development of municipally owned power distribution systems for these purposes. Nevertheless, despite PASNY's unprecedented mission and noble efforts, actual development of the hydroelectric potential of northern New York State was stymied by opposition from the private utilities and by treaty difficulties with Canada. As expressed in its 1937 annual report, the authority was concerned that the utilities and aluminum industry (a high-load user and competitor for development of hydroelectric facilities) were attempting to block or appropriate its custody for the St. Lawrence project. Delay in public development was attributed to the international ownership of the resource to be exploited, as well as to the "tremendous and far-flung nature of the combination of private interests determined to thwart any public power enterprise which does not accept its terms." In PASNY's opinion:

> The influence of these private interests extends to all forms of so-called big business so that its opposition may disguise itself in a score of different costumes. . . .
>   These interests, representing combined power and industrial monopolies, are concerned with the profits derived from monopoly rates

and prices. They know no national boundaries and their tendency is to favor areas in which private power undertakings are encouraged to the detriment of those seeking cheaper electricity through public developments.[95]

As an example, the authority singled out the Mellon family (with extensive holdings in upstate aluminum production) as a major manipulator of utility rates and service agreements.

Public Power for Private Profit

It was not until 1954, when Robert Moses became chair of the authority, that PASNY moved forcefully into energy production. A year earlier the Federal Power Commission issued the necessary construction license to PASNY following a treaty settlement with Canada for development of the St. Lawrence Seaway. Moses himself was no stranger to power politics. In 1934 an inflamed utility industry frantically sought to stem the New Deal promise of independent municipal access to hydropower. It put up Moses as the Republican guber-natorial candidate against Herbert Lehman, FDR's successor and chief sponsor of legislation authorizing localities to condemn and acquire private utility property within their jurisdiction. While Moses' campaign was a disaster, the utilities, through political pressure, intimidation, and ultimately PASNY allocation, successfully thwarted municipal appropriation of, and direct access to, Niagara and St. Lawrence power.[96] With PASNY finally given the green light for resource development, Moses accepted the PASNY directorship on condition that he alone would nominate the other four governor-appointed authority trustees. Under his leadership the New Deal promise of a socially progressive policy focusing on the stimulation of domestic consumption and municipal control of power resources was compromised. Soon thereafter PASNY abandoned any pretense to influence the retail rate charged by the private utilities purchasing power from it under long-term, low-cost, wholesale agreements.

Upon taking office Moses moved the authority's headquarters from Albany to New York City. His close ties with the city's financial community helped PASNY gain much-needed access to the bond market. The $335 million issue for development of the St. Lawrence project was quickly grabbed up. Four years later, in 1958, a $720 million bond issue for construction of the Niagara power project sold out in just four days, making it at the time the fastest moving and largest revenue-backed offering in the nation's history.[97] PASNY received a federal license for the mammoth 2,400-megawatt (Mw—1985-installed capacity) Niagara project following federal requirements that 50 percent of the generated power be allocated on a priority basis "to public bodies and nonprofit cooperatives within economic transmission distances," with 20 percent of this preference power made available to neighboring states.[98]

Over the past three decades PASNY continued to stray from its ideological origins as a yardstick against which to measure the social efficiency of private power production. With easy access to tax-exempt financing, freedom to set its own rates independent of Public Service Commission review, and the power to override local land use controls, PASNY became an important institution perpetuating, rather than challenging, monopoly utility control over power production and, in turn, urban development. In the intervening years PASNY's legislative mandate was broadened to allow for the financing, construction, maintenance, and operation of any type of electric-generating and transmission facility, including fossil fuel, nuclear, and pumped-storage projects. By 1984 PASNY was the largest supplier of electricity in the state, responsible for 32 percent of the total amount generated. Its 6.79 Mw of installed capacity was spread among six major facilities, including the Niagara and St. Lawrence projects, a pumped-storage facility, two nuclear reactors, and an oil-fired plant (Map 4.1).[99]

In addition to the highly rated tax-free investment potential, PASNY assistance for private accumulation took several other forms. To begin, the main projects initiated by PASNY, including the 40-mile St. Lawrence power project and the Niagara power project, were of a magnitude beyond the financing capacity of the private sector. The resulting electric output, marketed well below the bulk wholesale rate charged by the private utilities, was largely committed at cost to the private utilities for resale, or to high-load industries, such as chemical and metal production.

Under Moses' direction PASNY first began the policy of selling power at low bulk rates to upstate utilities and a few large-scale industries. With Moses successfully warding off challenges by the Municipal Electric Utilities Association, the authority came on line, in 1962, with firm industrial contracts for 64 percent of the St. Lawrence power and 46 percent of the Niagara power. The bulk of the remainder was given to private utility contracts. Clearly the intent, if not the letter, of the legislation authorizing PASNY development of Niagara and St. Lawrence resources was violated as PASNY, collaborating with the private utilities, repeatedly advised and pressured local governments not to form their own municipal systems in order to be eligible for the reserved hydropower. By 1982 only a few dozen small municipal systems had been established, the majority prior to Moses' directorship, and these served merely 2 percent of the state's population.[100] In the St. Lawrence city of Massena, a voter-approved referendum authorizing a bond issue to takeover Niagara Mohawk facilities under the earlier New Deal legislation was bitterly opposed by the utilities and PASNY, thereby precipitating a series of state and federal licensing challenges to PASNY's authority and practices.

In 1982 the U.S. share of the Niagara power capacity (actually varying with the amount of water permitted to go over the falls) went to several preferred customers: Niagara Mohawk (789 Mw), New York State Electric and Gas (294 Mw), and Rochester Gas and Electric (152 Mw). Large-scale Niagara-based industries, including metal refining and chemical companies congregating in the region to take advantage of the lower-cost hydroelectric power, received most of the remaining capacity.[101] The 912-Mw St. Lawrence power project sold the bulk of its 1982 output to Niagara Mohawk (112 Mw—reserved for

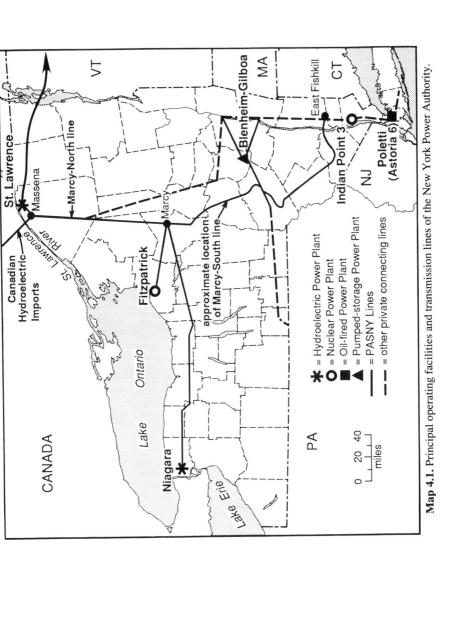

Map 4.1. Principal operating facilities and transmission lines of the New York Power Authority.

preference users), the Aluminum Corporation of America (ALCOA—174 Mw), Reynolds Aluminum (200 Mw), the state of Vermont (100 Mw), and the city of Plattsburgh (60 Mw). In 1985 more than one-half of St. Lawrence power sales went to just two firms (ALCOA and Reynolds).[102]

Municipal utility systems, labor unions, neighboring states, and local rural electric cooperatives have all opposed the major low-rate, long-term leases given to upstate utilities and industries. This contest for public power heated up during the 1970s. With the steep rise in oil prices, the hydropower marketed by PASNY was less than one-tenth the cost of the nuclear- and fossil fuel-generated power sold by the private utilities. As a consequence, the utilities eagerly sought to purchase more PASNY power beyond the initial low-cost allocation they were supposed to deliver to domestic and preference customers. Several municipalities, including New York City, Syracuse, and Erie County, formed their own public utilities in order to be eligible for preferential allocation.

The Federal Energy Regulatory Commission (formerly the Federal Power Commission) still monitors PASNY's compliance with the federal acts authorizing the Niagara project. In 1978 it sided with the Municipal Electric Utilities Association of New York and ruled that the authority had not reserved enough power for preference customers represented by the association. Two years later the commission ruled against PASNY's attempt to limit service to municipal systems established prior to 1962. Moreover, in 1984, the New York courts declared that PASNY had violated the lowest possible cost mandate for delivery of hydropower to residential users (passed through the private utilities) when excess Niagara and St. Lawrence revenue was used to plan for a nuclear plant. This contest for inexpensive power was temporarily settled when the Federal Energy Regulatory Commission allowed PASNY to switch Niagara's residential preference customers over to St. Lawrence power. Industrial and other nonpreference users received additional allocations from the James A. FitzPatrick nuclear plant and from other PASNY projects not subject to federal review for hydropower. Finally, the fossil fuel- and nuclear-dependent downstate municipalities and utilities (i.e., Con Ed and the Long Island Lighting Company—LILCO) were partially consoled by PASNY contracts to deliver imported Canadian hydropower, the promise of reallocation when the original upstate contracts expire between 1985 and 1990, and motions to take over financially troubled downstate facilities already under construction.[103]

Picking Up the Pieces: PASNY Enters the Nuclear Age

PASNY is frequently in a position to purchase unprofitable or partially completed power projects and transmission lines from the state's private utilities. The power produced is largely committed for resale to the private sector. For example, in 1956 Niagara Mohawk finally acceded to PASNY development of Niagara Falls. This came about after the authority agreed to a preferential 50-year lease with the utility in return for the right to acquire the remnants of a 365-Mw powerhouse that had been demolished by a rockslide. With Niagara

Mohawk's blessing, the Federal Power Commission designated PASNY as the sole Niagara developer when industry in the utility's service region threatened to relocate in the face of escalating energy costs. The resulting allocation came on line in January 1961 with Niagara Mohawk granted 250 Mw to promote expansion of industry in its Niagara service area. This came in addition to the 445 Mw the utility received as replacement power for the 31 companies on line to receive power from its own ill-fated plant.[104]

Nelson Rockefeller vigorously promoted nuclear power in response to aesthetic objections raised by environmentalists to fossil fuel and pumped-storage projects. Prior to widespread discussion of the difficulties associated with nuclear waste disposal in the late 1960s, many environmental advocates, including the Sierra Club, supported the Rockefeller stand on nuclear power. In 1968, as chair of a national task force on the role of electric power companies in environmental protection, brother Laurance Rockefeller went so far as to propose construction of an underground nuclear plant on Welfare (Roosevelt) Island in New York City.[105]

In 1959 a seminal report to Governor Rockefeller, prepared with assistance from General Electric and Westinghouse, stressed the significance of increased power generation to the state's industrial development and urban expansion. Playing to the governor, the report concluded that *"New York State requires big use, big units, big transmission lines and big ideas."*[106] Responding in his characteristically forceful manner, Rockefeller created a state Atomic Research and Development Authority in 1962 (later renamed the Atomic and Space Development Authority). In West Valley, 40 miles southeast of Buffalo, the new authority set up the Western New York Nuclear Service Center as the nation's only operational commercial nuclear fuel reprocessing facility. A private firm (Nuclear Fuel Services—later sold to Getty Oil) was subcontracted to construct and operate the project on state property, thereby evading local planning and zoning approval. Reprocessing began in 1966. Most of the spent fuel came from the federal Hanford Plant (Washington State), since private commercial operations were not advanced enough to take advantage of the service. In 1973 operations were stopped for modernization and expansion. The facility never reopened because more stringent federal safeguards and declining investor support made it prohibitively expensive to complete and operate.[107]

By 1969 local opposition to nuclear power plant construction had reached a point where Governor Rockefeller, relying on the state power of eminent domain, instructed the Atomic and Space Development Authority to preacquire plant sites for lease to the private utilities. In his estimation:

> Nearly all methods of maintaining clean land, air, and water in our society require electric power. Improved management of the environment [would] therefore call for greater supplies of electric power. For this reason, a forward-looking program to select and provide acceptable sites for future nuclear power plants in the State is a necessary adjunct to other measures being undertaken in many areas, to preserve and improve the environment.[108]

With the Atomic and Space Development Authority bogged down with a costly cleanup of the West Valley site, primary responsibility for the governor's commitment to nuclear power fell to PASNY. Through the governor's control of board appointments, the authority came to subsidize the nuclear industry in general, as well as the private utilities, whose partially completed reactors it purchased when the economic recession of the early 1970s led to a severe squeeze on private financing.

Throughout his administration Rockefeller tended to accept the utilities' own optimistic demand projections. Originally favoring private provision of nuclear power at a time when the utilities still viewed the new source of power as a lucrative venture, Rockefeller agreed to direct PASNY participation only after U.S. Senator Robert Kennedy challenged the governor's aid formula as a counterproductive measure designed to monopolize private profit at public expense while denying PASNY's own entry into the nuclear field.[109] The resulting "compromise" proved extremely beneficial to the utilities. They were assured that PASNY-produced nuclear power would be resold to them at low, guaranteed rates. In addition, the Atomic and Space Development Authority would assist the private sector in site acquisition for nuclear plants, conduct basic research and development for the nuclear industry, and directly pay for landscaping, noise reduction, and other aesthetic, health, and safety improvements not considered essential for power production. PASNY nuclear power sales, beyond what the private utilities would purchase, were further limited to large-scale bulk users whose own electric expenses were at least 10 percent of their operating costs.[110]

PASNY never got around to building its own plants. By 1970 the nuclear expansion program of the private utilities was suffering from high cost overruns due to mounting public opposition, regulatory delays, and a worsening recession contributing to a weak bond market and high capital costs. This situation prompted Rockefeller to honor his commitment by calling on PASNY to take over several financially troubled and still incomplete reactors and nuclear expansion programs. The 800-Mw FitzPatrick nuclear plant, located near Oswego on Lake Ontario, was completed by PASNY in 1975 following purchase of the construction site and reactor plans from Niagara Mohawk. The utility, in turn, was contracted to run the plant, delivering power along its own transmission lines to its clients. These included the six other investor-owned utilities and the major industrial firms Niagara Mohawk lured to its service area through low-cost, long-term electric contracts.[111] Niagara Mohawk, in effect, received tax-free financing for a project it could not complete, thus permitting it access to power at a much lower expense than if left to its own generation.

In time Con Ed became another major recipient of state support. Then the largest and richest private utility in the nation, it had a reputation of overcharging its New York City and Westchester customers (who paid the highest electric rates in the country). In 1974 PASNY purchased two of Con Ed's financially troubled and partially completed plants, a nuclear facility at Indian Point on the Hudson (35 miles north of New York City), and the oil-fired

Astoria 6 power plant in Queens. PASNY agreed to sell the major portion of the output back to the utility. The utility's financial reserve notwithstanding, chair Charles Luce promulgated rumors of imminent bankruptcy, leading to the PASNY bailout. Although a direct state purchase of all Con Ed voting stock could have been accomplished in 1974 at a price close to that paid for the two troubled projects, this proposal never received serious attention, and Con Ed's subsequent "recovery" was spectacular.[112]

By the 1980s, PASNY's original (1931) charge to consider industry as only a "secondary purpose" had long been forgotten in the interstate battle for investment. A "Juice for Jobs" program was formalized whereby inexpensive PASNY power would be used to attract and hold employment. This came in response to a threat by Grumman Aircraft, Long Island's largest employer, to locate planned administration and engineering facilities in Georgia unless the state, through PASNY, sweetened the pot through a preferred power allocation. Shearson Lehman (of American Express) also received access to FitzPatrick power (supposedly reserved for high-load industry) when it threatened to locate its headquarters across the Hudson, rather than at Battery Park City. In a similar and successful bluff, the Madison Square Garden Corporation, a subsidiary of Gulf and Western, received low-cost PASNY power and tax breaks totaling $50 million in return for an agreement not to move its New York Nicks (basketball) and New York Rangers (hockey) teams to New Jersey's Hackensack Meadowlands Stadium.[113]

As a final expression of support for private profit and expansion of production facilities, PASNY stepped in as developer of last resort when the utilities, faced with mounting local opposition on environmental and social grounds, were unable to push projects through a hostile regulatory system. This latter function deserves closer attention because it is a clear indication of the real quiet evolution in land use control overlooked by liberal planning reform advocates of a more visible "quiet revolution" through direct state facility siting legislation.

Local Opposition to PASNY Projects

Up until 1976 the New York State Power Pool, formed by the private utilities and PASNY, was the principal source of data used to justify capital expansion in siting decisions. Creation of the Power Pool permitted a coordination and sharing of production and delivery systems among the utilities, and they became more centralized and committed to larger and more expensive plants. This tendency was also fostered by a cost-plus system of rate regulation whereby the utilities were allowed to directly pass on to the ratepayers expenses incurred in facility construction plus a guaranteed rate of return based upon overall capital investment. In brief, more expensive plants yielded greater profits.

As was characteristic of much of the nation's utility industry during the 1960s, the demand projections offered by the Power Pool were not challenged by the state Public Service Commission. As a result, New York's utilities received permission to embark upon a massive and ill-fated program of capital expansion. Whereas in 1959 the largest private power plant in the state was only 350 Mw, by the mid-1960s, with active encouragement and assistance from the governor, the private utilities had several large nuclear and pumped-storage projects in the 1,000- to 2,000-Mw range planned or under construction.[114]

The rate of growth in energy consumption in New York State peaked in 1970. By 1974, when new capacity was coming on line, this figure was down. The result was emergence of considerable excess capacity, which continues today.[115] In 1976, after years of inaccurate forecasts by the Power Pool, the State Energy Office was established to formulate an energy policy stressing conservation while providing an independent estimate of future demand binding on siting and licensing procedures. Whereas the pressure of state assessment was quite useful, forcing the private utilities away from more unreasonable long-range commitments, the State Energy Office did not reevaluate projects already under construction.

Con Ed had the most aggressive expansion program. Rejecting the opportunity to purchase inexpensive hydropower from the Niagara Falls project (in 1958) and from Churchill Falls, Quebec (1964), the utility embarked on its costly coal-fired, pumped-storage, and nuclear expansion programs.[116] The utility's position was understandable given the then-current rate-pricing structure. The result was that Con Edison bypassed the cheaper hydropower, even though this would have lowered consumer rates, in favor of a system resulting in higher service charges and profits. The bubble finally burst during the economic recession of 1973-74. As demand drastically fell, and fuel prices rose, the utility was forced to sell the Indian Point 3 and Astoria 6 plants to PASNY. By this time Con Ed and its fellow utilities were mired in environmental litigation as consumers and ratepayers united to fight off the rate increases as well as destruction of their personal consumption space.

In 1962 Con Ed announced plans for a massive 2,020-Mw pumped-storage project atop Storm King Mountain near Cornwall on the Hudson, 50 miles north of New York City. In the early 1960s, when the Storm King proposal was first under consideration, the utility was having difficulty meeting the daytime demand of the "electric revolution" then sweeping Manhattan's office district, with its central air conditioning, computers, and electric typewriters. Con Ed's infamous "brown outs," at the time common in the metropolitan area, were a direct result of the utility's earlier refusal to link up with PASNY power in deference to its own, more profitable, generating system. However, the postwar shift in peak demand from night (home) to day (office) use also created a situation where excess energy could be stored at night in high reservoirs for release when demand was greatest. In effect the utility proposed to pump river water up to a 240-acre reservoir 1,000 feet above the river and behind Storm King Mountain. During the day the release of 8 billion gallons through a 2-mile, 40-foot tunnel through the mountain to a river powerhouse would generate 2,000 Mw for 11 hours. This was an amount deemed sufficient to meet the then-current shortfall.[117]

The Storm King project, however, was to be located in a scenic area long favored as a country retreat by upper-class residents and recreationists. This clash of production needs with consumption space resulted in a challenge by the Scenic Hudson Preservation Conference, thus setting the stage for one of the longest environmental battles ever waged in the nation's courts (Chapter 6).[118] Although the commonly accepted distinction of being the "birthplace" of the modern environmental movement is open to debate, Storm King did serve as a cause célèbre among the well-funded and preexisting landscape and historic preservation interests active in the Hudson Valley.

Nelson Rockefeller was a major proponent of the project. As governor, he was forced into a lengthy series of administrative and legal maneuvers to support the proposal.[119] Although the Storm King proposal ultimately failed, Rockefeller successfully labored to assure Con Ed's access to other inexpensive sources of power (Chapter 6). In addition to the creation of a Hudson River Valley Commission, designed to lobby for "socially necessary" and "environmentally acceptable" projects such as Storm King, Rockefeller instructed PASNY to provide pumped-storage and nuclear power-generating facilities after Storm King and several other private projects became entangled in environmental litigation. With a proven record of low-cost delivery, PASNY had the added advantage of eminent domain, allowing it to override local regulations blocking its projects.[120]

In 1968 PASNY proposed a pumped-storage facility near Gilboa, site of a small hamlet destroyed in 1919 by construction of New York City's Schoharie Reservoir (Map 4.1). Despite PASNY's assurance that the project would bring economic development to the north Catskill agrarian county of Schoharie, residents were upset and viewed the facility and its connecting transmission lines as yet another intrusion born of extraregional power demands. In 1969 the project received a federal operating license and a few years later began delivering power to upstate utilities (since Con Ed was not yet approved as one of PASNY's customers). In 1971 a second 1,000-Mw pumped-storage project and accompanying transmission line, designed to meet Con Ed's alleged needs, were suggested for North Blenheim, a hamlet a few miles downstream from the Gilboa site. Outraged local residents and farmers, whose land would be condemned for the project, forced PASNY to abandon the proposal. The authority's futile attempt to muster support for the project through provision of adjoining parks and recreational amenities (consumption space) had not mollified those whose homes and farms would be flooded. Although eclipsed at the local level by PASNY's power of eminent domain, they were bolstered by the 1970 National Environmental Policy Act (NEPA) requiring the Federal Power Commission to prepare an environmental impact statement for major projects that it licensed.[121]

The project was resurrected in 1973 for Breakabeen, yet another hamlet a few miles downstream from North Blenheim. Here destruction of 900 acres of what the state Office of Planning Services had designated as the "highest viability farmland" became the decisive issue, in particular as the state had recently enacted an agricultural districting law designed to protect prime farming areas. Finally, in 1976, PASNY proposed that a 500-acre reservoir behind a 3.6-mile earth dam be constructed at Prattsville in neighboring Greene County, with the existing Schoharie Reservoir serving as the lower catch basin. In 1985, following ten years of court challenges, the Federal Energy Regulatory Commission denied the license on grounds that the project failed to meet state water quality standards for wildlife and, in particular, threatened the highly rated fishing in creeks emptying out of the Schoharie Reservoir. Local residents and sports enthusiasts had prevailed.[122]

The Armor Is Pierced

In 1962 Rachel Carson's *Silent Spring* was published. It dealt with the ubiquitous spread of pesticides throughout the environment.[123] Although certainly not alone in sounding the alarm, within a few years her masterpiece was hailed as the most significant contribution of its generation. Seemingly overnight, residents across the nation awoke to discover that environmental contamination was not just an unpleasant feature of the degraded production space and central-city slums left behind. Suddenly the threat appeared everywhere: in the water they drank, the air they breathed, and the food they ate. The sanctum of private suburban consumption space had been breached and a national political movement thus was born (Chapter 6).

NEPA took effect in 1970, the same year that the Earth Day Teach-In involved millions of people in one of the largest grassroots displays of political and social concern ever organized in this nation. NEPA's most important provision required that an environmental impact statement (EIS) be prepared for major federal actions significantly affecting the human environment. Among the actions included were licensing procedures by the Nuclear Regulatory Commission (for nuclear power plants), by the Federal Power Commission (for all power plants, transmission lines, and storage projects in or adjoining any of the streams or water bodies over which Congress has jurisdiction), and by the U.S. Army Corps of Engineers (for encroachment on a navigable stream). As a consequence, major energy facilities, whether constructed by a private or public entity, would now be subject to stringent environmental review procedures. Power plants also had to meet the requirements of the Federal Clean Air Act of 1970 and the Federal Water Pollution Control Act of 1972.[124] Local residents and those opposed to power plants, transmission lines, and other major land uses attracting federal attention now had some powerful weapons with which to attack the armor of eminent domain worn by the state's public authorities.

By the early 1970s concern over the impact of large power-generating projects had spread beyond parochial issues, such as damage to property values, to embrace a much broader statewide and even national constituency. The state's public authorities, and in particular PASNY, were no longer politically sheltered from the growing environmental backlash against heretofore feebly regulated development. From now on their projects would also come under the jurisdiction of newly enacted environmental quality review legislation. With the private sector continuing to unload unprofitable and locally unwanted ventures on PASNY, the authority found itself burdened by mid-decade with several controversial projects that the private sector could not complete or site on its own. In addition to the aforementioned pumped-storage projects and several partially completed nuclear power plants purchased from Niagara Mohawk and Con Ed, PASNY was saddled with a problematic 765-kilovolt (kv) transmission line running from Massena (near the St. Lawrence) to Marcy (near Utica—Map 4.1). PASNY accepted responsibility for constructing the 155-mile line to be used for the import of Quebec hydropower from Con Ed when the latter ran into financing problems and vociferous local opposition over route selection. With its power of eminent domain, ease of access to investment capital, and exemption from demonstrating public need under licensing procedures, PASNY was a likely candidate for the controversial project.

However, whereas earlier transmission lines from the Niagara and St. Lawrence projects had been sited over the objections of local municipalities, the coalition of farmers, environmentalists, and students formed to fight the Massena-to-Marcy line now had the federally mandated review procedures through which to work. They thus forced major realignments to the line and also managed to have the state legislature remove PASNY's immunity from demonstration of need.[125]

PASNY's battles with environmentalists and landowners were not confined to just transmission lines and pumped-storage projects. In 1975 the authority sought approval for a 1,200-Mw nuclear facility at Cementon in Greene County. This was designed to supply power to the New York Metropolitan Transportation Authority as well as to several upstate utilities having siting problems. The proposed reactor, to be located on a scenic stretch of the Hudson, met with broad local resistance (Chapter 6). When coupled with declining demand projections, escalating capital costs, and growing national attention to the environmental impact of nuclear power development following the Three Mile Island disaster, the opposition was sufficient to force PASNY to abandon the venture in 1979.[126] On Staten Island a 700-Mw coal- and refuse-fired plant, announced by the authority in 1978, was approved by the New York State Board on Electric Generation Siting and the Environment despite continuing opposition from New York City. The city, however, refused to abide by the decision. Through delays in infrastructure connections (water, gas, and transportation), over which it still had authority, the city managed to block construction and PASNY subsequently withdrew its application.[127]

SPECIAL FACILITY SITING LEGISLATION IN NEW YORK STATE

By the early 1970s it was already evident that PASNY could no longer be counted on to push power projects through an increasingly complicated regulatory process where hostile local consumption interests had standing to participate. The authority (and, by inference, other public authorities) had lost its shield as an agent of the real quiet revolution. The alternative of state site selection in advance of need, as promoted by Rockefeller for nuclear plants through his Atomic and Space Development Authority, had also proven insufficient. Environmentalists and local opponents were still able to block plant construction through recourse to the newly enacted federal and state environmental legislation. In any case, the major problem confronting the utility industry was not land assembly for facility development, but rather uncertainty and delay arising from a complex regulatory process and the resulting escalation in capital costs required to ride out the lengthy process leading to plant approval.[128]

In response to this impasse, utilities, business lobbies, and other forces of production came somewhat reluctantly to the conclusion that direct state preemption of local land use regulation coupled, where possible, with regulatory streamlining was now warranted. In effect, controversial developments (power plants, transmission lines, hazardous waste treatment facilities, and others previously sited by local governments and, where necessary, by heretofore inconspicuous authorities) were now automatically thrust into the state arena due to the new federal and state regulations. From a development perspective then, the local level of regulation was, at best, a redundant level of bureaucracy. With the siting crisis of the early 1970s, power plants and hazardous waste management facilities received the most attention across the nation.

Power Plant Siting

At the national level the Nixon administration responded to the "energy crisis" with a proposal for states to establish one-stop power plant siting agencies. The threat of federal preemption of state and local decisions was held out should the states fail to accept their "fair share" of the nation's electric generation needs.[129] Although federal legislation never passed, the states began enacting power plant siting laws on their own.[130]

New York was one of the first to do so, prompted by an aggressive governor and industry frustration over environmental delay tactics. In 1970 Article 7 of the Public Service Law was enacted. It vested in the Public Service Commission authority for gas and electric transmission line siting, together with the power to preempt local regulations standing in the way of commission-approved projects.[131] This was followed two years later by Article 8 of the Public Service Law, which created the New York State Board on Electric Generation Siting and the Environment (hereafter also referred to as the board). The board consisted of designated representatives of the Public Service Commission, the State Energy Office, the Departments of Environmental Conservation and Commerce (all governor appointees), and one "private citizen" residing in the area proposed for a power plant.[132] Under the new law, PASNY and the utilities were required to prepare full applications and environmental impact statements on two sites for all steam generation electric plants of 50 Mw or more. The board's final authority for siting decisions would be binding on other state agencies and local governments.

The liberal planning reform movement leaves us with the impression that the state energy facility siting movement sweeping the nation in the 1970s was in response to broad popular disenchantment with the local level of regulation.[133] To be sure, power plant opponents were active on a state or regional level, especially where local regulation was overly accommodating to development. Nevertheless, by this period municipal resistance to large-scale energy development was sufficiently widespread that the opposition frequently had the regulatory means available at the local level to block construction (e.g., at Storm King; Cementon; for the Massena-to-Marcy transmission line; and on Staten Island, where the PASNY plant was actually approved by the state siting board).

In New York State environmental and social advocates were already well organized through the Storm King and Schoharie battles. Here Articles 7 and 8 were a compromise between the utilities and environmental and home rule advocates, rather than a reflection of broad popular pressure for reform. In return for a formalized system of public participation, extension of the siting laws to include the state power authority, and, by 1976, an independent assessment (by the State Energy Office) of demand binding on siting decisions, the utilities secured state preemption of obstructive local regulations and a consolidated state permit hearing process. Joining with the municipal lobbyists, environmentalists actually sought a greater role for local governments in the siting process. On Long Island, for example, environmental advocates, far from spearheading the push for preemption, joined with local residents and Suffolk County in forceful opposition to LILCO's Shoreham nuclear facility as it neared completion. Despite these protests, the plant was certified by the siting board. Even among those environmental groups favoring a single unified state hearing board (e.g., New York's Environmental Planning Lobby), none suggested complete state preemption of local regulation.[134]

In retrospect, following more than 15 years in application, Article 8 had many impacts unforeseen by its original sponsors and opponents. On the one hand, the requirement of an independent forecast of electric power demand (added as an amendment to Article 8) forced the New York State Power Pool to adopt a more conservative outlook and assisted the industry in adjusting to declining rates of energy consumption and the escalating cost of capital. Thus, for example, Rochester Gas and Electric could not build a nuclear plant on Lake Ontario in the Town of Sterling when the long-range forecast predicted a generating surplus for the 1980s. Under forced consideration of alternate generation systems and sites, New York State Electric and Gas's application for a nuclear plant on Lake Cayuga ended in a license for a cost-effective coal-fired plant on Lake Ontario, while LILCO's proposal for a double reactor at Jamesport (Long Island) was approved as a single coal-fired plant.[135] On the other hand, the law, designed ostensibly to speed the review process and bypass "unreasonable" local opposition, actually served to focus the diffuse but growing public opposition to siting proposals. Environmentalists no longer found local input necessary to hinder project approval. Joining now with statewide consumer advocates concerned about rate escalation accompanying capital expansion, they were quick to exploit the new legislation and alliance for maximum impact.[136]

As the current situation stands, the power plant siting process has ground to a halt. While uncertainty and delay due to local and environmental challenges had exacted a toll, the major reason for the lack of commitment to new plants springs from the utilities' ongoing financial crisis, in no small part associated with broad partnership in Niagara Mohawk's Nine Mile Two nuclear plant and with LILCO's Shoreham debacle. Over a decade behind schedule and more than 1,000 percent over original projected costs, the two plants may well rank as the two most expensive commercial power plants ever built per kilowatt output. With PASNY's access to relatively inexpensive Quebec hydropower, flexibility in setting rates, and lower capital borrowing costs, the authority will probably maintain its dominance in power generation and import for private distribution, even as it attempts to ward off demands from the private utilities that it assume responsibility for the two troubled reactors.[137]

Hazardous Waste Facility Siting

In addition to power plants and transmission lines, several other noxious types of land use required state intervention were they to be located. In 1976 legislation was enacted for state siting control over liquefied natural gas terminals.[138] With Staten Island the only targeted candidate for such a terminal, local opposition was minimal. The provision of hazardous waste treatment, storage, and disposal facilities, however, was of far greater concern, especially following the 1978 discovery of the Hooker chemical dump at Love Canal in Niagara Falls.

Industry in New York State generates approximately 400,000 tons of hazardous waste each year. Of this amount, over 90 percent is produced by less than 100 firms. About one-third of the total generated originates in Erie and Niagara counties, where the chemical and metal-refining firms were drawn through PASNY's provision of inexpensive hydroelectric power. Although the state has several commercial waste disposal facilities and provides better treatment for a greater share of its wastes than the national average, almost one-third of the wastes generated statewide receives improper treatment or no treatment at all.[139] Under new, stricter federal and state regulations adopted over the last decade, the treatment shortfall may well rise.

One form of public reaction to Love Canal and similar hazardous waste horror stories appeared through restrictive local land use controls and other measures designed to stall new waste disposal siting. At Love Canal irate residents led by Lois Gibbs formed the Love Canal Homeowners Association to lobby for state and federal remedial action. Organized on a purely political platform, with no claim to hotly debated scientific expertise, the grassroots effort quickly escalated, spinning off allied groups at other waste sites across the state and nation.[140] By 1979 the impasse had reached a point where a report to the Environmental Protection Agency concluded that the loss of faith by local communities in the ability of state and federal governments to solve environmental problems, while also protecting local interests, was the primary obstacle to implementing a successful hazardous waste treatment and siting program.[141]

In New York State, as elsewhere, the major lobby groups for industrial production were frustrated by federal and state regulations and by the growing local hostility to the siting of chemical plants, waste disposal sites, and other potentially hazardous facilities. In 1980 they united to form the Business Council of New York State. The Business Council became the dominant voice for industry in Albany and a major force shaping state hazardous waste policy. Through its Public Policy Institute, set up to conduct "solid and objective research," the Business Council successfully lobbied for state preemption of local land use regulations necessary to site an otherwise approved waste disposal facility.[142] With statewide environmental organizations leery of individual municipal control, particularly in industrial communities and where noxious public dumps already existed, conditions were ripe for legislative action.

Earlier, in 1970, the Environmental Facilities Corporation (EFC) was created by Rockefeller as a public authority with responsibility to assist in the construction and operation of air and water pollution control facilities. In 1980 the legislature directed the EFC to oversee construction of a high-capacity, privately run, disposal-incineration facility on state-owned land. Public landownership was considered necessary to bypass land use regulations that would be hastily enacted in localities under consideration for the plant.[143] In addition, state ownership of, and assumption of liability for, the plant was a significant goal for industries because they thought it would reduce public concern over site maintenance.

Subsequently an exhaustive search began to site the recommended high-technology facility. Attention eventually focused on Rochester Gas and Electric's 2,800-acre Sterling site on Lake Ontario in Cayuga County. By 1983 progress on the project had ground to a halt with the electric company hesitant to sell the potential power plant site, and the state under pressure from local and environmental concerns to abandon its plan and focus instead on measures designed to reduce the amount of hazardous waste generated in the production process.

While the Sterling waste treatment proposal collapsed, land use legislation first enacted in 1978 directs the governor to establish a hazardous waste disposal siting board whenever an application is received from the private sector or a public agency to construct a hazardous waste management, disposal, or treatment facility. The board is composed of five state agency heads and, depending upon the location of the proposed facility, only two local representatives. Operating in a manner similar to the New York State Board on Electric Generation Siting and the Environment, the ad hoc hazardous waste siting board holds consolidated hearings with the Department of Environmental Conservation and other state agencies and has final decision on project approval. Local control over the siting process is further diminished through a 1987 amendment to the siting act removing municipal ability to require conformity with local land use regulations in place at the time a facility is proposed. Now no municipal government may require any siting or operational condition, including conformity with local zoning and land use ordinances, for a facility that has been certified by the state siting board.[144]

CONCLUSION

With the state's industrial economy in a deep recession and hazardous waste producers operating at reduced capacity, the pressure for additional waste disposal sites slackened somewhat following the Sterling debacle. As of 1987 the hazardous waste siting board had yet to locate a facility, and the only projects under consideration, a proposal by the EFC to bury polychloridated biphenyls (PCBs) dredged from the Hudson and a new incinerator at an existing commercial waste management site, were only slowly advancing.[145] In this respect, industrial malaise had a greater immediate impact on power plant, waste disposal, and other types of large-scale infrastructure development than the administrative "red tape," and "obstructionist" environmental tactics cited by the corporate-sponsored wing of the liberal planning reform movement.[146]

Today, as in the past, pressure for reform continues to articulate with the pace of economic expansion and the local resistance to the environmental, social, and fiscal strains accompanying growth. Whereas public authorities in New York State and elsewhere have been a fundamental component of this land use reform effort, and still continue to enjoy strong support from business concerns both as investment vehicles and as agents of the real quiet evolution, they are now coming under more critical review as consumer advocates and local consumption interests challenge their former autonomy. With state special facility siting legislation at best an unreliable alternative to the use of public authorities for infrastructure, energy, and industrial development (due to more accessible and visible public participation), production interests are in a quandary where local interests cannot be won over by the promise of more jobs or tax revenues.

One important outcome of this stalemate was a move by project sponsors to have the federal courts and executive branch intervene on behalf of those controversial developments that can be declared of national significance. As consumption interests captured local and then state political power, federal intervention to facilitate economic development became the next logical extraregional arena in which to dilute spatially focused consumption movements. For example: the Carter administration proposed a Nuclear Siting and Licensing Act in 1978 to reassert federal authority and facilitate plant siting when individual states enacted restrictive ordinances on nuclear power development. More recently, there was a series of federal court rulings limiting the ability of individual communities to reject toxic waste facilities acceptable under guidelines of the federal toxic substance control and siting laws.[147]

As emphasized in this chapter, environmental groups and consumption interests generally resisted the push for state preemption of municipal land use regulation through use of public authorities, and they only reluctantly supported state facility siting legislation when confronted with growth-oriented municipal administrations. Whereas the antigrowth forces played only a minor role in the promotion of these two agencies of development, it is with the third element in New York's arsenal of regional land use mechanisms, i.e., designation of "critical" environmental, resource, and development areas, where we find the clearest expression of consumption and environmental support. In Chapter 5 critical area designation is addressed. Although most of the quiet revolution literature centers on critical area protection to support the popular view that state intervention is a recent phenomenon born of environmental concern, even here we find input from development forces. As we shall see, the designation of special areas requiring state intervention is not the unqualified expression of environmental concern portrayed in the literature. Rather it is another manifestation of the dual pressures placed upon the State (at all levels) in a system where production and consumption require one another and yet, in their actual spatial realization, are often antagonistic.

NOTES

1. See John Delafons, *Land Use Controls in the United States*, 2d ed. (Cambridge, MA: MIT Press, 1969); Leonard Downie, Jr., *Mortgage on America* (New York: Praeger, 1974); Marion Clawson, *Suburban Land Conversion in the United States* (prepared for Resources for the Future) (Baltimore: Johns Hopkins University Press, 1971); and Mark Gottdeiner, *Planned Sprawl* (Beverly Hills, CA: Sage, 1977).

2. Cf. Fred Bosselman and David Callies, *The Quiet Revolution in Land Use Control* (prepared for the U.S. Council on Environmental Quality) (Washington, DC: Government Printing Office, 1971); William Reilly, ed., *The Use of Land: A Citizen's Policy Guide to Urban Growth* (Report by the Task Force on Land Use and Urban Growth, sponsored by the Rockefeller Brothers Fund) (New York: Thomas Y. Crowell, 1973); American Law Institute, *A Model Land Development Code* (Washington, DC: American Law Institute, 1975); and Robert Healy, *Land Use and the States* (prepared for Resources for the Future) (Baltimore: Johns Hopkins University Press, 1976).

3. Annmarie Walsh, *The Public's Business: The Politics and Practices of Government Corporations* (Cambridge, MA: MIT Press, 1978), p. 4. See also Jameson Doig, "'If I See a Murderous Fellow Sharpening a Knife Cleverly . . .': The Wilsonian Dichotomy and the Public Authority Tradition," *Public Administration Review* 43 (July-August 1983):294.

Annmarie Walsh provides the most thorough history and critique of the use of public authorities to promote business-serving projects as in the "public interest." Her main concern involves the lack of effective economic and political tests of the efficiency and accountability of public authorities. Since many authorities produce goods and services under monopoly or controlled scarcity conditions, management efficiency is not contingent on consumer choice (Walsh, *Public's Business*, pp. 6ff.). Furthermore, the claim to efficiency by virtue of self-support is, in her opinion, a convenient fiction used to protect administrative autonomy. In practice many authorities, including the Urban Development Corporation and the Metropolitan Transportation Authority, are heavily subsidized through direct legislative grants during difficult periods and when they undertake projects with only limited revenue-producing potential. See also New York State, Office of the Comptroller, *Statewide Public Authorities: A Fourth Branch of Government?* New York State Comptroller's Studies on Issues in Public Finance, 2 vols. (Albany: Office of the Comptroller, 1972), 1:10-11.

4. Walsh, *Public's Business*, pp. 14-22. See also Robert Caro, *The Power Broker* (New York: Vintage Books, 1975), p. 615.

5. Walsh, *Public's Business*, p. 14. See also James Weinstein, *The Corporate Ideal in the Liberal State: 1900-1918* (Boston: Beacon Press, 1968), on the National Civic Federation.

6. Doig, "If I See a Murderous Fellow," p. 295. At the national level the Tennessee Valley Authority (created in 1933), Federal Home Loan Bank Board (1934), St. Lawrence Seaway Corporation (1954), Corporation for Public Broadcasting (1957), U.S. Postal Service (1970), and Amtrak (1970) are several well-known public authorities chartered by Congress.

7. Walsh, *Public's Business*, pp. 5, 118-19.

8. Ibid., pp. 5-6, 306-7. In New York State local governments may establish authorities on their own. However, a special act of the state legislature is required to form a local or state authority with power to incur debt *and* collect rentals, fees, and tolls for services provided (New York State, Department of State, *Local Government Handbook*, 2d ed. [Albany: Department of State, 1982], pp. 139-40).

9. U.S., Bureau of the Census, *1977 Census of Governments*, Governmental Organizations, vol. 1 (of 7), no. 1 (Washington, DC: Government Printing Office, 1978). See Victor Jones, "Bay Area Regionalism," in *The Regionalist Papers*, 2d ed., ed. K. Mathewson (Southfield, MI: Metropolitan Fund, 1977), pp. 133-59, on special purpose agencies in the San Francisco Bay Area.

10. New York State, Office of the Comptroller, *Statewide Public Authorities*, 1:i (introductory letter to the legislature from Comptroller Arthur Levitt). By 1981 the state's authority debt had mushroomed to five times that of the state through its own general obligation bonds. This peak was spurred on, in part, through creation of the Municipal Finance Corporation to assist New York City's reentry into the bond market during its fiscal crisis (Annmarie Walsh and James Leigland, "The Only Planning Game in Town," *Empire State Report* 9 [May 1983]:6, 10).

11. *Business Week*, "Borrowing Gets Harder and the Demand Intensifies," October 26, 1981, pp. 154-55. See also Walsh, *Public's Business*, pp. 149-54.

General obligation municipal and state bonds have been used to finance infrastructure and services (including job training, vocational education, and health care programs) that develop human capital. In a tight bond market, however, these bond offerings were at a competitive disadvantage against authority bonds used to finance development for direct use by private enterprise. This situation was sapping investment needed for continued economic growth and presented a crisis for capital as a class. With support from business organizations and other representatives of collective class interest, the Reagan administration indicated its intent to curb the tax-exempt status of industrial development bonds. Nevertheless, even here large-scale individual interests prevailed and the proposed cut only affected bond offerings of $10 million or less, used primarily to fund construction by merchant and competitive (small-scale) firms (*Business Week*, "Borrowing Gets Harder," p. 154).

12. See James O'Connor, *The Fiscal Crisis of the State* (New York: St. Martin's Press, 1973), pp. 180-83; and Manuel Castells, *The Economic Crisis and American Society* (Princeton, NJ: Princeton University Press, 1980), pp. 69-72, 124-25, 152-53.

13. Walsh, *Public's Business*, pp. 158-61. Even here bond investors were saved through government subsidies and higher authority tolls (ibid., p. 158). See Michael Blumstein, "The Lessons of a Bond Failure," New York *Times*, August 14, 1983, pp. III-1, 24; and *Business Week*, "The Fallout from 'Whoops,'" July 11, 1983, pp. 80-82, 86-87, on the failure of Washington Public Power Supply System to service a $2.25 billion obligation, the initial issue on a much larger $24 billion nuclear power plant construction program.

14. Annmarie Walsh and James Leigland, "The Authorities: $24 Billion in Debt and Still Growing," *Empire State Report* 9 (July 1983):33, 35.

15. Walsh, *Public's Business*, p. 302.

16. Cf. *Business Week*, "Special Report: State and Local Government in Trouble," October 26, 1981, p. 151; and Doig, "If I See a Murderous Fellow," p. 297. See also Robert Wood, *1400 Governments: The Political Economy of the New York Metropolitan Region* (Cambridge, MA: Harvard University Press, 1961); Michael Danielson and Jameson Doig, *New York: The Politics of Urban Regional Development* (Berkeley and Los Angeles: University of California Press, 1982), pp. 181-83; Moody's Investors Service, *Moody's Municipal & Government Manual*, 2 vols. (New York: Moody's Investors Service, 1981), 2:2385; and Caro, *Power Broker*, p. 930.

17. Frederick Bird, *A Study of the Port of New York Authority* (New York: Dun & Bradstreet, 1949), p. 34.

18. Caro, *Power Broker*, pp. 615-19, 623-30; and Bird, *Port of New York Authority*, pp. 44-50.

19. Joan Aron, "The New York Interstate Metropolis," in *Regional Governance: Promise and Performance. Volume 2: Case Studies*, Advisory Commission on Intergovernmental Relations, 8 vols. (Washington, DC: Government Printing Office, 1973), p. 207; Walsh, *Public's Business*, pp. 172-75; and Walsh and Leigland, "Only Planning Game in Town," p. 7.

20. Moody's Investors Service, *Moody's Municipal & Government Manual*, 2 vols. (New York: Moody's Investors Service, 1987), 2:3865.
    Ronan, a close associate of Nelson Rockefeller throughout his administration, received numerous personal financial "gifts" for his allegiance. Appointed as the first chair of the Metropolitan Transportation Authority (MTA) in 1968, he also served as chair of the Port Authority (1974-77) and sat on the board of the Power Authority of the State of New York (Walsh, *Public's Business*, pp. 267, 270; and Danielson and Doig, *Politics of Urban Regional Development*, pp. 232, 248-49).

21. Walsh, *Public's Business*, p. 14. President Eisenhower was specifically referring to the federal Tennessee Valley Authority.

22. Caro, *Power Broker*, pp. 918-19, 967-74; and Walsh, *Public's Business*, p. 155.

23. Walsh, *Public's Business*, pp. 89-90; Walsh and Leigland, "Only Planning Game in Town"; and Bird, *Port of New York Authority*. In 1931 the authority took

over operation of the preexisting Holland Tunnel (connecting lower Manhattan and Jersey City). The two states transferred the large revenue producer to the authority to help it through early credit difficulties.

24. Moody's Investors Service, *Municipal & Government Manual* (1987), 2:3872-73; Walsh and Leigland, "Only Planning Game in Town," p. 7; and Walsh, *Public's Interest*, pp. 89-90.

25. Fitch Investors Service Inc., *The Port Authority of New York and New Jersey, Municipal Bond Report*, no. 286 (December 3, 1981); and Walsh, *Public's Business*, pp. 99-102.

26. See Caro, *Power Broker*, pp. 1135-49; and Danielson and Doig, *Politics of Urban Regional Development*, pp. 227-33. The MTA is the nation's least representative major transit authority. All of its members are appointed by the governor (Walsh, *Public's Business*, p. 189).

27. Myer Kutz, *Rockefeller Power* (New York: Simon and Schuster, 1974), pp. 190-94; Betty Hawkins, "New York's Environmental Impact Tussle," *Empire State Report* 1 (February-March 1975):64-67, 93-95; and Danielson and Doig, *Politics of Urban Regional Development*, pp. 134-36.

28. Ralph Richardson, Jr. and Gilbert Tauber, eds., *The Hudson Basin: Environmental Problems and Institutional Response* (Report sponsored by the Rockefeller Foundation), 2 vols. (New York: Academic Press, 1979), 1:56-57; Kutz, *Rockefeller Power*, p. 195; and Hawkins, "Environmental Impact Tussle," pp. 66-67.

29. Michael Dorman, "The Bigger They Are," *Empire State Report* 9 (May 1983):16-18. The Queens committee has also challenged MTA and UDC activities.

30. Moody's Investors Service, *Municipal & Government Manual* (1987), 2:3865-69; Fitch Investors Service, *Port Authority*; and Danielson and Doig, *Politics of Urban Regional Development*, pp. 244-50. See Regional Plan Association of New York, *Financing Public Transportation, Regional Plan News*, no. 98 (1976), for the suggestion (subsequently implemented) that tolls and gasoline taxes be raised to fund mass transit.

31. Port Authority of New York and New Jersey. Committee on the Future, *Regional Recovery—The Business of the Eighties* (New York: Port Authority of New York and New Jersey, 1979); Isabel Wilkerson, "Dean Witter Agrees to Lease 24 Floors of the Trade Center," New York *Times*, July 9, 1985, pp. B1, 4; and Peter Goldmark, Jr., "The Economy of the New York-New Jersey Metropolitan Region," in *New York State Today: Politics, Government, Public Policy*, ed. P. Colby (Albany: State University of New York Press, 1985), pp. 257-65.

32. See Walsh, *Public's Business*, p. 223; Caro, *Power Broker*, pp. 1140-41; and Danielson and Doig, *Politics of Urban Regional Development*, pp. 227-44.

33. Ari Goldman, "State Agencies Take Command of Conrail Lines," New York *Times*, January 3, 1983, p. B4; and New York *Times*, "Coliseum Complex Is Put Up for Sale," February 5, 1985, p. B3. The New York Coliseum was built on land condemned by Moses in his capacity as New York City's Coordinator of Construction, one of many powerful positions he held (Jeanne Lowe, *Cities in a Race with Time* [New York: Random House, 1967], p. 49). As the city's primary exhibition hall it would, in any case, become obsolete once the UDC's new Jacob Javits Exposition and Convention Center opened.

34. James Underwood and William Daniels, *Governor Rockefeller in New York:*

The Apex of Pragmatic Liberalism in the United States (Westport, CT: Greenwood Press, 1982), pp. 164-65; and Walsh, *Public's Business*, p. 263.

35. New York State, Office of the Comptroller, *Statewide Public Authorities*, vol. 1.

36. Eugene Gleason and Joseph Zimmerman, "Executive Dominance in New York State" (Paper presented at the Annual Meeting of the Northeastern Political Science Association, Saratoga Springs, New York, November 11, 1978), pp. 21-22.

37. Hawkins, "Environmental Impact Tussle," p. 64; and Walsh, *Public's Business*, pp. 263-64.

38. Walsh, *Public's Business*, p. 129.

39. New York State, Moreland Act Commission on the Urban Development Commission and Other State Financing Agencies, *Restoring Credit and Confidence* (Albany: Moreland Act Commission, March 31, 1976), pp. 77, 83.

40. Nelson Rockefeller as quoted by Joel Stashenko, "Rocky's 'Edifice Complex,'" Syracuse *Herald American*, October 6, 1985, pp. B1, 2. Perhaps fitting, the architectural inspiration came to Rockefeller from the Dalai Lama's palace at Lhasa, Tibet (ibid).

41. Kutz, *Rockefeller Power*, p. 97; Peter Collier and David Horowitz, *The Rockefellers: An American Dynasty* (New York: Holt, Rinehart and Winston, 1976), pp. 472-74; Stashenko, "Rocky's 'Edifice Complex'"; and William Kennedy, "Everything Anybody Ever Wanted," *The Atlantic* 251, no. 5 (1983):77-88. Today a major process of gentrification spurred by the plaza is continuing to drive low-income residents out of the area as nearby rental rates soar.

42. See Kutz, *Rockefeller Power*; and Marvin Dunn, "The Family Office: Coordinating Mechanism of the Ruling Class," in *Power Structure Research*, ed. W. Domhoff (Beverly Hills, CA: Sage, 1980), pp. 17-45, on the Rockefeller family as a powerful kinship group and for an instrumental interpretation of State activities under its direction.

43. See Richard Barnett and Ronald Müller, *Global Reach* (New York: Simon and Schuster, 1974), pp. 235-36; and David Kotz, *Bank Control of Large Corporations in the United States* (Berkeley and Los Angeles: University of California Press, 1978), pp. 134-35, 149.

44. According to Annmarie Walsh, Rockefeller was impatient and frustrated with the "impossibly bureaucratic" state Department of Public Works. His authorities allowed him to "build faster and more to his taste" by avoiding annual legislative appropriations and the multiple-permit approval process from state agencies normally required for public construction (Walsh, *Public's Business*, pp. 265-66).

45. Cf. Robert Connery and Gerald Benjamin, eds., *Governing New York State: The Rockefeller Years*, *The Academy of Political Science* 31 (May 1974); and Kutz, *Rockefeller Power*, for two opposing views on the personal benefit Rockefeller derived through his political activities, with the former totally ignoring his ties with corporate and financial capital and seeing the governor's actions as purely in the public interest.

46. On housing policy in the capitalist State: David Harvey, "Labor, Capital and Class Struggle around the Built Environment in Advanced Capitalist Societies," in *Urbanization and Conflict in Market Societies*, ed. K. Cox (Chicago: Maaroufa Press, 1978), pp. 9-38; idem, "The Urban Process under Capitalism," *International Journal of Urban and Regional Research* 2 (1978):101-31; Ann Markusen, "Class and Urban Social

Expenditure: A Marxist Theory of Metropolitan Government," in *Marxism and the Metropolis*, 2d. ed., ed. W. Tabb and L. Sawers (New York: Oxford University Press, 1984), pp. 82-100; Manuel Castells, *The Urban Question* (London: Edward Arnold, 1977); and Richard Walker, "A Theory of Suburbanization: Capitalism and the Construction of Urban Space in the United States," in *Urbanization and Urban Planning in Capitalist Society*, ed. M. Dear and A. Scott (New York: Methuen, 1981), pp. 383-429.

47. See Barry Checkoway, "Large Builders, Federal Housing Programs and Postwar Suburbanization," in *Marxism and the Metropolis*, 2d ed., ed. W. Tabb and L. Sawers (New York: Oxford University Press, 1984), pp. 152-73; Marc Weiss, "The Origins and Legacy of Urban Renewal," in *Urban and Regional Planning in an Age of Austerity*, ed. P. Clavel, J. Forester, and W. Goldsmith (New York: Pergamon Press, 1980), pp. 53-80; and Richard Walker and Michael Heiman, "Quiet Revolution for Whom?" *Annals of the Association of American Geographers* 71 (March 1981):67-83.

48. For early national reform proposals: Fred Tuemmler, "Zoning for the Planned Community," *Urban Land* 13, no. 4 (1954):3-8; Committee for Economic Development, *Guiding Metropolitan Growth* (New York: Committee for Economic Development, 1960); Fortune Magazine, *The Exploding Metropolis* (Garden City, NY: Doubleday, 1958); Urban Land Institute, *New Approaches to Residential Land Development*, Technical Bulletin no. 10 (Washington, DC: Urban Land Institute, 1961); Charles Harr, "Regionalism and Realism in Land-Use Planning," *University of Pennsylvania Law Review* 105 (1957):515-37; and Richard Babcock, "The Chaos of Zoning Administration: One Solution," *Zoning Digest* 12 (1960):1-4. Although slum clearance was progressing at a rapid pace, subsequent renewal was not forthcoming.

49. Conference on Metropolitan Area Problems, *Metropolitan Area Problems, News and Digest* 1 (1957):1-2; and Rockefeller Brothers Fund, *The Challenge to America: Its Economic and Social Aspects*, Special Studies Project Report 4, America at Mid-century Series (Garden City, NY: Doubleday, 1958), pp. 44-48.

50. Connery and Benjamin, *Governing New York State*, p. 259; also Mel Scott, *American City Planning since 1890* (Berkeley and Los Angeles: University of California Press, 1971), pp. 458-59.

51. Walsh, *Public's Business*, pp. 63, 138.

52. National Advisory Commission on Civil Disorders, *Final Report* (Washington, DC: Government Printing Office, 1968), pp. 257-63; President's Committee on Urban Housing, *A Decent Home* (Final Report of the President's Committee on Urban Housing) (Washington, DC: Government Printing Office, 1968); and National Commission on Urban Problems, *Building the American City* (Washington, DC: Government Printing Office, 1968). See Chapter 1 and Walker and Heiman, "Quiet Revolution for Whom?" for an overview of the origins and programs of the liberal planning reform movement during the 1960s and of its impact on federal policy. For additional recommendations that federal and state governments intervene to remove barriers to private-sector provision of planned unit developments and new communities: Advisory Commission on Intergovernmental Relations, *Urban and Rural America: Policies for Future Growth* (Washington, DC: Government Printing Office, 1968); American Institute of Planners, *New Communities*, Background Paper no. 2 (Washington, DC: American Institute of Planners, 1968); and American Law Institute, *Model Land Development Code*.

53. Robert Connery, "Nelson Rockefeller as Governor," *Governing New York State: The Rockefeller Years, The Academy of Political Science* 31 (May 1974):11; Connery and Benjamin, *Governing New York State*, p. 262; and Eleanor Brilliant, *The Urban Development Corporation* (Lexington, MA: Lexington Books, 1975), pp. 21-22.

54. William Reilly and S. J. Schulman, "The Urban Development Corporation: New York's Innovation," *The Urban Lawyer* 1, no. 2 (1969):138; and Brilliant, *Urban Development Corporation*, p. 76.

55. Rockefeller's advocacy for the UDC enabling legislation, against extensive opposition from the state legislature and local governments, was among the most pronounced expressions of political muscle exercised during his administration (Vincent Moore, "Politics, Planning, and Power in New York State: The Path from Theory to Reality," *Journal of the American Institute of Planners* 37 [March 1971]:73; and Louis Loewenstein, "The New York State Urban Development Corporation— Forgotten Failure or a Precursor of the Future?" *Journal of the American Institute of Planners* 44 [July 1978]:262).

56. New York State, Moreland Act Commission, *Restoring Credit*, p. 104. By 1972 the UDC controlled 90 percent of the state's Section 236 housing grants, much to the chagrin of municipal housing authorities (Brilliant, *Urban Development Corporation*, p. 51). See Walker and Heiman, "Quiet Revolution for Whom?" on the federal New Communities Program.

57. New York State, Moreland Act Commission, *Restoring Credit*, p. 103; and Moore, "Politics, Planning, and Power," p. 74.

58. Jack Newfield and Paul DuBrul, *The Abuse of Power: The Permanent Government and the Fall of New York* (New York: Viking Press, 1977), p. 25; and New York State, Moreland Act Commission, *Restoring Credit*, pp. 128-33.

59. Moore, "Politics, Planning, and Power," p. 73; and Walsh, *Public's Business*, pp. 272-73.

60. Newfield and DuBrul, *Abuse of Power*, p. 24.

61. New York State, Moreland Act Commission, *Restoring Credit*, p. 128.

62. Moore, "Politics, Planning, and Power," p. 75. Also Louella Jacqueline Long and Vernon Robinson, *How Much Power to the People? A Study of the New York State Urban Development Corporation's Investment in Black Harlem* (New York: Urban Center, Columbia University, 1971), pp. 74-76; and Reilly and Schulman, "Urban Development Corporation." The subsidiaries were set up pursuant to either the state's business corporation law (primarily for nonsubsidized commercial, industrial, and middle-income housing), or the not-for-profit corporation law and the private housing finance law (for subsidized and nonprofit construction).

63. Michael Danielson, *The Politics of Exclusion* (New York: Columbia University Press, 1976), p. 312; and Brilliant, *Urban Development Corporation*, pp. 17-19, 67-71. For favorable comments from the liberal planning reform movement: Reilly, *Use of Land*, pp. 259-61; Richard Babcock and Fred Bosselman, *Exclusionary Zoning: Land Use Regulation and Housing in the 1970s* (New York: Praeger, 1973), pp. 213-18; Raymond, Parish, Pine and Weiner Inc., *The Role of Local Government in New Community Development* (prepared for the Office of Policy Research and Development, U.S., Department of Housing and Urban Development) (Washington, DC: Department of Housing and Urban Development, 1978), pp. 71-79; and Reilly and Schulman, "Urban Development Corporation."

64.   Danielson, *Politics of Exclusion*, pp. 145, 312-20. See also Harvey Kaiser, *The Building of Cities* (Ithaca, NY: Cornell University Press, 1978), p. 86, on upstate business support for the UDC's new community program.

65.   Judith Getzels, Peter Elliot, and Frank Beal, *Private Planning for the Public Interest: A Study of Approaches to Urban Problem Solving by Nonprofit Organizations* (Chicago: American Society of Planning Officials, 1975), pp. 28-29; and Kaiser, *Building of Cities*, p. 86.

66.   On liberal planning advocacy for new communities and other large-scale, publicly assisted, development projects: Walker and Heiman, "Quiet Revolution for Whom?"; and Checkoway, "Large Builders."

67.   New York State, Office of Planning Coordination and the Urban Development Corporation, *New Communities for New York* (Albany: Office of Planning Coordination, 1970), pp. 2, 53, 57-58.

68.   See Robert Dormer, "Three New Towns," *Journal of Housing* 36, no. 2 (1979):86-89.

69.   New York State, Office of Planning Coordination, *The Buffalo-Amherst Corridor*, pamphlet (Albany: Office of Planning Coordination, 1969).

70.   See Bill Fulton, "The New Town That Works," *Planning* 46 (1980):12-13; Marty McMahon, "Radisson: For Some an American Dream," Syracuse *Herald American*, September 9, 1984, pp. L1, 3; and Kenneth Thompkins, "Radisson: Honoring the Plan," Syracuse *Post-Standard*, November 16, 1984, pp. A1, 2. As of July 1984, Radisson had approximately 1,000 middle- and upper middle-income homes, with 180 subsidized units available for the elderly and low-income families.

71.   Ari Goldman, "Audit Says Roosevelt Island Is a Burden to the Taxpayer," New York *Times*, March 21, 1980, p. B1.

72.   Charles Bennett, "Mayor Has a Plan Rivaling State's to Improve Cities," New York *Times*, March 3, 1968, pp. A1, 36; and Raymond, Parish, Pine and Weiner, *Role of Local Government*, p. 78.

73.   On the Harlem controversy: Long and Robinson, *How Much Power to the People?*; and Kutz, *Rockefeller Power*, pp. 104-8.

74.   Brilliant, *Urban Development Corporation*, pp. 132-46; and Danielson, *Politics of Exclusion*, pp. 315-21.

75.   Brilliant, *Urban Development Corporation*, pp. 137, 142-43.

76.   For example: Danielson, *Politics of Exclusion*, pp. 145, 312-15; and Raymond, Parish, Pine and Weiner, *Role of Local Government*, pp. 78-79.

77.   Robert Lindsey, "Fast Growing Suburbs Act to Limit Development," New York *Times*, December 2, 1985, p. A10.

78.   New York State, Office of Planning Coordination and the Urban Development Corporation, *New Communities*, p. 57; also Walsh, *Public's Business*, p. 161.

79.   New York State, Moreland Act Commission, *Restoring Credit*, p. 141; and Brilliant, *Urban Development Corporation*, pp. 101-2.

80.   Kutz, *Rockefeller Power*, p. 15; Loewenstein, "Forgotten Failure?" p. 265; and Walsh, *Public's Business*, p. 275.

81.   Loewenstein, "Forgotten Failure?" pp. 266-67.

82.   On the origins of this "crisis" and on attempts to resolve it in a manner benefiting large-scale financial and corporate interests: Newfield and DuBrul, *Abuse*

of Power, Roger Alcaly and David Mermelstein, eds., *The Fiscal Crisis of American Cities: Essays on the Political Economy of Urban America with Special Reference to New York* (New York: Vintage Books, 1977); and Eric Lichten, "The Development of Austerity: Fiscal Crisis in New York City," in *Power Structure Research*, ed. W. Domhoff (Beverly Hills, CA: Sage, 1980), pp. 139-71.

83.   According to the UDC's defenders, the banks pushed default on the UDC largely to discipline the state legislature for overturning the covenant preventing the Port Authority from engaging in nonprofit-making enterprises (Loewenstein, "Forgotten Failure?" p. 264).

84.   Frank Smeal as quoted by Loewenstein, "Forgotten Failure?" p. 268. Smeal was also active in the financial community's coordinated response to New York's fiscal crisis and the disciplining of its militant public employee unions (Lichten, "Development of Austerity").

85.   Until its default the UDC concentrated on housing, and some 30,000 units were constructed at a cost of over $1.5 billion, with only $200 million given to industrial and commercial construction. Following the 1975 reorganization, however, subsidized public projects were relegated to a back burner and only 5 percent of the funds went to residential projects, with middle- and upper middle-income apartments dominating (as at Battery Park City and Radisson) (Joseph Fried, "Good-bye Slum Razing: Hello Grand Hyatt," New York *Times*, July 15, 1979, p. IV-6; and Moody's Investors Service, *Municipal & Government Manual* [1987], 2:3909).

86.   New York State, Urban Development Corporation, *Annual Report for 1977* (covers the period January 1, 1975 to December 31, 1977) (New York: Urban Development Corporation, 1978); idem, *Annual Report for 1979* (New York: Urban Development Corporation, 1980); Arthur Greenspan, "UDC Goes High-Tech," *Empire State Report* 9 (March 1983):28-31; and Martin Gottlieb, "From Public Housing to Private Incentive," New York *Times*, January 27, 1985, p. I7. There is now a strong critique of the effectiveness of tax credits, public financing, industrial parks, and other supply-side incentives used to stimulate private investment. See Doreen Massey and Richard Meegan, "Industrial Restructuring versus the City," *Urban Studies* 15, no. 3 (1978):286-87; and Bennett Harrison and Sandra Kanter, "The Political Economy of States' Job-Creation Business Incentives," *Journal of the American Institute of Planners* 44 (October 1978):424-35. Critics contend that the incentives constitute a regressive redistribution of income from taxpayers to the corporate sector and generate little or no new investment that was not already planned in the absence of such subsidies.

87.   Martin Gottlieb, "U.D.C. Chief Steering Agency into New Area," New York *Times*, April 13, 1983, pp. B1, 3; idem, "New Delay Seen in Redeveloping Times Sq. Area," New York *Times*, September 20, 1985, p. B3; and Greenspan, "UDC Goes High-Tech."

88.   On the temporary ascendancy of capitalist control during periods of crisis through the transformation of the State structure: O'Connor, *Fiscal Crisis of the State*; and Castells, *Economic Crisis*.

89.   New York State, Moreland Act Commission, *Restoring Credit.* As Walsh and Leigland document, the UDC, instead of only being allowed to build out as the commission recommended, has instead gone ahead and branched out (Walsh and Leigland, "The Authorities").

90.   Allan Talbot, *Power along the Hudson* (New York: E. P. Dutton, 1972), p.

60; and Richard Hellman, *Government Competition in the Electric Utility Industry* (New York: Praeger, 1972), p. 9. The seven major private electric utility companies in New York State represent a consolidation of approximately 900 separate companies once serving the state (New York State, Governor's Committee on Power Resources, *Report to Governor Nelson A. Rockefeller* [Albany: Governor's Committee on Power Resources, December 15, 1959], p. 17).

91. Hellman, *Government Competition*, pp. 10-12; and Walsh, *Public's Business*, p. 103.

92. Hellman, *Government Competition*; and Walsh, *Public's Business*, p. 103.

California was an early leader in public power production with seven municipal power and light agencies established by 1900. Many more came on line during the 1930s following successful battles with investor-owned utilities for access to federal and state hydroelectric power (Walsh, *Public's Business*, p. 105).

93. Laws of New York (1931, Chapter 772, Section 5).

94. See Hellman, *Government Competition*, pp. 78-81.

95. Power Authority of the State of New York, *Annual Report for 1937* (Albany: Power Authority of the State of New York, March 1938), pp. 11. 14.

96. See Caro, *Power Broker*, pp. 402-25; James Brennan, "An Overview of the New York State Power Authority," in *The Future of the Power Authority of the State of New York*, Report from Joseph Ferris (chair of the Assembly Joint Subcommittee on Public Power), vol. 1 (of 2) (Albany: New York State, Legislative Commission on Science and Technology, 1984); and Power Authority of the State of New York, *Annual Report for 1953* (Albany: Power Authority of the State of New York, February 1954). Plattsburgh's incorporation of New York State Electric and Gas facilities was the only major success under Lehman's legislation (Brennan, "Overview," 1:2).

In 1962 Moses resigned in protest as chair of PASNY following a bitter struggle with Governor Rockefeller over control of the State Council of Parks, where Nelson succeeded in having his brother Laurance replace Moses as chair (Caro, *Power Broker*, pp. 1073-75).

97. Power Authority of the State of New York, *Annual Report for 1962* (Albany: Power Authority of the State of New York, 1963); and Moody's Investors Service, *Municipal & Government Manual* (1981), 2:2356.

98. New York State, Legislative Commission on Expenditure Review, *Power Authority of the State of New York*, Program Audit (Albany: Legislative Commission of Expenditure Review, November 1984), p. 2; and New York Power Authority, *Annual Report for 1985* (Albany: New York Power Authority, 1986), p. 26. See also Richard Longshore, "The Power Authority of the State of New York: Accountability and Public Policy," Ph.D. diss., Syracuse University, 1981, pp. I-47–I-58, on the Niagara project.

Moses' preference for the private utilities was clear through contracts with them for Niagara power. These typically ran longer than those negotiated with the independent municipal systems (Brennan, "Overview," 1:3).

99. New York Power Authority, *Annual Report 1985*, pp. 26-27; and New York State, Legislative Commission on Expenditure Review, *Power Authority*, pp. S-1, S-7.

100. Longshore, "Accountability and Public Policy," p. I-60; Kennedy Maize, "New York Hydro Wars," *Empire State Report* 10 (October 1984):9-12; Paulette Mandelbaum, "Affecting New York's Energy Future," *Empire State Report* 11 (July

1985):48; and Brennan, "Overview." According to a critical state assembly overview:

> Considering its origins, the Power Authority might be presupposed, at a minimum, to be neutral in its attitudes toward struggles between the investor-owned utilities, the municipally owned utilities, and municipalization movements. However, beginning with Robert Moses, the Authority has allied itself with the investor-owned utilities to conspire against public power and the hopes and dreams of its very own creators. (Brennan, "Overview," 1:6)

101.   Moody's Investors Service, *Municipal & Government Manual* (1981), 2:2356-57; Power Authority of the State of New York, *Annual Report for 1981* (Albany: Power Authority of the State of New York, 1982), pp. 25-26; and Longshore, "Accountability and Public Policy," p. I-58.

102.   Moody's Investors Service, *Municipal & Government Manual* (1981), 2:2356; and New York Power Authority, *Annual Report 1985*, p. 44. With one of the most energy-intensive production processes in the industrial world, the aluminum companies garnered public power for the thousands of jobs they provided in economically depressed northern New York.

103.   New York State, Legislative Commission on Expenditure Review, *Power Authority*, pp. 2, 11-13.

104.   Longshore, "Accountability and Public Policy," pp. I-48–I-58; Hellman, *Government Competition*, pp. 95, 98, 100; and Maize, "Hydro Wars." Niagara Mohawk, Rochester Gas and Electric, and New York State Electric and Gas also receive some Niagara hydropower for resale to their domestic and rural residential customers under limited-profit terms set by the 1957 federal license.

105.   Nelson Rockefeller, *Our Environment Can Be Saved* (Garden City, NY: Doubleday, 1970), p. 76; and David Bird, "Nuclear Power Plant Proposed beneath Welfare Island," New York *Times*, October 7, 1968, pp. A1, 93.

106.   New York State, Governor's Committee on Power Resources, *Report to Rockefeller*, p. 15 (emphasis in original).

107.   Donald Gilligan, "The Time Bomb South of Buffalo," *Empire State Report* 3 (January 1977):3-11; Gene Rochlin, Marjorie Held, Barbara Kaplan, and Lewis Kruger, "West Valley: Remnant of the AEC," *Bulletin of the Atomic Scientists* 34, no. 1 (1978):17-26; and *New York State Environment*, "NFS Announced Plans to Abandon in 1976—in Cattaraugus County—Only Commercial Nuclear Fuel Reprocessing Plant in USA" (December 1976):1, 4.

> By 1976, when Getty Oil announced plans to abandon the project, over 600,000 gallons of high-level toxic wastes were stored at the site in carbon steel tanks, with an estimated useful life of only 40 years. Negotiations then got underway, with the federal Department of Energy agreeing to cover the major portion of the $1 billion estimated cleanup cost (*New York State Environment*, "Plans to Abandon Nuclear Fuel Reprocessing Plant"; and Richard Beer, "The Tombstone of Nuclear Power?" *Seven Days*, March 28, 1977, pp. 2, 5-6).

108.   New York State, Atomic and Space Development Authority, *Nuclear Power Siting Program: Phase 1: State-wide Survey* (Albany: Atomic and Space Development Authority, c. 1970), p. 2. See also Bill Kovach, "Governor Offers Aid on Atomic Plants," New York *Times*, September 6, 1969, p. A23.

109. Cf. Rockefeller, *Environment Can Be Saved*, pp. 73-76; New York State, State Energy Office, *New York State Energy Master Plan*, Draft (Albany: State Energy Office, August 1979); New York *Times*, "Kennedy Attacks State Power Plan," July 27, 1967, p. A14; Sidney Schanberg, "Rockefeller Shifts Stand on Control of Atomic Power," New York *Times*, May 5, 1968, pp. A1, 57; and Longshore, "Accountability and Public Policy," pp. II-5–II-19.

110. Schanberg, "Rockefeller Shifts Stand."

111. See Power Authority of the State of New York, *Annual Report for 1978* (Albany: Power Authority of the State of New York, 1979), pp. 7-9; Walsh, *Public's Business*, p. 108; and Longshore, "Accountability and Public Policy," pp. II-18–II-19.

In 1985 ALCOA was the largest recipient of FitzPatrick power followed by Con Ed. The utilities could add the relatively inexpensive FitzPatrick power (compared to their own generation costs) to their general delivery system subject to withdrawal, when needed, for the benefit of public bodies and nonprofit cooperatives (New York Power Authority, *Annual Report 1985*, p. 44; and New York State, Legislative Commission on Expenditure Review, *Power Authority*, p. 12).

112. See Walsh, *Public's Business*, p. 108; David Andelman, "$500-Million Aid to ConEd Is Agreed upon in Albany," New York *Times*, April 25, 1974, pp. A1, 23; and Newfield and DuBrul, *Abuse of Power*, pp. 284-90. In 1985 Con Ed was the largest recipient of power from the two plants, followed by the New York MTA, New York City (for its public buildings), and the city's housing authority. The private utility was granted a rate increase to make up for the loss of these public customers (New York Power Authority, *Annual Report 1985*, p. 44).

113. E. J. Dionne, Jr., "Carey Signs Bill Providing Tax Benefits for Madison Square Garden," New York *Times*, July 8, 1982, p. B7; Andrew Sherry, "The Low-Profile N-Plant," Syracuse *Herald American*, July 28, 1985, pp. E1, 4; and Power Authority of the State of New York, *Annual Report for 1984* (Albany: Power Authority of the State of New York, March 1985), pp. 3-4.

114. New York State, Governor's Committee on Power Resources, *Report to Rockefeller*. As late as 1975 PASNY and the private utilities were enthusiastically promoting an additional 28,000 Mw of installed capacity by 1995, effectively doubling the state's 1974 generation. Three-quarters of this would come from 16 new nuclear plants (Power Authority of the State of New York et al., *Nuclear Power for the Empire State: A Position Paper in Support of Nuclear Power* [prepared by the Power Authority and the state's major private utilities] [New York: Power Authority of the State of New York, 1975]).

115. New York State, Department of Public Service, *An Energy Almanac: New York State 1960-1980* (Albany: Public Service Commission, 1976), p. 2; and New York State, Office of the Comptroller, *Program Review: State Energy Office. Executive Department. August 26, 1976-April 30, 1980* (Albany: Office of the Comptroller, 1980).

The 1978 Power Pool report lowered the demand forecast for the fifth straight year. At 29,580 Mw, the projected peak required capacity for 1990 was actually 13.9 percent below the 1977 estimate. With 29,000 Mw already installed or under construction, it appeared that the 1990 peak would be provided for, and there was talk of selling future excess capacity to out-of-state utilities (New York State, Legislative Commission on Energy Systems, *Legislating for Energy Independence*

[Albany: Legislative Commission on Energy Systems, 1978], p. 58). See also New York State, State Energy Office, *Master Plan.*

116. See Newfield and DuBrul, *Abuse of Power,* pp. 272-73.

117. Talbot, *Power along the Hudson,* pp. 72-89.

118. Scenic Hudson Preservation Conference v. Federal Power Commission, 354 F. 2d 608 (2d Cir. 1965), cert. denied 384 U.S. 941 (1966).

119. Talbot, *Power along the Hudson,* provides the most thorough discussion of the Storm King controversy. Cf. Kutz, *Rockefeller Power,* pp. 156-71; William Rogers, *Rockefeller's Follies: An Unauthorized View of Nelson A. Rockefeller* (New York: Stein and Day, 1966), pp. 85-118; and Rockefeller, *Environment Can Be Saved,* pp. 78-79.

120. PASNY's power had already been demonstrated in 1957 through the unprecedented condemnation of 1,400 acres of the Tuscarora Indian Reservation for the Niagara project. The seizure was ultimately upheld in the U.S. Supreme Court (Longshore, "Accountability and Public Policy," pp. I-51–I-55).

121. Cf. Schoharie County Cooperative Extension Service, *People and Power: An Impact Study of Power Projects in Schoharie County* (Cobleskill, NY: Schoharie County Cooperative Extension Service, 1972); and Cliff Spieler, "A Philosophy of Power," *The Catskills* (Spring 1973):41-44. The cooperative extension study stressed the sense of powerlessness felt by local residents when confronting a public authority immune from many of the regulations faced by private developers. See also Carl Phillips, "The Effect on Employment in Schoharie County of the Projects of the State Power Authority of New York" (Study done for Assemblyman Charles Cook [105th District, New York] by the class of Industrial and Labor Relations 368 conducted by Professor Clark Hamilton, School of Industrial and Labor Relations, Cornell University, 1977); Tom Miner, "Pumped Storage at Prattsville," *New York State Environmental News* (Atmospheric Sciences Research Center, State University of New York at Albany) 7, no. 2 (1980):1-6; and Longshore, "Accountability and Public Policy," pp. II-21–II-28.

In 1972 the Greene County Planning Board, joined by the Sierra Club, successfully sued PASNY and the Federal Power Commission to block construction of the 345-kv transmission line accompanying the North Blenheim proposal (Greene County Planning Board v. FPC, 455 F. 2d 412, 422, n.24, 2 ELR, 20017, 20021, n.24 [2d Cir. 1972]). See William Hillhouse II, "The Federal Law of Water Resources Development," in *Federal Environmental Law,* ed. E. Dolgin and T. Guilbert (prepared for the Environmental Law Institute) (St. Paul, MN: West Publishing, 1974), pp. 900-907, 912-16, on licensing procedures of the Federal Power Commission.

122. Miner, "Pumped Storage"; Harold Farber, "City Now against Using Reservoir for Power," New York *Times,* April 4, 1982, p. A39; idem, "Power Authority Is Denied Permit to Build a Plant," New York *Times,* April 10, 1982, p. A26; and New York *Times,* "State Power Agency Denied U.S. License for Upstate Project," July 14, 1985, p. A24. Local residents also anticipated the loss of the New York City reservoir from their tax base should PASNY take title to the project.

123. Rachel Carson, *Silent Spring* (Boston: Houghton Mifflin, 1962).

124. For descriptions of the major federal environmental laws and their significance for energy siting decisions: Hillhouse, "Law of Water Resources Development"; and U.S., Council on Environmental Quality, *Environmental Quality:*

The Tenth Annual Report of the Council on Environmental Quality: 1979 (Washington, DC: Government Printing Office, January 1980).

125. Laws of New York (1978, Chapter 760); Harold Farber, "Controversy over Power Lines Spreads across Upstate New York," New York *Times*, May 22, 1979, p. A49; Richard Grover, "People Power: It Can Make a Difference," *Planning News* (New York Planning Federation) 42 (March-April 1978):1, 6, 7; and Longshore, "Accountability and Public Policy," pp. II-71–II-79.

   In 1985 PASNY received state and federal approval for a new 345-kv line to connect the Marcy substation with Con Ed's distribution station at East Fishkill (southern Dutchess County—Map 4.1). Running for 200 miles through eight counties along the western and southern edge of the Catskills, the line, now under construction, has galvanized resistance all along the intended route (Harold Farber, "Ex-City Residents Lead Opposition to New Powerline Upstate," New York *Times*, August 30, 1982, p. B2; New York Power Authority, *Annual Report 1985*, p. 23; and Sara Rimer, "Power Line for City Stirs Rural Anger," New York *Times*, December 30, 1986, pp. B1, 3).

126. Power Authority of the State of New York, *Annual Report 1978*; and New York State, Legislative Commission on Expenditure Review, *Power Authority*, p. 7. In a precedent-setting move, the Nuclear Regulatory Commission recommended against granting a license. Scenic preservation was a major factor in this decision (Chapter 6).

127. Power Authority of the State of New York, *Annual Report 1984*, p. 29.

128. See the statement by Charles Luce (chair of the board for Con Ed), "Power for Tomorrow: The Siting Dilemma," *Environmental Law* 1 (1970):60-71; and Association of the Bar of the City of New York: Special Committee on Electric Power and the Environment, *Electricity and the Environment: The Reform of Legal Institutions* (St. Paul, MN: West Publishing, 1972), pp. 22-23.

129. H.R. 5277, 92d Cong., 1st sess., 1971. See also Reilly, *Use of Land*, p. 205.

130. By 1979, 32 states had power plant siting boards (Joan Aron, "Intergovernmental Politics of Energy," *Policy Analysis* 5 [Fall 1979]:455-56).

131. Article 7 of the Public Service Law: Laws of New York (1970, Chapter 272). In 1972 the county and several town governments in Orange County unsuccessfully challenged Public Service Commission approval of a Con Ed transmission line under the new act (New York State, Public Service Commission, *Annual Report for 1972* [Albany: Public Service Commission, 1973]).

132. Article 8 of the Public Service Law: Laws of New York (1972, Chapter 385). Article 8 was similar to California's Warren-Alquist Act of 1975 (the California Energy Resources Conservation and Development Act). Both called for an independent assessment of power demand and for a single state agency with authority for final siting decisions. See Aron, "Politics of Energy."

133. Cf. Robert Healy and John Rosenberg, *Land Use and the States* (prepared for Resources for the Future), 2d ed. (Baltimore: Johns Hopkins University Press, 1979), pp. 26-27, 218-19; Reilly, *Use of Land*, p. 26; and Fred Bosselman, Duane Feurer, and Charles Siemon, *The Permit Explosion: Coordination of the Proliferation* (Washington, DC: Urban Land Institute, 1976), pp. 4, 51-53.

134. See Luce, "Power for Tomorrow," p. 67, on the significance of consolidated permit proceedings and state preemption to the utility industry; and Frederick Inscho, "An Analysis of Power Plant Siting Policy in New York State," Ph.D. diss., State

University of New York at Buffalo, 1978, pp. 28-29, 101-2, on the split within environmental ranks over support for the legislation in New York State. See also New York State, Temporary State Commission on the Environmental Impact of Major Public Utility Facilities, *Final Report* (Albany: Temporary State Commission on the Environmental Impact of Major Public Utility Facilities, 1971), pp. 4-5.

135. New York State, Public Service Commission, *Annual Report for 1977* (Albany: Public Service Commission, 1978), p. 21; and Paulette Mandelbaum, "Who Runs New York's Power Plant?" *Empire State Report* 8 (May 1982):29-31.

136. New York State, Legislative Commission on Expenditure Review, *State Environmental Permits*, Program Audit (Albany: Legislative Commission on Expenditure Review, July 1977), pp. S-4, 13-16; and Steve Lawrence, "Only One Power Plant Has Been Approved in New York State since the Legislature Created the Siting Board in 1972," *Empire State Report* 4 (January 1978):14-17. Under Article 7 progress on transmission line siting far outpaced new plant siting under Article 8.

137. Power Authority of the State of New York, *Annual Report 1984*, pp. 14-15; James Cook, "Nuclear Follies," *Forbes*, February 11, 1985, pp. 85, 88; and Michael Oreskes, "State Aid Urged in Cuomo Plan for Nine Mile 2," New York *Times*, May 8, 1984, p. B1. On Long Island ratepayers and county officials are lobbying for a complete state or Power Authority purchase of financially troubled LILCO, while the utility is pushing for a more modest Power Authority takeover of the Shoreham plant.

138. Article 27 (Title 17) of the Environmental Conservation Law: Laws of New York (1976, Chapter 892).

139. New York State, Hazardous Waste Treatment Facilities Task Force, *Final Report* (Albany: Hazardous Waste Treatment Facilities Task Force, September 1985), p. v; and ERM-Northeast, *Hazardous Waste Facilities Needs Assessment, Summary Report and Appendices* (prepared for New York State, Department of Environmental Conservation, Division of Solid and Hazardous Waste) (Albany: Department of Environmental Conservation, 1985).

Under state law (Chapter 638 of the Laws of New York, 1978), hazardous wastes are defined as wastes that "may cause or significantly contribute to an increase in mortality or an increase in serious irreversible or incapacitating reversible illness, or pose a substantial present or potential hazard to human health or the environment when improperly treated, stored, transported, disposed or otherwise managed."

140. John Worthley and Richard Torkelson, "Intergovernmental and Public-Private Relations in Hazardous Waste Management: The New York Example," in *The Politics of Hazardous Waste Management*, ed. J. Lester and A. Bowman (Durham, NC: Duke University Press, 1983), pp. 102-11.

141. Centaur Associates, *Siting of Hazardous Waste Management Facilities and Public Opinion* (Report to the U.S. Environmental Protection Agency) (Washington, DC: Environmental Protection Agency, Office of Solid Waste, 1979); and U.S., Council on Environmental Quality, *Tenth Annual Report*, p. 187.

142. Public Policy Institute of New York State, *Meeting the Challenges of Hazardous Waste in New York State* (Albany: Business Council of New York State, 1981), p. i. According to the institute, "Siting is, in the main, a public education program and not a technical difficulty" (ibid., p. 31).

143. See New York State, Hazardous Waste Disposal Advisory Committee, *A Comprehensive Program for Hazardous Waste Disposal in New York State* (Albany:

Environmental Facilities Corporation, 1980); and *New York State Environment*, "High-Tech Hazardous Waste Treatment Facility Planned for Cayuga County," 10 (June 1981):2-4. In general, environmental forces favored a state-run facility, while industry favored a privately operated facility with state assumption of liability.

144.   Article 27 (Title 2) of the Environmental Conservation Law of New York State (Part 361); and Laws of New York (1987, Chapter 618).

145.   Harold Farber, "Upstate Town Resisting Role as PCB Burial Site," New York *Times*, January 3, 1986, p. B2. The PCBs originated from two General Electric plants in the Town of Fort Edward. The local group Citizen Environmentalists Against Sludge Encapsulation (Cease), organized to fight burial in the town, was typical of the marriage between self-professed environmental concerns and local consumption interests.

146.   See Walker and Heiman, "Quiet Revolution for Whom?"

147.   See Aron, "Politics of Energy"; and Philip Shabecoff, "Ruling May Stall Efforts to Block Toxic Dumps," New York *Times*, November 6, 1985, p. A16.

5

Critical Area Protection
and the Ideology of Nature

In this and the following chapters I continue examining state response to popular protest over the negative social and environmental impacts of land development. Here the focus is on state designation of "critical" environmental, resource, and development areas. Designation of critical conservation and development areas is the third element in New York's arsenal of regional land use regulatory mechanisms. As covered in the preceding chapter, the other two are use of public authorities to bypass local control of infrastructure provision, and selective state preemption of local regulation on a project-specific basis. Some of New York's best-known examples of state intervention in land use regulation are reviewed here, beginning in this chapter with attempts to set aside the Adirondack and Catskill mountains as watershed and recreation preserves, and continuing in the next with state demarcation of the Hudson Valley region as a critical area.

With the environmental protection movement scoring several impressive victories over the past two decades, particularly along the coast and in fragile mountain regions, the liberal planning reform literature is quick to point to critical area protection in support of the view that state intervention in land development is a recent phenomenon born of popular environmental concern. Yet, even here, as evident through the demarcation of the Adirondack forest preserve in the 1880s, we find input from production forces. Moreover, business interests do not merely bargain over the content of legislation designed to protect critical areas; rather, as in the past, they actively sponsor reform when it is conducive to their own goals. Insofar as protection of critical areas presents both opportunities and problems for production concerns, liberal land use reform goes further and actively seeks a balance between protection of environmentally significant areas and accommodation of socially desirable development.

This apparent contradictory push, both for development and for preservation, is actually one of the most ubiquitous features of liberal land use reform. The suggested reform is itself a response to the tension between capitalist production and consumption. Thus, production requires consumption for the realization of profit (exchange value), for without consumption there would be no basis for production, and yet consumption, when expressed through use value in the landscape, tends to present barriers to further expansion of production (Chapter 1).

NATURE AS PERSONAL CONSUMPTION SPACE

To understand the position taken by production and consumption interests in the protection of critical environmental areas, and the state role in mediating between the two, we must first step back and consider how the "environment" and "nature," the self-proclaimed objects of most critical area planning efforts, are socially defined. Most conceptions of "nature" within the physical and social sciences recognize the complex of biotic, physical, and climatic forces affecting an individual or a community. A more critical interpretation emphasizes the creation and modification of nature, as well as our commonsense conception of it, as articulating with a particular mode of production and with the social relations engendered. To take a well-known example: the commonsense view of parks, wilderness, and even of suburban greenbelts and backyards sees them as special environments from which the messy forces of production are banished. This view also accepts the protection of nature in these environments as a refuge where alienated individuals, be they workers or bourgeois owners and managers, can escape from the vigors of the workplace, there to consume the hard-earned fruits or ill-gotten gains, depending on one's point of view, of their efforts (Chapter 1).

In addition to being subjectively perceived as a refuge from the production system, nature in the form of leisure and residential consumption space objectively serves as the locus for family life and as a container for reproduction of the workforce. In this manner, the cognitive separation of space into production and consumption zones, including areas for residence, recreation, and reproduction, results from and helps to support capitalist production.

Ideology can be succinctly defined as the manner or context of thought characteristic of an individual, group, or culture. The conception of nature is itself but one of many expressions of an ideology. As with all ideologies, the specific capitalist ideological concept of nature as a refuge from production is reproduced through social practice. To the point, we cannot even acquire understanding of nature, nor knowledge of the consumption space containing this nature, without first entering into social relations. This occurs because our everyday understanding, including knowledge of nature and of human-environmental interactions, is socially produced through engagements involving experience, education, and practice. Our commonsense knowledge, in turn, helps reproduce the social systems through which this understanding is acquired. In this manner, a critique of commonsense knowledge becomes a critique of the social systems generating this knowledge.[1]

Although social position in the production system tends to dominate in the process of socialization, it is not the sole determining force in socialization or in the acquisition of knowledge and understanding. Other social institutions—some predating capitalism, such as the church and patriarchy—also influence our knowledge of nature. Nevertheless, in the absence of a true revolutionary break with existing knowledge and practice, our current understanding of nature tends to support continuation of existing dominant production relations, that is to say, capitalism. This is because most commonsense conceptions of human-environmental interaction, as those, for example, embodied in the liberal planning reform movement, reproduce knowledge of nature generated in a class-stratified production system. Here, following the famous dictum of Marx and Engels: "The ideas of the ruling class are in every epoch the ruling ideas: i.e. the class, which is the ruling material force of society, is at the same time its ruling intellectual force."[2]

In this manner the intersubjective (shared) meaning we ascribe to nature is produced by conscious social practice and yet, our experience is interpreted for us by institutions under capitalist class control. To illustrate, the identification of nature in popular literature, park planning, and even in academic discourse, with landscapes for spiritual, psychological, and biological rejuvenation lying beyond the urban fringe, is an interpretation of nature accepted and promoted by dominant elites as nonthreatening to an urban-based production system where life in the workplace is hazardous and alienating. Simultaneously, even though thousands of workers are exposed daily to toxic substances at the workplace, and typically in concentrations far exceeding those permitted for the surrounding environment, the established media still tend to define the "environmental crisis" as a contamination of this surrounding "nature" and not of the workplace.

Nature worship and psychological communion with natural forces preceded capitalism and were common features of aboriginal life and of organic (premechanistic) feudal cosmology. While perhaps receiving a biblical sanction, the dichotomy between human beings and nature only became widely accepted in European urban centers during the seventeenth century. This was the era when the mechanized view of nature as dead and available for human exploitation replaced the earlier organic view of nature as alive and integrated with the human body and spirit. The new conception of nature as an external object, divorced from human essence and character, was itself a radical departure from the classical and pre-Enlightenment interpretation of nature as a process, the undeveloped potential, if you will, of the human body and soul. In classical thought, for example, the arcadian landscape was accepted as a symbol of the normal process whereby society should develop, while pastoralists, together with the environment created by pastoralism, were identified with collective social values.[3]

The revolutionary mechanistic view of nature as dead was fostered and accepted by the emerging capitalist order because it permitted objectifying nature as a mere input into the production system to be exploited for commodity production and for human benefit. With the growth of the capitalist mode of production, new divisions appeared in social life and landscape assessment. For example: human alienation from nature in urban production districts was accompanied by workers' alienation from the product of their efforts; an aesthetic dichotomy emerged between the industrialized urban areas, where nature was transformed by labor into commodities, and what was considered the scenic rural countryside; and a view of work time as distinct from private leisure and residential (family) time took hold.[4]

The psychological alienation resulting from the vulgar materialism required by capitalist commodity production contributed, in turn, to a secondary view of nature as a place of refuge, escape, and leisure relaxation from the social and environmental turmoil generated by industrial production. Historically this focus on nature as a place of sanctuary from the dreary urban industrial scene, to be protected in pastoral, wilderness, and later in residential, landscapes, actually blossomed in Western Europe during the romantic period of the eighteenth century. Antecedents, however, could already be found in the sixteenth- and seventeenth-century experience of the rural peasantry. This was the period during which common land was being transformed into a private commodity. Thus, the classical ideology of nature as an arcadian process was already being compromised in favor of a new interpretation whereby nature became the refuge from which the impoverished peasants had been driven.

In England realization of the bucolic landscape as a refuge had to await the eighteenth century, when the wealthy landed class established great landscape parks and estates as private "natural" retreats from the expanding production system and social discord of London and the emerging production centers. Over time the bourgeoisie also came to embrace nature recovered, restored, and protected in personal recreation and residential districts, even as their industries were transforming nature into commodities elsewhere. As Raymond Williams documents, the very concept of rural landscapes as pleasing prospects for those able to afford the luxury of residing there gained strength as production areas in industrial nations became undesirable for both work and residence.[5]

Of course elite landscape tastes had to be forced upon the impoverished agrarian populace who unwittingly found themselves thrust into the new social and economic order of capitalist production. Following the enclosure movement, commodification of agriculture, and agrarian mechanization, the resulting rural landscape had become a composite of private pastoral retreats set in a countryside from where many, now landless, inhabitants had been driven to move toward the emerging urban industrial centers.

Whether or not we accept David Lowenthal and Hugh Prince's observation that "passion for the countryside [was] perhaps strongest where the cities [were] most bleak," it appears that the working class also came to share this commonsense view of nature as a refuge.[6] While we have only scant record of the actual environmental preference of the working class during the eighteenth and nineteenth centuries, the situation remains that bourgeois landscape tastes dominated literary and intellectual thought and, ultimately, everyday social practice, at least as recorded through park, rural, resort, and urban planning.

Nature as a refuge remained a private goal for the bourgeoisie during most the nineteenth century. However, the acceptance of nature as a refuge began to permeate popular consciousness already by midcentury. In industrial districts this coincided with the decline in agrarian subsistence and in household production, and with the rise of large-scale commodity production and mass consumerism characteristic of the new corporate-industrial stage of capitalist development. By the end of the century the ideological and spatial separation between the realms of individual consumption and production was well under way.

Over the last century rising material affluence, improved transportation, and a host of other public and private factors enabled the bourgeoisie as well as the working class to realize nature, in the form of leisure and residential consumption space, as a refuge from production. Nevertheless, insofar as the spatial demarcation between production and consumption was itself a response to inherent contradiction contained within the capitalist mode of production, its attainment remained problematic (Chapter 1). Thus the drive for continued economic expansion, characteristic of capitalist production relations, tended to compromise the physical and psychological integrity of sanctified consumption space. Responding to the social and environmental deterioration accompanying urban development, popular protest movements arose to defend this space. Contemporary expressions of this defense included the local antigrowth sentiment found in many wealthy residential districts, inner-city battles to prevent urban renewal of working-class neighborhoods, and the environmental movement to protect critical consumption (use value) resource areas such as aquifer recharge areas and recreation preserves.

On the one hand, these antidevelopment movements present serious barriers to further property development and expansion in the forces of production. Here production interests would aim to curtail the demarcation and defense of consumption space. On the other, producers are also consumers of renewable resources and, as such, favor protection of the resource base upon which they depend. Moreover, producers have a vested interest in the shelter, education, and other consumption concerns of their own labor force where these affect wage demand and productivity.

In brief, the identification and defense of consumption space, and the protection of lands supporting the availability of other renewable resources and the reproduction and the productivity of labor, present both solutions and barriers to expansion of capitalist production. Such is the nature of structural contradiction (Chapter 1). This ambivalence over the value of designated and protected consumption space results in uneven support by production interests for state protection of critical environmental areas. Contrary to much of the conventional planning literature, there is no readily identifiable public interest in state or regional planning for critical environmental areas. Rather, as events in the Adirondacks, the Hudson Valley (Chapter 6), and elsewhere suggest, the position taken by production as well as consumption interests is historically and spatially specific to the issue and participant interests involved.

THE ADIRONDACK MOUNTAINS: AN AREA OF SPECIAL STATE CONCERN

Occupying the northeastern quadrant of New York, the Adirondack Mountain massif ranges from the gently rolling hills of the south and west to the high peaks region of the northeast (Map 5.1).[7] Over 40 of the Adirondack mountains rise above 4,000 feet, with Mt. Marcy at 5,344 feet, the highest point in the state. The Adirondacks are remnants of an ancient Precambrian uplift, more closely related to the Laurentian Shield of Canada than to the neighboring Appalachian ranges.

Covering some 6 million acres, of which 2.5 million (42 percent) are state held and the remainder in private ownership, the Adirondack "Park" encompasses the mountain massif. The park itself is approximately the size of the state of Vermont and yet contains less than one-fourth of that state's population. Its mountains embrace the headwaters of three major drainage basins (those of the Hudson, Black, and Mohawk rivers), as well as sections of the St. Lawrence River and Lake Champlain drainage basins. As identified with the Adirondack Park boundary, the heavily forested park contains over 2,300 lakes and ponds, 1,000 miles of rivers, and 30,000 miles of brooks and streams.[8] Considered the most extensive remaining wilderness area in the eastern United States, the park region is unique in North America for the extent of riparian habitat in close proximity with mountainous terrain. This significance becomes even more apparent when one realizes that it is within a day's drive, by automobile, of some 55 million people.

The Area Left Behind Becomes a Tonic for Urban Alienation

With an extremely short growing season, shallow soils, and rugged terrain, the central Adirondack region was bypassed by the colonial settlers of the Hudson, St. Lawrence, and Mohawk river valleys. The opening of the Erie Canal in 1825 did little to improve the area's attraction, since an easy access to the rich agricultural areas of Ohio and the upper Midwest was now available. By the mid-nineteenth century, however, the logging industry had moved into the heretofore unmapped wilderness, having already denuded much of northern New England of the desirable white pine. Between 1850 and 1860 the virgin Adirondack forests helped propel New York to lead the nation in production of cut timber.[9] Most of the cutting occurred in the winter, with logs sledded out to holding ponds. With considerable ecological disruption the pond dams were broken during the spring runoff, and the logs floated to sawmills at Glens Falls and other surrounding communities.

Contemporaneous with the arrival of logging, tanning, mining, and other resource-extraction operations, the region also attracted the attention of urban-based artists, writers, and wealthy vacationers. They sought a more remote setting than that afforded by the popular Catskill Mountains and Hudson River

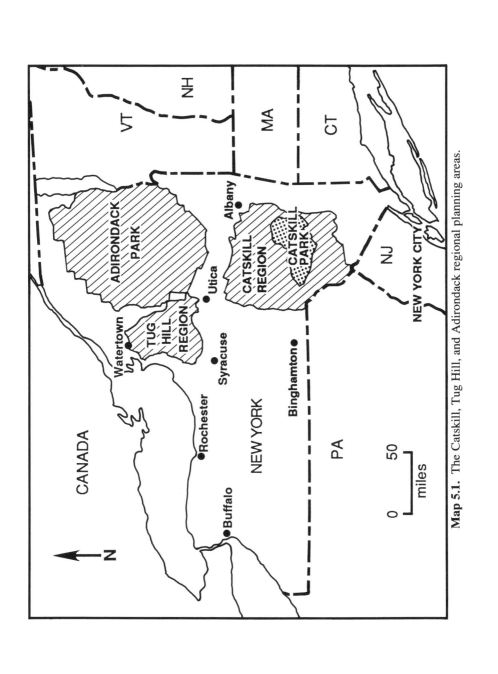

Map 5.1. The Catskill, Tug Hill, and Adirondack regional planning areas.

Valley resorts, or by the fashionable Saratoga spa at the southeastern edge of the Adirondacks. With its vast unlogged stretches, the Adirondacks provided Thomas Cole and other romantics of the Hudson River School of Landscape Painting with some of the last wilderness settings available in the east before a second generation of landscapists, led by Albert Bierstadt and Thomas Moran, moved west in search of new excitement. The well-known Philosophers' Camp, established during the summer of 1858, enabled Louis Agassiz, James Russell Lowell, Ralph Waldo Emerson, William J. Stillman, and several other luminaries of the period to enjoy a comfortable taste of the wilderness surrounding Follensby Pond north of Long Lake, in the heart of the Adirondacks.[10]

Inspired by Joel T. Headley's *The Adirondack; or, Life in the Woods* (1849), wealthy urban vacationers began summer sojourns to well-stocked wilderness camps and hunting lodges set up for their rest and relaxation. For those less inclined to rough it, several large hotels, such as the exclusive Ft. William Henry on Lake George, first appeared in the 1850s. Following the 1869 publication of William H. H. Murray's popular guide, *Adventures in the Wilderness; or, Camp-Life in the Adirondacks*, the trickle turned to a flood as middle-class vacationers flocked by rail, steamship, and coach to a multitude of hotels and family vacation camps set up at Lake George, Schroon Lake, Lake Placid, Blue Mountain Lake, and other popular destinations.[11]

The "rush to the wilderness" by "Murray's fools" caused some consternation among sports enthusiasts and others more appreciative of the seclusion afforded by the Adirondacks. Denunciations of Murray and his flood of gullible commoners soon appeared in the Boston and New York papers. As described by a present-day Adirondack historian:

> It was to be the beginning of the end for the old Adirondack wilderness. Writers turned out guidebooks, map-makers prepared tourist maps of the Adirondacks, hotels went up, and private camps erupted along the lake-shores. Railroads reached around and into the Adirondacks, steamboats puffed along its lakes. Within fifteen years avenues of access and clusters of culture had so penetrated the wilderness as to transform much of it into a sort of middle-landscape, something which, though certainly not urban, was not quite the same thing as wilderness, either. It was an environment of informal social life with a touch of rustic fashion, of luxury hotels and the family vacation, of pet deer and chained bears, of game preserves and managed forests, of manicured landscaping around summer camps, and all of it civilized, however discreetly and however wrapped about in birchbark, balsam boughs, and cedar pillows.[12]

Henri Lefebvre's theory of leisure in a capitalist society considers development of leisure space as commodity production for sale to alienated and bored urbanites. The social division of labor is rigidly reproduced in the production of leisure space, from public beaches and ball parks for the working class to the exclusive estates and hunting reserves of wealthy bankers and industrialists. As the quest for leisure space takes the form of a commodity fetishism, consumers, whatever their class origins, tend to see only the product sought and ignore the social relations and exploitation generated or reproduced through the production of leisure space.[13] Moreover, once acquired for their use value, leisure space and consumption amenities are defended by consumers against further exploitation by the forces of production, including producers of more consumption services. As revealed by the colorful social history of the Adirondacks, attempts by nonnative consumers to protect it as a park for leisure space, removed from both outside as well as local production forces, generated social conflict that continues to this day.

During the latter half of the nineteenth century the wealthy upper class, many of whom were financiers and railroad tycoons, established great private reserves in the forests, safe and secure from the clamor of surrounding logging practices and the social "rabble" in more developed vacation spots. The fabled estates of the Rockefellers, Morgans, Harrimans, Vanderbilts, Whitneys, and others were monuments to the rigid social order taking hold in the Adirondacks.[14]

At the other end of the social ladder, local inhabitants found themselves cut off by no trespassing signs from familiar hunting and trapping lands and were left to seasonal employment as housekeepers, game managers, caretakers, and tourist guides. Exclusive private clubs were also established. The most famous was the Lake Placid Club, founded in 1891 by Melvil Dewey, originator of the Dewey Decimal Classification System. Well-known for its stern rules of discrimination, the club helped establish Lake Placid as the social center of the region and as a bastion of anti-Semitism. By the mid-1890s some 45 sporting clubs and estates had posted almost 1 million acres. These were patrolled by armed guards against the ever-eager trappers and game and timber poachers of nearby hamlets.[15]

While most of the great estates were broken up or reverted to philanthropic and institutional uses over the ensuing years, several survive intact to the present. In 1970 the Temporary Study Commission on the Future of the Adirondacks estimated that seven individuals and three clubs still held tracts in excess of 10,000 acres each. Organized in 1890 by wealthy New York City sportsmen, the Adirondack League Club became the most extensive. Growing to some 200,000 acres by the turn of the century—making it, at the time, the largest private sporting estate in the nation—it continues to this day as the Adirondacks' biggest estate (approximately 54,000 acres).[16]

Captured by E. L. Doctorow in his popular novel *Loon Lake*, the Adirondacks' gilded age of large estates (1870-1915) already carried with it a strong undercurrent of social unrest.[17] As was the earlier case in Great Britain, social conflict in the Adirondacks took the form of local opposition to the imposition of what was locally perceived as outside bourgeois consumption tastes. In 1903, for example, a reclusive P. Dexter was murdered under suspicious circumstances following a long feud with natives over the posting of his 7,000-acre estate in the township of Santa Clara. Soon thereafter the local class animosity made national headlines when adjoining landowner William Rockefeller, brother of John D. Rockefeller, Sr., attempted to force a few families off inholdings within his newly acquired preserve. Although

Rockefeller eventually won the battle, he may have lost the war. Local residents refused to help put out a fire, suspected as the work of an arsonist, engulfing some 40,000 acres of his enormous estate.[18]

The bitterness felt by local residents at the imposition of extraregional demand for wilderness as leisure space continues to this day. It is particularly intense where preservation is seen as interfering with local livelihood, be it in the logging and trapping of yesteryear or, more recently, in second home construction and other types of commercial development.[19] Nevertheless, while protection of consumption concerns from local development schemes is commonly accepted as the basis for state intervention in the Adirondacks, consumption alone was not the original sponsor of state action. In addition to the reproduction of social order, and as a tonic for urban workplace alienation, park designation favors capitalist production in other ways. Park protection, for example, may support the commodification of leisure services or assist as a conservation measure to save select resources from short-term exploitation while surrounding areas are invaded by production. In the next section this private production interest behind public landscape preservation will be covered.

Consumption and Production Interests Unite to Save the Forest

Following the Revolutionary War, New York State held original title to most of the Adirondack territory. However, with land practically given away to speculators and railroad and lumber interests, graft and corruption helped reduce the size of these holdings to a mere 681,374 acres by 1885.[20] In 1867 a chemical process was discovered whereby softwoods, particularly the Adirondack red spruce, could be rendered into paper pulp. Soon thereafter the Adirondack logging industry took off on a new boom. By 1885 two-thirds of the original forest had been logged at least once. The onslaught was so intense that for a brief period around 1900 New York State led the nation in production of paper pulp.[21] Logging practices were extremely wasteful, and little attention was given to soil erosion, regeneration, or future land productivity. Devastating fires swept thousands of acres. Often originating in the slash left behind by clear-cutting or from engine sparks once the railroads penetrated the mountains in the 1870s, the conflagrations frequently invaded the remaining state lands and private estates.

In addition to wood products, the Adirondacks provided the young nation with an important source of iron ore. Port Henry on Lake Champlain had one of the first blast furnaces, built in 1822, and the iron used for the U.S.S. *Monitor* was mined in Essex County. As late as 1880, despite problems with ore contamination from ilmenite (later a source for titanium oxide), the eastern Adirondacks still furnished 15 percent of the nation's iron ore.[22] Soon thereafter the South and upper Midwest took off as major ore producers since they were closer to the coking coal required for steel production and had better quality ore. By the turn of the century iron mining and production were discontinued throughout most of the Adirondacks, leaving behind a severely denuded landscape wherever the railroads had penetrated to ore concentrations.

Although romantic artists and writers made an early plea for preservation of the Adirondack wilderness as a source of spiritual and physical enlightenment for the weary traveler, a political constituency for preservation only emerged in the latter half of the nineteenth century. Samuel Hammond, a wealthy Albany lawyer who sought out the Adirondacks "to lay around loose for a season vagabondizing among the wild and savage things of the wilderness," was perhaps the first to propose state constitutional protection for a vast wilderness in the central Adirondacks.[23] Expressing the dominant bourgeois goal of separating and balancing leisure and production spaces, Hammond also applauded the march of civilization and economic development. In areas ill suited for development the wilderness, then, was to be left as a refuge for the alienated laborer or, in his case, the harried businessman.

In a burst of wishful thinking, an 1864 New York *Times* editorial neatly extolled Hammond's sense of balance in the Adirondacks:

> Within an easy day's ride of our great City, as steam teaches us to measure distance, is a tract of country fitted to make a Central Park for the world. The jaded merchant, or financier, or *litterateur*, or politician, feeling excited within him again the old passion for nature, (which is never permitted entirely to die out), and longing for the inspiration of physical exercise, and pure air, and grand scenery, has only to take an early morning train, in order, if he chooses, to sleep the same night in the shadow of kingly hills, and waken with his memory filled with pleasant dreams, woven from the ceaseless music of mountain streams. . . .

With reference to the Adirondack Railroad Company's construction of a new line into the "heart of the wilderness," the editorial goes on to anticipate a day soon when

> the Adirondack region will become a suburb of New York. The furnaces of our capitalists will line its valleys, and create new fortunes to swell the aggregate of our wealth; while the hunting-lodges of our citizens will adorn its more remote mountain-sides and the wooded islands of its delightful lakes. It will become to our whole community, on an ample scale, what the Central Park now is on a limited one. . . .
>
> . . . In spite of all the din and dust of furnaces and foundries, the Adirondacks, thus husbanded, will furnish abundant seclusion for all time to come; and will admirably realize the true union which should always exist between utility and enjoyment.[24]

Following the 1864 publication of *Man and Nature*, George Perkins Marsh's landmark study of human-caused environmental disruption, sports enthusiasts and industrialists alike had reason to support the preservation of critical watershed and habitat to help conserve the natural resources utilized.[25] Soon thereafter downstate business interests, concerned over the impact of destructive logging practices on the state's water supply, joined with the estate owners and a growing number of sports, fishing, and hunting clubs to demand an end to exploitation.

In what can best be described as a temporary coalescence of extraregional bourgeois production and consumption interests, an alliance was formed to prevent further encroachment on state forest lands by real estate speculators, small-scale "chipper" logging firms, and other local competitive capital interests. Thus it came to pass that the New York Board of Trade and Transportation, organized in 1873 by New York City's major trade and wholesale firms, took the Adirondacks under its wing. The board was alarmed by reports that poor land management and extensive forest fires were responsible for stream sedimentation and watershed destruction contributing to dangerously low water levels and sandbars. While important mill sites and domestic water supplies on the upper Hudson were threatened, the major concern of the board was the Erie-Hudson transportation corridor. With total annual tonnage carried on the canal peaking as late as 1880, the merchants were acutely aware that should the nonwinterized canal be obstructed by sedimentation and low water levels, they would be completely dependent upon the New York Central Railroad running parallel to the canal through the Mohawk Valley.[26]

In 1883, the board joined with the New York (State) Chamber of Commerce and Brooklyn's Constitution Club (another business organization) to lobby the state legislature for permanent protection, by eminent domain if necessary, of the central Adirondacks. The New York *Herald Tribune* and the New York *Times* were also major forces behind this alliance. Following extensive fire damage and a severe drought, final impetus for state action arose when the Adirondack Railroad Company announced its intention to lumber 500,000 additional acres purchased by its predecessor from the state at prices as low as five cents per acre.[27]

In 1883 the state legislature prohibited further sale of state land in the Adirondack region and established a senate committee to investigate the need for additional action. Under pressure from the business lobbyists, Governor Hill signed a bill on May 15, 1885 declaring that all state lands then owned or thereafter acquired within 14 Adirondack and Catskill counties would be known as the state forest preserve. The state preserve was to be kept forever as "wild forest lands" and neither leased nor sold to any public or private corporation.[28] This was a significant event in U.S. environmental history, heralding the first instance of widespread wilderness preservation for utilitarian resource conservation.[29]

The Adirondack Park was actually created in 1892. It originally consisted of all state forest preserve land within a region delineated by a blue line that was drawn in 1890 on a map of a then-proposed Adirondack park. Within this 2.8 million-acre region, the state was to acquire title to additional acreage through tax default and purchase. The core park holdings were to be "forever reserved, maintained and cared for as ground open for the free use of all the people for their health and pleasure, and as forest lands necessary to the preservation of the headwaters of the chief rivers of the State, and a future timber supply."[30] In 1912 the Adirondack Park came to imply all land, both public and private, within the blue line. Since 1892 the area enclosed by the blue line has more than doubled to encompass nearly 6 million acres, spread out over all or parts of 12 Adirondack counties.

Although state holdings in the Adirondacks were granted a measure of protection through the acts of 1885 and 1892, Governor Flower encouraged continued sale of state timber through legislative amendment. Inefficient management by the state Forest Commission set up to administer the reserve resulted in additional loss of state land to speculators. Concurrently, fires started by timber poachers and squatters on state lands spread to neighboring private estates and commercial forests. Led by the Board of Trade and Transportation, the metropolitan commercial interests gathered media and public support for the unprecedented constitutional protection of the forest preserve. They were assisted in this effort by the Adirondack Park Association, formed in 1890 by prominent state business leaders, wealthy Adirondack estate owners, and the operators and physicians of Adirondack tuberculosis sanatoriums and health spas. Sports clubs were also strong supporters of this measure, since camping, hunting, and fishing were encouraged as appropriate activities in the state forest preserve.[31]

On January 1, 1895 Article 7, Section 7 of the state constitution (now Article 14, Section 1) went into effect. Originally drafted by the Board of Trade and Transportation and enthusiastically approved by the legislature and the voters, the well-known "forever wild" clause states:

> The lands of the state, now owned or hereafter acquired, constituting the forest preserve as now fixed by law, shall be forever kept as wild forest lands. They shall not be leased, sold or exchanged, or be taken by any corporation, public or private, nor shall the timber thereon be sold, removed, or destroyed. . . .[32]

Through this action, New York became the first state in the nation to provide constitutional protection for a natural resource area. Although the protection of production interests in water and lumber supply were motivating forces behind constitutional defense of the forest preserve, public sentiment, as first fashioned by wealthy estate owners and sports enthusiasts, and later expressed in camping guides and media reports, came to accept the Adirondacks as a special place set aside from the surrounding forces of urbanization and production.

Over the ensuing years there have been dozens of proposals to open the preserve to multiple use, yet only a few limited amendments concerned with servicing recreation and consumption interests through highway, ski resort, and reservoir impoundments have passed. The Association for the Protection of the Adirondacks, founded in 1902 by the Adirondack League and other large estate owners, including J. P. Morgan, William Rockefeller, Harry Payne Whitney, and Alfred G. Vanderbilt, defended the forest preserve through many of these amendment battles. Accused by local inhabitants of being a rich man's club, the association, to this day, still holds its meetings in the Wall Street area. The Adirondack Mountain Club was another major defender of the state preserve. It was founded in 1921 in a log cabin on the roof of the original Abercrombie & Fitch sporting goods store in Manhattan. Although the hiking club today has a broad middle-class membership, the original charter members were well-to-do bankers, attorneys, estate owners, doctors, and hotel operators.[33]

During the 1920s fears that most of the Adirondack Park would be converted to private estates prompted the state Conservation Commission to publicize and provide for public camping in the state preserve. The preserve itself more than tripled in size through periodic bond acquisitions. Constituting some 42 percent of the park's area, this public land has been managed since 1970 by the New York State Department of Environmental Conservation (DEC).

In spirit, the original battle to protect and enlarge the Adirondack forest preserve was in line with the utilitarian conservation movement of the turn of the century. The Adirondack situation, however, parted company with the national conservation movement of the Roosevelt administration through the strong initial support by large-scale corporate business and commercial concerns for preservation, together with controlled leisure access to the Adirondack forest. Elsewhere the corporate and industrial resource users backing the national conservation movement typically favored a more aggressive multiple-use program, including timber, mining, and range management, in addition to watershed protection and leisure access.[34]   Whereas conservationists, such as Gifford Pinchot, and preservationists, including John Muir, bitterly opposed one another on other public land use designations, we find much less conflict in the Adirondacks between conservation for production inputs and preservation for leisure consumption access.

This amiable collusion of extraregional production and consumption interests in support of preservation in the Adirondacks was somewhat unique. The situation was possible because the Adirondacks, with the exception of scattered mining operations and the forest industry, offered remarkably few opportunities for intensive production or industrial investment. The logging industry was, and continues to be, the largest private landowner in the park. With those small-scale loggers (chippers) dependent upon state holdings effectively removed from the picture, the remaining larger-scale private timber companies usually supported designation of state land as a preserve. In practice, the timber companies profited from the sale of logged-over areas to sports clubs, resort owners, and even to the state reserve itself. On the consumption side, while the golden age of the large private estate passed with the First World War, with many camps reverting to philanthropic use or subdivided into smaller resorts, heirs frequently maintained an active interest in Adirondack preservation. Furthermore, with the arrival of the family vacation and the private automobile in the 1920s, and the construction of thousands of campsites and small resort rooms, a much broader class of consumers came to use and appreciate the Adirondacks as leisure space.

With few large-scale capital concerns actively interested in Adirondack investment, the unity of external production with consumption interests in support of preservation was to hold for most of the park's recent history. However, as events in the Hudson River Valley would indicate (Chapter 6), this ideal spatial accommodation, both for leisure consumption through preservation and for production through development, could not hold up in areas more conducive to economic development. Even in the Adirondacks, the stage was set for inevitable social conflict, as impoverished local inhabitants came to the conclusion, whether justified or not, that protection of upper- and middle-class consumption interests interfered with their own means of livelihood.[35] They were joined in opposition to preservation by locally based competitive capital concerns, represented by small-scale construction, retail trade, and service enterprises.

The Specter of Vacation Home Sprawl

The contemporary era of state concern with development in the Adirondacks arrived with the postwar second home market. Encouraged by increased mobility, expanded leisure time, rising family income, and low mortgage rates, the national vacation home industry had its boom years during the 1960s and early 1970s before collapsing, along with the rest of the real estate market, in the 1973-75 economic slump. Florida, Colorado, Hawaii, California's coastal zone, the Lake Tahoe Basin, Arizona, Vermont, and Maine received the brunt of the real estate speculation and poor land management techniques accompanying market expansion. This sparked a slew of state land use legislation designed to curtail the worst externalities of second home construction and rural land speculation. Overlooking social tension and state intervention already present in the area since the last century, liberal planning reformers and analysts tend to focus only on this contemporary period in the Adirondacks as New York's contribution to the "quiet revolution."[36]

While many of its second homes were built by the upper class prior to the Second World War, New York State, with an affluent and growing middle class, did not escape the postwar boom. In 1970 the state still had a larger percentage (10.1 percent) and greater number of households owning second homes than any other state in the nation. The state's coastal and mountain areas were popular destinations, and in 1970 New York ranked second only behind Michigan in the absolute number of second homes contained within its borders.[37]

Although only a minor market considering its size, the Adirondacks also caught the attention of land speculators. With only 10 percent of the private land under any local land use regulation, they were encouraged by extremely permissive or nonexistent zoning and subdivision regulations, and by the low cost of land.[38] Early in 1972 the notorious Horizon Corporation, subject of the largest land sale fraud case in the history of the Federal Trade Commission, purchased 24,300 acres in the unzoned Town of Colton. The company announced plans to subdivide the tract into 7,000 lots and provide for a recreation community of approximately 30,000 people. The scale would be similar to that of the 18,500-acre "Ton-da-lay" complex proposed by a Connecticut developer for the Town of Altamont near Tupper Lake.[39]

Alarmed by the possible social and environmental impacts from large projects such as these, and by additional residential and recreation development pressure following the 1968 completion of the Adirondack Northway (Interstate 87), downstate preservationists joined forces with several Adirondack estate owners to lobby for state action to prevent unregulated development on private land in the park. While not appreciated by preservationists at the time, groundwork for this endeavor had already been laid by Laurance Rockefeller, brother of then Governor Nelson Rockefeller.

From Laurance Rockefeller's "Modest Proposal" to Creation of the Temporary Study Commission

In 1967 Laurance commissioned a private study calling for creation of a 1.7 million-acre national park (with 1.1 million acres already state held) in the core of the Adirondacks.[40] Then known as the "Dean of the American Conservation Movement," Laurance's influence on the shaping of national recreation policy was nothing short of phenomenal. At the time, he was chair of the State Council of Parks and of the Hudson River Valley Commission (appointed to both positions by his brother), past chair of the seminal federal Outdoor Recreation Resources Review Commission and of Johnson's White House Conference on Natural Beauty, commissioner and vice-president of the Palisades Interstate Park Commission, and a founding director or trustee in over a dozen other environmental and conservation organizations including the Conservation Foundation, the Population Council, and Resources for the Future. Laurance's report was drafted by Conrad Wirth, a close Rockefeller associate and past director of the National Park Service. Although carrying the prestige of Laurance's support, the national park proposal met with near universal opposition. Conservationists challenged Laurance's emphasis on intensive recreation development for public park lands; hunters and fishers feared a loss of access to the state forest preserve should it become a national park; local governments dreaded the loss in tax revenues, as the state at least made payments in lieu of taxes on the forest reserve; while timber companies and estate owners were threatened with a loss of their property.[41]

A variety of motives were attributed to Laurance's Adirondack proposal. Supporters cited his sincere and generous contribution to conservation causes. Detractors focused on the personal profit he derived from private resort development adjacent to public parks, many of which his own family helped establish, such as in the Grand Tetons in Wyoming and on St. John Island in the U.S. Virgin Islands.[42] Although direct financial gain was not cited as a specific motivation for Laurance's Adirondack report, the fact remains that upon receiving the proposal Governor Rockefeller immediately established a study commission to examine the issues raised. On September 19, 1969 the governor created, through executive order, a Temporary Study Commission on the Future of the Adirondacks. It was assigned the task of reviewing the economic and environmental problems of the Adirondack Park and developing alternatives to serve the needs and interests of the citizens of the entire state.

As embodied in the commission's membership, attention to the interests of the broader statewide constituency would take precedence over more parochial local concerns. Among the 13 members of the "blue-ribbon" commission, Peter Paine, Jr., a Wall Street attorney, and Richard Lawrence, Jr., a wealthy Adirondack businessman and landowner, were two of the most outspoken environmentalists. Other commission members included attorney Frederick Sheffield and surgeon Julien Anderson, both from New York City; the famous commentator and explorer Lowell Thomas; Adirondack newspaper publisher James Loeb; Rockefeller protégé and later DEC commissioner Henry Diamond; Elmira businessman Howard Kimball, Jr.; former Albany Congressman Leo O'Brien; state Senator, wealthy Hudson Valley environmentalist, and undaunted defender of Article 14, R. Watson Pomeroy; Frederick O'Neal, who was labor's "representative" as head of Actors' Equity; and Robert Hall, newspaper writer and editor. Harold Jerry, Jr., a well-known preservationist and later executive director of the Wilderness Society, served as staff director for the commission. The most influential member was the commission's chair, Harold Hochschild. A seasonal Adirondack estate resident since 1904, Hochschild was past chair of American Metal Climax (AMAX) and founder of the Adirondack Museum at Blue Mountain Lake.[43] For the sake of its members and supporters, most of the commission's meetings were held in New York City and Albany.

The commission's concern with preservation and with the aesthetic and ecological integrity of the park, to the relative neglect of local production and consumption interests, was evident in its final report. Released late in 1970, the report concluded that second home subdivisions posed a grave threat to the future social and ecological integrity of the Adirondacks.[44] Denoting the extremely low population levels found in most of the park's 87 town(ship)s lying wholly or partially within the blue line (only 19 had populations over 2,500), the commission discovered that only a few exercised even the most rudimentary types of subdivision control.

The prevailing pattern of private landownership lent, in the commission's view, a sense of urgency to the situation. Of the approximately 3.5 million acres of private land then within the park, 626 owners held almost 2 million acres, or 53 percent. This was interspersed in a complex patchwork with state-held lands. Although over 60 percent of the park's private land was held by nonresident owners, both individual and corporate, the commission held that it was essential to control the actions of small native landowners as well, since the accumulated effect of their actions, if left unregulated, would upset the park's integrity.[45]

The physical and biological need for control of land use within the region derived from the inability of shallow Adirondack soils to assimilate waste, high soil erodibility, and the severe development restrictions posed by the park's extensive riparian habitat. Additional justification for regulation came through a state interest in retaining the "parklike" atmosphere and the economic resource base of the area, dependent as it was upon tourism and the timber industry.

Reviewing the state's historical interest in the Adirondacks as a watershed and recreation destination, and drawing reference to the precedent set by other states, such as Hawaii and Vermont, the commission found that "massive" state action was necessary to protect the park from unregulated development on private land and misguided management of state land. Reliance on local municipalities to plan for and implement effective land use controls was unwise because, in the commission's view, local attempts to enhance the property tax base would jeopardize open space preservation.[46]

The Birth of the Adirondack Park Agency

The commission's principal recommendation called for statutory creation of an independent, bipartisan, Adirondack Park Agency (APA) within the executive branch and under the governor's control. The APA would have land use planning and development control powers over use of both state and private lands within the park. The newly created Department of Environmental Conservation would administer state land, and the agency would share responsibility with local governments for private land regulation.

Over strenuous objections from local inhabitants and politicians, the Republican-dominated state legislature overwhelmingly passed the Adirondack Park Agency Act in June of 1971.[47] Strong support came through downstate newspapers, such as the New York *Times*, and from statewide and national conservation organizations including the Sierra Club, Wilderness Society, Audubon Society, Adirondack Mountain Club, and Association for the Protection of the Adirondacks. By and large, the environmental groups most active in the APA fight had a membership with family incomes well above the state average while, at the local level, the few Adirondack residents vocal in their support for a strong state role in private land use regulation were wealthy retirees and those whose social and business connections sheltered them from the wrath of impoverished neighbors.[48]

As drafted by the commission, the act created a nine-member agency consisting of two cabinet (ex-officio) members representing the Office of Planning Services and DEC, together with seven private citizens. All were appointed by the governor and four had to be park residents. As with the commission, Nelson Rockefeller selected an agency that would be receptive to statewide consumption interests in the Adirondacks. Thus, Peter Paine and Richard Lawrence (the new agency chair) continued on as agency members. They were joined by Mary Prime, an ardent local environmentalist; John Stock, a representative of the local timber industry not opposed to state regulation; and by the two state members, Richard Wiebe and Henry Diamond, both of whom answered directly to Rockefeller. The agency's core staff also came over from the commission. In this manner the agency was stacked in favor of environmental protection. The only original local agency member opposing state regulation resigned after submitting a minority report to the agency's private land use plan.[49]

The new agency was assigned the task of preparing a state land management plan by July 1, 1972, and a private land use plan for the park's 92 towns and 14 villages (the Park Agency Act had expanded the blue line), together with recommendations for implementation, by January 1973. While acknowledging local production and consumption concerns, the agency's commitment to dominant extraregional aesthetic and recreation concerns was evident in its official charge. Thus, the planning process had to encourage "optimum overall conservation, protection, preservation, development and use of the unique scenic, and natural resources of the Adirondack park. . . . [and in addition] . . . recognize the major state interest in the conservation, use and development of the park's resources and the preservation of its open space character. . . ."[50]

The Adirondack Park State Land Master Plan was signed by the governor on July 26, 1972.[51] Development of the private land plan proved more complex. The planning process had to encourage preservation of the "parklike" atmosphere of the region while still allowing enough latitude to permit some livelihood for the permanent residents of the park and a continuing regulatory role for local governments. After an intense political struggle, during which the governor vetoed a locally sponsored bill designed to delay implementation of the agency's private land use plan, the legislature approved the Adirondack Park Land Use and Development Plan on May 22, 1973, to become operative on August 1, 1973.[52]

The agency's private land use plan was the most extensive and, to this day, is still the most stringent state land use control effort in the nation. Nelson Rockefeller's strong support for this unusual effort came through agency appointments and legislative maneuvering. With an eye continuously focused on the White House, Rockefeller was resolved to be identified with one of the most ambitious state planning and development control efforts in the nation. His position was strengthened by overwhelming extraregional support for the plan. In the cities outside the park almost every major newspaper joined with growing and newly formed environmental organizations to support firm state action and immediate legislative approval of the plan.

Most states involved in regional land use regulation separate policy formation (state) from implementation (local). That the Adirondack Park Agency (APA) managed to preserve an inordinate and broad measure of state dominion over routine implementation derived mainly from agency and state administrators perceiving little need for local consensus from the sparsely populated and politically weak region. In the absence of countervailing local participation, the APA preempted local development approval throughout most of the 6 million-acre park. Much to the chagrin of local residents, it imposed more detailed regulations, with lower thresholds in size and ecological impact, than land use programs found in other "quiet revolution" states, including Hawaii, Vermont, California (along the coast and at Lake Tahoe), Florida, and Oregon.[53]

The Ideology of Designing with Nature

In preparing the private land use plan the agency's staff utilized the ecological planning approach first popularized by Ian McHarg of the University of Pennsylvania. Using a resource overlay method screening the development capability for biological, physical, and public facilities (e.g., historic sites, scenic vistas, and proximity to existing development), this method identifies those select locations best suited for development and suggests areas where growth restrictions should be imposed.

McHarg's approach, also termed "ecological determinism," buries economic and social differences among competing interest groups under an idealism that humans should organize their activities in a manner consistent with the "objective" limits of the natural world.[54] Working on a watershed, river basin, or any other ecologically definable scale, this "rational" level of planning ignores political boundaries. As a consequence, it usually requires regional or state intervention to implement. However, regional land use control, as it typically involves intervention by a larger unit of government, proposes major shifts in economic and political power. Local development interests, long dominant in rural planning and land use decisions, are keenly aware of the threat posed by regional intervention.

McHarg's "designing with nature" materially benefits larger-scale or extraregional interests, whether prodevelopment or propreservation, that cannot secure local municipal approval for their goals and, moreover, have the means to ride out short-term swings in the real estate market. It is often rejected by local residents intent on land uses that may not be "rational" from a long-term or sustainable-yield perspective. For example, local farmers and their government representatives, still dreaming of quick speculative gains, refused McHarg's demonstration project in the late 1960s at the Brandywine Creek watershed outside of Philadelphia. At the other end of the continent, a planning team led by disciples of McHarg discovered that technical proficiency was no substitute for political savvy, as the long-awaited Lake Tahoe Regional Plan collapsed under a flood of local opposition.[55]

William Whyte, an admirer of McHarg, correctly pointed out that designing with nature can protect a favored way of life or a resource use under pressure against development while, in the long run, generate as much or more return for the landowner as can premature sale to urban speculation.[56] Such appears to be the case in Hawaii. Here the state's major corporate agricultural concerns, in their bid to control market release of land for urban uses, are among the strongest supporters of the pioneering state effort to regulate land use according to environmental limitations.

The quest for economic gain was not as obvious in the Adirondacks insofar as the larger tracts of private timber and estate land did not abut urban development. Although controlled release of land for optimum return was not a major factor, the desire to stay in business with assured access to use value in the resource base and the possibility of protecting one's consumption space led the large timber companies and estate owners to support the agency's planning process. Furthermore, as was the case at Lake Tahoe, Brandywine, and other areas where the McHarg approach had been applied, in the Adirondacks the more numerous small-scale landowners, realtors, and developers rejected the process in favor of what they perceived as more immediate and tangible gains.

Implementing the Private Land Use Plan

With strong extraregional support and tacit approval from the park's major landholders, the APA staff was able to implement McHarg's methodology despite vociferous opposition from local residents. As adopted by the state legislature, the private land use plan consisted of a map classifying nonstate land into six categories of use and an accompanying text prescribing guidelines for the overall intensity, type, and character of development, and the extent of land use permitted in each (Table 5.1). Land use categories were assigned primarily on the basis of physical ability to withstand development, protection of open space and critical environmental resources, existing land use, and proximity to the park's hamlet and service centers.[57] The shoreline restrictions of the plan, applicable to all lakes, ponds, and navigable (by canoe) rivers and streams, provided minimum lot width and setback standards and limitations on removal of vegetation.

Table 5.1

THE ADIRONDACK PARK LAND USE AND DEVELOPMENT
PLAN: DENSITY GUIDELINES[a]

Type of land area	Principal buildings per square mile[b,c]	Approximate percentage of private land[c]	Average lot size[c] (acres)
Hamlet	no restriction	2	no restriction
Moderate-intensity use	500	3	1.3
Low-intensity use	200	8	3.2
Rural use	75	34	8.5
Resource management	15	53	42.7
Industrial	no restriction	undefined	not applicable

[a]As adopted under the Adirondack Park Agency Act of 1973 (Article 27 of the Executive Law as amended on May 22, 1973 by Chapter 348, Laws of New York).

[b]Principal buildings are counted as single family homes, mobile homes, large tourist cabins (in excess of 300 square feet), ten motel or hotel units within a single structure (if each unit is under 300 square feet), etc.

[c]Adopted from New York State, Adirondack Park Agency, "Overall Intensity Guidelines," *Comprehensive Report,* vol. 1 (of 2) (Ray Brook, NY: Adirondack Park Agency, 1973); and New York State, Adirondack Park Agency, *Comprehensive Report: Adirondack Park Agency,* 2 vols. (Ray Brook, NY: Adirondack Park Agency, 1976; reprinted, Lake Placid *News,* March 4, 1976, Section 2).

Plan implementation envisioned towns and villages assuming a larger share of responsibility once agency-approved comprehensive local land use plans and methods for implementation, including zoning and subdivision regulations, were adopted. The plan established a project review and permit system as the principal method of administration. All Class A regional projects representing proposed development having a regional impact, such as large subdivisions, mineral extraction, ski centers, and campgrounds, would be reviewed by the agency regardless of whether the local government had an approved land use program. Where a local program met with agency approval, all development not listed as a Class A project would come under local review jurisdiction. In localities without such approval, the agency would also review Class B regional projects entailing numerous smaller-scale developments. The delineation of Class A and Class B projects would depend upon the land use area for which they were proposed. Thus, for example, in the least restricted areas (hamlets), only subdivisions of 75 lots or more were considered Class A projects while, at the other extreme, in resource management areas, single-family dwellings were classified as Class B, and subdivisions of two or more lots as Class A projects.[58]

The APA considered attainment of exclusive local review jurisdiction over Class B projects and the privilege of distributing overall intensity guidelines within each land use parcel as the principal advantages of an approved local land use program. In addition, data gathered through a local planning effort could be used to justify amendments to the plan's regional map.[59] Through the agency, state technical and financial assistance was also available to cooperating municipalities. Optimistic claims of the agency notwithstanding, these incentives were apparently insufficient, and the local response to the agency's planning program was dismal. While a majority of the park's towns and villages accepted planning assistance, by 1978 only three had local land use programs approved by the APA and subsequently adopted by local authorities.[60] With critics focusing on local cooperation as a test of agency success, the APA was forced to recognize partially completed programs containing a land use element as sufficient for initial delegation of review powers. Even with these concessions, local reluctance to participate continued as the so-called rewards were not considered worth the effort nor the indignation of local residents, the overwhelming majority of whom still opposed the agency's presence.

Although APA administrators considered economic impact in project review, they were not obligated to weigh the virtues of environmental protection against economic development. Administrative decisions based on natural resource limitations defined through the regional planning process were easier to support when social and economic externalities did not have to be accounted for. In comparison with efforts in other areas to control development (e.g., Vermont, Oregon, and the Lake Tahoe Basin), the APA had little need for local consensus on its programs and policies. There were more members of environmental organizations in the state than residents in the Adirondack Park. As long as the agency's downstate constituency was able to turn back locally sponsored amendments to the agency act, the APA could give primacy to environmental conservation and attendant recreation pursuits.[61]

The Triumph of Consumption

With the closing of the canal transportation era and constitutional protection extended to the forest preserve, extraregional production interest in the Adirondacks also declined. Over the same period the park became accessible and affordable for millions of working-class families. At the creation of the Temporary Study Commission in 1968 the Adirondacks were already receiving over 8 million visitors a year.[62] During the early 1970s this figure continued to grow as skiing, boating, backpacking, snowmobiling, and other outdoor recreation pursuits gained in popularity.

Today the Adirondacks attract a broad economic cross-section of the population, from wealthy elites who still maintain camps and clubs in the mountains, to inner-city children bused to fresh-air and charity camps in the forest. The primary objective of contemporary state intervention in the Adirondacks is protection of this leisure space consumed by millions from haphazard or poorly planned subdivision and development projects favored by a much smaller and politically weak minority. This commitment to leisure space comes across in the opening paragraph of the legislative findings and purposes establishing the agency (as amended in 1973):

> The Adirondack Park is abundant in natural resources and open space unique to New York and the eastern United States. The wild forest, water, wildlife and aesthetic resources of the park, and its open space character, provide an outdoor recreation experience of national and international significance. Growing population, advancing technology and an expanding economy are focusing ever-increasing pressures on these priceless resources.[63]

On occasion recreation even takes precedence over the sanctity of the preserve itself; e.g., constitutional amendments have been passed allowing tree removal for public campsites and ski trails.

The attention to preservation for consumption is also apparent in the structure of the agency's permit approval process. With local governments inclined to accept almost any development promising to improve the tax base and bolster employment, the Adirondack regulatory process allows all local ordinances to remain operative, whether agency approved or not. As a consequence, developers have to meet both agency and local regulations in towns and villages with unapproved local programs. This situation sets the Adirondack program apart from state intervention championed by liberal reformers for areas where defense of consumption amenities hamper economic development. In the latter situation, as with Florida's Environmental Land and Water Management Act, Maryland's Power Plant Siting Act, New Jersey's Hackensack Meadowlands Reclamation Act, and New York State's own power plant and hazardous waste siting acts, the state can override local disapproval of development considered to be regionally beneficial.[64]

The Political Economy of Local Reaction
to the Adirondack Park Agency

The Adirondack Park Local Government Review Board was created by amendment to the Adirondack Park Land Use and Development Plan as a favor to local legislators. It contains one member appointed by each of the park's 12 county governments. Although empowered with only advisory functions, the review board has long served as a focal point for local opposition to the agency. Claiming that the APA was "the most hated agency in Northern New York," the review board concluded in its 1979 report to the state legislature that Adirondack citizens "have been overpowered by a superior outside force which only proves that the State of New York can subdue and misuse a minority people."[65] In the most comprehensive survey of local reaction to the regulatory process yet undertaken, Charles Zinser found that among all the Adirondack towns, only in the Town of Lake George could the overall attitude of local government officials (supervisors, tax assessors, planning board chairs, etc.) be considered slightly positive. In the aggregate for the municipal officials in the park, opponents of the plan outnumbered supporters eight to one and for realtors it was approximately four to one.[66]

These ratios alone might overstate local opposition insofar as municipal political domination by realtors and developers, those most likely affected by land use regulation, is a fact of life in most Adirondack communities. The true extent of local dissent is more apparent through the results of a recent survey of landowner reaction to the agency's plan. This survey is more representative because the overwhelming majority of Adirondack permanent residents also own their homes or the land they sit upon. Here the survey found 60 percent of the year-round permanent resident landowners opposing the plan while only 27 percent of the nonpermanent landowners disapproved. Support for the plan was highly correlated with income, leading the Cornell University research team to characterize support for the plan in terms of a "white collar-blue collar" split.[67]

A strong case is made by the agency and its supporters that with less than one-quarter of the park's area owned by local residents, outside public and private landowning interests have a legitimate concern when supporting resource conservation and open space protection. These conditions notwithstanding, the Adirondacks, already one of the most economically depressed regions in the state and, in terms of personal income, on par with the poverty found in Appalachia, have been singled out for special treatment.[68] Furthermore, the assumption that working-class and moderate-income families prefer open space and aesthetic preservation to the more intensive recreation and second home development favored by many local residents is, for now, an act of faith, particularly considering the high participation rates by "blue-collar" workers in motorboating, fishing, skimobiling and other more consumptive recreation pursuits.

No doubt, many local residents blame the agency for conditions chronic to the state and national economies. Figures released by the state Board of

Equalization and Assessment demonstrate that the drastic decline in real estate transactions and construction within the park during the 1973-75 collapse of the housing industry in New York State approximated that found in other rural regions, including Tug Hill and the Catskills.[69] Although used by the APA to bolster the position that the agency was not responsible for the local decline in construction, these data can be misleading if left uninterpreted. They fail to consider opportunities lost due to the imposition of land use controls in an area otherwise receiving what might have been a rate of construction exceeding state norms. With 10.4 percent of the Adirondack labor force engaged in construction in 1970 (compared with a state average of 4.8 percent), and with unemployment rates then more than twice the state average, even a minor adjustment to the rate of construction could have had a large employment impact.[70]

One may or may not accept the agency's claim that its actions did not significantly influence the level of real estate activity during the 1973-75 recession. Nevertheless, the original justification advanced for state intervention in the control of private land use (to prevent extensive subdivision and second home development from compromising the park's open space and natural resource qualities) was weakened by the allegation that existing levels of activity were not significantly altered by the agency's presence.

Actually the large-scale outside developers were the exception in the Adirondacks. Although the APA's eagerly awaited study of the local real estate market made no mention of the size of individual projects coming before it for review, support for this conclusion could be drawn from this study. Between August 1, 1973 and December 31, 1975 new applications were received for 6,861 principal buildings (or lots for same) from a total of 1,093 applicants. The distribution was spread among 340 applications for single-family dwellings, 543 for subdivisions, and the rest for campgrounds, mobile home courts, and industrial and commercial projects. Furthermore, the 3 applications for large-scale projects (Ausable Acres, Loon Lake Estates, and Valmont Village) together accounted for 3,164 of the 6,861 principal buildings (lots) applied for, leaving 3,697 building lots spread among 1,090 applicants.[71] From a survey of developers applying for 5 lots or more, Zinser estimated that over three-quarters of the developers were permanent park residents or living in the immediate periphery of the park. Of these, nearly two-thirds considered the plan's overall economic impact to be "very negative" and contributing to a decline in leisure home construction, local employment, and the property tax base.[72]

Local resentment against the agency peaked between 1974 and 1976 when the newly formed League for Adirondack Citizens' Rights held "speak-outs" across the park, organized protest rallies in Albany, and spread the impression that the agency was a plot by Rockefeller, wealthy estate owners, and "rabid" environmentalists to lock up the Adirondacks and drive off impoverished residents. These opinions were strengthened by the agency's policy of excluding the public, media, and even the Local Government Review Board from its meetings, a procedure setting the agency aside from proceedings in most other states where regional development control agencies held open meetings and actively encouraged citizen participation.[73]

Although there was no evidence of a conspiracy to drive off local inhabitants, state intervention in support of extraregional consumption during the 1970s did have the effect of restricting local production interests. Tempers cooled with the appointment of an Adirondack town supervisor and, later, a local minister to chair the agency, and with the streamlining in agency scrutiny of single-family and small-scale projects. A slow increase in nonnative residents further helped to moderate local antipathy in areas where the newcomers, who tended to be more sympathetic to agency protection of consumption space, were politically active. Finally, belated attempts by the agency to address local economic development concerns through the hiring of an economic planning consultant and a major attempt during 1983-84 to solicit local public input into a new program to define agency goals also contributed to declining resentment.[74] These reforms notwithstanding, widespread local hostility to the agency remains a fact of political life in the Adirondacks. More recently, local suspicions were even heightened by a 1986 state bond proposal allowing for major additions to the state forest preserve, and by a report from the Adirondacks' most influential preservation advocate requesting that the state purchase scenic easements (prohibiting further development) on 2 million additional acres of private land.[75]

Stung by repetition of widespread horror stories in individual dealings with the agency and by continuing local antagonism to its planning programs, the agency already in its first comprehensive report reached a conclusion still maintained today. Thus the pivotal 1973 private land use act was judged "basically sound, though within the Adirondack Park it remain[ed] controversial and widely misunderstood."[76] Expressing a view popular among regional planning reform advocates, planning analyst Frank Popper agreed with the agency, noting that "local people, who might be hostile to any plan, have been especially hostile to this one because they could not understand it."[77]

Popper's conclusion carried the assumption that had residents been able to understand the private land use plan, they would have been inclined to more favorably support agency activities. The evidence, however, does not support this supposition. Local resistance to the agency was frequently strongest in towns and villages with prior planning and zoning experience. Furthermore, the first three towns with agency-approved local planning programs were the thinly populated towns of Indian Lake and Hague, neither with any prior planning or zoning experience, and Greenfield, only a small portion of which lies within the blue line. Although initial local comprehension of the APA planning process could be characterized as incomplete, it appears that traditional material concerns were better indicators of local reaction than progress made toward understanding a common interest in park conservation. These included the anticipated impact of agency regulation on local employment and property values, and the perceived strength of the specific incentives offered by the agency for compliance. In turn, the low material incentives for compliance supported an ideological position among the Adirondack natives that they had been deprived of the cherished right of use (or abuse) of property enjoyed by residents elsewhere across the state.[78] With logging and mining practices, once the gravest threats to the wilderness, now in compliance with state regulations and actually declining in significance, Adirondack natives came to realize that, in the eyes of the state, they had become the real "enemy" from which the woods had to be saved.[79]

The Rationale behind Local Resistance to Critical Area Protection

The liberal planning reform literature portrays local hostility to rational and technically proficient regional plans as having a basis in local inability to comprehend complex management systems. According to this reform ideology, contradiction and political conflict are not necessary aspects of social life but, rather, derive from short-sighted and incomplete conceptualization of self-interest as it accords with a broader, and more objective, public interest.[80] As a case in point, proponents of open space conservation in the Adirondacks suggest that the Adirondack economy is typical for a rural area peripheral to industrial production and consumer markets. As such, it is best suited to serve extra-regional recreation and primary resource needs. According to the Temporary Study Commission on the Future of the Adirondacks, all parties should agree that "in the long run, the measures proposed by the Commission to maintain the wild forest character of the Park and to channel development along proper lines will enhance the economic well-being of Adirondack residents."[81]

Well, perhaps so, but not by chance. In many ways this characterization has become a self-fulfilling prophecy. Measures adopted by state authorities already in the last century reinforced the Adirondacks as a forest preserve set aside for leisure consumption, and this trend continues to the present. The study commission, for example, placed heavy emphasis on private commercial forests as "vital to the Adirondack economy," and yet only 3.1 percent of the park's 1970 labor force was engaged in the combined fields of agriculture, forestry, and fisheries. According to the APA's own calculations, more than three times as many individuals derived primary employment from construction in 1970 as from the forests and agriculture.[82]

At the peak extension of farmland in New York State during the 1880s and 1890s, a mere 18 percent of the state was forested. Protection of sensitive watersheds from further disruption fueled production concern with the Adirondacks during this period. Today 60 percent of the state is forested.[83] With most significant Adirondack headwaters now protected in the state forest preserve and with the decline in mining and logging activity, attention by production interests to Adirondack preservation has also waned.

For an area considered peripheral to urban development, it now appears that fear of overt environmental disruption and the need for resource conservation are, by themselves, no longer sufficient to warrant the extent of state regulation found in the Adirondacks. As a result, the agency and its supporters must rely upon the long-standing parallel perception of the Adirondacks as a unique refuge set apart from everyday production activities. As eloquently captured by a passage in the agency's first comprehensive plan, preservation of the park's open space, free from development, is at the very base of the contemporary regulatory process:

> The protection of natural open space is fundamental to the Land Use and Development Plan. . . . Open space protection is often indistinguishable from resource protection. . . . Indeed, open space may of itself be considered a natural resource.
>
> Yet open space is something more than the sum of its parts. Its values are psychological and aesthetic, as well as physical and biological. Open space involves a sense of wilderness, of natural expanse and abundance, of sweeping scenic beauty, which transcends the qualities and tolerances of the soils, slopes, wildlife, vegetation and hydrological resources. . . . Natural resources can sometimes withstand a degree of development that would drastically alter the open space character of an area.
>
> Adirondack open spaces are perceived differently. From a highway, open space is the undisturbed bog or pond or distant mountains seen from a passing car. From a hilltop, open space is the panorama of other hills and lakes and valleys. From a lake, it may be an undisturbed natural shoreline against a backdrop of undisturbed forests and mountains; from a river or riverbank, it is the long stretch of stillwater backed up behind a beaver dam; from the foot path through the meadow or woods, open space is simply that which insulates the user from the man-made world beyond.[84]

Small wonder then that the agency and its program are "misunderstood" by those whose own livelihood and consumption space may be circumscribed to meet these needs. The tendency by local governments to seek larger tax bases, the accommodation of locally powerful real estate and development interests, the quest for employment—in short the Adirondack urbanizing process itself—is quite similar to that found in surrounding communities. The major difference between Adirondack and external urbanization is the special regulations imposed by the state to control development in the designated open space preserve. As acknowledged by the agency, these development standards stem more from aesthetic judgments and from the quest to protect consumption amenities than from actual threats to public health and safety posed by development itself.

Given the depressed local economy and, as yet, the low level of economic development, conflict between expansion of the forces of production and defense of consumption space may not be apparent to the casual observer. Certainly production and consumption dialectically generate one another and may even coexist temporarily in space, as occurred during the latter part of the nineteenth century through the fight to create the original state forest preserve. Nevertheless, unity is at best temporary in a dynamic economy. It is, of course, the social externalities of an alienating production system, sending millions off to consume nature as a tonic for urbanization, that generate the observed social conflict in the Adirondacks today.

Here, as other areas where critical reserves are set aside for rest and relaxation, the spatial separation of consumption from production space can only be a temporary solution to problems born of a production system driven by the quest for profit and premised upon expansion. For example, the ecological integrity of the park is currently undergoing production pressure in the form of "acid precipitation." This occurs as sulfur and nitrogen oxides from fossil fuel combustion, often hundreds of miles away, mix with water vapor and enter the local hydrological system as sulfuric and nitric acids. With much of the area devoid of natural buffering agents such as limestone, the acid readily leaches scarce mineral nutrients, as well as toxic metals, out of the already poor soils. In this manner the acid has been implicated as a primary cause for a near-total loss of fish life in hundreds of Adirondack lakes and ponds.[85]

In conclusion, local response to the imposition of regional planning and development control in the Adirondacks is consistent with an economic system stressing private property rights coupled with the quest for personal material gain. The dichotomy between local economic interests on the one hand, and regional or statewide concern with critical area planning for environmental quality and moreover for recreation space on the other, arises not from any parochial misunderstanding of some fictitious common public interest. Rather it derives from persistent demands placed on an unreceptive local populace by an expanding production system. The "nogrowth" sentiment sweeping affluent suburban areas in the path of urban expansion is actually the flip side of local clamor in the Adirondacks for economic and urban development. Both impulses derive from contradiction inherent in a system where consumption is conceptually isolated from production, and where private goals are at variance with State attempts to provide separate areas appropriate for production and for consumption. In the Adirondacks, residents are merely responding to the imposition of outside consumption tastes originating in the last century among the bourgeoisie and accepted in this century by the working class. In this situation consensus remains an illusion, because education on liberal planning norms and patient attention to local participation cannot pave over real social differences. Short of direct purchase of existing private property rights, strong extraregional political coercion will be required for many years to come as the state struggles to set the Adirondacks aside as a critical area somehow removed from the process of economic development in the world beyond.

The continuing animosity expressed by local residents toward state planning and the regulation of private lands in the Adirondack Park appears to support the geographic dichotomy between regional public concerns and local parochial goals portrayed by the liberal planning reform literature. The situation, however, is more complex. In the Adirondacks local production concerns are actually attempting to service the outside consumption demands of a wider populace, while extraregional business interests, although no longer as active as in the past, still recognize a value in maintaining the Adirondacks as a "park," available for the leisure consumption use of their workforce.

The Adirondacks are not the only region where the state declared and attempted to plan for a critical area. As uncovered in the sections to follow, state attention to critical area protection in the Catskill and Tug Hill regions also takes a unique form as it responds to a regionally specific mix of local and extraregional production and consumption interests generating alliances that defy a simple local "parochial" versus regional "public" split.

THE FAILURE OF REGIONAL PLANNING AND DEVELOPMENT CONTROL IN THE CATSKILLS

With 34 peaks over 3,500 feet, the Catskill Mountains of southeastern New York were an impressive and familiar sight for nineteenth-century Hudson River steamboat travelers.[86] Many visitors were drawn to the Catskill Mountain House. Established in 1823, this fabled resort was one of the nation's first vacation destinations. It was situated on a ledge 2,250 feet above the river valley. From here it commanded a sweeping view and was therefore considered a mandatory stop on the Grand Tour of America's scenic wonders then undertaken by wealthy Europeans.[87] At the Mountain House, Thomas Cole, James Fenimore Cooper, Washington Irving, and other celebrated Hudson Valley artists and authors could relax among all the comforts of a well-appointed hotel while recording the supposedly wild splendors of the mountains behind and the river below.

Throughout the nineteenth century the northeast escarpment of the Catskills, above the village of Catskill, supported a major vacation complex geared to upper-class needs and tastes. This occurred even as thousands of acres of hemlock in adjoining valleys and coves were clear-cut for their bark, then used to tan leather hides. Most of the visitors came for the season, to marvel, and perhaps sketch or record in their diaries the scenes made famous by the artists. They also came to escape the congestion, heat, yellow fever, malaria, and the other environmental and social discomforts of the valley lowlands and the crowded metropolis some 125 miles downriver.

The ideology of escape to nature was promoted by ever-popular guide books and by the numerous resort hotels, steamboat lines, and after midcentury, by the railroads established in the region. Visitors were carefully shielded from the disagreeable facts of production in the landscape due to tanning, logging, subsistence farming, and mining. They were told when and where to look, so as to best appreciate a scene already made famous by the artists. In this manner U.S. literati and bourgeoisie did not so much return to the land, for they rarely had agrarian roots, as they actually turned toward an idealized nature for spiritual and recreational release.

Recreational use of the Catskills was closely related to the social history of New York City. By 1880 over 2 million people lived within a day's travel of the mountains. Nevertheless, insufficient means and overt ethnic discrimination largely limited resort use to wealthy Anglo-Protestants. By the turn of the century, however, union victories in wage and hour demands succeeded in allowing organized labor to enjoy at least a day's outing by steamboat to numerous picnic sites at the foot of the cliffs, while successful business managers or brokers might aspire to a week or two at one of the mountain houses perched high above.

In the end anti-Semitism and changing tastes undercut the mountain hotels. During the 1920s the southwestern fringe of the Catskills, in Sullivan County, was developed as one of the largest concentrations of resort hotels in the world. Beginning with the conversion of farm homes into boarding houses, hotels here specifically catered to the Jewish working class and their dietary restrictions. In the interim, scenery alone was no longer sufficient to recommend the once-exclusive mountain hotels, and they were abandoned for the Adirondacks, Newport (Rhode Island), Long Island's Hamptons, Palm Beach (Florida), and other more glamorous resorts. For their part, the unionized workers could care less for the scenery. Situated among the rather ordinary hills and valleys in an area not even considered part of the Catskills until twentieth-century tourist brochures proclaimed otherwise, the Sullivan County resorts were given to much more active leisure consumption through boating, golf, tennis, skiing, and similar exercises.[88]

With recreation space primarily limited to the northeastern edge (Greene County) and, later, the southwestern fringe just outside the mountains, the central Catskill region did not have the appeal of the Adirondacks when the state forest preserve was established in 1885. That state holdings in the Catskills were included at all was largely the result of the indefatigable efforts of Cornelius Hardenbergh, an Ulster County assemblyman. He was incensed by an act holding the county responsible for state taxes levied on tax-delinquent property that, by law, reverted to the county. In 1884 he successfully sponsored legislation having existing lands obtained by the county at tax sales and all future tax-delinquent land automatically revert to the state. Only applicable to the Catskill counties of Ulster, Greene, and Sullivan, with Delaware added in 1888, these lands would be included as part of the state forest preserve, to be protected, together with state-held land in the Adirondacks, as forever wild.[89] Most of the original 33,893 acres of state land were clustered in northern Ulster County, forming the foundation for the Catskill forest preserve.[90]

Although originally lacking the organized production, estate, and recreation concerns with resource conservation found in the Adirondacks, the Catskills were soon recognized as integral to the well-being of the New York City metropolitan region. Already in 1891 the state forest commissioner charged with preserve management was recommending additional purchase for recreation use. In 1904 the legislature established the boundary of a Catskill Park within which the state would concentrate acquisition efforts. Through additional bond purchases and boundary enlargement, the park grew to its current 705,500 acres (Map 5.1), encompassing 272,917 acres of state-held land (38 percent of the total).[91]

In 1907 construction began on New York City's first Catskill reservoir. Eight years later the valves were opened and 250 million gallons a day began flowing from the Ashokan Reservoir on Esopus Creek to the city.[92] In 1924 the Schoharie Reservoir, just outside the park, was added to this magnificent system. Eventually the city came to rely on Catskill sources for 89 percent of its water supply (1.5 billion gallons a day), with approximately four-fifths of the park and the major portion of the surrounding area draining into the system.[93]

With the city purchasing thousands of acres of sensitive watershed to secure the high quality of its supply, much of the Catskill region was de facto protected as open space and available for nondegrading recreational access, such as hiking, boating, and fishing. In this manner the Catskill landscape and economy were given to servicing extraregional recreation and water consumption requirements. Following the collapse of the hemlock-based tanning industry and the decline in logging, timber production, and bluestone quarrying in the late nineteenth century, only a few local production concerns, mostly in poultry and dairy farming, remained to compete with extraregional consumption interests for land use.[94]

This calm was not to last. Having successfully supported creation of the Temporary Study Commission on the Future of the Adirondacks and assured a guiding role in its deliberations, the state's environmental preservation and regional planning advocates turned attention to other areas where a state presence in land use development might be exercised. Long favored as a recreation destination by residents of metropolitan New York City, and now under increasing pressure from second home development and even suburbanization, the Catskill region became the next likely candidate.

By the early 1970s the seven-county Catskill region was receiving approximately 7 million vacationers a year. This figure was just shy of the Adirondack total.[95] Moreover, six of New York City's seven principal reservoirs were in five of the region's counties. Outside production concerns were also taking an interest in the area. In 1973 the New York State Power Pool, on behalf of the utility industry, optimistically estimated that the seven-county Catskill region would become a major electric power producer. Through a combination of nuclear, hydro, and conventional fossil fuel plants, the region could anticipate a phenomenal 22-fold growth in electric power output, from a mere 450 megawatts in 1970 to some 10,000 megawatts by 1990.[96]

Organized primarily through the Mid-Hudson Pattern for Progress and (representing metropolitan New York City) the Regional Plan Association of New York (RPA), downstate business interests supported state intervention and regional land use control necessary to site energy facilities, protect critical watersheds, and, at least for the RPA, preserve the Catskills as a major open space and recreation destination for urban workers (Chapters 2 and 3). Favoring creation of a permanent Catskill agency with power to preempt local land use control, the RPA argued that open space preservation and protection of recreation amenities were essential.

> The economy of the New York Urban Region depends heavily on attracting employees of large corporations to live in the Region. The natural countryside surrounding this largest urban area of the nation is an important asset in that attraction. The most cited reason for corporations leaving New York City is the difficulty in getting middle management to come to New York to work—and outdoor recreation opportunities are among the most vital reasons of people who prefer other areas. We must not lose these assets we have (and we should publicize them more).
>   Protection of special places from urbanization is unlikely if left to localities. . . .[97]

Although this business support was significant, primary impetus for comprehensive regional planning and land use control in the Catskills originated with local estate owners and with the state's environmental lobbyists. Created in 1969 by several affluent local families, the nonprofit Catskill Center for Conservation and Development initiated the drive for a Catskill study commission, modeled loosely after the Adirondack experience. The center was particularly concerned about the high rate of land subdivision occurring in towns lacking any planning, zoning, or subdivision regulations.

With native opposition to state activities in the Adirondacks not yet organized or obvious, Catskill legislators initially welcomed the center's proposal. By and large they supported the 1971 legislation creating a Temporary State Commission to Study the Catskills (hereafter also referred to as the Catskill commission).[98] Municipal consent was secured through the commission's responsibility to examine development potential and social and economic conditions, in addition to environmental issues.[99] Moreover, the Catskill commission, unlike the Adirondack commission and later the Adirondack Park Agency, was under direct legislative control. As a consequence, it would have to be more accommodating to local interests as expressed by local legislators.

As redefined in 1973, the 4 million-acre study area had a permanent population of approximately 375,000 in 1970.[100] Boundaries were liberally drawn to enclose the Catskill Mountains and adjoining foothills. With the Catskill Park at the core, the region's borders were adjusted to the Hudson River on the east and to the Delaware River on the southwest. Six and one-half counties were included in the final study region: Ulster, Sullivan, Greene, Delaware, Ostego, and Schoharie counties, and the rural half of Albany County (Map 5.1).

The governor (Rockefeller) and the senate and assembly leaders each appointed three members to the Catskill commission. Serving as volunteers without compensation except for expenses, the nine-member commission was supposedly representative of local interests, since six members had to be residents of the affected counties. As with the Adirondack Park Agency and much to the chagrin of local agriculture, development, and business interests, residence alone proved a poor substitute for social allegiance. Of the ten who eventually served on the commission, four were attorneys living mostly on the periphery or completely outside of the region, and two others were a corporate president and a stock broker. The vice-president of the Catskill Center also served on the commission. The region's resort industry and labor interests had only one spokesperson each, and the leading production concern in the region, agriculture, had no principal representative. Finally, the only commission member actually living within the Catskill Park itself was then a director of the Mid-Hudson Pattern for Progress and of the Catskill Center, as well as owner of the state's largest ski area. The commission's chair, Kirby Peake, actually lived in Westchester County and, as many other members, had a strong recreation interest in the Catskills. Through an exceptionally candid listing in the commission's final report of member interests we learn that conservation for leisure consumption appeared to dominate member affiliations. Several even went so far as to have themselves listed as "ardent angler," "sportsman," and "conservationist."[101]

Charged with a more comprehensive task for a more diverse region than the Adirondack commission, the Catskill commission realized from the start that it could ill-afford to ignore public participation in its activities. The consumption bent of its commissioners notwithstanding, the staff attempted to balance competing production demands from the powerful local real estate, construction, resort, and agriculture industries with extraregional concern for open space preservation, watershed protection, and environmental conservation. Torn between local production and regional leisure consumption interests, the commission, in its final report, could only offer a broad list of proposals designed to appease each of these constituencies. Its central recommendation was a two-year extension of its mission, which would be sufficient to implement a land use program of the sort called for by the American Law Institute's Model Land Development Code (Chapter 1). "Areas of critical regional significance" (e.g., floodplains, mountaintops, poorly drained soils, prime agriculture and forest lands) and "projects of critical regional significance" (e.g., major highways, power plants, large industrial plants, and residential developments) were to be designated through a county and regional process. Local municipalities would prepare land use regulations with assistance from, and for approval by, a strengthened county planning board. The county board would ensure that the regional interest in protection of critical areas and in the prompt siting of economically beneficial development was served. A Catskill Region Agency would be created to coordinate efforts, provide planning assistance, and lobby for Catskill interests at regional and state levels. Unlike the APA, it was to have a dual purpose in economic development and in land use conservation. Furthermore, it would implement regional plans and economic and social programs only if local governments would "default their initial opportunity."[102]

The commission's report drew heavily from an earlier plan prepared by the Catskill Center. Promoted as "a citizen's plan," seeking "progressive change . . . through mutual exchange and understanding. . . . [by charting]. . . the only sensible course for the future," the center's proposal first suggested the American Law Institute model and creation of the Catskill agency. Although not part of the commission's final report, the center's recommendation of "disincorporation of the smaller villages, and their merger with the towns in which they [were] located. . . . [so as] . . . to effect more coordinated and responsive administrative units. . . ." fomented local concern.[103]

Released in April of 1975, the commission's final report had the misfortune of arriving during the worst economic recession to hit New York since the Great Depression. Failing to gather sufficient grassroots backing, the commission fell victim to emerging local fears of another Adirondack Park Agency-style takeover. Farmers, realtors, and resort owners were particularly incensed and formed the nucleus of an antiplanning constituency that survives to this day.[104]

The commission lacked a discernible broad-based constituency. The state's numerous environmental organizations, divided over specific policy recommendations, mustered only weak support.[105] Furthermore, for the urbanizing fringe of the region, the state's larger-scale production concerns, and in particular the utility industry, failed to rally behind the vague promise of assistance in overcoming local opposition to the siting of projects of "critical" regional significance. By 1975 they already had specific state siting legislation for their needs and could turn to the state's public authorities for assistance with the provision of housing, transmission lines, power plants, and other inputs into the production process (Chapter 4). With local construction and resort industries already in a tailspin and offended by the commission's characterization of their future as marginal, the region's progrowth interests also saw little value in adding what they perceived as yet another layer of bureaucracy to the land development process. The most significant extraregional activity in the Catskills, safeguarding the New York City water supply, was already well served through prior state and city land purchase and control. Finally, the 4 million-acre region under study was far larger than the core Catskill Park, and many residents and communities could not identify with the Catskill region. In the end, local concerns successfully persuaded their representatives and, in turn, a sympathetic state legislature, to oppose recertification of the commission.

Over the intervening years since the commission's demise, the state Department of Environmental Conservation continued some of the commission's planning activities, particularly on state lands and with respect to natural resource conservation. Concurrently, there has been an increase in land subdivision activity, particularly in towns with little or no regulation. Although the deleterious environmental impact and the exorbitant cost of servicing poorly planned and inaccessible plots are obvious, communities are slow to respond with regulations, in part because local politics are dominated by construction and real estate interests.

Sidestepping public regulation, a most intriguing experiment surfaced in 1984, when the media discovered that Larry Rockefeller, son of Laurance Rockefeller, had over the past eight years quietly purchased 4,000 acres of inactive farmland along the remote Beaverkill Valley in the western reaches of the Catskill Park (Ulster and Sullivan counties). Although proclaimed as one of a "new breed of conservationists," Larry was very much in the conservation brokerage tradition of his father because he purchased the land prior to commercial subdivision, set very stringent development restrictions, and repackaged it into lots ranging from 10 to 100 acres. Putting Ian McHarg's "designing with nature" into practice, the junior Rockefeller managed to generate a profit on land sales, raise the property tax base, and, according to local critics, gentrify a valley wherein the long-time residents who sold out to him could stay on as tenants in subsidized apartments.[106] This private approach to the protection of critical environmental areas as personal consumption space harks back to the great landscape estates of eighteenth-century Europe and of the nineteenth-century Adirondacks. As at Beaverkill, it would only succeed where the forces of urbanization and production were still some distance away, while local concerns were willing to be bought out or were forced out by higher land prices.

THE TRIUMPH OF REGIONAL PLANNING
ON THE TUG HILL PLATEAU

In 1972 a third and final commission to study the need for regional planning and rural land use control was created for the Tug Hill district, a 1.3 million-acre rural area spread across 39 towns and parts of 4 counties west of the Adirondacks (Map 5.1). As defined by the planning jurisdiction of the Temporary State Commission on Tug Hill (hereafter also referred to as the Tug Hill commission), the region stretches some 40 miles east to west and 50 miles north to south. This roughly corresponds to the broad and relatively flat block of tilted sedimentary rock known as the Tug Hill Plateau, together with surrounding foothills and low-lying forests. The plateau itself rises gently from the west to a height of 1,900 feet along its eastern escarpment. Standing in the path of winter storms as they cross unfrozen Lake Ontario and pick up moisture, the plateau offers an ideal site for orographic precipitation and is reputed to receive the highest annual snowfall (200 to 300 inches a year) of any area in the United States east of the Rocky Mountains. At its core lies a vast roadless semiwilderness. Most of the region's 90,100 residents (1980 census) live in scattered towns and hamlets on the periphery of the plateau.[107]

With the region offering little opportunity for manufacturing investment and remote from major markets, Tug Hill's population peaked around 1870, at the height of the logging boom then sweeping northern New York. This level was not again reached for more than a century, when exurbanites were drawn to Tug Hill as an inexpensive retirement and second home location, while the southern fringe of the region came within the commute shed of the Syracuse and Rome-Utica metropolitan areas. By the early 1970s most of the Tug Hill region was held as low-quality commercial forest land, with the state owning some 12 percent in reforestation or game management tracts, and much of the remainder given to dairy and other small agricultural holdings.[108] Although nearly wild at its core, the Tug Hill Plateau also failed to attract much attention from statewide environmental organizations. In part it lacked the spectacular beauty and appeal of the more popular Adirondack and Catskill mountains as a recreation destination, and it was also more distant from the downstate New York City metropolis. As a consequence, Tug Hill was not portrayed as facing the critical development pressures of these better-known districts.

With the exception of the depressed logging industry, the Tug Hill region was largely bypassed as an area of concern by both extraregional production and (leisure) consumption interests. As a result, and quite unlike the situation in the Adirondacks and Catskills, the impetus for state intervention actually arose with the area's own elected local and state representatives, who were eager for development planning assistance. Concern was also expressed that with only 7 of the 39 Tug Hill towns having zoning ordinances, the municipalities were incapable of protecting long-range local interests against a mammoth 55,000-acre second home project then proposed by the Horizon Corporation for the core area. With many town budgets already strained to the breaking point by the unusually high cost of road maintenance, snow removal, and other services required by remote second homes that were converted into year-round residences, the officials were worried that the Horizon project would not generate enough tax resources nor jobs for local residents to justify acceptance. In addition, local residents, many of whom hunted and fished in the project area (on Georgia-Pacific land), feared a loss of access to this consumption space should the project move forward.[109]

Although largely disinterested in, or unaware of, changing events, local residents at least acquiesced to the creation of the Tug Hill commission. They vaguely perceived it as protecting their own consumption amenities and preferred way of life, while also attracting state attention to the economic plight of the area's four leading industries—dairying, forestry, wood processing, and recreation. Locals also realized that land speculation accompanying unplanned development would increase the price of accessible private forest land while threatening the future of the local industries upon which they still depended.[110]

The request for state assistance fell on fertile ground since, at that time, local consumption and production interests neatly coincided with a broader state interest in open space preservation and attention to expanding recreation opportunities. As a result, the 1972 act creating the Temporary State Commission on Tug Hill passed the state legislature by wide margins and was signed into law by Governor Rockefeller.[111] With the governor and the senate and assembly leaders each appointing three members, the commissioners over the ensuing years have been regional residents committed to a defense of local production and consumption interests.[112]

Working in cooperation with local governments and attempting to avoid the antagonism characteristic of the Adirondack and Catskill relationships, the Tug Hill commission staff emphasized grassroots planning with extensive public participation. Released in February 1976, the resulting plan's primary goal was to find measures to "keep Tug Hill the way it is"; its major supporting aims were preserving "home rule" and curbing "the growing cost of government."[113] Surviving through subsequent state budget appropriations, the commission focused on regional planning with technical assistance for cooperating municipalities. By 1980 it had successfully fostered formation of several cooperative planning boards involving two-thirds of the region's towns. Under commission guidance local adoption of planning and zoning ordinances substantially increased.[114]

Preemption of municipal land use regulations was never seriously considered in Tug Hill, due as much to an absence of clear state interest in the region as to any pressure for an override from outside production or consumption concerns. In many ways the Tug Hill commission operates more like a regional planning board, particularly since local participation in, and response to, planning proposals are voluntary. Nevertheless, attempts are made to coordinate local decisions in a manner benefiting the region's interest in environmental, resource base, and cultural conservation. At least in practice the Tug Hill experience may achieve many of the same goals sought by more forceful regional planning and development agencies, such as the Adirondack Park

Agency. Politically, however, the Tug Hill approach can only work in those remote rural areas meeting two basic criteria. First, the forces of production cannot yet be sufficiently developed for local production and consumption forces to clash for control of scarce land resources. This situation, by itself, is characteristic of many economically deprived rural regions. Second, the area must not yet be targeted by larger-scale regional- or state-level production or consumption forces at variance with local desires.

This combination, long the result of sheltered isolation, may now be changing. Symbolically, the opening volley is in the form of acid precipitation, originating mainly in the industrialized Ohio River Valley, and through the locally unpopular 765-kilovolt Massena-to-Marcy transmission line of the New York Power Authority, portions of which cross the eastern edge of the region (Chapter 4). More recently the northern section of the region is under the influence of a major military expansion at nearby Fort Drum. With the stationing of the new light infantry division expected to draw 30,000 new residents to the area, the Tug Hill commission is busy assisting and coordinating local response through new and strengthened land use regulations.[115]

The fort expansion, in turn, prompted state creation of the North Country Development Authority in 1986 to help provide the necessary infrastructure to service the anticipated population increase. Operating as a public authority, with state power of eminent domain, revenue-backed bond financing, and so forth (Chapter 4), the authority has pushed ahead with plans to site, construct, and operate a regional solid waste disposal landfill in the Town of Rodman within the Tug Hill district. This proposal has forced the Tug Hill commission into the politically uncomfortable position of having to respond to requests from affected local residents for assistance in opposing the site location, presumably on environmental grounds, while also having to acknowledge the legitimacy of an authority composed of county-appointed commissioners, operating under a state mandate, and committed to regional economic development.[116]

Outside consumption interests are also on the ascent as the proportion of land held by absentee owners has been rising dramatically in recent years. As in the Adirondacks, there is a tendency for these nonresident property owners to petition local officials in order to better service their primary interest in preservation for leisure and retirement consumption, thereby restricting some local production concerns such as logging or construction. On the political front, the commission's original sponsors, the well-connected Republicans Assembly-man Crawford and Senator Barclay, no longer serve in the state legislature.

As a result of these pressures, the Tug Hill commission is drifting toward entanglement in new local versus regional, state, and even national, interest debates. Lacking the means or even the will to coerce local municipalities to accept unpopular outside production and consumption demands, the commission as presently constructed has little choice but to present the local response to broader intrusions born of a dynamic production system. In so doing, it may further evolve into a popularly supported environmental and social amenity advocate, while distancing itself from the regional preemption approach to state intervention championed by the liberal planning reform movement for areas where defense of local interests threatens expansion of production or consumption space serving a broader population. Thus, in time, the state, under pressure from the new outside production and consumption interests, may move to abolish, preempt, or alter the commission should it be perceived as unresponsive to extraregional concerns. Should this occur, it might terminate one of the few successful examples in New York State where rural production and consumption concerns are united in support of regional land use planning.

CONCLUSION: THE TURNING POINT IN POPULAR SUPPORT FOR STATE PREEMPTION OF LOCAL REGULATION

During the heyday of environmental legislation in the early 1970s a coalition of environmental organizations, good government reformers (e.g., the League of Women Voters), and professional planners had a dominant hand in drafting much of New York's critical area protection legislation. In addition to the major Adirondack Park Agency Act, and the more modest Catskill effort, their influence was pronounced through passage of the Tidal Wetlands Act of 1973, the Freshwater Wetlands Act of 1975, and legislation calling for the reclamation of mined lands, protection of prime agricultural land, and designation of wild and scenic rivers.[117] Each of these measures passed without much attention from the larger development and business concerns, and opposition was largely limited to locally affected property owners.

New York's coastal zone management program is another example of critical area land use legislation. As defined in accord with requirements of the Federal Coastal Zone Management Act (PL92-583), New York's coastal zone includes the shoreland and adjoining sensitive areas along the St. Lawrence and Hudson rivers (as far north as Troy), and lands bordering the Great Lakes, the Atlantic Ocean, and Long Island Sound. In comparison with other coastal states such as California, Oregon, and Texas, New York's program is quite weak by itself.[118] In deference to the powerful home rule interests dominating suburban Long Island and Great Lakes-St. Lawrence politics, the coastal zone legislation provides only the minimum additional state review of local land use decisions required for federal certification and funding. With tidal wetlands protection, agricultural zoning, liquefied natural gas and power plant siting, endangered species legislation, and other measures already in place, neither consumption nor production interests rallied behind the coastal program, nor did they press for a stronger comprehensive program.

The State Environmental Quality Review Act (SEQR) was enacted in 1975. It had a more comprehensive focus and, as a consequence, attracted greater resistance from the prodevelopment forces than did critical area protection. Modeled after the National Environmental Policy Act of 1969, SEQR required all state and local agencies, including private subcontractors, to prepare environmental impact statements on any of their actions having a significant environmental effect. These reports would be taken into consideration, for example, when licensing private activities involving wetland development, groundwater discharge, air contaminant release, and stream disturbance.[119]

SEQR's passage marked a turning point in the (extraregional) environmentalists' assessment of local land use regulation. The act guaranteed the public's right to participate in major development decisions. With a second level of state review secured for most fragile areas, and participation in state decisions now assured, environmentalists began to reassess the local role. From now on they would selectively champion local land use regulation when it opposed state-mandated siting of energy, hazardous waste, and other types of noxious land uses (Chapter 4). Contrary to the portrayal by the liberal planning reform literature, New York's environmental advocates, whether locally or regionally focused, had already by the mid-1970s grown suspicious of state intervention in land use regulation (Chapter 6). That they had reached this turn of mind was due, in large measure, to their experience with the Hudson River Valley Commission.

NOTES

1. Andrew Sayer, "Epistemology and Conceptions of People and Nature in Geography," *Geoforum* 10, no. 1 (1979):19-43; and Karl Marx and Frederick Engels, "Feuerbach: Opposition of the Materialist and Idealist Outlook" (1845), in *The German Ideology*, Karl Marx and Frederick Engels, ed. and intro. by C. J. Arthur (New York: International Publishers, 1977), pp. 39-95. See also Hans Enzenzberger, "A Critique of Political Ecology," in *Political Ecology*, ed. A. Cockburn and J. Ridgeway (New York: Time Books, 1974), pp. 371-93; and Richard Walker, "Editor's Introduction," *Antipode* (Special Issue on Natural Resources and the Environment) 11, no. 2 (1979): 1-16.

2. Marx and Engels, "Feuerbach," p. 64.

3. See Kenneth Olwig, *Nature's Ideological Landscape* (London: George Allen & Unwin, 1984). On premechanistic conceptions of nature in western societies: cf. Clarence Glacken, *Traces on the Rhodian Shore* (Berkeley and Los Angeles: University of California Press, 1967); and Carolyn Merchant, *The Death of Nature* (San Francisco: Harper & Row, 1980). On the biblical roots of western attitudes toward the environment: Lynn White, Jr., "The Historical Roots of Our Ecological Crisis," *Science* 155 (March 10, 1967):1203-7. For refutations of White's shallow reading: Yi-Fu Tuan, "Our Treatment of the Environment in Ideal and Actuality," *American Scientist* 58 (May-June 1970):244-49; and Rene Dubos, "Conservation, Stewardship and the Human Heart," *Audubon Magazine* 74 (September 1972):20-28.

In rural districts given to subsistence activities, the older organic and classical cosmology unifying humans with nature, and not separating family life, reproduction, or consumption from the working environment, persisted well into the nineteenth century. This was the period when capitalist commodity production penetrated the last vestiges of agrarian life in North America and northern Europe.

4. See Karl Marx, *Grunrisse: Foundations of the Critique of Political Economy* (1858) (London: Harmondsworth/Penguin, 1973), pp. 489-90; Howard Parsons, *Marx*

and Engels on Ecology (Westport, CT: Greenwood Press, 1977); and Edmond Preteceille and Jean-Pierre Terrail, *Capitalism, Consumption and Needs* (1977; English ed., New York: Basil Blackwell, 1985).

5. Raymond Williams, *The Country and the City* (New York: Oxford University Press, 1973). See also H. C. Darby, "The Changing English Landscape" (1951), in *Man, Space, and Environment*, ed. P. English and R. Mayfield (London: Oxford University Press, 1972), pp. 37-39; Alfred Schmidt, *The Concept of Nature in Marx* (London: New Left Books, 1971); and Karen Olwig and Kenneth Olwig, "Underdevelopment and the Development of 'Natural' Park Ideology," *Antipode* 11, no. 2 (1979):16-25. While the hunting parks and private estates of England's aristocracy date from the tenth century, the romantic invention of landscape as a pleasing setting in which to retire from the ills of urban life only arose during the eighteenth century.

6. David Lowenthal and Hugh Prince, "English Landscape Tastes," in *Man, Space, and Environment*, ed. P. English and R. Mayfield (London: Oxford University Press, 1972), p. 82. See also Lucia White and Morton White, *The Intellectual versus the City* (Cambridge, MA: Harvard University Press, 1962).

Working- and lower-class disinterest with contemporaneous bourgeois environmental concerns is well known. In part this stems from bourgeois attention to the welfare of nature and of other species to the relative neglect of immediate human welfare and contamination in working-class residential and production districts. Where the working class adopted the bourgeois view of nature as a refuge and passion for suburban residential districts as distinct from the workplace, it was usually with a more active mechanized consumption of nature than was characteristic of bourgeois tastes.

7. Adirondack means "bark eater" in the Iroquois tongue, a term of derision possibly used by the Indians to describe the neighboring Algonquians of the area. See Alfred Donaldson, *A History of the Adirondacks*, 2 vols. (New York: Century, 1921), 1:34-36; and William Douglas, "The Eastern Forests," in *The American Heritage Book of Natural Wonders* (New York: American Heritage Publishing, 1963), p. 56.

8. Eleanor Brown, *The Forest Preserve of New York State: A Handbook for Conservationists* (Glens Falls, NY: Adirondack Mountain Club, 1985), pp. 13, 16-17. Over 200 lakes are 10 or more acres in size (Douglas, "Eastern Forests," p. 55).

The 1984 estimated permanent population for the Adirondack Park was approximately 120,000 residents (New York State, Adirondack Park Agency, *1984 Annual Report* [Ray Brook, NY: Adirondack Park Agency, 1985], p. 12).

9. Jane Keller, *Adirondack Wilderness* (Syracuse, NY: Syracuse University Press, 1980), p. 92.

10. Thomas Cole's *Schroon Mountain, Adirondacks* (1838, Cleveland Museum of Art); Sanford Gifford's *Twilight in the Adirondacks* (1864, Adirondack Museum); and Charles Cromwell Ingham's *The Great Adirondack Pass—Painted on the Spot* (1838, Adirondack Museum) are representative pieces from the Hudson River school. Winslow Homer's *Two Guides* (1876, Sterling and Francine Clark Art Institute) depicts another profession, in addition to logging, available to the area's inhabitants once the wealthy tourists began arriving.

On artists and philosophers in the Adirondack wilderness: Donaldson, *History of the Adirondacks*, 1:172-89; and Hans Huth, *Nature and the American* (1957) (Lincoln: University of Nebraska Press, 1972), pp. 96-98.

11. Joel Tyler Headley, *The Adirondack; or, Life in the Woods* (New York: Baker and Scribner, 1849); and William H. H. Murray, *Adventures in the Wilderness; or Camplife in the Adirondacks* (Boston: Fields, Osgood, 1869). During the 1830s Charles Fenno Hoffman, editor of the New York *Mirror* and later of the *American Monthly*, was one of the first people to praise the Adirondacks as a fitting destination for gentlemen in search of wild scenery. See William Chapman White, *Adirondack Country* (New York: Duell, Sloan and Pearce; Boston: Little, Brown, 1954), pp. 101-20; Huth, *Nature and the American*, p. 81; and Philip Terrie, *Forever Wild: Environmental Aesthetics and the Adirondack Forest Preserve* (Philadelphia: Temple University Press, 1985), pp. 44-67.

12. William Verner, "Wilderness and the Adirondacks—An Historical View," *The Living Wilderness* 33 (Winter 1969):35, 37. See also Donaldson, *History of the Adirondacks*, 1:190-201; Frank Graham, *The Adirondack Park: A Political History* (New York: Alfred A. Knopf, 1978), pp. 23-30; Wardner Cadbury, "Introduction," in *Adventures in the Wilderness* (1869), W. H. H. Murray (Syracuse, NY: Syracuse University Press, 1970); and Keller, *Adirondack Wilderness*, pp. 117-46. By 1890 the Adirondack native resident population was already quite close to its current level and, as today, primarily engaged in resource extraction, construction, and visitor-serving occupations.

13. Henri Lefebvre, *Everyday Life in the Modern World* (London: Harper & Row, 1971); idem, *The Survival of Capitalism* (London: Allison and Busby, 1976).

14. Donaldson, *History of the Adirondacks*, 2:93, 144-47, and 1:74-75; White, *Adirondack Country*, pp. 136-52; and Graham, *Adirondack Park*, pp. 37-44.

15. Donaldson, *History of the Adirondacks*, 1:320-29; White, *Adirondack Country*, pp. 136-51; and Anthony D'Elia, *The Adirondack Rebellion* (Onchiota, NY: Onchiota Books, 1979), pp. 11-13.

16. Temporary Study Commission on the Future of the Adirondacks, "Private Land Inventory," in *The Future of the Adirondacks, Private and Public Land,* Technical Report 1A (Albany: Temporary Study Commission on the Future of the Adirondacks, 1970; reissued [in 2 vols.], Blue Mountain Lake, NY: Adirondack Museum, 1971), 2:55; and Donaldson, *History of the Adirondacks*, 2:159-62. The Adirondack League Club was an early supporter of scientific forestry and game management on its land, and a major force behind efforts to preserve state holdings as "forever wild."

The 54,000-acre figure comes from the 1970 records of the state Board of Equalization and Assessment as reported by New York State, Adirondack Park Agency, "Large Landowner Survey" (Adirondack Park Agency, Ray Brook, NY, c. 1972, Mimeographed), p. 5.

17. E. L. Doctorow, *Loon Lake* (New York: Random House, 1980).

18. White, *Adirondack Country*, pp. 151-52; and Donaldson, *History of the Adirondacks*, 2:142-49.

Curiously Frank Graham's "political history" of the Adirondack Park makes no mention of native resistance to estate expansion and claims that the 1903 fire was due to train sparks and sloppy forestry practices on adjoining state lands (Graham, *Adirondack Park*, p. 154). Laurance Rockefeller conceived of, and contributed funds for, Graham's work (ibid., pp. ix-x).

19. On the "rebellion" by local inhabitants against what was, and still is, perceived as the intrusion of outside aesthetics and leisure tastes: D'Elia, *Adirondack*

Rebellion; League for Adirondack Citizen's Rights, *Adirondacker's Survival Kit*, reprints and pamphlets (Ausable Forks, NY: Black Brook Town Hall, c. 1976); and Richard Liroff and Gordon Davis, *Protecting Open Space: Land Use Control in the Adirondack Park* (Cambridge, MA: Ballinger Publishing, 1981), pp. 142-43.

20. Donaldson, *History of the Adirondacks*, 1:151-58, 214-24; and Graham, *Adirondack Park*, pp. 75-76, 92-94, 106, 154.

21. Actual cutting peaked in the Adirondacks in 1905 when over 700 million board feet (about 3.5 million trees) were cut. By this time, however, New York was no longer the leading pulp producer, and even the major New York City dailies were turning to bountiful Canadian supplies for newsprint (Keller, *Adirondack Wilderness*, pp. 94-96).

22. Ibid. pp. 99-108. See also Harold Hochschild, *Township 34* (printed by Harold Hochschild [1952] and available from the Adirondack Museum, Blue Mountain Lake, NY), pp. 20-22.

23. Samuel Hammond, *Wild Northern Scenes; or, Sporting Adventures with the Rifle and the Rod* (New York: Derby and Jackson, 1857), pp. x, 23.

24. New York *Times*, editorial, August 9, 1864, p. 4.

25. George Perkins Marsh, *Man and Nature; or, Physical Geography as Modified by Human Action,* rev. ed. (New York: Charles Scribner, 1871); also Graham, *Adirondack Park*, p. 67-68. Keller observes that Marsh had the Adirondacks in mind when extolling the utilitarian values of watershed protection, soil conservation, and leisure pursuits that accompany forest preservation *(Adirondack Wilderness*, p. 157).

Verplanck Colvin, chief state land surveyor in the Adirondacks from 1865 until 1900, was the most persistent voice for a timber preserve. In a stream of reports to the state legislature, he argued that conservation measures be taken and a "park" be established in the central Adirondacks (Donaldson, *History of the Adirondacks*, 2:162ff.; and Norman Van Valkenburgh, "The Creation of the Forest Preserve," *The Conservationist* 39 [May-June 1985]:10-15).

26. Donaldson, *History of the Adirondacks*, 2:170-200; Graham, *Adirondack Park*, pp. 96-106; and James E. Vance, Jr., *Capturing the Horizon: The Historical Geography of Transportation* (New York: Harper & Row, 1986), p. 128.

The New York Board of Trade and Transportation soon became the coordinating agent for other conservation groups working to preserve the Adirondack forests, a role it continued to maintain for over 50 years (New York State, Department of Conservation, *The Adirondacks: New York's Forest Preserve and a Proposed National Park* [Albany: Department of Conservation, 1967], p. 6).

27. New York State, Department of Conservation, *New York's Forest Preserve*, p. 6; and Hochschild, *Township 34*, p. 176.

28. Laws of New York (1885, Chapter 283, Sections 7 and 8); also Donaldson, *History of the Adirondacks*, 2:171-85. Initially the preserve included 681,374 acres in the Adirondacks and 33,893 acres in the Catskills (Harold Farber, "A Centennial Celebration of the Adirondacks," *New York Times Magazine*, March 21, 1985, pp.52ff.).

29. Thirteen years earlier, President Grant approved the designation of 2 million acres in Wyoming as Yellowstone National Park. Here the major concern was to protect the area's scenic "curiosities" from private acquisition and exploitation, rather than for aesthetic preservation or utilitarian conservation (Roderick Nash, *Wilderness and the American Mind,* rev. ed. [New Haven, CT: Yale University Press, 1973], pp.

108-13; and Huth, *Nature and the American*, pp. 152-61). Until John Muir led the successful campaign to establish Yosemite National Park in 1890 for the expressed purpose of wilderness aesthetics and protection, most preservationists found allies in commercial interests, such as the railroads (which provided access to, and recreation services in, preserved areas).

30. Laws of New York (1892, Chapter 707, Section 1); also Donaldson, *History of the Adirondacks*, 2:180-84.

31. Donaldson, *History of the Adirondacks*, 2:182-96; Verner, "Wilderness and the Adirondacks," pp. 38, 42; and Graham, *Adirondack Park*, pp. 126-32. During the 1880s Dr. Edward Livingston Trudeau established Saranac Lake (in the high peaks region) as the location of one of the leading tuberculosis sanatoriums and the first tuberculosis laboratory in the world (White, *Adirondack Country*, pp. 165-78).

32. New York, 1938. Article 14, Section 1 of the state constitution, as amended (originally Article 7, Section 7, 1895). On the history of Article 14:   Ralph Semerad, "Article XIV," in *The Future of the Adirondacks, Private and Public Land,* Technical Report 1B (Albany: Temporary Study Commission on the Future of the Adirondacks, 1970; reissued [in 2 vols.], Blue Mountain Lake, NY: Adirondack Museum, 1971), 2:5-21.

33. Graham, *Adirondack Park*, p. 147; Donaldson, *History of the Adirondacks*, 2:193ff.; Verner, "Wilderness and the Adirondacks," p. 44; Brown, *Forest Preserve of New York State*, pp. 52-55; and Arthur Newkirk, "Early ADK Conservationists," *Adirondac* (Adirondack Mountain Club) 49 (January 1985):34-36.

34. See Samuel Hays, *Conservation and the Gospel of Efficiency* (Cambridge, MA: Harvard University Press, 1959), on the utilitarian purpose behind the conservation movement and on its support from large-scale industrial enterprise.

35. Olwig and Olwig, "'Natural' Park Ideology"; and James Overton, "A Critical Examination of the Establishment of National Parks and Tourism in Underdeveloped Areas: Gros Morne National Park in Newfoundland," *Antipode* 11, no. 2 (1979):34-47, provide some of the best recent analyses of park protection, the production of leisure consumption space, and the social conflict generated.

36. Cf. Fred Bosselman and David Callies, *The Quiet Revolution in Land Use Control* (Prepared for the U.S. Council on Environmental Quality) (Washington, DC: Government Printing Office, 1971), pp. 295-99; Robert Healy and John Rosenberg, *Land Use and the States* (prepared for Resources for the Future), 2d ed. (Baltimore: Johns Hopkins University Press, 1979), pp. 181, 186-88; Frank Popper, *The Politics of Land-Use Reform* (Madison: University of Wisconsin Press, 1981), pp. 81-83; William Reilly, ed., *The Use of Land: A Citizen's Policy Guide to Urban Growth* (Report by the Task Force on Land Use and Urban Growth, sponsored by the Rockefeller Brothers Fund) (New York: Thomas Y. Crowell, 1973), pp. 279, 282; and Michael Heiman, "An Evaluation of State Land Use Planning and Development Control in the Adirondacks" (Master's thesis, Department of Natural Resources, Cornell University, 1975).

37. American Society of Planning Officials, *Subdividing Rural America: Impacts of Recreational Lot and Second Home Development* (prepared for the U.S. Council on Environmental Quality) (Washington, DC: Government Printing Office, 1976), pp. 136-38.

38. See New York State, Adirondack Park Agency, *Land Use Planning for the Adirondack Park*, pamphlet (Ray Brook, NY: Adirondack Park Agency, 1974); and Temporary Study Commission on the Future of the Adirondacks, *The Future of the Adirondack Park* (Albany: Temporary Study Commission on the Future of the Adirondacks, 1970; reissued [in 2 vols.], Blue Mountain Lake, NY: Adirondack Museum, 1971), 1:27.

39. On the Horizon and Ton-da-lay proposals: Liroff and Davis, *Protecting Open Space*, pp. 161-62, 169-70; and Graham, *Adirondack Park*, pp. 248-49. On Horizon's mammoth projects in the Southwest and Florida: Leonard Downie, Jr., *Mortgage on America* (New York: Praeger, 1974), pp. 138, 146-47. On the land fraud case: *Land Use Planning Report*, "FTC Cites Horizon Corp. on $375-million Land Fraud," October 8, 1979.

40. Ben Thompson, Roger Thompson, and Conrad Wirth, *A Report on a Proposed Adirondack Mountains National Park* (issued by Laurance Rockefeller) (New York: Rockefeller Center, 1967). See also New York State, Department of Conservation, *New York's Forest Preserve*. The term "modest," used to describe Rockefeller's proposal, comes from the Rockefeller-funded political history of the Adirondack Park (Graham, *Adirondack Park*, p. 219).

41. Liroff and Davis, *Protecting Open Space*, pp. 16-18; and Graham, *Adirondack Park*, pp. 219-29.

42. Cf. Myer Kutz, *Rockefeller Power* (New York: Simon and Schuster, 1974), pp. 48-49, 149; Olwig and Olwig, "'Natural' Park Ideology"; and Alvin Moscow, *The Rockefeller Inheritance* (Garden City, NY: Doubleday, 1977), pp. 193-95.

43. Liroff and Davis, *Protecting Open Space*, pp. 11, 18; Graham, *Adirondack Park*, pp. 236-41; and Holly Nelson and Alan Hahn, *State Policy and Local Influence in the Adirondacks* (Ithaca, NY: Center for Environmental Research, Cornell University, 1980).

44. Temporary Study Commission on the Future of the Adirondacks, *Future of the Adirondack Park*, 1:27.

45. Ibid., pp. 26-28.

46. Ibid., pp. 26, 32, 63-64, 83.

47. The Adirondack Park Agency Act of 1971 (Article 27 of the Executive Law, Sections 800-819, as amended by Chapter 706, Laws of New York [1971]).

48. Nelson and Hahn, *State Policy and Local Influence*; and Liroff and Davis, *Protecting Open Space*, pp. 22-26.

49. Liroff and Davis, *Protecting Open Space*, p. 26; and Heiman, "Evaluation of State Land Use Planning," pp. 78-79.
 Accepting locus of residence for political allegiance, Frank Popper erroneously concludes that strong local representation on the agency favors local economic concerns since, "given the park's chronic poverty, these members generally can be expected to favor development proposals" (*Politics of Land-Use Reform*, p. 107).

50. The Adirondack Park Agency Act of 1971 (Article 27 of the Executive Law, Section 801, as amended by Chapter 706, Laws of New York [1971]).

51. New York State, Adirondack Park Agency, *Adirondack Park State Land Master Plan* (Ray Brook, NY: Adirondack Park Agency, 1972).

52. The Adirondack Park Agency Act of 1973 (Article 27 of the Executive Law, Sections 801-819, as amended by Chapter 348, Laws of New York [1973]).

53. See Heiman, "Evaluation of State Land Use Planning," pp. 78-83.

54. Ian McHarg, "Ecological Determinism," in *Future Environments of North America*, ed. F. Fraser Darling and J. P. Milton (Garden City, NY: Natural History Press, 1966), pp. 526-38; idem, *Design with Nature* (Philadelphia: Falcon Press/ Natural History Press, 1969); and New York State, Adirondack Park Agency, *State Land Master Plan.*

55. For a review of the Brandywine experience: Ann Strong, *Private Property and the Public Interest: The Brandywine Experience* (Baltimore: Johns Hopkins University Press, 1975). For a self-critical examination of the planning process at Lake Tahoe: Charles Finkelstein and Laurence Baxter, *Planning and Politics: A Staff Perception of the Tahoe Regional Planning Agency*, Institute of Government Affairs, Environmental Quality Series Report no. 21 (Davis: University of California, 1974).

56. William H. Whyte, *The Last Landscape* (Garden City, NY: Doubleday, 1968), pp. 182-95.

57. New York State, Adirondack Park Agency, *Adirondack Park Land Use and Development Plan and Recommendations for Implementation* (Ray Brook, NY: Adirondack Park Agency, 1973); and idem, *Comprehensive Report: Adirondack Park Agency*, 2 vols. (Ray Brook, NY: Adirondack Park Agency, 1976; reprinted, Lake Placid *News*, March 4, 1976, Section 2).

58. New York State, Adirondack Park Agency, *Land Use and Development Plan*; idem, *Comprehensive Report*, vol. 1. For an update on the agency project review process as amended: Liroff and Davis, *Protecting Open Space*, pp. 26-39.

59. New York State, Adirondack Park Agency, *Local Planning and Land Use Controls in the Adirondacks: A Handbook for Local Governments* (Ray Brook, NY: Adirondack Park Agency, 1975), pp. 6-8.

60. New York State, Legislative Commission on Expenditure Review, *Adirondack Park Planning and Regulation*, Program Audit (Albany: Legislative Commission on Expenditure Review, April 1978), pp. 23-25. For two contrasting views of program success: cf. New York State, Adirondack Park Agency, *1978 Annual Report* (Ray Brook, NY: Adirondack Park Agency, 1979); and Adirondack Park Local Government Review Board, *A Return to Basic Problems: 1979 Annual Report* (Loon Lake, NY: Adirondack Park Local Government Review Board, 1979). See Heiman, "Evaluation of State Land Use Planning," on initial local reaction to the agency's program and for an evaluation of the different incentives offered for local compliance.

61. Although statewide support for the agency remained steadfast over the ensuing years, the agency, under Albany's direction, has become more involved in economic development planning. Tourism, crafts, dairying, and other activities compatible with environmental preservation are favored. See Farber, "Centennial Celebration"; and New York State, Adirondack Park Agency, *1984 Annual Report.*

62. Temporary Study Commission on the Future of the Adirondacks, *Future of the Adirondack Park*, 1:72. Recreation use of the forest preserve peaked during the mid-1970s as the "baby boomers" flooded the forest. By 1980 recorded use of state campgrounds in the Catskill and Adirondack forest preserves had actually fallen 46 percent from the level reached in 1970 (Brown, *Forest Preserve of New York State*, p. 56).

63. The Adirondack Park Agency Act of 1973 (Article 27 of the Executive Law, Section 801, as amended by Chapter 348, Laws of New York [1973]).

64. On these programs: Bosselman and Callies, *Quiet Revolution*; Healy and Rosenberg, *Land Use and the States*; and Popper, *Politics of Land-Use Reform*.

65. Adirondack Park Local Government Review Board, *1979 Annual Report*, pp. 1, 9. See also Liroff and Davis, *Protecting Open Space*, pp. 129-45, on the review board's history of opposing the imposition of development control in the Adirondacks.

66. Charles Zinser, *The Economic Impact of the Adirondack Park Private Land Use and Development Plan* (Albany: State University of New York Press, 1980), pp. 71, 104, 234.

67. Charles Geisler, Susan Kenney, and Roger Vlieger, "Sources of Inholder Opposition to Land Use Management in the Adirondack Park of New York" (Paper presented at the Annual Meeting of the Rural Sociological Society, College Station, TX, August 22-25, 1984) (available from the Department of Rural Sociology, Cornell University, Ithaca, NY); and Charles Geisler, et al., *Adirondack Landowners Survey*, Department of Rural Sociology Bulletin no. 145 (Ithaca, NY: Department of Rural Sociology, Cornell University, 1985), p. 33.

68. For comparisons between unemployment rates for Adirondack counties and those for the rest of the state: New York State, Legislative Commission on Expenditure Review, *Planning and Regulation*, pp. 9-10; and Paul Eberts, *Socioeconomic Trends in Rural New York State: Toward the 21st Century* (Albany: New York State, Legislative Commission on Rural Resources, 1984).

69. New York State, Adirondack Park Agency, *Adirondack Park Economic Profile: Phase Two: Recent Trends and Factors Affecting the Adirondack Real Estate Market* (Ray Brook, NY: Adirondack Park Agency, 1976); New York State, Legislative Commission on Expenditure Review, *Planning and Regulation*, pp. 11-13; and New York State, Board of Equalization and Assessment, *Adirondack Park Real Property Tax Base Study*, Final Report (Albany: Board of Equalization and Assessment, 1978).

In 1973 New York State had 79,470 housing starts. By 1975 this figure had fallen 59 percent to a low of 32,623 starts. During the same period the Adirondack Park itself had a 54 percent decline in housing starts, while the Catskill counties experienced a 56 percent decline (New York State, Adirondack Park Agency, *Economic Profile*, p. 6).

Comparing this data with local opinion on the plan's impact, Zinser concluded that municipal officials and others opposed to the agency's presence seriously underestimated the effect of the 1974-75 recession and rising fuel prices upon employment and construction in the park. Simultaneously they exaggerated the contribution of the agency's plan to economic malaise (Zinser, *Economic Impact of the Adirondack Park Plan*, pp. 49, 55, 143-71).

70. See New York State, Adirondack Park Agency, *Comprehensive Report*, vol. 1, Table 36. In 1970 the unemployment rate for the Adirondack Park stood at 8.2 percent, more than double the figure for the rest of the state (ibid., vol. 2, Table 35). The Adirondacks also had one-third again more families below or near the poverty level (as defined by the U.S. Department of Agriculture) than the state as a whole (ibid., vol. 2, Table 38).

71. Cf. ibid., vol. 1, Table 1; idem, *Economic Profile*; and Zinser, *Economic Impact of the Adirondack Park Plan*, p. 125. Of the three large subdivisions, only

Ausable Acres survived. The other two went bankrupt, largely in response to agency-related delays and an inability to profitably meet the density standards set (Zinser, *Economic Impact of the Adirondack Park Plan*, p. 125).

72. Zinser, *Economic Impact of the Adirondack Park Plan*, pp. 136-37.

73. League for Adirondack Citizen's Rights, *Adirondacker's Survival Kit*; Adirondack Park Local Government Review Board, *Annual Report—1975*, section 1, finding no. 6, Representation on Adirondack Park Agency (Loon Lake, NY: Adirondack Park Local Government Review Board, 1975); and Zinser, *Economic Impact of the Adirondack Park Plan*, p. 76. See also D'Elia, *Adirondack Rebellion*; Graham, *Adirondack Park*, p. 254-57; Liroff and Davis, *Protecting Open Space*, pp. 142-45; Elaine Moss, ed., *Land Use Controls in New York State* (prepared for the Natural Resources Defense Council) (New York: Dial Press, 1975), pp. 125-29; and Popper *Politics of Land-Use Reform*, p. 111.

74. See Geisler et al., *Adirondack Landowners Survey*; New York State, Adirondack Park Agency, *1984 Annual Report*; and Mary Esch, "APA Now Trying to Promote Economic Development," *Leader-Herald* (Gloversville-Johnstown, NY), August 14, 1985, p. 7.

75. Liroff and Davis, *Protecting Open Space*, p. 145; Adirondack Park Local Government Review Board, *1979 Annual Report*; idem, *The Blue Line Review* (Adirondack Park Local Government Review Board) 4 (March 1986); and Kim Elliman, "Keep the Adirondack State Park 'Forever Wild,'" editorial, New York *Times*, December 7, 1985, p. A27. The Adirondack Council, chief proponent for expansion of the forest preserve, represents a coalition of five major preservation organizations, including the Wilderness Society and the Association for the Protection of the Adirondacks, together with 3,400 individual members. Established in 1975, its three current directors all came from the park agency's own staff (Adirondack Council, *A Special Report: State of the Park 1986*, Fourth Annual Report [Elizabethtown, NY: Adirondack Council, 1986]).

76. New York State, Adirondack Park Agency, *Comprehensive Report*, vol. 1, section 4, New Initiatives, first paragraph.

77. Popper, *Politics of Land-Use Reform*, p. 83; also Graham, *Adirondack Park*, pp. 257-59.

Finkelstein and Baxter, *Planning and Politics*, describe the difficulties encountered by the Lake Tahoe regional planning staff with local rejection of their "objective" and "scientific" planning process. They also accept insufficient public comprehension of the plan's complexities as a basis for local reaction and overlook real differences in economic and social goals.

78. Heiman, "Evaluation of State Land Use Planning," pp. 113-60; Keller, *Adirondack Wilderness*, pp. 213-24; Liroff and Davis, *Protecting Open Space*, pp. 117-21; and New York State, Legislative Commission on Expenditure Review, *Planning and Regulation*, pp. 36-42.

79. Keller, *Adirondack Wilderness*, pp. 216-17.

80. See Chapter 1. The Rockefeller Task Force on Land Use and Urban Growth, to cite an example, suggests that "there are probably few other fields in which citizens, *adequately informed* about problems and alternative solutions, can be so helpful to public decision-makers as in the field of urban growth" (Reilly, *Use of Land*, p. 10, emphasis added).

81. Temporary Study Commission on the Future of the Adirondacks, *Future of the Adirondack Park*, 1:68.

82. Cf. ibid., 1:57; and New York State, Adirondack Park Agency, *Comprehensive Report*, vol. 2, Table 36. Even considering the important secondary employment multipliers from wood processing (e.g., lumber and furniture), the Adirondacks fare rather poorly since most of the value added on forest resources occurs outside of the region (see Shanna Ratner and Peter Ide, *Strategies for Community Economic Development through Natural Resource Use in Northern New York*, Economics Resource Paper 85-10 [Ithaca, NY: Department of Agricultural Economics, Cornell University, 1985]).

83. Brown, *Forest Preserve of New York State*, p. 11.

84. New York State, Adirondack Park Agency, *Comprehensive Report*, vol. 1, section 2, The Adirondack Park Agency Program.

85. See Arthur Johnson, "Acid Deposition: Trends, Relationships, and Effects," *Environment* 28 (May 1986):6-11, 34-39.

86. Brown, *Forest Preserve of New York State*, p. 144. At 4,204 feet, Slide Mountain is the highest peak in the massif.

87. See Roland Van Zandt, *The Catskill Mountain House* (New Brunswick, NJ: Rutgers University Press, 1966).

88. See Betsy Blackmar, "Going to the Mountains: A Social History," in *Resorts of the Catskills,* Architectural League of New York and Gallery Association of New York State (New York: St. Martin's Press, 1979); and Eric Freedman and Roger Klingman, "The Catskills," *Empire State Report* 9 (June 1983):13-23.

89. Laws of New York (1884, Chapter 551); Laws of New York (1885, Chapter 283); Laws of New York (1888, Chapter 520). See also Tom Miner, "For Our Children's Children," *The Conservationist* 39 (May-June 1985):60-65; and Brown, *Forest Preserve of New York State*, p. 28. In effect the tables had been turned since now the state would make payments in lieu of taxes on forest preserve land to the local governments.

90. Farber, "Centennial Celebration," p. 56.

91. Laws of New York (1904, Chapter 233); and Farber, "Centennial Celebration," p. 56.

92. New York City, Board of Water Supply, *Catskill Water Supply: A General Description and Brief History* (New York: Board of Water Supply, 1917).

93. Brown, *Forest Preserve of New York State*, pp. 3-6.

94. Despite declining productivity, the larger Catskill region remained a major agricultural supplier for nearby metropolitan centers. In 1973 the farm dollar value in the seven-county region was nearly as large as that for all of New Jersey (New York State, Temporary State Commission to Study the Catskills, *The Future of the Catskills: Final Report of the Temporary State Commission to Study the Catskills* [Albany: Temporary State Commission to Study the Catskills, 1975], p. 16).

95. Cf. ibid., p. 55; and Temporary Study Commission on the Future of the Adirondacks, *Future of the Adirondack Park*, p. 72.

96. New York State, Temporary State Commission to Study the Catskills, *Future of the Catskills*, pp. 25-27. See Chapter 4 on unfulfilled power projections by the state's utilities during the 1960s and 1970s.

97. Regional Plan Association of New York, "Catskill Resources Management Commission Being Debated by New York Legislature," *The Region's Agenda* 6 (June 1977):1.

98. Laws of New York (1971, Chapter 688, Section 2); also Alan Hahn and Cynthia Dyballa, "State Environmental Planning and Local Influence: A Comparison of Three Regional Natural Resource Management Agencies," *Journal of the American Planning Association* 47 (July 1981):328; and Brown, *Forest Preserve of New York State*, p. 47.

99. See New York State, Temporary State Commission to Study the Catskills, *Future of the Catskills*, pp. 3, 13-15.

100. Ibid, p. 4.

101. Ibid, p. i; and editorial in *The Catskills,* "Our Future Awaits" (Winter 1972-73):40-44. Executive Director Albert Hall was listed as "career conservationist."

102. New York State, Temporary State Commission to Study the Catskills, *Future of the Catskills*, pp. 10-15.

103. Catskill Center for Conservation and Development, *The Catskill Center Plan* (Hobart, NY: Catskill Center for Conservation and Development, 1974), p. 7 (from the introduction by Peter Borrelli), and pp. 64-65.

104. Hahn and Dyballa, "State Environmental Planning and Local Influence," p. 328; and New York *Times*, "Planning Fought by Catskill Farmers," August 11, 1985, section 1, p. 44.

105. According to Hahn and Dyballa, "The commission apparently saw its emphasis on economic development as well as natural resource protection as evident of responsiveness to regional concerns. However, it did not cater to any specific interests and apparently ended up pleasing no one sufficiently to mobilize their wholehearted support" ("State Environmental Planning and Local Influence," pp. 328-29).

106. Michael Winerip, "One Man's Efforts Conserve Catskills Valley," New York *Times*, February 19, 1984, pp. A1, 2. See idem, "Cheap Land in Catskills Not Always a Bargain," New York *Times*, September 7, 1984, pp. A1, B4, on recent land sale activity.

107. See New York State, Temporary State Commission on Tug Hill, *Interim Report* (Watertown, NY: Temporary State Commission on Tug Hill, 1974); idem, *The Tug Hill Region: Preparing for the Future: Report of the Temporary State Commission on Tug Hill* (Watertown, NY: Temporary State Commission on Tug Hill, 1976); and Benjamin Coe and Thorton Ware, "The Tug Hill Experience," *Planning News* (New York Planning Federation) 41 (March-April 1977).

108. New York State, Temporary State Commission on Tug Hill, *Interim Report*; idem, *Tug Hill Region*, pp. 36-40.

109. New York State, Temporary State Commission on Tug Hill, *Tug Hill Region*, pp. 12, 16. See also Elizabeth Marsh, *Cooperative Rural Planning: A Tug Hill Case Study* (Watertown, NY: Temporary State Commission on Tug Hill, 1981), p. 25; and Cynthia Dyballa, "The Tug Hill Commission: A Cooperative Approach to Regional Planning" (Master's thesis, Department of Natural Resources, Cornell University, 1979). Just prior to the creation of the Tug Hill commission, the Horizon project was abandoned as economically unfeasible given the then-collapsing vacation home market.

110. League of Women Voters of New York State, *Making Land Use Decisions in New York State* (New York: League of Women Voters of New York State, 1975), p. 41; and Hahn and Dyballa, "State Environmental Planning and Local Influence."

111. Laws of New York (1972, Chapter 972).

112. Of the first nine commissioners, four held local public offices, and all except Assemblyman Crawford (sponsor of the commission) resided in the study area. Of the nine, three were local businessmen, and all had a primary commitment to home rule and local interests. See Cynthia Dyballa, Lyle Raymond, Jr., and Alan Hahn, *The Tug Hill Program: A Regional Planning Option for Rural Areas* (Syracuse, NY: Syracuse University Press, 1981), pp. 69-70.

113. New York State, Temporary State Commission on Tug Hill, *Tug Hill Region*, pp. 14, 48.

114. Hahn and Dyballa, "State Environmental Planning and Local Influence," pp. 329-30; and Dyballa, Raymond, and Hahn, *Tug Hill Program*, pp. 80-110.

115. On extraregional production pressures in the Tug Hill region: Benjamin Coe, "Tug Hill Revisited," *Planning News* 43 (July-August 1979):1, 6-7; and Richard Grover, "People Power: It Can Make a Difference," *Planning News* 42 (March-April 1978):1, 6-7. On the impact of the military expansion: Benjamin Coe, "Meeting the Needs of Rural Communities Governed by Part-Time Officials" (Paper prepared for the Region I/II Conference of the American Society for Public Administration, held in Albany, NY, October 22, 1986 (available from the Temporary State Commission on Tug Hill, Watertown, NY).

116. Norah Machia and Paul Foy, "Tug Hill Commission 'Wimps' on Garbage," Watertown *Daily Times*, April 24, 1987, pp. 1, 12; and *Tug Hill Commission Newsletter* (Watertown, NY), "Tug Hill Issues Multiply" (June 1987):1, 3-4.

117. The Tidal Wetlands Act (New York State Environmental Conservation Law, Article 25) mandates a local permit system under DEC review for any alteration of a tidal wetland up to ten feet in elevation above mean sea level. The Freshwater Wetlands Act (New York State Environmental Conservation Law, Article 24) establishes a similar process for any dredging, diking, or filling that involves wetlands of 12.35 acres or more. Approximately 25,000 acres are covered by the tidal program and over 1.3 million by the freshwater wetland program (New York State, Department of Environmental Conservation, *Land Resources Management and Related Programs of the New York State Department of Environmental Conservation*, 3 vols. [Albany: Land Resources Planning Group, Department of Environmental Conservation, 1976], p. 8; see also Moss, *Land Use Controls in New York State*).

118. New York's coastal legislation authorizes a procedure whereby the DEC designates critical coastal erosion areas with local governments responsible for drafting the safeguarding legislation. See Mitchel Abolafia, "Coordinating for the Collective Good: A Study of Coastal Zone Planning," *Administration & Society* 11 (August 1979):172-92; New York State, Department of State, *New York State Coastal Management Program: Draft Environmental Impact Statement* (Albany: Department of State, 1976); and Joseph Heikoff, *Marine and Shoreland Resources Management* (Ann Arbor, MI: Ann Arbor Science Publishers, 1980).

119. See Deborah Hoard, "The Substantive Duties of Local Governments under the New York State Environmental Quality Review Act" (Master's thesis, Department of Natural Resources, Cornell University, 1978).

Landscape Preservation
and Social Conflict
in the Hudson Valley

With a rich history of social conflict dating from the colonial period, New York's Hudson River Valley is perhaps the nation's most celebrated battleground between the forces of production and those seeking protection of leisure and residential consumption amenities. Recent state attempts during the Rockefeller administration to coordinate land development in the valley and balance these opposing concerns provide yet another overlooked example of New York's quiet evolution in land use control. As with the use of public authorities and special facility siting legislation, this quiet evolution entails an ongoing process of regulatory centralization, usually with support from production concerns, when a local defense of consumption amenities presents barriers to capital expansion. And, as is often the case, state intervention to facilitate economic expansion is tempered by competing demands on the public sector to assist with the defense of threatened consumption space. These requests may even arise from the very individuals and institutions that have a vested production interest in the landscape. Such is the nature and irony of the contradictory relationship with nature intrinsic to the capitalist mode of production (Chapters 1 and 5).

Governor Rockefeller's creation of the Hudson River Valley Commission (HRVC) provides an interesting case study of the liberal attempt to balance production concerns with self-professed environmentalism, as expressed through a defense of consumption space. In particular, the commission appears as an endeavor to mollify concern by the valley's wealthy landowners in protecting a privileged lifestyle from the ravage of poorly planned urban development, while also ensuring that public investment in energy, transportation, and residential development required for continued capital accumulation could continue. This agenda challenges the conventional explanation for regional intervention focusing on consumer demand and is also at variance with a strict Marxist interpretation of State action centered on production requirements. The HRVC case study can also be used to enlarge the boundaries of traditional Marxist analysis by demonstrating that social movements opposed to the expansion of production may arise from bourgeois, as well as working-class, defense of consumption space. Finally, the HRVC presents a provocative study for development of a Marxist theory of the State. It thus appears that Rockefeller's commission not only addressed *structural* contradiction besetting capitalist production in the valley—in this case where a social movement based upon protection of bourgeois consumption amenities generated barriers to continued production—but, moreover, did so in a manner bearing the apparent mark of *instrumental* self-enrichment for the Rockefeller family.

PRODUCTION CONFRONTS CONSUMPTION: FROM PRIVATE SOLUTIONS TO PUBLIC INTERVENTION

The Hudson River flows some 315 miles from its source high on the flank of Mt. Marcy, the state's tallest mountain, to its mouth at New York Harbor. The river has two distinct sections. Above Troy, where the Mohawk River and Erie Canal enter, the rushing river encounters many waterfalls. Many grist, iron, saw, and textile mills were established here during the eighteenth and nineteenth centuries. Near Troy, however, the river enters a drowned valley enlarged by Pleistocene glaciers. As a result, the lower half of the river is subject to ocean tides and has a bed lying below sea level. With some dredging between Albany and Hudson, oceangoing vessels can navigate as far as the Albany-Troy area where goods may be loaded or unloaded for transport through the Mohawk Valley via the Erie Canal (completed in 1825) (Map 6.1). Taken together, the Hudson and Mohawk valleys provide the only navigable break through the Appalachian Mountains in the United States. Since pioneering days these valleys served as the most significant transportation corridor between the Great Lakes and the Atlantic Ocean.

Stretching approximately 150 miles from New York City to the Albany-Troy area, and 10 to 20 miles in width between the Catskill and Palisades highlands on the west and the Taconics on the east, the Hudson River Valley was a primary location during colonial times for Dutch and British crown grants to favored subjects. The revolutionary government honored many of these grants in exchange for loyalty. As a result, the valley emerged at the beginning of the nineteenth century as one of the few centers in the northern United States where tenant farmers confronted a genuine landed segment of capital interests whose social standing was tied to landownership.

In Albany and Rensselaer counties the 700,000-acre Rensselaerswyck Manor had several thousand tenants by the early 1800s, while to the south the Livingston Manor covered 160,000 acres along the Hudson in Columbia County. From 1751 until the Civil War thousands of tenant farmers struggled to gain freehold property rights to some 2 million acres in the Hudson and Mohawk river valleys.[1] Industrial capitalists sided with the farmers when attacking the landed aristocracy as a parasite class thwarting productive enterprise and investment. With this support, the farmers had some measure of success. Following the removal of property ownership as a basis for male suffrage in 1822 and the violent Anti-Rent Movement of 1839-45, tenant farmers gained limits on

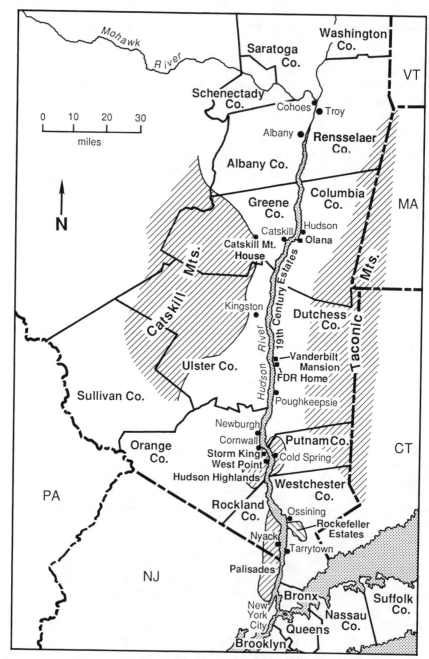

Map 6.1. Hudson Valley landmarks.

eviction proceedings and stricter estate tax and inheritance laws. However, with portions of the valley now opened to a competitive market in landownership and the decline in agricultural production once cheaper midwestern produce began to flood the market, control recentralized somewhat. Elsewhere, small remnants of the older estates remained intact among descendants of the original landlords.

Although the Hudson Valley gave birth and inspiration to the young nation's first indigenous school of painting, the popular acceptance of the Hudson River school as depicting a wilderness condition actually found in the valley and adjoining Catskill Mountains was itself mistaken. Apparently serving as an inspiration for Thomas Cole, the "wild shores" of the Hudson already ran through the heart of what was referred to as "the breadbasket of the nation" from the close of the Revolutionary War until the 1820s, when the Erie Canal provided access to the newer wheat-growing regions of western New York and, later, the Midwest.[2] By the 1840s, at the peak of the Hudson River school's influence, the intensely settled valley was swarming with Europeans and wealthy Americans on the Grand Tour of America's "wild wonders." Steaming up the "wild" Hudson they were apparently oblivious to intense commercial steamboat use of one of the nation's leading thoroughfares and to the squalid living conditions of the nearby tenant farmers.

To the immediate west, the Catskill counties were alive by the 1820s with lumbering, tanning, mining, and farming activities. The mountainous terrain had been opened for commercial exploitation through an intricate system of canals and turnpikes. On the opposite bank major forges and ironworks were established at Troy, Hudson, Cold Spring, Poughkeepsie, and Peekskill, while other Hudson River towns were given to brick making, quarrying, and cement production. Nevertheless, in their rush to fulfill the growing European and American demand for views of a romantic wilderness, Cole and his contemporaries, including Asher B. Durand, Frederick E. Church, and poet William Cullen Bryant, although personally troubled by the destruction, often overlooked or screened out the burnt-over fields, stinking tanneries, polluted streams, clamorous sawmills, and other production intrusions.[3] Their success was phenomenal, and luxurious mountaintop hotels, such as the well-known Catskill Mountain House, were erected to provide a comfortable experience for the itinerant wilderness traveler in search of famous scenes. Here, perched high above the valley on the hotels' verandas, and clutching well-worn guidebooks suggesting the best positions and times to view God's creation so as to avoid the disagreeable facts of production, the bourgeoisie could imagine an idealized rural landscape curiously devoid of social struggle and human suffering. According to the noted Catskill historian Alf Evers:

> Pilgrims en route to the Mountain House might hold their noses as tanners' wagons passed by or rub their eyes when the smoke of forest fires made the mountain air thick and biting, yet they could console themselves by reflecting that they were in the midst of what the best authorities certified to be a wilderness Garden of Eden into which only the famous Mountain House intruded.[4]

Attracted by the possibility of large landholdings, a new breed of Hudson Valley landowners emerged during the latter half of the nineteenth century. Their fortunes were derived from industrial and financial activities rather than through land inheritance. Represented by the Rockefellers, Harrimans, and Vanderbilts, these new owners were primarily concerned with estate ownership for their own residence and leisure consumption, often linked with additional holdings in the Adirondacks and at Newport for a summer retreat. They were only marginally interested in Hudson property for rent or productive investment. Many of the largest estates were located on the more level east side of the river in Dutchess and Columbia counties. This location permitted stunning views across to the rugged Catskill Mountains.[5]

Following completion of the first railroad line along the east bank of the river in 1851, the lower Hudson, from the Hudson Highlands in the vicinity of West Point south, fell within the commute shed of New York City. Thereafter many wealthy merchants, industrialists, bankers, and others whose presence in the city was a daily requirement moved north from their Manhattan abodes to estates clustered along the river districts of Westchester and Putnam counties. Here they created a privileged landscape removed from the social turmoil and environmental contamination of their urban workplace. This spatial demarcation between production and consumption, however, could no longer be guaranteed solely through private action. With new consumption and industrial demands being made upon the valley's natural resources, state regulation would now be necessary to protect this idyllic setting. It was with the arrival of the new gentry and suburban commuters that public attempts were finally made to prevent further production intrusion into the Hudson Valley landscape.[6]

With the introduction of dynamite in the 1870s the riverfront from Poughkeepsie to New York City experienced an increase in rock quarrying and stone crushing. Local estate owners rallied behind park preservation to prevent noise pollution and scenic destruction. In addition, parks could stall land speculation and suburbanization. Historic preservation of old battlesites, forts, and mansions became a rallying cause for action. This was somewhat ironic because the original Hudson River artists, to whom many activists made reference, often celebrated the lack of a prior historic and cultural association in the landscape. In the 1890s J. Pierpont Morgan, then vice-president of the American Scenic and Historic Preservation Society, convinced several wealthy associates to join with him to support both private donation and public purchase of land in the lower valley for scenic production. The movement to protect New Jersey's Palisades Cliffs from further quarrying was led by the Palisades Protection Association. The association was organized by wealthy business and financial leaders with homes on Westchester County's opposing shore. The movement's narrow social origin was apparent as the New York *Times*, in numerous editorials, lamented the public's indifference to the desecration.[7] In 1900 the preservation forces succeeded in having New York and New Jersey establish the Palisades Interstate Park Commission with the power to condemn and acquire land for recreation purposes.

The Palisades Interstate Park was finally dedicated in 1909 after nearly a decade of struggle by landowners atop the Palisades, who resisted condemnation of their own residential property. With the Morgans, Rockefellers, and Harrimans donating the initial $15 million for acquisition, additional state bond appropriations were supplemented by further land dedications from these families. The Palisades Interstate Park system eventually spread to cover thousands of acres in several dispersed units along the west shore, with an accumulated 40 miles of protected parkland reaching to the Hudson Highlands at Storm King Mountain.[8]

In 1936 the Hudson River Conservation Society was established by wealthy valley residents to acquire scenic easements and guard against further quarrying in and along the river. More recently, in 1962, Consolidated Edison, then the nation's largest private utility, announced plans to construct a 2,020-Mw pumped-storage facility atop Storm King Mountain, a particularly scenic spot on the river (Chapter 4). This action was successfully challenged by the Scenic Hudson Preservation Conference. The conference was formed by local land-owners as a splinter group from the Hudson River Conservation Society when the society's board, with the backing of the governor's brother Laurance, voted not to oppose the controversial project following assurances from the utility that there would be no overhead transmission lines across the river.[9] Employing nineteenth-century lithographs from the Hudson River school in its brochures, the Scenic Hudson coalition soon expanded to include the Sierra Club, Izaak Walton League, Wilderness Society, Audubon Society, and numerous hunting and fishing clubs. The latter were concerned over the threat to the Hudson's prized striped bass fishery. Even the city of New York, served by Con Ed, opposed the project, allegedly because the blasting would threaten the Catskill Aqueduct running through Storm King Mountain.[10]

While arguably the birthplace of the contemporary environmental move-ment, Storm King was certainly the birthplace of the environmental litigation movement. Its significance for consumption movements was profound. Now, for the first time, the nation's highest courts agreed that aggrieved parties without economic concerns, but with aesthetic, recreational, and other nontan-gible interests, could sue and thereby freely participate in the defense of the environment.

Following almost two decades of legal battles, an agreement to abandon the Storm King plan was finally reached in 1981 between the state, the U.S. Environmental Protection Agency, environmental organizations, the Nuclear Regulatory Commission, and those utilities maintaining plants along the Hudson. In return for abandoning the pumped-storage project, donating the land for a state park, scheduling water withdrawal so as to minimize fish loss, and sponsoring continuing research on the river, the utilities were relieved of a federal requirement to install closed-cycle cooling systems.[11] This decision was furthered by declining power demand and by an earlier commitment from the Power Authority to purchase several financially ailing Con Ed power plants and to tie the utility into its existing power grid (Chapter 4). Finally, the environmental groups were faced with a dilemma. They acknowledged the devastation wrought by cooling withdrawal, which, within a 20-mile stretch from Newburgh to Haverstraw Bay, drew in a majority of the river's freshwater flow. Nonetheless, they did not welcome the visual impact of the six huge cooling towers proposed as the solution. In the end, the aesthetic wing of the coalition won, and the fish and their habitat, although safer than before, were partially compromised.[12]

Scenic preservation also figured prominently in the Nuclear Regulatory Commission's deliberations on the Power Authority's 1,200-Mw nuclear facility proposed at Cementon (on the Hudson), in southern Greene County. A major concern was that the enormous cooling towers required by the plant would spoil the stunning view across the river from Olana, the magnificent estate of Hudson artist Frederick E. Church and by then a state historic landmark. The 1979 resolution was precedent setting as the first environmental impact statement ever issued by the NRC staff recommending against the licensing of a nuclear power plant. That the denial rested in large measure upon scenic and aesthetic objectives demonstrated how politically powerful consumption interests had become and the still considerable significance attached to bourgeois landscape ideology as cultivated in the valley.[13] In an impassioned defense of the valley's visual resources, Carl Petrich of Oak Ridge National Laboratory (under contract to prepare the impact statement for the NRC) referred to the valley's stunning landscape as helping us to discover the very roots of our aesthetic sensibilities:

> The human preference is for controlled vistas—tamed nature. . . . We need wilderness for raw inspiration, but for our front yards, our local parks, for the daily refreshing of our spirits, we prefer the American landscape prototype: the nineteenth century Hudson River estate and its derivatives.[14]

As events would prove at Storm King, Cementon, and elsewhere along the river, this spirited defense of nature as residential and recreational space presented serious obstacles to capital expansion, once again prompting state intervention.

THE HUDSON RIVER VALLEY COMMISSION

Despite his family's long-standing support for open space and scenic preservation in the Hudson Valley, Governor Nelson Rockefeller was a strong proponent of Storm King and of the nuclear power plant expansion in the valley envisioned by Con Ed during the 1960s. In 1965, Nelson appointed a commission "to enhance the river's recreational, industrial, historic, scenic, cultural, residential and esthetic values, and preserve these values for the future."[15] The idea for the commission came through the New York State Council of Parks, then under the leadership of Laurance Rockefeller. With Laurance as its first chair and Laurance's associate Conrad Wirth (later replaced by Rockefeller cousin Alexander Aldrich) as executive director, the Hudson River Valley Commission was designed to demonstrate the governor's commitment to environmental integrity while also supporting the governor's call for "socially necessary" and "environmentally acceptable" projects such as Storm King. Constituting a "who's who" of Hudson Valley power and influence, early commission members included ex-governor and philanthropist W. Averell Harriman; Henry T. Heald, president of the Ford Foundation; Marian Sulzberger Heiskell, wife of the chair of Time Inc. and daughter of the publisher of the New York *Times*; Alan Simpson, president of Vassar College; Thomas Watson, Jr., chair and president of IBM; landscape critic William H. Whyte, who, together with Wirth, was directly employed by Laurance's American Conservation Association; famed conservationist and commentator Lowell Thomas (later replaced by actress Helen Hayes); Frank McCabe, president of the National Commercial Bank and Trust Co. of Albany, in which many state funds were deposited; and George Yerry, local president of the Building and Construction Trades Council.[16] An advisory committee, drawn from major industrial and utility interests in the valley and from other Rockefeller associates, was also appointed by the governor to help the commission achieve the proper balance between landscape preservation and economic development. The committee included the presidents or operating managers from most of the significant industrial concerns impacting the valley, such as the U.S. Gypsum Co., Con Ed, the New York Central Railroad, the Tarrytown Chevrolet plant of General Motors, and Orange and Rockland Utilities.[17]

With broad-based popular concern over urban sprawl, water pollution, and scenic deterioration still several years away, Nelson's commission emerged as an innovative state attempt to mediate bourgeois consumption amenities, later embraced by a wider constituency, and production concerns in the valley. The governor, however, was not the only politician seeking recognition as a Hudson Valley mediator. A few months prior to the Rockefeller effort Democratic Congressman Richard Ottinger proposed a bill establishing a Hudson Highlands National Scenic Riverway from Yonkers to Newburgh. Challenging the Rockefeller administration's commitment to environmental conservation, Ottinger's bill was designed to block construction of the Storm King project and a proposed Hudson River Expressway. Stepping into the fray, Secretary of Interior Steward Udall supported a successful Ottinger bill giving the secretary review power for three years over all federal licensing actions in the valley, including federal participation in transportation and energy projects. At hearings before the Subcommittee on National Parks and Recreation of the House Committee on Interior and Insular Affairs, Conrad Wirth, himself a former director of the National Park Service, tried to assure the audience that the Udall-Ottinger proposal was not necessary because the valley would be safe under New York's control. The latter, of course, could be equated with Rockefeller control and, according to Wirth, the family's strong commitment to environmental conservation was beyond reproach.[18]

Dominating both houses of the state legislature, Nelson moved quickly to nullify federal action. In 1965 and 1966 bills were passed attempting to formalize the HRVC as an interstate planning and development agency.[19] Nelson rejected a contending federal compact with equal representation from New York and New Jersey as inviting "a paralysis of development" and as producing a "narrow view that recognized only recreation and scenic beauty as important considerations." He acted unilaterally and endowed his commission with only a more limited ability to comment formally on public and private development within a one to two mile viewshed on either side of the main river as it emerged from the Adirondack Park.[20] Although only advisory, Rockefeller's HRVC did retain power to withhold comment and thus delay local action for 60 days so as to publicize its position and bring public pressure upon local authorities and, where applicable, upon state and federal licensing agencies or sponsors. Beyond project review, the commission focused most of its attention on comprehensive planning for a wider region embracing a large portion of the Hudson and Mohawk (the major Hudson tributary) watersheds.

The HRVC played a significant role as a reform organization created to address specific forms of contradiction arising out of the capitalist process of urban development. On the one hand, the environmental and landscape preservation forces were initially encouraged by the commission's strong support for open space, park, and trail development. On the other, developers, labor unions, and larger industrial concerns welcomed the commission's approval of massive investment in roads, utilities, schools, factories, commercial centers, and other infrastructure considered necessary to accommodate a near doubling of the region's population then envisioned by the end of the century.[21] Working with a large and well-funded staff of architects and landscape planners, and pioneering planning innovations such as cluster zoning, planned unit developments, new communities, billboard ordinances, and, in particular, negotiated settlement with developers, the commission successfully spread the Rockefeller view that urban development was acceptable if aesthetically pleasing.

Focusing almost exclusively on aesthetics and neglecting the biological, social, and physical impacts of development, the commission rarely rejected project proposals. On the contrary, it accepted urban expansion as "vital" and strove to redesign poorly planned proposals to make them visually acceptable and physically accessible. Along the Manhattan shoreline, for example, the commission approved the controversial ·filling of the Hudson to service office and high-income residential construction and to accommodate massive redevelopment proposed by the Regional Plan Association and the Downtown-Lower Manhattan Association (Chapter 3). This was portrayed as offering New York City "a great second chance" to provide access to the waterfront. To the north, a 345-kv transmission line in Rockland County won commission approval following aesthetic realignment, while a fossil fuel power plant at Newburgh was approved "upon the condition that the design of the plant would be reconsidered from the vantage point of the River."[22]

THE CHALLENGE TO ROCKEFELLER DOMINATION
OF THE ENVIRONMENTAL MOVEMENT

During the late 1960s, there was a surge in environmental activism. One branch, represented by student protests, led to the Earth Day Teach-In of 1970. It focused on the incompatibility of energy- and capital-intensive production with environmental quality. Although more radical than the movements concerned with protection of individual consumption space, the campus-based activism presented less of an immediate problem for the expansion of capital. The other branch took hold among middle- to upper middle-class homeowners. This consumption-based movement was also bolstered by new evidence of the damage caused by air and water pollution. Its principal concern, however, was that continued energy, transportation, and residential development, whether visually pleasing or not, was contaminating personal residential and leisure space. In the Hudson Valley the most visible manifestation of this sentiment occurred as an antigrowth movement. Although most New York State communities continued to welcome urban growth as contributing to their tax base, the nogrowth sentiment took hold among affluent suburban towns and villages in Westchester and Rockland counties and in the Hudson Valley portions of Putnam, Orange, Dutchess, and Ulster counties. The 1972 affirmation by state and federal courts of the controlled growth plan implemented by the Hudson Valley town of Ramapo was a high-water mark in local rejection of urban growth.[23]

With the antiurban sentiment threatening to stall the sizable public and private investment still envisioned for the lower and mid-Hudson, the Rocke-fellers strove to direct this "new mood" (as they termed it) toward a resolution supporting continued capital accumulation. They worked through the HRVC, the State Council of Parks, and other state agencies under executive control, as well as through their own Task Force on Land Use and Urban Growth. In effect, however, this new social movement, with its inclination to confront business and development interests, proved too popular and politically active for them to control. As a result, Laurance's brand of conservation, focusing on scenic beauty and design mediation with production concerns, was largely confined during the 1970s and 1980s to the reports of the Conservation Foundation, the Rockefeller Task Force on Land Use and Urban Growth, the Jackson Hole Preserve, and other liberal planning reform organizations the family continued to support (Chapter 1).[24]

By the early 1970s, New York State was entering its worst economic recession in 40 years. With demand projections and urban growth down, the state's utilities, developers, and industrial concerns had less use for design and siting assistance from the HRVC. Concurrently, Scenic Hudson and the valley's other environmental groups were challenging the commission's commitment to environmental integrity, eventually forcing it to abandon support for Storm King.

The state legislature terminated financial support for the Hudson River Valley Commission during the 1971-72 budget crisis; soon thereafter, the commission ceased operations as an independent agency. Although the Rockefeller-inspired attempt to link environmental protection with negotiated accommodation of development was rejected by the public, the valley's wealthier residents still supported open space and historic preservation. This concern prompted the Department of Environmental Conservation to coordinate its extensive project review powers in the valley, with an aim of protecting scenic and historic resources.[25] Over the intervening years, as federal and state regulations dramatically reduced the river's pollution, public support for preservation broadened, prompting many river communities to redevelop their long-neglected industrial properties as riverfront parks and commercial districts.

STORM KING AND THE HUDSON RIVER EXPRESSWAY

State-sponsored regional land use planning aims to further economic expansion because it supports continued urban development while attempting to address the negative externalities generated. As a result, the State perpetuates capitalism and the social structure engendered; in particular, capital, as a class, benefits. Nevertheless, State activities are not always collectively rational. At times various factions of capital or labor can dominate portions of the State apparatus, including the courts or legislative process, to pursue private goals, whether for consumption or for production purposes; to cite an example: consumption interests worked through the courts to block construction of the Storm King project. In response, Con Ed successfully persuaded the Power Authority to help supply the electricity otherwise delivered by Storm King (Chapter 4).

Before accepting a structuralist (class- or social structure-preserving) interpretation of the activities of the Hudson River Valley Commission and, by analogy, the liberal planning reform movement that it represents, we should carefully examine the commission in practice and Rockefeller's relationship with it. On the microlevel, Rockefeller's association with the commission provides an interesting study of conflict inherent in production expansion and consumption protection faced by a single, albeit unusual, individual and his family. In this manner the tension is indicative of the contradiction faced by capital as a class and by the mode of production (capitalism) generating this class (Chapter 1). While the proposed solutions strove to reduce manifestations of this structural contradiction, they were accomplished in a way that appears to instrumentally aid the Rockefeller family's private interests in the valley.

The commission's strange silence on Storm King, the most obvious threat to the valley's environmental integrity, invites further examination. The governor's strenuous aversion to a federal environmental presence in the valley was prompted, in part, by his enthusiastic support for the pumped-storage project and by his desire to speed it past the federal permit review process.[26] Many conservationists and long-term associates of the governor were shocked and confused by his defense of Storm King. Some of Nelson's critics suggested that his instructions to the commission about Storm King were informed by family interests, since the Rockefellers were the largest shareholders in Con Ed, guiding many of the early mergers leading to creation of the conglomerate.[27] Nonetheless, though demonstration of personal material gain is necessary for an instrumental (self-serving) explanation of the governor's actions, it is not sufficient. The Rockefeller family controls such vast financial resources that direct self-benefit seems incomplete as an interpretation. This tremendous wealth, in turn, has been used to bolster the popular view that the governor, and would-be president, was beyond petty personal self-enrichment. Although political power can also be considered as an instrumental objective, the governor's strong support of increased energy production, even at the expense of alienating members of his own class living in the valley, probably reflected what he considered to be the state's responsibility to guarantee adequate electrical power for continued urban development and capital accumulation in the New York metropolitan region.

Support for an instrumental interpretation of Nelson Rockefeller's actions becomes stronger, however, when we examine the commission's defense of the proposed Hudson River Expressway. Running along the densely settled east bank of the river, from the New York Thruway at Tarrytown north to Ossining, the 10.4-mile highway spur was presented by Rockefeller's staff as an alternative to an earlier proposal to extend Interstate 87. Prepared during the Harriman administration, the original alignment ran several miles to the east behind the river towns, and right through the Rockefeller family's 3,668-acre estate at Pocantico Hills in Westchester County (Map 6.2). In contrast, Rockefeller's alternative would run in and along the river. Approximately 40 percent of the highway would be on some 9.5 million cubic yards of fill placed in the Hudson at a location considered to be one of the most important fish-breeding shoals along the river. Projected to cost over $120 million, the Rockefeller alignment, at the time, was one of the most expensive highway projects per mile ever proposed in the state.[28] Anticipating opposition from local conservation interests, Rockefeller's staff included extensive recreation development with the highway. The 400-boat marina, fishing piers, swimming pools, and other facilities suggested would be in addition to a 165-acre public dedication by the Rockefeller family for a riverfront park.[29]

Since federal funding for the project would entail environmental and social impact assessment while also opening up the procedure to public participation, Nelson's staff initially sidestepped the potentially damaging review process and quietly steered state authorization for the expressway through the legislature. In highly unusual and possibly illegal proceedings, local officials and residents were not informed of the authorizing legislation; no public hearings were held; and the bills sailed through the senate and assembly and were signed by the governor without hearings by their highway committees, supporting memoranda, designation of authorship, and other features normally indicating the purpose and impact of proposed legislation.[30]

A month later, in July 1965, the Hudson River Valley Commission was created with responsibility for reviewing projects that might adversely affect the

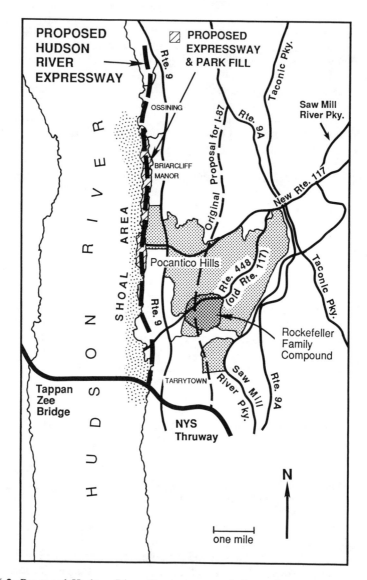

Map 6.2. Proposed Hudson River Expressway and alternative routes in relation to Rockefeller estate at Pocantico Hills (Westchester County).

Source: Adapted from U.S. Congress, House, Committee on Merchant Marine and Fisheries, Subcommittee on Fisheries and Wildlife Conservation, *Hearings on: The Impact of the Hudson River Expressway Proposal on Fish and Wildlife Resources of the Hudson River and Atlantic Coastal Fisheries*, 91st Cong., 1st sess., June 24-25, 1969 (Washington, DC: Government Printing Office, 1969), p. 121.

valley's natural resources. Initially caught off guard, local officials and residents in the towns slated for riverfront demolition became aware that the commission, with its mandatory procedure for a public hearing, presented a last possible barrier before the bulldozers. The commission itself was not informed about the expressway until notice of its realignment was leaked to the press. It nevertheless quickly rallied behind the proposal as an "excellent means for providing much greater visual access to the River for motorists." In an attempt to calm local critics, the commission stressed its own professional competence in environmental analysis and embraced the riverfront park proposal.[31]

Eight hundred anxious persons jammed the long-delayed state public information hearing on the expressway. Chaired by the HRVC and the state Department of Public Works, it was held in June 1967, two years after the expressway was first authorized by the legislature. The local residents and small businesses whose homes and shops would be condemned for the highway were joined by sports and environmental groups. The latter were appalled by the tremendous amount of fill required for a highway slicing through the very center of what was considered one of the most scenic stretches of the Hudson. With the exception of the highway officials presenting the route, all of the speakers at the meeting voiced opposition to the expressway. As the route unfolded, it appeared that most of the neighborhoods slated for demolition along the riverbank were low- to middle-income. For more than a century, laborers and servants working for the estates on the hills resided here. With the state making no mention of relocation assistance, Ossining and North Tarrytown would lose a major portion of their black homeowning communities.[32]

A year later, in June 1968, the commission held its own obligatory hearing prior to rendering a decision; only 2 of 43 speakers favored the expressway. Nevertheless, despite overwhelming public opposition, the HRVC unanimously rubber-stamped the Rockefeller proposal the following month. This vote was not surprising since a confidential memorandum prepared by Executive Director Alexander Aldrich six months prior to the commission's hearing assured the governor that "it is extremely unlikely that the Commission will disapprove the road in its final findings. There is ample precedent for this kind of approval following a public hearing."[33]

Although eventually caving in under intense pressure from the governor, Secretary Udall, in his capacity to review federal licensing permits in the valley, initially sided with Congressman Ottinger in opposing the expressway. As outlined in a memorandum prepared by the U.S. Bureau of Recreation (part of the Department of the Interior), entitled "Benefits to the Rockefeller Estate from the Expressway," the new route would just nick the northwest corner of the Rockefeller estate in an area slated by the family for large-scale office, apartment, and commercial development. In addition to putting developable portions of the estate within a reasonable commute from New York City without splitting the estate, the Hudson River Expressway proposal included companion legislation to relocate the old state Route 117 meandering through the estate to a peripheral location (Map 6.2).[34]

With the Sierra Club, Village of Tarrytown, NAACP, Scenic Hudson Preservation Conference, and other social and environmental advocates joining to block federal permit approval, the confrontation moved to the federal courts. The main litigant, known as the Citizens Committee for the Hudson Valley, was a local consumption organization composed of white middle-income property owners whose residences would be disturbed by the proximity of the expressway. A decision was reached in 1969 enjoining the U.S. Army Corps of Engineers from approving a permit for the required fill and diking.[35] Continuing without federal funding or approval, Nelson attempted to go it alone. The project was finally killed in 1971 when voters soundly defeated a $2.5 billion transportation bond issue authorizing state funds for the highway.[36] As the region was already adequately served by several north-south highways, the final debate was carried by a growing concern that the additional thoroughfare was unnecessary.

With the exception of the governor and his handpicked staff (in the Departments of Environmental Conservation and Public Works, and on the Hudson River Valley Commission), the Hudson River Expressway failed to generate support from either production or consumption interests. As a consequence, one might conclude that the governor either erred through arrogance or, more likely, sought personal financial gain and protection of his own consumption space. In any case, his stand was certainly a major political liability. Moreover, the demarcation between a structural and an instrumental interpretation of the governor's actions is itself spurious (Chapter 3). The properties of any social system are expressed and reproduced through everyday practice. A class or individual members (agents) of that class, acting in their own self-interest, also tend to perpetuate the social system giving rise to their social demarcation, together with that system's internal contradiction. Nelson Rockefeller's actions with respect to the commission and valley development supported continued capital accumulation, together with a vociferous local defense of consumption space by valley residents (a manifestation of contradiction), even as his instructions tended to benefit more select family interests.

Resigning in the fall of 1973 to prepare for his final presidential bid, Nelson sought to mend severed ties to the politically powerful and wealthy Hudson Valley conservation community. With the next generation of Rockefellers displaying little interest either in developing or in maintaining the Pocantico Hills estate, the family abandoned many of the proposals for intense commercial development. Instead, it began to dedicate some of the peripheral parcels of the estate as public park land, a move that also helped to divest the family of the heavy tax burden for open space preservation.[37]

Direct Rockefeller control over public policy in the Hudson Valley declined after the governor's resignation. Family influence, however, continued through Laurance Rockefeller's Task Force on Land Use and Urban Growth and, more specifically, via the Hudson Basin Project. The $500,000 project was initiated in 1973 by the Rockefeller Foundation as an experiment promoting a regional perspective on environmental issues in the 44-county river basin covering half of the state.[38] It was staffed by the Mid-Hudson Pattern (for Progress), a private, nonprofit, regional planning advocate funded by larger-scale Hudson Valley business enterprises (Chapter 3). The aesthetics of development, a recurrent Rockefeller theme, was singled out as the major environmental concern hindering broader popular acceptance of necessary urban growth. Accepting the large expansion in residential construction, power generation, and industrial development then projected for the valley, the project suggested that "contemporary problems are too broad in scope to be dealt with by local governments acting individually, and if this inability is eroding confidence in government, then the present balance may need reassessing."[39] This support for a centralization of land use regulation was directly in line with the liberal land use reform movement then sweeping the nation (Chapter 1).

Focusing on public professionalism, rationality, responsibility, and regionalism as means whereby controversial land use issues could be de-politicized, the project condemned adversary court battles that delayed "socially beneficial" development. In their place it promoted negotiated settlement and public assistance through grants, incentive bonuses, new zoning techniques, and, where necessary, through the use of eminent domain to facilitate larger-scale development and overcome local opposition.[40]

Released in 1976, the three-year study received only scant attention from public and private decision makers. At the local level, the liberal position recommending negotiation in place of confrontation was dismissed by residents who had just won resounding battles against energy and highway forces supported by the most politically powerful family in the state. Furthermore, for the region as a whole, declining growth projections and continuing depression in the real estate market had rendered most of the project's recommendations obsolete. By the time the real estate market picked up again, in the mid-1980s, nogrowth and slow-growth forces were firmly entrenched in many Hudson Valley communities with several of them placing moratoria on new subdivision developments.[41]

A "LEISURE-CLASS" ORIGIN FOR ENVIRONMENTALISM?

We can now turn to William Tucker's scathing polemic attacking "environmentalism" as a phenomenon of the "leisure class," to use a term first popularized by Thorstein Veblen in 1899.[42] Tucker's work is important because it is the best-known analysis of the Storm King controversy, as well as the most-cited critique of consumption-based environmental movements.

Tucker defines environmentalism by its attention to upper-class consumption amenities and space. Failing to probe the structure and basis for attention by production and consumption interests to environmental issues, he delineates a very narrow social basis for what constitutes an environmental movement. Although neglected or disregarded by analysts such as Tucker, laborers fighting for safer and healthier workplace conditions, and inner-city residents resisting urban renewal for transportation or office development are other examples of environmental battles waged over production and consumption space. Furthermore, production concerns can also support environmental preservation, as when the New York Board of Trade and Transportation lobbied for constitutional protection of the Adirondack forest preserve and, more recently, when the Regional Plan Association encouraged open space preservation in the Catskills (Chapter 5).

The strength of Tucker's analysis rests on his recognition of the parochial consumption-based motivation for action by the Scenic Hudson Preservation Conference and the problems it presented for expansion of the forces of production ("progress"). Both Veblen and Tucker were taken by the tenacity of working-class aspiration to "leisure-class" status. Grafting social psychology onto political economy, they accepted this "pecuniary emulation" (after Veblen) as a basic human characteristic. Leaping from individuals to institutions, however, Tucker summarily denigrated all other motivations for opposition to the Storm King project as just a desire to be equated with this aristocratic cause and for the respectability thus conferred.[43] New York City's opposition to the proposal as a threat to its water supply and the very real threat posed by the project to the estuary's multimillion-dollar commercial fisheries could not be so easily dismissed. Moreover, Tucker and Veblen both paid insufficient attention to the process whereby leisure-class or, more precisely, ruling-class ideas and goals acquire the strength of commonsense notions and are disseminated among a broader populace (Chapter 5).

Tucker, like Veblen before him, designates imprecise pseudoclasses drawn solely from a description of consumption characteristics and an assumption of consumer sovereignty. He thereby fails to link these attributes to the dominant mode of production. Class distinctions are first and foremost rooted in the production process (Chapter 1). Nevertheless, our perception of class may be influenced and reinforced through the sphere of consumption as, for example, in the institution of homeownership. Although groupings based upon general consumption characteristics, such as leisure class or middle class, are pervasive commonsense understandings, these are also chaotic generalizations as used by Tucker because they rest upon unnecessary (contingent) relations instead of necessary (internal) social relations. Once we structurally connect production with consumption (e.g., consumption is necessary to realize exchange value and profit from production, and consumption is the sphere of social reproduction of the labor force, without which production could not occur), we can appreciate why social movements that focus on defense of consumption amenities are both a logical outcome of the capitalist production system, as well as a potential barrier to its expansion.[44]

Finally, Tucker overlooks real intraclass conflict arising from personal attention to production as well as consumption requirements. This is patently obvious in the Storm King controversy. Here Rockefeller, Tucker's "aristocrat among aristocrats," betrayed his leisure-class origins and actually supported the project.[45] Tucker is not alone in his misconception. Focusing on consumer-environmental elites, many critics of contemporary environmental movements recognize, but cannot account for, the irony that the same consumer elites fighting to defend their leisure and residential space are often promoting development in other areas.

THE DEFENSE OF NATURE AS CONSUMPTION SPACE: FORCE FOR RADICAL CHANGE OR SAFETY VALVE FOR THE ESTABLISHED ORDER?

The foregoing examination of attempts to centralize the regulation of development in so-called critical environmental areas supports several conclusions. Although not necessarily exclusive to capitalism, the widespread conception of nature as a place removed from production is a historically specific product of our mode of production and of the social forces and relations generated. Thus, as in the Hudson Valley and the Adirondacks, we tend to view nature as a place for leisure and recreation, set aside as a refuge for biological (family) reproduction, spiritual rejuvenation, and psychological re-creation. With the rise of industrial capitalism, defense of nature appropriated as leisure and residential space is understandable given our strong attachment to nature as a refuge from, as well as a reward for, toil in an alienating production system where the majority own only their own labor power. Today we tend to define ourselves according to what and how we consume (nature) through recreation and residential activities, rather than by our class position in the production process (Chapters 1 and 5). However, this defense of nature as consumption space can generate barriers for further expansion of the forces of production. In time, the public sector, or State, steps in to balance production requirements and the popular defense of consumption amenities. The State is, in the first instance, designed to defend and maintain the institutions (such as a legal system premised upon the sanctity of private property) supporting the dominant social structure constituting the existing mode of production.

Now, for a while the same space might be able to serve both production and consumption interests as, for example, a working farm that also is perceived as open space by nearby residents. Indeed, no single space can be absolutely defined as production or consumption without considering how different people use and conceive of that area. One person's work space might be another's residential or recreation space. Consider a ski area or winery. This spatial convergence is itself indicative of the dialectical relationship between production and consumption. After all, every consumption space is built or, in the extreme case of a wilderness area, is at least delineated and guarded, by some worker or park manager. Moreover, consumption is required to reproduce the labor power necessary for production (Chapter 1). However, as in all dialectical relations, there is also a tension in this relationship. Accordingly, commodity production for exchange value will, over time, tend to challenge consumptive use value in the landscape. This occurs, for example, when the farmer applies noxious chemicals to the land or runs farm machinery at early hours disturbing nearby residents; other examples include the successful winery moving toward mass production, ski area expansion threatening fragile mountain areas enjoyed by hikers, and further residential construction challenged by existing subdivision homeowners. In brief, the demarcation between production and consumption in the landscape is only a heuristic device for understanding people's relationship with a specific space. Nevertheless, it is an important distinction because without it we cannot readily account for the social makeup and commitment of contemporary environmental movements concerned with the use of land.

The day-to-day practice of land use regulation and the content of specific programs advocated by local residents, preservationists, developers, and other interests reflect the geographically specific and socially unique history of culturally, economically, and environmentally defined regions such as the Hudson River Valley, the Adirondacks, and Tug Hill. Nonetheless, State response still accords with the broader set of demands placed upon the public sector under the capitalist mode of production. From a structural perspective, State intervention in land use development is required to correct inherent tendencies toward disarray in capitalist urban development arising from the private appropriation of surplus value (Chapter 1). In the process, the State helps reproduce the social relations of production. Centralized land use regulation, often through the designation of state-regulated "critical environmental areas," is just one example of State intervention. As in the Hudson Valley, social movements to protect parochial consumption amenities can also block regional economic development, thereby prompting regional intervention.

The State, at all levels, is not, however, an autonomous regulator only operating in the interest of system maintenance. With various social factions coalescing around consumption as well as production interests, the State's controlling mechanisms can be captured by specific sectors to present class or subclass ideologies and needs as the collective interest. In the Adirondack Park, where locally consumed leisure and residential space did not yet clash with local production, antagonistic extraregional preservation consumers captured the State apparatus to overwhelm local support for development and establish the Adirondack Park Agency. In contrast, local production interests prevailed over disorganized extraregional preservation forces in the Catskills, and they actually coalesced with local as well as the broader regional consumption concerns in the Tug Hill area. In the latter instance, both local and regional concerns shared a more active interest in land use through hunting, snowmobiling, fishing, and camp maintenance, thus assuring a more amiable alliance between local and extraregional interests than found in the Adirondacks or in the Catskills. On occasion, regulatory and review mechanisms can be captured by even more select interests. The Hudson River Valley Commission is an extreme example of a State review agency under the virtual control of a single, albeit powerful, family that was used to support continued economic development (system maintenance) in a manner apparently benefiting family interests.

Finally, from the Hudson Valley experience we realize that for the individual in our society social protest over the impact of capitalist development need not only arise in the workplace, as many orthodox Marxists would have us believe. It can also arise from a defense of consumption space or of nature as consumption space. This can come from the working class, as well as from the bourgeoisie and managerial strata whose own lifestyle and sphere of consumption may be threatened by production. Such is the irony of the structural contradiction arising from the social (class-defining) nature of capitalist production and the private appropriation of the use and exchange values generated (Chapter 1). With a conflict in loyalty occurring between support for continued economic expansion and the quest for a refuge safe and secure from the social and environmental externalities generated, individuals can be driven toward private positions in opposition to their own collective class interest in continued development of the forces of production. This ambivalent tension is common to many environmental and nogrowth movements in the United States.

The stage, thus, is set for new alliances as the defense of consumption against the forces of production cuts across class lines. Those of us committed to the pursuit of equitable, secure, and meaningful production, as well as consumption, experiences might exploit these opportunities. We must, however, be vigilant. Simplistic reform as offered, for example, by the now-familiar conservation-*and*-development approach to regional land use control and critical area designation, should be avoided where it attempts to balance bourgeois production and consumption demands at the expense of broader social concerns.

NOTES

1. David Ellis, *Landlords and Farmers in the Hudson-Mohawk Region, 1790-1850* (Ithaca, NY: Cornell University Press, 1946); Henry Christman, *Tin Horns and Calico* (1945) (New York: Collier Books, 1961); and Allan Heskin, *Tenants and the American Dream* (New York: Praeger, 1983) cover the fascinating history of commercial life and social conflict in the Hudson Valley during the late eighteenth and early nineteenth centuries. On private landownership in Great Britain as a basis for the demarcation of class interest and on its role in social formation: Doreen Massey and Alejandria Catalano, *Capital and Land: Landownership by Capital in Great Britain* (London: Edward Arnold, 1978).

2. The pivotal history by Roderick Nash appears to accept Cole's romantic depiction of the "wild" Hudson as existing reality (*Wilderness and the American Mind*, rev. ed. [New Haven, CT: Yale University Press, 1973], p. 81). On settlement in the Hudson Valley: cf. Raymond O'Brien, *American Sublime: Landscape and Scenery of the Lower Hudson Valley* (New York: Columbia University Press, 1981); Ellis, *Landlords and Farmers*; and Donald Meinig, "Geography of Expansion, 1785-1855" (1966), in *Geography of New York State*, ed. J. Thompson (Syracuse, NY: Syracuse University Press, 1977), pp. 154-55.

By 1820, prior to the opening of the Erie Canal or the arrival of Thomas Cole upon the scene, Albany (at 12,630 population) had already grown to become the largest inland city and sixth largest city in the nation (Meinig, "Geography of Expansion," p. 155).

3. Kenneth Warren, *The American Steel Industry 1850-1970: A Geographic Interpretation* (Oxford, UK: Clarendon Press, 1973); Kenneth La Budde, "The Mind of Thomas Cole" (Ph.D. diss., University of Minnesota, 1954), p. 93; and O'Brien, *American Sublime*, pp. 168, 190. Cole's lament over the destruction was largely confined to his prose.

4. Alf Evers, *The Catskills: From Wilderness to Woodstock* (Garden City, NY: Doubleday, 1972), p. 379; also pp. 445-49.

5. John Reed, *The Hudson River Valley* (New York: Clarkson N. Potter, 1960), pp. 18-19; and Harold Eberlein and Cortland Van Dyke Hubbard, *Historic Houses of the Hudson Valley* (New York: Architectural Book Publishing, 1942), pp. 271-72.

6. O'Brien, *American Sublime*, pp. 141-45, 186-90; and Roland Van Zandt, *Chronicles of the Hudson: Three Centuries of Travelers' Accounts* (New Brunswick, NJ: Rutgers University Press, 1971), pp. 271-72.

7. O'Brien, *American Sublime*, pp. 22, 193ff; also New York *Times*, "To Save the Palisades," editorial, November 25, 1894, p. 17.

8. O'Brien, *American Sublime*, pp. 7, 241-59.

9. In 1964 the society's board of directors had to reverse their position and oppose the project following unexpected opposition from the membership (Allan Talbot, *Power along the Hudson* [New York: E. P. Dutton, 1972], p. 107).

10. Ibid., pp. 84-96, 105, 191; Joseph Sax, *Defending the Environment: A Strategy for Citizen Action* (New York: Alfred A. Knopf, 1971), pp. 131-33; Myer Kutz, *Rockefeller Power* (New York: Simon and Schuster, 1974), pp. 156-72; and Scenic Hudson Preservation Conference, *Scenic Hudson News* (New York: Scenic Hudson Preservation Conference, 1974).

11. On the compromise reached: Ross Sandler, "Settlement on the Hudson," *The AMICUS Journal* 3 (Spring 1981):42-45; and Bob Henshaw, "Compromise Agreement Ends Hudson River Controversy," *New York State Environment* (Department of Environmental Conservation) 10, no. 6 (1981):3. Over the intervening years the Hudson has gotten much cleaner due to the departure of brick, cement, and limestone industries from most of the riverbank and to the imposition of secondary municipal sewage systems in accord with the 1972 Federal Clean Water Act (Cf. Sara Rimer, "Long-Abused Hudson Thrives Again," New York *Times*, November 6, 1986, pp. B1, 9; and U.S., Department of the Interior, Bureau of Outdoor Recreation, *Focus on the Hudson* [Washington, DC: Government Printing Office, 1966], p. 9).

12. Had it been built, the Storm King project would have doubled the existing fish loss on the Hudson due to water withdrawal (Sandler, "Settlement on the Hudson," pp. 42-43).

13. Carl Petrich, "Aesthetic Impact of a Proposed Power Plant on an Historic Wilderness Landscape" (Paper presented at the National Conference on Applied Techniques for Analysis and Management of the Visual Resource, Incline Village, NV, April 23-25, 1979; reprinted in *Our National Landscape* [Berkeley, CA: Pacific Southwest Forest and Range Experiment Station, 1979], pp. 477-84); Mary Pratt, "Power Plant Decisions," *New York State Environmental News* (Atmospheric Sciences Research Center, State University of New York at Albany) 7, no. 7 (1980):4-5; and Power Authority of the State of New York, *Annual Report for 1981* (Albany: Power Authority of the State of New York, March 1982).

14. Petrich, "Aesthetic Impact of a Proposed Power Plant," p. 482.

15. New York State, Hudson River Valley Commission, *The Hudson: Report of the Hudson River Valley Commission, 1966* (Iona Island, Bear Mountain, NY: Hudson River Valley Commission, 1966), p. 4; see also Kutz, *Rockefeller Power*, pp. 165, 172-73. Prior to legislative authorization, the commission was supported through dis-

cretionary funds in the executive budget and by a grant from Laurance's American Conservation Association (Kutz, *Rockefeller Power*, p. 172).

16. Marquis—Who's Who, *Who's Who in the East*, 10th ed. (Chicago: Marquis—Who's Who, 1967); also New York State, Hudson River Valley Commission, *Report 1966*, p. 94; idem, "Members of the Hudson River Valley Commission," *Hudson River Valley Commission Newsletter* (Tarrytown, NY) 1, no. 1 (1966):2; William Rogers, *Rockefeller's Follies: An Unauthorized View of Nelson A. Rockefeller* (New York: Stein and Day, 1966), pp. 195-200; and Kutz, *Rockefeller Power*, pp. 171-72.

17. Rogers, *Rockefeller's Follies*, pp. 196-98; and New York State, Hudson River Valley Commission, *Report 1966*, p. 88.

18. PL89-605 (Hudson River Compact Act); and H.S. 3012 (a bill to create the Hudson Highlands Scenic Riverway—1965); also Kutz, *Rockefeller Power*, pp. 172-73; and Talbot, *Power along the Hudson*, pp. 140-47. Udall appeared unconvinced. An internally circulated Department of Interior investigation of Laurance uncovered that he had "infiltrated" 11 environmental organizations and "controlled," through funding and appointments of his staff and associates, some two dozen more (as quoted in Talbot, *Power along the Hudson*, p. 143).

19. Laws of New York (1965, Chapter 560, The Hudson River Corridor Act); and Laws of New York (1966, Chapter 345, as amended, The Hudson River Valley Commission Act).

20. Nelson Rockefeller as quoted in Kutz, *Rockefeller Power*, p. 176. Cf. U.S., Department of the Interior, Bureau of Outdoor Recreation, *Focus on the Hudson*; and New York State, Hudson River Valley Commission, *Report 1966*, pp. 94-100, for the contending proposals.

In 1968 the legislature established a Genesee River Valley Commission and a St. Lawrence-Eastern Ontario Commission. Both regional review commissions were modeled after the Hudson River Valley Commission for areas where there was far less development controversy. See New York State, Joint Legislative Committee on Metropolitan and Regional Areas Study, *Governing Urban Areas: Strengthening Local Governments through Regionalism* (annual report of the committee) (Albany: Joint Legislative Committee on Metropolitan and Regional Areas Study, 1968), pp. 130-34.

21. See New York State, Hudson River Valley Commission, *Report 1966*, pp. 4-11; and Marshall Stalley, "Environmental Planning and the Defunct Hudson River Valley Commission," *Landscape Architecture* 62 (July-August 1972):327-30, 348. By 1967 the commission's budget had ballooned 300 percent to three-quarters of a million dollars (New York State, Hudson River Valley Commission, *Annual Report* [Tarrytown, NY: Hudson River Valley Commission, 1968]).

22. New York State, Hudson River Valley Commission, *Report 1966*, p. 28; and idem, *Annual Report* (Tarrytown, NY: Hudson River Valley Commission, 1969), pp. 24-26.

23. Golden v. Planning Board of Town of Ramapo, 30 N.Y. 2d 359, 334 N.Y.S. 2d 138, 285 N.E. 2d 291 (1972), appeal dismissed, 409 U.S. 1003 (1972).

24. Peter Collier and David Horowitz, *The Rockefellers: An American Dynasty* (New York: Holt, Rinehart and Winston, 1976), pp. 399-402; and New York *Times*, "Rockefellers Expand Bid to Protect Hudson Valley's Essence," October 25, 1987, p. A35. See Richard Walker and Michael Heiman, "Quiet Revolution for Whom?" *Annals of the Association of American Geographers* 71 (March 1981):67-83, on the

Conservation Foundation, the Rockefeller Task Force on Land Use and Urban Growth, and other Rockefeller-sponsored expressions of the liberal planning reform movement. See also Chapter 1, n. 7.

25. New York State, Department of Environmental Conservation, *The Hudson River Valley: A Heritage for All Time*, pamphlet (Albany: Department of Environmental Conservation, 1979); and idem, *The Hudson River Study* (prepared by Raymond, Parish, Pine and Weiner Inc.) (Albany: Department of Environmental Conservation, 1979).

26. See Nelson Rockefeller, *Our Environment Can Be Saved* (Garden City, NY: Doubleday, 1970), pp. 78-79, for a defense of his position; and New York State, Hudson River Valley Commission, *Report 1966*, p. 78, for the recommendation that the Storm King project be relocated to a less scenic site should "a feasible alternative" be found. Even this rearguard proposal was only in reaction to the U.S. Court of Appeals overturning the Federal Power Commission's license for Storm King on grounds that the FPC had failed to adequately consider alternative means of power generation (Scenic Hudson Preservation Conference v. Federal Power Commission, 354 F. 2d 608 [2d Cir. 1965], cert. denied 384 U.S. 941 [1966]).

27. U.S. Congress, House, Congressional Information Service, *Analysis of the Philosophy and Public Record of Nelson A. Rockefeller, Nominee for Vice-President of the United States* (prepared for Committee on the Judiciary, 93d Cong., 2d sess.) (Washington, DC: Government Printing Office, 1974), pp. 93-94, 97. Cf. Kutz, *Rockefeller Power*, pp. 164-65; and Rogers, *Rockefeller's Follies*, pp. 86-87.

28. Rogers, *Rockefeller's Follies*, pp. 131-63; and Sax, *Defending the Environment*, pp. 64-83, cover the expressway controversy. See also Shaul Amir, *Conservation Kills a Highway: The Hudson River Expressway Controversy*, Research on Conflict in Locational Decisions, no. 4 (Philadelphia: Regional Science Department, University of Pennsylvania, 1970); and A. Q. Mowbray, *Road to Ruin* (New York: Lippincott, 1969). The old alignment would have passed within 200 yards of Nelson's home and 100 yards of Laurance's residence (U.S. Congress, House, Committee on Merchant Marine and Fisheries, Subcommittee on Fisheries and Wildlife Conservation, *Hearings on: The Impact of the Hudson River Expressway Proposal on Fish and Wildlife Resources of the Hudson River and Atlantic Coastal Fisheries*, 91st Cong., 1st sess., June 24-25, 1969, Series no. 91-10 [Washington, DC: Government Printing Office, 1969], pp. 121-22). The calculation of Pocantico's size is found in Rogers, *Rockefeller's Follies*, pp. 135, 143.

29. U.S. Congress, House, Committee on Merchant Marine and Fisheries, Subcommittee on Fisheries and Wildlife Conservation, *Impact of the Hudson River Expressway Proposal*, pp. 5ff.

30. Ibid., pp. 122-23.

31. New York State, Hudson River Valley Commission, *Report 1966*, pp. 64-65; and Rogers, *Rockefeller's Follies*, p. 171. The proposal to beautify controversial public projects, such as the Westside Highway (Chapter 3) and New York City's North River Pollution Control Plant (also built in and along the Hudson), with improved public access and recreation facilities is a long-standing goal promoted by the Rockefeller-sponsored wing of the liberal planning reform movement. Cf. New York State, Hudson River Valley Commission, *Report 1966*, p. 28; William Reilly, ed., *The Use of Land: A Citizen's Policy Guide to Urban Growth* (Report by the Task Force on Land Use and

Urban Growth, sponsored by the Rockefeller Brothers Fund) (New York: Thomas Y. Crowell, 1973); William H. Whyte, *The Last Landscape* (Garden City, NY: Doubleday, 1968); Robert Healy, *Environmentalists and Developers: Can They Agree on Anything?* (Washington, DC: Conservation Foundation, 1977); and Rockefeller, *Environment Can Be Saved.*

    32. Amir, *Conservation Kills a Highway*, pp. 7-11; Kutz, *Rockefeller Power*, pp. 180-85; Mowbray, *Road to Ruin*, pp. 172-73; and U.S. Congress, House, Committee on Merchant Marine and Fisheries, Subcommittee on Fisheries and Wildlife Conservation, *Impact of the Hudson River Expressway Proposal*, pp. 97, 186-88.

    33. U.S. Congress, House, Committee on Merchant Marine and Fisheries, Subcommittee on Fisheries and Wildlife Conservation, *Impact of the Hudson River Expressway Proposal*, pp. 124-25, 196-97.

    34. Ibid., pp. 114-15, 121, 195, 207-9. See also Sax, *Defending the Environment*, pp. 64-82; and Rogers, *Rockefeller's Follies*, pp. 162, 166, 175, 187. The relocation of state Route 117 had been a pet project of the family since the 1930s, when John D. Rockefeller, Jr. first offered to pay for the undertaking (Kutz, *Rockefeller Power*, p. 179).

    35. Citizens Committee for the Hudson Valley et al. v. Volpe et al., 302 F. Supp. 1083, 1 ELR, 20001 (S.D.N.Y. 1969), aff'd, 425 F. 2d 97, ELR (2d Cir. 1970), cert. denied 400 U.S. 949 (1970). Sax, *Defending the Environment*, pp. 127-30, provides an overview of the complex legal maneuvering leading to the decision. See also William Hillhouse II, "The Federal Law of Water Resources Development," in *Federal Environmental Law*, ed. E. Dolgin and T. Guilbert (prepared for the Environmental Law Institute) (St. Paul, MN: West Publishing, 1974), pp. 915-16, on the corps' role in the Hudson River Expressway case; and Amir, *Conservation Kills a Highway*, on the social makeup of the opposition.

    36. Kutz, *Rockefeller Power*, p. 189.

    37. U.S. Congress, House, Committee on the Judiciary, *Philosophy of Nelson Rockefeller*, pp. 93-94, 97; Collier and Horowitz, *Rockefellers*, pp. 511-17, 564; and Virginia Franklin, "At Pocantico Hills, a Question of Taxes," New York *Times*, November 25, 1981, Section 22, p. 26.

    38. See Ralph Richardson, Jr. and Gilbert Tauber, eds., *The Hudson Basin: Environmental Problems and Institutional Response* (Report sponsored by the Rockefeller Foundation), 2 vols. (New York: Academic Press, 1979); Hudson Basin Project, *Final Report of the Hudson Basin Project* (published by and for the Rockefeller Foundation) (New York: Hudson Basin Project, 1976); and Bente King, "Critique of the Hudson Basin Project" (Master of Professional Studies thesis, Department of Natural Resources, Cornell University, 1975).

    39. Richardson and Tauber, *Hudson Basin*, 1:67. See also Hudson Basin Project, *Final Report*, pp. 93-97.

    40. Hudson Basin Project, *Final Report*, pp. 76, 108-16; and Hudson Basin Project, Land Use/Human Settlement Task Force, *Task Force Report* (published by and for the Rockefeller Foundation) (New York: Hudson Basin Project, 1976), pp. 118-19. See also Hudson Basin Project, *Final Report*, pp. 258 ff., for the application of these proposals to the siting of large-scale energy projects.

    41. Sara Rimer, "In Dutchess, Fear of the Future," New York *Times*, October 17, 1986, pp. B1, 5.

42. Cf. William Tucker, "Environmentalism and the Leisure Class," *Harper's* 255 (December 1977):49-56, 73-80; and Thorstein Veblen, *The Theory of the Leisure Class: An Economic Study of Institutions* (New York: Charles Scribner's Sons, 1899). See also William Tucker, *Progress and Privilege: America in the Age of Environmentalism* (Garden City, NY: Anchor Press, 1982).

43. Tucker, "Environmentalism and the Leisure Class"; idem, *Progress and Privilege*; and Veblen, *Theory of the Leisure Class*.

44. On the link between production and consumption, and on the barriers that consumption in its actualization can present for production: Edmond Preteceille and Jean-Pierre Terrail, *Capitalism, Consumption and Needs* (1977; English ed., New York: Basil Blackwell, 1985); David Harvey, "Government Policies, Financial Institutions and Neighborhood Change in United States Cities," in *Captive Cities*, ed. M. Harloe (London: John Wiley, 1977), pp. 123-39; Manuel Castells, *The City and the Grassroots* (Berkeley and Los Angeles: University of California Press, 1983); Ira Katznelson, *City Trenches* (New York: Pantheon, 1981); and James O'Connor, *Accumulation Crisis* (New York: Basil Blackwell, 1984). See also Chapter 7.

45. Tucker, "Environmentalism and the Leisure Class," p. 54.

Conclusion: From Liberal Planning in the "Public Interest" to Progressive Land Use Reform

Throughout this book an interpretation of individual and group positions on land use reform has been presented focusing on production and consumption activities. As all human activity may be categorized as involving production and consumption, this interpretation, in and of itself, is neither startling nor revolutionary. What is important is the realization that through an understanding of the necessary relation that production and consumption have with each other and, in turn, with the mode of production, an explanation can now be proffered for the various positions on land use reform that is historically specific, empirically grounded, and capable of being monitored as capitalism evolves according to its internal contradiction (Chapter 1). As a result, the idealist impulse typically offered by the liberal planning reform literature as explanation for land use attitudes, captured, for example, through the individual's quest for homeowning status, aesthetic appreciation, and environmental quality, can now be reinterpreted and grounded through an understanding of the basic social relations and necessary components comprising the dominant mode of production.

The capitalist mode of production is, of necessity, growth oriented. This drive results from the private appropriation of surplus value in a competitive market. Growth can also be ascribed to consumer demand for more goods and services. Consumption cannot, however, have an essence independent from supply (or production). Although the incentive for expansion lies primarily with the pressures placed on private producers in a competitive market, production cannot proceed without consumption. In this manner, consumer demand for commodities bears a necessary relationship with production, one that is dialectic, conditioning, as well as being conditioned by, production (Chapter 1).

Insofar as production and consumption are dialectically related, there is a perpetual tension between the two spheres of human consciousness and activity. The conflict is particularly acute as production and consumption take, or are perceived as taking, spatial forms. In this situation the necessary expansion of the forces of production under capitalism threatens the sanctity of those areas set aside and used for consumption, while the realization of consumption through land use frequently presents barriers for expansion of production.

Liberal planning reform, when calling for a centralization of land use regulation, attempts to reduce this tension. On the one hand, liberal reform strives to pacify social movements fighting to protect residential, leisure, and other consumption amenities from the intrusion of further production. This is done through an identification of specific goals, such as open space, environmental protection, and quality housing, with a broader public interest that can only be attained at the regional level of planning and regulation, and with specific types of land use relegated to appropriate areas. On the other hand, liberal planning reform attempts to provide the infrastructure, services, and other resources, including housing for labor, necessary for further production. Thus, local communities are encouraged to enact ordinances and policies accommodating these requirements. Where local jurisdictions are unable to service urban expansion, or where local politics have been captured by social movements seeking to protect more parochial consumption amenities, liberal reform suggests a centralization of regulation through municipal consolidation or the more select state preemption of local responsibility and authority for the provision of public facilities and the siting of private projects.

This commitment to expanding production and containing the externalities generated is captured by the "conservation-and-development" (or the "consumption-and-production") approach to land use reform. Although possible in any production system, including communism, where expansion of the forces of production generates popular protest, the conservation-and-development approach is ubiquitous in capitalism. This tendency may be traced to the necessary and relentless drive for economic expansion under capitalism, which must be accommodated and cannot be halted without compromising the very structural conditions, such as the presence of a competitive market, defining that mode of production. Thus, in a sense, while a nogrowth or steady-state economy could respect the sanctity of established nature, residential, and other consumption preserves, capitalism could never adjust to this equilibrium on a large scale. To do so would require such drastic modification of the competitive market, control of individual initiative to produce, and reallocation of private wealth necessary to preserve social harmony in a system without material expansion that the result could no longer be recognized as capitalism.

Supported primarily by production concerns through private foundations, university research centers, and civic organizations, liberal land use reform can scarcely challenge private ownership and control of the means of production. Failing to uncover and address the underlying social structure giving rise to contradiction and crisis, liberal planning reform can only offer ad hoc remedies for, and not prevent the generation of, contradiction as it takes new economic, social, and environmental forms (Chapter 1). Thus constrained, liberal planning reform traces the social ills and environmental problems accompanying urban growth to an inappropriate level of regulation rather than to structural contradiction. As a result, the liberal solution proposed is technical rather than structural, or social. Typically the local level of regulation is questioned, with real and competing positions on land use either ignored or subsumed under a broader regional "public interest." Refocusing on the original possessor of police power over land use, liberal reformers refer to the state level of planning and regulation as the appropriate, autonomous, coordinating mechanism. Through the pluralist political process, reformers feel that the agency of the state can be pressured by the variety of affected interests (comprising the majority of citizens) to accommodate a broader public agenda where more select concerns may also be embraced.

Too many urban and regional planning analysts are still captive of this liberal reform ideology equating social and environmental ills with a technical malfunction in the land use regulatory process, rather than recognizing these negative externalities as expressions of underlying contradiction inherent in the mode of production. Concentrating on the level of land use regulation rather than on content, conventional analysis often mistakes the geographic scale, or locus, of regulation as the very essence of social conflict over land use reform. This is captured, for example, by the local-versus-regional, urban-versus-rural, and sunbelt-versus-frostbelt debates so common in the literature. Accepting the liberal prognosis and prescription, conventional analysis all too often bypasses existing social and economic differences between and within social classes operating at any geographic scale. While the emphasis on state-level reform is proper given the legal structure of our land regulatory system, the notion that social harmony can be achieved at this autonomous layer of regulation is itself a myth.

Since the scale of capitalist development has been increasing during the past century and large-scale production and development concerns are finding the local level of regulation unsuited to their needs, there has been a tendency for liberal reformers and their corporate sponsors to favor a centralization of land use regulation. This tendency, however, should not be mistaken for a rule. Consumption concerns, be they environmental groups, nogrowth advocates, sports organizations, or homeowner associations, can also push for a centralization of regulation to further goals antagonistic to production interests. Moreover, local governments are often accommodating to economic growth at whatever level they can handle. As demonstrated through New York State's experimentation with regional planning in metropolitan areas, the use of public authorities, designation of critical areas, and facility siting legislation, regional or state preemption of local planning or zoning can take many forms and serve diverse purposes.

Where social protest over land development threatens to stifle urban development, liberal reformers are challenged to prepare a new agenda for policy reform claiming to speak for popular dissatisfaction while also arranging the elements of a new growth ensemble. Contrary to liberal reformers' claims, the recent surge in state regulation, commonly identified as a "quiet revolution," is not a new phenomenon directed by a unified environmental movement intent on protecting consumption amenities and space against the ravage of urban development. Rather it is the latest expression of an ongoing *evolution* whereby a more centralized authority is called on to address, and when under liberal influence, to balance, competing goals of economic expansion and defense of consumption as these take their historically specific spatial forms in the U.S. political economy. Insofar as the accommodation of growth via centralized regulation has already been continuing since the turn of the century, often under the guidance of private planning advocates accepted as serving in the public interest and via the activities of public authorities shielded from public scrutiny or participation, the change in land use control may more accurately be termed a *quiet evolution.*

State intervention, when under liberal control, attempts to balance the most vociferous objections to growth, often debased to the more manageable question of aesthetics, while ensuring that expansion continues in more appropriate areas. However, as consumption and production bear a necessary and dialectical relationship to one another, expansion of the former will invariably threaten to compromise realization of the latter. As a result, balance between the two through centralized land use control appears, at best, temporary and enigmatic.

In practice, much of the push for planning reform stretches back to the turn of the century when business attempted to evade barriers to urban development and accumulation arising as the scale of development increased and more units of local government adopted restrictive land use controls. More recently, sports, homeowner, environmental, and other consumption interests have also joined the dialogue, lobbying for state intervention and centralized regulation when local ordinances are perceived as too accommodating to growth. Today the situation is variable, with many production- and consumption-based social movements seeking to control that sector and level of the State apparatus most amenable to their goals. On occasion production interests prevail, as seen through utility and manufacturing support for New York State's hazardous waste and energy facility siting legislation or through the activities of politically sheltered public authorities.   In other instances consumption concerns successfully slow economic expansion, be this through state intervention, as in the Adirondacks, or through local legislation and, if need be, state and federal court challenges, as in the Hudson Valley and with the Westway highway proposal.

This evidence suggests that it is not the level or form of regulation that is the real issue, but rather the substance of regulatory control that is important. What matters is the accessibility and behavior of the politicians and regulators, and the legal process at the various levels of government. In other words, regional versus local control is chiefly a tactical and technical question, depending on the issue and the interests at stake. Where one takes a position depends largely on where one's interests have the best chance of prevailing. This is no less true of production interests than it is of consumption interests.

We should not presume that regional land use reform is necessarily synonymous with the public's interest, however that is defined. Alternatively, existing local political systems, dominated by small-scale developers and local consumption interests, have many pernicious aspects when we consider democratic control, racial equality, and social justice. Furthermore, local social movements focused on protection of consumption amenities can undermine working-class unity, as occurs when existing homeowners, working through local zoning and subdivision regulations, frustrate the provision of rental housing for nonpropertied segments of the working class.

The problem then is, first of all, one of political strategy in a situation of intense conflict over social goals, where class loyalty is compromised through private positions on both production and consumption issues. Contrary to the liberal proclamation, there is no clear unitary "public interest" and that is precisely the problem. Pretending that one exists only serves as an ideological screen for the pursuit of one group's interests over another's.

Once we recognize the futility of defining a common interest in property development and land use regulation in a production system with inherent social and material differences, how should progressive reform proceed? Most participants in land use reform will support, even if sanctimoniously, a goal of democratic participation in land development, where those affected at least have the standing and the resources to participate. As such, we should anticipate and recognize real social divisions so as not to blindly force our will on, or submit to the will of, others through the assumption of social harmony where none exists.

As the evidence from New York State demonstrates, there are many competing interests in the land development process. Where one stands, as an environmentalist, developer, or social reformer, depends more on the immediate circumstances and propensity of securing one's goals from a specific level of decision making than from some ahistoric realization of a higher and more harmonious regional level of public interest. Nevertheless, property development, like all social investment, needs to be socially planned. But how can power be centralized and democracy maintained?

This issue should be raised, particularly in a state such as New York, where much of the public investment and regional land use decisions are made behind closed doors either by private enterprises or by governor-appointed commissions and authorities. Drawing upon historic practice and observable events, and grounded in necessary relationships rather than on idealist impulse, the explanation offered in the preceding chapters for centralized land use regulation uncovers the private interest in public planning, while questioning the public interest in private planning. Thus, it offers a more realistic interpretation of land use reform than what passes as conventional wisdom. Furthermore, it exposes the origins of a liberal reform ideology largely functioning to interpret and shape legitimate social protest over land use into a form useful for continued accumulation. A danger exists that popular protest seeking to establish greater democratic governance over the shape and pace of land development will be suppressed, or at least induced, into supporting reform antithetical to its own interests. Recognition of this pitfall is required for the development of more democratic and socially progressive alternatives.

Progressive land use reform may be recognized as the encouragement of individual and group participation in, and control over, the physical and social forces affecting one's life as mediated through land use, and in such a manner as to minimize coercive pressure on other groups and individuals. Acknowledging the complexity of struggle over land use as alliances form and movements are established that not only cut across class lines, but even lead individuals to pursue private aims in opposition to collective class goals, what are the implications for collective action in support of progressive reform?

To start, we would have to acknowledge the definite split that has appeared in the practical consciousness of America's working class, between the politics of work or production, and the politics of community or consumption. Certainly the Democratic progrowth coalition, long dominant in our central cities, rested upon organized labor, even as urban renewal destroyed working-class residential districts, thereby generating neighborhood resistance.[1] Given this division in consciousness as a fact of contemporary ideology and political life, it appears that consumption-based social movements are a two-edged sword in the fight for progressive land use reform. In their conservative form they cater to and reproduce ethnic, racial, income, and other social divisions. These divert attention away from development of the critical class consciousness required to bring about necessary change in the mode of production for a more socially just, environmentally stable, and economically secure society.

Alternatively, consumption-based social movements may come to realize the connection between their own specific struggle and the requirements of a dynamic production system dependent upon the very process of growth and transformation now threatening their security. If so, those protesting the process of land development may turn from specific rearguard action to actually challenge the social structure responsible for the pressures they are now facing. The conservative side of consumption-based social movements is illustrated through exclusionary suburban zoning and subdivision regulation, or where working-class residential districts are divided and defended along racial and ethnic lines. The progressive potential of consumption may be found with the united challenge that working-class residents, environmentalists, and inner-city minorities raise before urban renewal where it accommodates central-city conversion for office expansion, or when local residents, farmers, utility ratepayers, and consumer advocates protest the construction of expensive and environmentally risky energy facilities and power lines.

Social theorists are divided on the potential of consumption-based movements to force significant social change. On the one hand, Marxists have, at least until recently, dismissed consumption-based conflict as displaced class struggle from the sphere of production or, worse, as an attempt by capitalists to divide and conquer the proletariat, with contradiction simply replicated in the sphere of consumption.[2] On the other hand, neo-Weberians, where they have come to appreciate and respect the political power of consumption-based social movements, have tended to recognize production-based class struggle at the national, or central, level of political activity (defined, for example, by battles over social security, working conditions, and minimum wage levels). Consumption-based struggle, however, is conceived of as being local and as having origins that may be independent from the broader process of capital accumulation.[3] Failing to acknowledge the necessary relation between production and consumption, the neo-Weberians must rely upon a dual explanation for land use reform, with the Marxist focus on class divisions informing central State intervention, and contingent Weberian categories informing local intervention. The result is a fractured explanation rather than the theoretical unity possible with the Marxist recognition of the necessary, yet dialectic, relation that consumption has with production. Finally, neo-Marxists have been sensitized by the Weberians to the actual experience and ideology of consumption advocates, who may not themselves recognize a link between production and consumption. As such, the Marxists have recently come to appreciate the revolutionary potential of consumption movements as they challenge capitalist hegemony both in the sphere of consumption and in the sphere of production.[4]

Recent critical analysis on consumption movements, whether leaning toward Marxist or Weberian interpretation, has been largely limited to studies of the working class. It thereby overlooks the potential barrier for production and the potential for antithetical consciousness among individual members of the bourgeoisie, whose own private consumption is also threatened by, and challenges a collective class concern with, continued accumulation. As a result, the full potential for a radical change in consciousness, as people come to realize that their own myopic consumption concerns are incompatible with the very same production process responsible for their livelihood, may neither be appreciated nor exploited for progressive land use reform. This is not to suggest that the bourgeoisie, as a class, can ever be the revolutionary force challenging a mode of production where it is dominant, nor to deny the revolutionary potential of the proletariat. Rather, for the more immediate goal of progressive land use reform, we should be aware that contradiction, as it takes a spatial form, affects all members of society, be they producers or consumers, the bourgeoisie or the proletariat. We also need to recognize that strategic alliances may temporarily cross class lines.

As in so many other areas of social life, this is a period of upheaval and transition in the institutions of property development and land use regulation. Consumption opens up new arenas for conflict leading to the more revolutionary change in the mode of production required for a socially just, environmentally stable, and materially secure society. The real quiet evolution in land use control has been to selectively centralize responsibility for land use regulation when the State is captured by local consumption interests not aligned with continued accumulation and expansion of the forces of capitalist production. Therefore, we must be wary of liberal reform equating regional planning and centralized regulation with some abstract rationality promising something for everybody, particularly at a time when disparate social groups are finally exerting their right to participate in local land use decisions after years of quiescence. The time has come to unmask the quiet evolution and encourage real revolutionary consciousness to emerge.

NOTES

1. See Ira Katznelson, *City Trenches* (New York: Pantheon, 1981); David Halle, *America's Working Man: Work, Home, and Politics among Blue-Collar Property Owners* (Chicago: University of Chicago Press, 1984); and John Mollenkopf, "The Postwar Politics of Urban Development," in *Marxism and the Metropolis*, ed. W. Tabb and L. Sawers (New York: Oxford University Press, 1978), pp. 117-52.

2. Cf. David Harvey, "The Urban Process under Capitalism," *International Journal of Urban and Regional Research* 2, no. 1 (1978):101-31; idem, "Labor, Capital and Class Struggle around the Built Environment in Advanced Capitalist Societies," in *Urbanization and Conflict in Market Societies*, ed. K. Cox (Chicago: Maaroufa Press, 1978), pp. 9-38; and Manuel Castells, *The Urban Question* (London: Edward Arnold, 1977).

3. See Peter Saunders, *Social Theory and the Urban Question* (New York: Holmes & Meier, 1981); and idem, "Why Study Central-Local Relations?" *Local Government Studies* 82 (March-April 1982):55-66.

4. See Edmond Preteceille and Jean-Pierre Terrail, *Capitalism, Consumption and Needs* (1977; English ed., New York: Basil Blackwell, 1985); Manuel Castells, *The City and the Grassroots* (Berkeley and Los Angeles: University of California Press, 1983); Katznelson, *City Trenches*; James O'Connor, *Accumulation Crisis* (New York: Basil Blackwell, 1984); and Jim Kemeny, "A Critique and Reformulation of the New Urban Sociology," *Acta Sociologica* 25 (1982):419-30.

Works Cited

Abolafia, Mitchel. "Coordinating for the Collective Good: A Study of Coastal Zone Planning." *Administration & Society* 11 (August 1979):172-92.

Adams, Thomas. *Planning the New York Region.* New York: Committee on Regional Plan of New York and Its Environs, 1927.

Adirondack Council. *A Special Report: State of the Park 1986.* Fourth Annual Report. Elizabethtown, NY: Adirondack Council, 1986.

Adirondack Park Local Government Review Board. *Annual Report—1975.* Loon Lake, NY: Adirondack Park Local Government Review Board, 1975.

————. *A Return to Basic Problems: 1979 Annual Report.* Loon Lake, NY: Adirondack Park Local Government Review Board, 1979.

————. *The Blue Line Review* (Adirondack Park Local Government Review Board) 4 (March 1986).

Advisory Commission on Intergovernmental Relations. *Urban and Rural America: Policies for Future Growth.* Washington, DC: Government Printing Office, 1968.

Alcaly, Roger, and David Mermelstein, eds. *The Fiscal Crisis of American Cities: Essays on the Political Economy of Urban America with Special Reference to New York.* New York: Vintage Books, 1977.

Alpert, Irvin, and Ann Markusen. "The Professional Production of Policy Ideology and Plans: An Examination of Brookings and Resources for the Future." In *Power Structure Research,* edited by W. Domhoff, pp. 173-97. Beverly Hills, CA: Sage, 1980.

American Institute of Planners. *New Communities.* Background Paper, no. 2. Washington, DC: American Institute of Planners, 1968.

————. *Survey of Land Use Planning Activity.* Prepared for the U.S. Department of Housing and Urban Development. Washington, DC: Government Printing Office, 1976.

American Law Institute. *A Model Land Development Code.* Washington, DC: American Law Institute, 1975.

American Society of Planning Officials. *Subdividing Rural America: Impacts of Recreational Lot and Second Home Development.* Prepared for the U.S. Council on Environmental Quality. Washington, DC: Government Printing Office, 1976.

Amir, Shaul. *Conservation Kills a Highway: The Hudson River Expressway Controversy.* Research on Conflict in Locational Decisions, no. 4. Philadelphia: Regional Science Department, University of Pennsylvania, 1970.

Andelman, David. "$500-Million Aid to ConEd Is Agreed upon in Albany." New York *Times*, April 25, 1974, pp. A1, 23.

Armstrong, Regina. *The Office Industry.* Prepared for Regional Plan Association of New York. Cambridge, MA: MIT Press, 1972.

Aron, Joan. "The New York Interstate Metropolis." In *Regional Governance: Promise and Performance. Volume 2: Case Studies*, Advisory Commission on Intergovernmental Relations, pp. 199-213. 8 vols. Washington, DC: Government Printing Office, 1973.

————. "Intergovernmental Politics of Energy." *Policy Analysis* 5 (Fall 1979): 451-71.

Asher, Charles. "Comment on Robert Moses." *New York Planning Review* (New York Metropolitan Chapter of the American Institute of Planners) 17 (Spring 1975):A11-13.

Ashton, Patrick. "Urbanization and the Dynamics of Suburban Development under Capitalism." In *Marxism and the Metropolis*, 2d ed., edited by W. Tabb and L. Sawers, pp. 54-81. New York: Oxford University Press, 1984.

Association of the Bar of the City of New York: Special Committee on Electric Power and the Environment. *Electricity and the Environment: The Reform of Legal Institutions.* St. Paul, MN: West Publishing, 1972.

Babcock, Richard. "The Chaos of Zoning Administration: One Solution." *Zoning Digest* 12, no. 1 (1960):1-4.

————. *The Zoning Game.* Madison: University of Wisconsin Press, 1966.

Babcock, Richard, and Fred Bosselman. *Exclusionary Zoning: Land Use Regulation and Housing in the 1970s.* New York: Praeger, 1973.

Barnett, Richard, and Ronald Müller. *Global Reach.* New York: Simon and Schuster, 1974.

Beer, Richard. "The Tombstone of Nuclear Power?" *Seven Days,* March 28, 1977, pp. 2, 5-6.

Bell, Daniel. *The Coming of Post-Industrial Society.* New York: Basic Books, 1973.

————. *The Cultural Contradictions of Capitalism.* New York: Basic Books, 1976.

Bennett, Charles. "Mayor Has a Plan Rivaling State's to Improve Cities." New York *Times,* March 3, 1968, pp. A1, 36.

Berman, Marshall. *All That Is Solid Melts into Air.* New York: Simon and Schuster, 1982.

Bhaskar, Roy. *The Possibility of Naturalism: A Philosophical Critique of the Contemporary Human Sciences.* Sussex, UK: Harvester Press, 1979.

Bird, David. "Nuclear Power Plant Proposed beneath Welfare Island." New York *Times,* October 7, 1968, pp. A1, 93.

Bird, Frederick. *A Study of the Port of New York Authority.* New York: Dun & Bradstreet, 1949.

Blackmar, Betsy. "Going to the Mountains: A Social History." In *Resorts of the Catskills*, Architectural League of New York and Gallery Association of New York State, pp. 71-98. New York: St. Martin's Press, 1979.

Blumstein, Michael. "The Lessons of a Bond Failure." New York *Times,* August 14, 1983, pp. III-1, 24.

Bosselman, Fred. *Alternatives to Urban Sprawl: Legal Guidelines for Governmental Action.* Prepared for the National Commission on Urban Problems. Technical Report no. 15. Washington, DC: Government Printing Office, 1968.

Bosselman, Fred, and David Callies. *The Quiet Revolution in Land Use Control.* Prepared for the U.S. Council on Environmental Quality. Washington, DC: Government Printing Office, 1971.

Bosselman, Fred, David Callies, and John Banta. *The Taking Issue.* Prepared for the U.S. Council on Environmental Quality. Washington, DC: Government Printing Office, 1973.

Bosselman, Fred, Duane Feurer, and Charles Siemon. *The Permit Explosion: Coordination of the Proliferation.* Washington, DC: Urban Land Institute, 1976.

Brennan, James. "An Overview of the New York State Power Authority." In *The Future of the Power Authority of the State of New York,* Report from Joseph Ferris (chair of the Assembly Joint Subcommittee on Public Power). Vol. 1 of 2. Albany: New York State, Legislative Commission on Science and Technology, 1984.

Brilliant, Eleanor. *The Urban Development Corporation.* Lexington, MA: Lexington Books, 1975.

Brown, Eleanor. *The Forest Preserve of New York State: A Handbook for Conservationists.* Glens Falls, NY: Adirondack Mountain Club, 1985.

Buffalo City Planning Association. *Annual Report.* Buffalo: Buffalo City Planning Association, 1947.

Burrows, Lawrence. *Growth Management: Issues, Techniques and Policy Implications.* New Brunswick, NJ: Center for Urban Policy Research, Rutgers University, 1978.

Business Week. "Borrowing Gets Harder and the Demand Intensifies." October 26, 1981, pp. 154ff.

———. "Special Report: State and Local Government in Trouble." October 26, 1981, pp. 135ff.

———. "The Fallout from 'Whoops.'" July 11, 1983, pp. 80-82, 86-87.

———. "The New York Market Settles Down to a Steady Boil." August 12, 1985, pp. 64-65.

———. "The Selling of Rockefeller Center." August 12, 1985, p. 65.

Cadbury, Wardner. "Introduction." In *Adventures in the Wilderness* (1869), William H. H. Murray. Syracuse, NY: Syracuse University Press, 1970.

California Land Use Task Force. *The California Land: Planning for the People.* Sponsored by the California Planning and Conservation Foundation. Los Altos, CA: William Kaufman, 1975.

Caro, Robert. *The Power Broker.* New York: Vintage Books, 1975.

Carson, Rachel. *Silent Spring.* Boston: Houghton Mifflin, 1962.

Castells, Manuel. *The Urban Question.* London: Edward Arnold, 1977.

———. *The Economic Crisis and American Society.* Princeton, NJ: Princeton University Press, 1980.

————. *The City and the Grassroots.* Berkeley and Los Angeles: University of California Press, 1983.

Catskill Center for Conservation and Development. *The Catskill Center Plan.* Hobart, NY: Catskill Center for Conservation and Development, 1974.

The Catskills. "Our Future Awaits." Editorial (Winter 1972-73):40-44.

Centaur Associates. *Siting of Hazardous Waste Management Facilities and Public Opinion.* Report to the U.S. Environmental Protection Agency. Washington, DC: Environmental Protection Agency, Office of Solid Waste, 1979.

Checkoway, Barry. "Large Builders, Federal Housing Programs and Postwar Suburbanization." In *Marxism and the Metropolis,* 2d ed., edited by W. Tabb and L. Sawers, pp. 152-73. New York: Oxford University Press, 1984.

Christman, Henry. *Tin Horns and Calico.* 1945. New York: Collier Books, 1961.

Clawson, Marion. *Suburban Land Conversion in the United States.* Prepared for Resources for the Future. Baltimore: Johns Hopkins University Press, 1971.

————. "Economic and Social Conflicts in Land Use Planning." *Natural Resources Journal* 15 (1975):473-89.

Coe, Benjamin. "Tug Hill Revisited." *Planning News* (New York Planning Federation) 43 (July-August 1979):1, 6-7.

————. "Meeting the Needs of Rural Communities Governed by Part-Time Officials." Paper prepared for the Region I/II Conference of the American Society for Public Administration, October 22, 1986, in Albany, NY. Available from the Temporary State Commission on Tug Hill, Watertown, NY.

Coe, Benjamin, and Thorton Ware. "The Tug Hill Experience." *Planning News* (New York Planning Federation) 41 (March-April 1977).

Cohen, Henry. "Planning Rationally for the City." In *Governing the City: Challenges and Options for New York*, edited by R. Connery and D. Caraley, pp. 179-92. New York: Praeger, 1969.

Cohen, R. B. "The New International Division of Labor: Multinational Corporations and the Urban Hierarchy." In *Urbanization and Urban Planning in Capitalist Society*, edited by M. Dear and A. Scott, pp. 287-315. New York: Methuen, 1981.

Collier, Peter, and David Horowitz. *The Rockefellers: An American Dynasty.* New York: Holt, Rinehart and Winston, 1976.

Committee for Economic Development. *Guiding Metropolitan Growth.* New York: Committee for Economic Development, 1960.

————. *Modernizing Local Government.* New York: Committee for Economic Development, 1966.

Committee on Regional Plan of New York and Its Environs. *Highway Traffic.* Regional Survey of New York and Its Environs, vol. 3 of 8. New York: Regional Plan of New York and Its Environs, 1927.

————. *Major Economic Factors in Metropolitan Growth and Arrangement.* Regional Survey of New York and Its Environs, vol. 1 of 8. New York: Regional Plan of New York and Its Environs, 1927.

————. *Public Recreation.* Regional Survey of New York and Its Environs, vol. 5 of 8. New York: Regional Plan of New York and Its Environs, 1928.

————. *Transit and Transportation.* Regional Survey of New York and Its Environs, vol. 4 of 8. New York: Regional Plan of New York and Its Environs, 1928.

————. "The Clothing and Textile Industries." In *Food, Clothing and Textile Industries Wholesale Markets and Retail Shopping and Financial Districts.* Regional Survey of New York and Its Environs (originally monographs nos. 7-9 of Economic Series), vol. 1B of 8. New York: Regional Plan of New York and Its Environs, 1928.

————. "The Printing Industry." In *Chemical, Metal, Wood, Tobacco and Printing Industries.* Regional Survey of New York and Its Environs (originally monograph no. 6 of Economic Series), vol. 1A of 8. New York: Regional Plan of New York and Its Environs, 1928.

————. *The Graphic Regional Plan.* Regional Plan of New York and Its Environs, vol. 1 of 2. New York: Regional Plan of New York and Its Environs, 1929.

————. *Neighborhood and Community Planning.* Regional Survey of New York and Its Environs, vol. 7 of 8. New York: Regional Plan of New York and Its Environs, 1929.

————. *Population, Land Values and Government.* Regional Survey of New York and Its Environs, vol. 2 of 8. New York: Regional Plan of New York and Its Environs, 1929.

————. *The Building of the City.* Regional Plan of New York and Its Environs, vol. 2 of 2. New York: Regional Plan of New York and Its Environs, 1931.

Commoner, Barry. "The Environmental Costs of Economic Growth." In *Economics of the Environment,* edited by R. Dorfman and N. Dorfman, pp. 261-83. New York: W. W. Norton, 1972.

Conference on Metropolitan Area Problems. *Metropolitan Area Problems. News and Digest* 1 (1957):1-2.

Connery, Robert. "Nelson Rockefeller as Governor." *Governing New York State: The Rockefeller Years. The Academy of Political Science* 31 (May 1974):1-15.

Connery, Robert, and Gerald Benjamin, eds. *Governing New York State: The Rockefeller Years. The Academy of Political Science* 31 (May 1974).

Cook, James. "Nuclear Follies." *Forbes,* February 11, 1985, cover and pp. 82-100.

Costikyan, Edward, and Maxwell Lehman. *New Strategies for Regional Cooperation: A Model for the Tri-State New York-New Jersey-Connecticut Area.* New York: Praeger, 1973.

Dahlberg, Jane. *The New York Bureau of Municipal Research: Pioneer in Government and Administration.* New York: New York University Press, 1966.

Danielson, Michael. *The Politics of Exclusion.* New York: Columbia University Press, 1976.

Danielson, Michael, and Jameson Doig. *New York: The Politics of Urban Regional Development.* Berkeley and Los Angeles: University of California Press, 1982.

Darby, H. C. "The Changing English Landscape" (1951). In *Man, Space, and Environment,* edited by P. English and R. Mayfield, pp. 28-41. London: Oxford University Press, 1972.

Delafons, John. *Land Use Controls in the United States.* 2d ed. Cambridge, MA: MIT Press, 1969.

D'Elia, Anthony. *The Adirondack Rebellion.* Onchiota, NY: Onchiota Books, 1979.

Dionne, E. J., Jr. "Carey Signs Bill Providing Tax Benefits for Madison Square Garden." *New York Times,* July 8, 1982, p. B7.

Doctorow, E. L. *Loon Lake.* New York: Random House, 1980.

Doig, Jameson. *Metropolitan Transportation Politics in the New York Region.* New York: Columbia University Press, 1966.

——. "'If I See a Murderous Fellow Sharpening a Knife Cleverly . . .': The Wilsonian Dichotomy and the Public Authority Tradition." *Public Administration Review* 43 (July-August 1983):292-304.

Domhoff, William. *The Powers That Be: Processes of Ruling Class Domination in America.* New York: Random House, 1978.

——. *Who Really Rules?* Santa Monica, CA: Goodyear Publishing, 1978.

Donaldson, Alfred. *A History of the Adirondacks.* 2 vols. New York: Century, 1921.

Dorman, Michael. "The Bigger They Are." *Empire State Report* 9 (May 1983):16-18.

Dormer, Robert. "Three New Towns." *Journal of Housing* 36, no. 2 (1979):86-89.

Douglas, William. "The Eastern Forests." In *The American Heritage Book of Natural Wonders.* New York: American Heritage Publishing, 1963.

Douglass, Harlan P. *The Suburban Trend.* New York: Century, 1925.

Downie, Leonard, Jr. *Mortgage on America.* New York: Praeger, 1974.

Downs, Anthony. *Opening Up the Suburbs.* New Haven, CT: Yale University Press, 1973.

Downtown-Lower Manhattan Association. *Recommended Land Use, Redevelopment Areas, Traffic Improvements.* New York: Downtown-Lower Manhattan Association, 1958.

——. *World Trade Center: A Proposal for the Port of New York.* New York: Downtown-Lower Manhattan Association, 1960.

——. *Major Improvements: Land Use, Transportation, Traffic—Lower Manhattan.* New York: Downtown-Lower Manhattan Association, 1963.

Dubos, Rene. "Conservation, Stewardship and the Human Heart." *Audubon Magazine* 74 (September 1972):20-28.

Duffus, R. L. *Mastering the Metropolis.* New York: Harper and Brothers, 1930.

Dunn, Marvin. "The Family Office: Coordinating Mechanism of the Ruling Class." In *Power Structure Research*, edited by W. Domhoff, pp. 17-45. Beverly Hills, CA: Sage, 1980.

Dyballa, Cynthia. "The Tug Hill Commission: A Cooperative Approach to Regional Planning." Master's thesis, Department of Natural Resources, Cornell University, 1979.

Dyballa, Cynthia, Lyle Raymond, Jr., and Alan Hahn. *The Tug Hill Program: A Regional Planning Option for Rural Areas.* Syracuse, NY: Syracuse University Press, 1981.

Eberlein, Harold, and Cortland Van Dyke Hubbard. *Historic Houses of the Hudson Valley.* New York: Architectural Book Publishing, 1942.

Eberts, Paul. *Socioeconomic Trends in Rural New York State: Toward the 21st Century.* Albany: New York State, Legislative Commission on Rural Resources, 1984.

Edel, Matthew. "Capitalism, Accumulation and the Explanation of Urban Phenomena." In *Urbanization and Urban Planning in Capitalist Society,* edited by M. Dear and A. Scott, pp. 19-44. New York: Methuen, 1981.

Elliman, Kim. "Keep the Adirondack State Park 'Forever Wild.'" New York *Times.* Editorial, December 7, 1985, p. A27.

Ellis, David. *Landlords and Farmers in the Hudson-Mohawk Region, 1790-1850.* Ithaca, NY: Cornell University Press, 1946.

Engels, Frederick. *The Condition of the Working Class in England.* 1844. London: Basil Blackwell, 1958.

Enzenzberger, Hans. "A Critique of Political Ecology." In *Political Ecology,* edited by A. Cockburn and J. Ridgeway, pp. 371-93. New York: Time Books, 1974.

Epstein, Jason. "The Last Days of New York." In *The Fiscal Crisis of American Cities: Essays on the Political Economy of Urban America with Special Reference to New York,* edited by R. Alcaly and D. Mermelstein, pp. 59-76. New York: Vintage Books, 1977.

ERM-Northeast. *Hazardous Waste Facilities Needs Assessment, Summary Report and Appendices.* Prepared for New York State, Department of Environmental Conservation, Division of Solid and Hazardous Waste. Albany: Department of Environmental Conservation, 1985.

Esch, Mary. "APA Now Trying to Promote Economic Development." *Leader-Herald* (Gloversville-Johnstown, NY), August 14, 1985, p. 7.

Evers, Alf. *The Catskills: From Wilderness to Woodstock.* Garden City, NY: Doubleday, 1972.

Farber, Harold. "Controversy over Power Lines Spreads across Upstate New York." New York *Times*, May 22, 1979, p. A49.

———. "City Now against Using Reservoir for Power." New York *Times,* April 4, 1982, p. A39.

———. "Power Authority Is Denied Permit to Build a Plant." New York *Times*, April 10, 1982, p. A26.

———. "Ex-City Residents Lead Opposition to New Powerline Upstate." New York *Times,* August 30, 1982, p. B2.

———. "A Centennial Celebration of the Adirondacks." *New York Times Magazine,* March 21, 1985, pp. 52ff.

———. "Upstate Town Resisting Role as PCB Burial Site." New York *Times,* January 3, 1986, p. B2.

Farr, Walter, Jr., Lance Liebman, and Jeffrey Wood. *Decentralizing City Government: A Practical Study of a Radical Proposal for New York City.* New York: Praeger, 1972.

Finkelstein, Charles, and Laurence Baxter. *Planning and Politics: A Staff Perception of the Tahoe Regional Planning Agency.* Institute of Government Affairs, Environmental Quality Series Report no. 21. Davis: University of California, 1974.

Fitch, Robert. "Planning New York." In *The Fiscal Crisis of American Cities: Essays on the Political Economy of Urban America with Special Reference to New York,* edited by R. Alcaly and D. Mermelstein, pp. 246-84. New York: Vintage Books, 1977.

Fitch Investors Service Inc. *The Port Authority of New York and New Jersey. Municipal Bond Report,* no. 286 (December 3, 1981).

Fortune Magazine. *The Exploding Metropolis.* Garden City, NY: Doubleday, 1958.

Franklin, Virginia. "At Pocantico Hills, a Question of Taxes." New York *Times,* November 25, 1981, Section 22, p. 26.

Freedman, Eric, and Roger Klingman. "The Catskills." *Empire State Report* 9 (June 1983): 13-23.

Fried, Joseph. "Good-bye Slum Razing: Hello Grand Hyatt." New York *Times,* July 15, 1979, Section 4, p. 6.

Frieden, Bernard. *The Environmental Protection Hustle.* Cambridge, MA: MIT Press, 1979.

Friedmann, John, and Clyde Weaver. *Territory and Function.* Berkeley and Los Angeles: University of California Press, 1980.

Fulton, Bill. "The New Town That Works." *Planning* 46 (January 1980):12-15.

Geisler, Charles, Susan Kenney, and Roger Vlieger. "Sources of Inholder Opposition to Land Use Management in the Adirondack Park of New York." Paper presented at the Annual Meeting of the Rural Sociological Society, August 22-25, 1984, in College Station, TX. Available from the Department of Rural Sociology, Cornell University, Ithaca, NY.

Geisler, Charles et al. *Adirondack Landowners Survey.* Department of Rural Sociology Bulletin no. 145. Ithaca, NY: Department of Rural Sociology, Cornell University, 1985.

Getzels, Judith, Peter Elliot, and Frank Beal. *Private Planning for the Public Interest: A Study of Approaches to Urban Problem Solving by Nonprofit Organizations.* Chicago: American Society of Planning Officials, 1975.

Giddens, Anthony. *Central Problems in Social Theory: Action, Structure and Contradiction in Social Analysis.* Berkeley and Los Angeles: University of California Press, 1979.

———. *A Contemporary Critique of Historical Materialism.* Berkeley and Los Angeles: University of California Press, 1981.

Gilligan, Donald. "The Time Bomb South of Buffalo." *Empire State Report* 3 (January 1977):3-11.

Glacken, Clarence. *Traces on the Rhodian Shore.* Berkeley and Los Angeles: University of California Press, 1967.

Gleason, Eugene, and Joseph Zimmerman. "Executive Dominance in New York State." Paper presented at the Annual Meeting of the Northeastern Political Science Association, November 11, 1978, in Saratoga Springs, NY.

Goldman, Ari. "Audit Says Roosevelt Island Is a Burden to the Taxpayer." New York *Times,* March 21, 1980, p. B1.

———. "State Agencies Take Command of Conrail Lines." New York *Times,* January 3, 1983, p. B4.

Goldmark, Peter, Jr. "The Economy of the New York-New Jersey Metropolitan Region." In *New York State Today: Politics, Government, Public Policy,* edited by P. Colby, pp. 257-65. Albany: State University of New York Press, 1985.

Goodman, Percival. "Lincoln Center, Emporium of the Arts." In *Urban Renewal: People, Politics, and Planning,* edited by J. Bellush and M. Hausknecht, pp. 406-14. Garden City, NY: Anchor Books, 1967.

Gordon, David. "Capitalist Development and the History of American Cities." In *Marxism and the Metropolis,* 2d ed., edited by W. Tabb and L. Sawers, pp. 21-53. New York: Oxford University Press, 1984.

Gottdeiner, Mark. *Planned Sprawl.* Beverly Hills, CA: Sage, 1977.

Gottlieb, Martin. "U.D.C. Chief Steering Agency into New Area." New York *Times*, April 13, 1983, pp. B1, 3.
———. "From Public Housing to Private Incentive." New York *Times*, January 27, 1985, p. I7.
———. "New Delay Seen in Redeveloping Times Sq. Area." New York *Times*, September 20, 1985, p. B3.
Graham, Frank. *The Adirondack Park: A Political History.* New York: Alfred A. Knopf, 1978.
Greenspan, Arthur. "UDC Goes High-Tech." *Empire State Report* 9 (March 1983): 28-31.
Grover, Richard. "People Power: It Can Make a Difference." *Planning News* (New York Planning Federation) 42 (March-April 1978):1, 6-7.
Grupp, Fred, Jr., and Alan Richards. "Variations in Elite Perceptions of American States as Referents for Public Policy Making." *American Political Science Review* 69 (September 1975):850-58.

Hahn, Alan, and Cynthia Dyballa. "State Environmental Planning and Local Influence: A Comparison of Three Regional Natural Resource Management Agencies." *Journal of the American Planning Association* 47 (July 1981):324-35.
Hall, Peter. *The World Cities.* 2d ed. New York: McGraw-Hill, 1977.
Halle, David. *America's Working Man: Work, Home, and Politics among Blue-Collar Property Owners.* Chicago: University of Chicago Press, 1984.
Hammack, David. *Power and Society: Greater New York at the Turn of the Century.* New York: Russell Sage Foundation, 1982.
Hammond, Samuel. *Wild Northern Scenes; or, Sporting Adventures With the Rifle and the Rod.* New York: Derby and Jackson, 1857.
Harr, Charles. "Regionalism and Realism in Land-Use Planning." *University of Pennsylvania Law Review* 105 (1957):515-37.
Harrison, Bennett, and Sandra Kanter. "The Political Economy of States' Job-Creation Business Incentives." *Journal of the American Institute of Planners* 44 (October 1978):424-35.
Harvey, David. *Social Justice and the City.* Baltimore: Johns Hopkins University Press, 1973.
———. "Government Policies, Financial Institutions and Neighborhood Change in United States Cities." In *Captive Cities,* edited by M. Harloe, pp. 123-39. London: John Wiley, 1977.
———. "Labor, Capital and Class Struggle around the Built Environment in Advanced Capitalist Societies." In *Urbanization and Conflict in Market Societies*, edited by K. Cox, pp. 9-38. Chicago: Maaroufa Press, 1978.
———. "The Urban Process under Capitalism." *International Journal of Urban and Regional Research* 2, no. 1 (1978):101-31.
Hawkins, Betty. "New York's Environmental Impact Tussle." *Empire State Report* 1 (February-March 1975):64-67, 93-95.
Hays, Forbes. *Community Leadership: The Regional Plan Association of New York.* New York: Columbia University Press, 1965.
Hays, Samuel. *Conservation and the Gospel of Efficiency.* Cambridge, MA: Harvard University Press, 1959.

————. "The Politics of Reform in Municipal Government in the Progressive Era." *Pacific Northwest Quarterly* 55, no. 4 (1964):157-69.

————. "Value Premises for Planning and Public Policy: The Historical Context." In *Land in America,* edited by R. Andrews, pp. 149-66. Lexington, MA: Lexington Books, 1979.

Headley, Joel Tyler. *The Adirondack; or, Life in the Woods.* New York: Baker and Scribner, 1849.

Healy, Robert. *Land Use and the States.* Prepared for Resources for the Future. Baltimore: Johns Hopkins University Press, 1976.

————. *Environmentalists and Developers: Can They Agree on Anything?* Washington, DC: Conservation Foundation, 1977.

Healy, Robert, and John Rosenberg. *Land Use and the States.* 2d ed. Prepared for Resources for the Future. Baltimore: Johns Hopkins University Press, 1979.

Heikoff, Joseph. *Marine and Shoreland Resources Management.* Ann Arbor, MI: Ann Arbor Science Publishers, 1980.

Heiman, Michael. "An Evaluation of State Land Use Planning and Development Control in the Adirondacks." Master's thesis, Department of Natural Resources, Cornell University, 1975.

Helburn, Nicholas. "Geography and the Quality of Life." *Annals of the Association of American Geographers* 72 (December 1982):445-56.

Hellman, Richard. *Government Competition in the Electric Utility Industry.* New York: Praeger, 1972.

Henshaw, Bob. "Compromise Agreement Ends Hudson River Controversy." *New York State Environment* (Department of Environmental Conservation) 10, no. 6 (1981):3.

Heskin, Allan. *Tenants and the American Dream.* New York: Praeger, 1983.

Hillhouse, William II. "The Federal Law of Water Resources Development." In *Federal Environmental Law,* edited by E. Dolgin and T. Guilbert, pp. 844-926. Prepared for the Environmental Law Institute. St. Paul, MN: West Publishing, 1974.

Hoard, Deborah. "The Substantive Duties of Local Governments under the New York State Environmental Quality Review Act." Master's thesis, Department of Natural Resources, Cornell University, 1978.

Hochschild, Harold. *Township 34.* Printed by Harold Hochschild, 1952. Available from the Adirondack Museum, Blue Mountain Lake, NY.

Hoover, Edgar, and Raymond Vernon. *Anatomy of a Metropolis.* Cambridge, MA: Harvard University Press, 1959.

Hudson Basin Project. *Final Report of the Hudson Basin Project.* Published for and by the Rockefeller Foundation. New York: Hudson Basin Project, 1976.

Hudson Basin Project, Land Use/Human Settlement Task Force. *Task Force Report.* Published by and for the Rockefeller Foundation. New York: Hudson Basin Project, 1976.

Huth, Hans. *Nature and the American.* 1957. Lincoln: University of Nebraska Press, 1972.

Inscho, Frederick. "An Analysis of Power Plant Siting Policy in New York State." Ph.D. dissertation, State University of New York at Buffalo, 1978.

Johnson, Arthur. "Acid Deposition: Trends, Relationships, and Effects." *Environment* 28 (May 1986):6-11, 34-39.

Johnson, David. "The Emergence of Metropolitan Regionalism: An Analysis of the 1929 Regional Plan of New York and Its Environs." Ph.D. dissertation, Cornell University, 1974.

———. "Seventy-five Years of Metropolitan Planning in the N.Y.-N.J.-Connecticut Urban Region. A Retrospective Assessment." Paper delivered at the Twenty-sixth Annual Meeting of the Association of Collegiate Schools of Planning, October 19, 1984, in New York City.

Jones, Victor. "Bay Area Regionalism." In *The Regionalist Papers*, 2d ed., edited by K. Mathewson, pp. 133-59. Southfield, MI: Metropolitan Fund, 1977.

Kaiser, Harvey. *The Building of Cities*. Ithaca, NY: Cornell University Press, 1978.

Kantor, Harvey. "Charles Dyer Norton and the Origins of the Regional Plan of New York." *Journal of the American Institute of Planners* 39 (January 1973):35-42.

Katznelson, Ira. *City Trenches*. New York: Pantheon, 1981.

Keith, John, and William Shore. *Public Participation in Regional Planning*. Report of the Second Regional Plan. New York: Regional Plan Association, 1967.

Keller, Jane. *Adirondack Wilderness*. Syracuse, NY: Syracuse University Press, 1980.

Kemeny, Jim. "A Critique and Reformulation of the New Urban Sociology." *Acta Sociologica* 25 (1982):419-30.

Kennedy, William. "Everything Anybody Ever Wanted." *The Atlantic* 251, no. 5 (1983):77-88.

King, Bente. "Critique of the Hudson Basin Project." Master of Professional Studies thesis, Department of Natural Resources, Cornell University, 1975.

Kotz, David. *Bank Control of Large Corporations in the United States*. Berkeley and Los Angeles: University of California Press, 1978.

Kovach, Bill. "Governor Offers Aid on Atomic Plants." New York *Times,* September 6, 1969, p. A23.

Kutz, Myer. *Rockefeller Power*. New York: Simon and Schuster, 1974.

La Budde, Kenneth. "The Mind of Thomas Cole." Ph.D. dissertation, University of Minnesota, 1954.

Land Use Planning Report. "FTC Cites Horizon Corp. on $375-Million Land Fraud." October 8, 1979, p. 319.

Lawrence, Steve. "Only One Power Plant Has Been Approved in New York State since the Legislature Created the Siting Board in 1972." *Empire State Report* 4 (January 1978):14-17.

League for Adirondack Citizen's Rights. *Adirondacker's Survival Kit*. Reprints and pamphlets. Ausable Forks, NY: Black Brook Town Hall, c. 1976.

League of Women Voters of New York State. *Making Land Use Decisions in New York State*. New York: League of Women Voters of New York State, 1975.

Lefebvre, Henri. *Everyday Life in the Modern World*. London: Harper & Row, 1971.

———. *The Survival of Capitalism*. London: Allison and Busby, 1976.

Ley, David. "Liberal Ideology and the Postindustrial City." *Annals of the Association of American Geographers* 70 (June 1980):238-58.

Lichten, Eric. "The Development of Austerity: Fiscal Crisis in New York City." In *Power Structure Research*, edited by W. Domhoff, pp. 139-71. Beverly Hills, CA: Sage, 1980.

Lichtenberg, Robert. *One-Tenth of a Nation.* Cambridge, MA: Harvard University Press, 1960.

Lindsey, Robert. "Fast Growing Suburbs Act to Limit Development." New York *Times*, December 2, 1985, p. A10.

Liroff, Richard, and Gordon Davis. *Protecting Open Space: Land Use Control in the Adirondack Park.* Cambridge, MA: Ballinger Publishing, 1981.

Loewenstein, Louis. "The New York State Urban Development Corporation—Forgotten Failure or a Precursor of the Future?" *Journal of the American Institute of Planners* 44 (July 1978):261-73.

Long, Louella Jacqueline, and Vernon Robinson. *How Much Power to the People? A Study of the New York State Urban Development Corporation's Investment in Black Harlem.* New York: Urban Center, Columbia University, 1971.

Longshore, Richard. "The Power Authority of the State of New York: Accountability and Public Policy." Ph.D. dissertation, Syracuse University, 1981.

Lowe, Jeanne. *Cities in a Race with Time.* New York: Random House, 1967.

Lowenthal, David, and Hugh Prince. "English Landscape Tastes." In *Man, Space, and Environment,* edited by P. English and R. Mayfield, pp. 81-112. London: Oxford University Press, 1972.

Lubove, Roy. *The Progressives and the Slums.* Pittsburgh: University of Pittsburgh Press, 1962.

————. *Twentieth-Century Pittsburgh: Government, Business and Environmental Change.* New York: John Wiley, 1969.

Luce, Charles. "Power for Tomorrow: The Siting Dilemma." *Environmental Law* 1, no. 1 (1970):60-71.

McAneny, George. *The Second Annual Report of the Regional Plan Association.* Presented at the Annual Meeting of the Regional Plan Association, May 31, 1931, in New York City. New York: Regional Plan Association of New York, 1931.

————. *The Sixth Annual Report of the Regional Plan Association.* Presented at the Annual Meeting of the Regional Plan Association, June 6, 1935, in New York City. New York: Regional Plan Association of New York, 1935.

————. *The Seventh Annual Report of the Regional Plan Association.* Presented at the Annual Meeting of the Regional Plan Association, May 28, 1936, in New York City. New York: Regional Plan Association of New York, 1936.

————. *The Eighth Annual Report of the Regional Plan Association.* Presented at the Annual Meeting of the Regional Plan Association, December 2, 1937, in New York City. New York: Regional Plan Association of New York, 1937.

————. *The Ninth Annual Report of the Regional Plan Association.* Presented at the Annual Meeting of the Regional Plan Association, December 1, 1938, in New York City. New York: Regional Plan Association of New York, 1938.

McHarg, Ian. "Ecological Determinism." In *Future Environments of North America,* edited by F. Fraser Darling and J. P. Milton, pp. 526-38. Garden City, NY: Natural History Press, 1966.

—————. *Design with Nature.* Philadelphia: Falcon Press/Natural History Press, 1969.

Machia, Norah, and Paul Foy. "Tug Hill Commission 'Wimps' on Garbage." Watertown *Daily Times,* April 24, 1987, pp. 1, 12.

McMahon, Marty. "Radisson: For Some an American Dream." Syracuse *Herald American,* September 9, 1984, pp. L1, 3.

Maize, Kennedy. "New York Hydro Wars." *Empire State Report* 10 (October 1984):9-12.

Makielski, S. J., Jr. *The Politics of Zoning.* New York: Columbia University Press, 1966.

Mandel, Ernst. *Late Capitalism.* 1972. English ed., London: Verso, 1978.

Mandelbaum, Paulette. "Who Runs New York's Power Plant?" *Empire State Report* 8 (May 1982):29-31.

—————. "Affecting New York's Energy Future." *Empire State Report* 11 (July 1985):7-8, 11-12, 46-48.

Markusen, Ann. "Class and Urban Social Expenditure: A Marxist Theory of Metropolitan Government." In *Marxism and the Metropolis,* 2d ed., edited by W. Tabb and L. Sawers, pp. 82-100. New York: Oxford University Press, 1984.

Marquis—Who's Who. *Who's Who in the East.* 10th ed. Chicago: Marquis—Who's Who, 1967.

Marsh, Elizabeth. *Cooperative Rural Planning: A Tug Hill Case Study.* Watertown, NY: Temporary State Commission on Tug Hill, 1981.

Marsh, George Perkins. *Man and Nature; or, Physical Geography as Modified by Human Action.* Rev. ed. New York: Charles Scribner, 1871.

Marx, Karl. *Grunrisse: Foundations of the Critique of Political Economy.* 1858. London: Harmondsworth/Penguin, 1973.

—————. *Capital: A Critique of Political Economy.* Vol. 1 of 3. 1867. Chicago: Charles H. Kerr, 1908.

—————. "Critique of the Gotha Programme" (1875). In *Karl Marx: The First International and After,* edited by D. Fernback, pp. 339-59. New York: Vintage Books, 1974.

Marx, Karl, and Frederick Engels. "Feuerbach: Opposition of the Materialist and Idealist Outlook" (1845). In *The German Ideology,* K. Marx and F. Engels, pp. 39-95. Edited and introduced by C. J. Arthur. New York: International Publishers, 1977.

Massey, Doreen, and Alejandria Catalano. *Capital and Land: Landownership by Capital in Great Britain.* London: Edward Arnold, 1978.

Massey, Doreen, and Richard Meegan. "Industrial Restructuring versus the City." *Urban Studies* 15, no. 3 (1978):273-88.

Mayer, Martin. "A Commercial Renaissance." In *New York New York '82.* Special advertising section, prepared by the Real Estate Board of New York. New York *Times,* October 31, 1982, pp. 6, 8-9, 10.

Meinig, Donald. "Geography of Expansion, 1785-1855" (1966). In *Geography of New York State,* edited by J. Thompson, pp. 140-71. Syracuse, NY: Syracuse University Press, 1977.

Merchant, Carolyn. *The Death of Nature.* San Francisco: Harper & Row, 1980.

Mid-Hudson Pattern for Progress. *Closing the Gap.* Annual Report for 1968. Poughkeepsie, NY: Mid-Hudson Pattern for Progress, 1969.

———. *New Directions for the '70s.* Annual Report for 1969. Poughkeepsie, NY: Mid-Hudson Pattern for Progress, 1970.

———. *Crisis to Opportunity.* Annual Report for 1973-74. Poughkeepsie, NY: Mid-Hudson Pattern for Progress, 1974.

———. *Electrical Energy and the Catskill Region.* Prepared for the New York State, Temporary State Commission to Study the Catskills. Poughkeepsie, NY: Mid-Hudson Pattern for Progress, 1974.

———. *Mid-Hudson Pattern for Progress, Inc.* Introductory brochure. Poughkeepsie, NY: Mid-Hudson Pattern for Progress, c. 1986.

Mid-Hudson Pattern for Progress, and Regional Plan Association of New York. *The Mid-Hudson: A Development Guide.* Poughkeepsie, NY: Mid-Hudson Pattern for Progress, 1973.

Mid-Hudson Pattern for Progress; New York State, Urban Development Corporation; and Regional Plan Association of New York. *Mid-Hudson Regional Development Program: A Partnership for Progress.* Pamphlet. Poughkeepsie, NY: Mid-Hudson Pattern for Progress, 1969.

Miliband, Ralph. *The State in Capitalist Society.* New York: Basic Books, 1969.

Miner, Tom. "Pumped Storage at Prattsville." *New York State Environmental News* (Atmospheric Sciences Research Center, State University of New York at Albany) 7, no. 2 (1980):1-6.

———. "For Our Children's Children." *The Conservationist* 39 (May-June 1985): 60-65.

Mollenkopf, John. "The Post-War Politics of Urban Development." *Politics and Society* 5 (1975):247-95.

———. "The Postwar Politics of Urban Development." In *Marxism and the Metropolis*, edited by W. Tabb and L. Sawers, pp. 117-52. New York: Oxford University Press, 1978.

Molotch, Harvey. "The City as a Growth Machine: Toward a Political Economy of Place." *American Journal of Sociology* 82 (1976):309-22.

Moody's Investors Service. *Moody's Municipal & Government Manual.* 2 vols. New York: Moody's Investors Service, 1981.

———. *Moody's Municipal & Government Manual.* 2 vols. New York: Moody's Investors Service, 1987.

Moore, Vincent. "Politics, Planning, and Power in New York State: The Path from Theory to Reality." *Journal of the American Institute of Planners* 37 (March 1971):66-77.

Moscow, Alvin. *The Rockefeller Inheritance.* Garden City, NY: Doubleday, 1977.

Moses, Robert. *Public Works: A Dangerous Trade.* New York: McGraw-Hill, 1970.

Moss, Elaine, ed. *Land Use Controls in New York State.* Prepared by the Natural Resources Defense Council. New York: Dial Press, 1975.

———. *Land Use Controls in the United States.* Prepared by the Natural Resources Defense Council. New York: Dial Press, 1977.

Mowbray, A. Q. *Road to Ruin.* New York: Lippincott, 1969.

Mumford, Lewis. "The Plan of New York 1." *The New Republic*, June 15, 1932, pp. 121-26.

———. "The Plan of New York 2." *The New Republic*, June 22, 1932, pp. 146-54.

Murphy, Justin. "Presidential Address Delivered at the Twenty-eighth Annual Meeting of the Downtown-Lower Manhattan Association." New York City, March 5, 1985. Mimeographed.

Murray, William H. H. *Adventures in the Wilderness; or Camplife in the Adirondacks.* Boston: Fields, Osgood, 1869.

Nash, Roderick. *Wilderness and the American Mind.* Rev. ed. New Haven, CT: Yale University Press, 1973.

National Advisory Commission on Civil Disorders. *Final Report.* Washington, DC: Government Printing Office, 1968.

National Commission on Urban Problems. *Building the American City.* Washington, DC: Government Printing Office, 1968.

Nelson, Holly, and Alan Hahn. *State Policy and Local Influence in the Adirondacks.* Ithaca, NY: Center for Environmental Research, Cornell University, 1980.

Nelson, Robert. *Zoning and Property Rights: An Analysis of the American System of Land-Use Regulation.* Cambridge, MA: MIT Press, 1977.

Newfield, Jack, and Paul DuBrul. *The Abuse of Power: The Permanent Government and the Fall of New York.* New York: Viking Press, 1977.

Newkirk, Arthur. "Early ADK Conservationists." *Adirondac* (Adirondack Mountain Club) 49 (January 1985):34-36.

New York City, Board of Water Supply. *Catskill Water Supply: A General Description and Brief History.* New York: Board of Water Supply, 1917.

New York City, Improvement Commission. *Report of the New York City Improvement Commission to the Honorable George B. McClellan.* New York: Kalkhoff, 1907.

New York City, Planning Commission. *The Lower Manhattan Plan.* Prepared by Wallace, McHarg, Roberts, and Todd; Whittlesey, Conklin, and Rossant; Voorhees and Associates Inc. New York: Planning Commission, 1966.

New York Power Authority. *Annual Report for 1985.* Albany: New York Power Authority, 1986.

New York State, Adirondack Park Agency. *Adirondack Park State Land Master Plan.* Ray Brook, NY: Adirondack Park Agency, 1972.

———. "Large Landowner Survey." Ray Brook, NY, c. 1972. Mimeographed.

———. *Adirondack Park Land Use and Development Plan and Recommendations for Implementation.* Ray Brook, NY: Adirondack Park Agency, 1973.

———. "Overall Intensity Guidelines." *Comprehensive Report.* 2 vols. Ray Brook, NY: Adirondack Park Agency, 1973.

———. *Land Use Planning for the Adirondack Park.* Pamphlet. Ray Brook, NY: Adirondack Park Agency, 1974.

———. *Local Planning and Land Use Controls in the Adirondacks: A Handbook for Local Governments.* Ray Brook, NY: Adirondack Park Agency, 1975.

———. *Adirondack Park Economic Profile: Phase Two: Recent Trends and Factors Affecting the Adirondack Real Estate Market.* Ray Brook, NY: Adirondack Park Agency, 1976.

———. *Comprehensive Report: Adirondack Park Agency.* 2 vols. Ray Brook, NY: Adirondack Park Agency, 1976. Reprinted in Lake Placid *News*, March 4, 1976, Section 2.

———. *1978 Annual Report.* Ray Brook, NY: Adirondack Park Agency, 1979.

————. *1984 Annual Report.* Ray Brook, NY: Adirondack Park Agency, 1985.

New York State, Atomic and Space Development Authority. *Nuclear Power Siting Program: Phase 1: State-wide Survey.* Albany: Atomic and Space Development Authority, c. 1970.

New York State, Board of Equalization and Assessment. *Adirondack Park Real Property Tax Base Study.* Final Report. Albany: Board of Equalization and Assessment, 1978.

New York State, Commission of Housing and Regional Planning. *Report of the Commission of Housing and Regional Planning to Governor Alfred E. Smith.* Albany: J. B. Lyon, 1926.

New York State, Department of Conservation. *The Adirondacks: New York's Forest Preserve and a Proposed National Park.* Albany: Department of Conservation, 1967.

New York State, Department of Environmental Conservation. *Land Resources Management and Related Programs of the New York State Department of Environmental Conservation.* 3 vols. Albany: Land Resources Planning Group, Department of Environmental Conservation, 1976.

————. *The Hudson River Study.* Prepared by Raymond, Parish, Pine and Weiner Inc. Albany: Department of Environmental Conservation, 1979.

————. *The Hudson River Valley: A Heritage for All Time.* Pamphlet. Albany: Department of Environmental Conservation, 1979.

New York State, Department of Public Service. *An Energy Almanac: New York State 1960-1980.* Albany: Public Service Commission, 1976.

New York State, Department of State. *New York State Coastal Management Program: Draft Environmental Impact Statement.* Albany: Department of State, 1976.

————. *Local Government Handbook.* 2d ed. Albany: Department of State, 1982.

New York State, Governor's Committee on Power Resources. *Report to Governor Nelson A. Rockefeller.* Albany: Governor's Committee on Power Resources, December 15, 1959.

New York State, Hazardous Waste Disposal Advisory Committee. *A Comprehensive Program for Hazardous Waste Disposal in New York State.* Albany: Environmental Facilities Corporation, 1980.

New York State, Hazardous Waste Treatment Facilities Task Force. *Final Report.* Albany: Hazardous Waste Treatment Facilities Task Force, September 1985.

New York State, Hudson River Valley Commission. *The Hudson: Report of the Hudson River Valley Commission, 1966.* Iona Island, Bear Mountain, NY: Hudson River Valley Commission, 1966.

————. "Members of the Hudson River Valley Commission." *Hudson River Valley Commission Newsletter* (Tarrytown, NY) 1, no. 1 (1966):2.

————. *Annual Report.* Tarrytown, NY: Hudson River Valley Commission, 1968.

————. *Annual Report.* Tarrytown, NY: Hudson River Valley Commission, 1969.

New York State, Joint Legislative Committee on Metropolitan and Regional Areas Study. *Governing Urban Areas: Strengthening Local Governments through Regionalism.* Annual report of the committee. Albany: Joint Legislative Committee on Metropolitan and Regional Areas Study, 1968.

New York State, Legislative Commission on Energy Systems. *Legislating for Energy Independence.* Albany: Legislative Commission on Energy Systems, 1978.

New York State, Legislative Commission on Expenditure Review. *State Environmental Permits.* Program Audit. Albany: Legislative Commission on Expenditure Review, July 1977.

————. *Adirondack Park Planning and Regulation.* Program Audit. Albany: Legislative Commission on Expenditure Review, April 1978.

————. *Power Authority of the State of New York.* Program Audit. Albany: Legislative Commission on Expenditure Review, November 1984.

New York State, Moreland Act Commission on the Urban Development Commission and Other State Financing Agencies. *Restoring Credit and Confidence.* Albany: Moreland Act Commission on the Urban Development Commission and Other State Financing Agencies, March 31, 1976.

New York State, Office of the Comptroller. *Statewide Public Authorities: A Fourth Branch of Government?* New York State Comptroller's Studies on Issues in Public Finance. 2 vols. Albany: Office of the Comptroller, 1972.

————. *Program Review: State Energy Office. Executive Department. August 26, 1976-April 30, 1980.* Albany: Office of the Comptroller, 1980.

New York State, Office of Planning Coordination. *The Buffalo-Amherst Corridor.* Pamphlet. Albany: Office of Planning Coordination, 1969.

————. *New York State Development Plan-1.* Albany: Office of Planning Coordination, 1971.

New York State, Office of Planning Coordination; and the Urban Development Corporation. *New Communities for New York.* Albany: Office of Planning Coordination, 1970.

New York State, Public Service Commission. *Annual Report for 1972.* Albany: Public Service Commission, 1973.

————. *Annual Report for 1977.* Albany: Public Service Commission, 1978.

New York State, State Energy Office. *New York State Energy Master Plan.* Draft. Albany: State Energy Office, August 1979.

New York State, Temporary State Commission on the Environmental Impact of Major Public Utility Facilities. *Final Report.* Albany: Temporary State Commission on the Environmental Impact of Major Public Utility Facilities, 1971.

New York State, Temporary State Commission to Study the Catskills. *The Future of the Catskills: Final Report of the Temporary State Commission to Study the Catskills.* Albany: Temporary State Commission to Study the Catskills, 1975.

New York State, Temporary State Commission on Tug Hill. *Interim Report.* Watertown, NY: Temporary State Commission on Tug Hill, 1974.

————. *The Tug Hill Region: Preparing for the Future: Report of the Temporary State Commission on Tug Hill.* Watertown, NY: Temporary State Commission on Tug Hill, 1976.

New York State, Urban Development Corporation. *Annual Report for 1977.* Covers the period January 1, 1975 to December 31, 1977. New York: Urban Development Corporation, 1978.

————. *Annual Report for 1979.* New York: Urban Development Corporation, 1980.

New York State Environment. "NFS Announced Plans to Abandon in 1976—in Cattaraugus County—Only Commercial Nuclear Fuel Reprocessing Plant in USA." (December 1976):1, 4.

————. "High-Tech Hazardous Waste Treatment Facility Planned for Cayuga County." 10 (June 1981):2-4.

New York *Times*. Editorial, August 9, 1864, p. 4.
————. "To Save the Palisades." Editorial, November 25, 1894, p. 17.
————. "Kennedy Attacks State Power Plan." July 27, 1967, p. A14.
————. "Coliseum Complex Is Put Up for Sale." February 5, 1985, p. B3.
————. "State Power Agency Denied U.S. License for Upstate Project." July 14, 1985, p. A24.
————. "Planning Fought by Catskill Farmers." August 11, 1985, Section 1, p. 44.
————. "Death of a Highway." Editorial, September 27, 1985, p. A30.
————. "Rockefellers Expand Bid to Protect Hudson Valley's Essence." October 25, 1987, p. A35.
Noble, David. *America by Design.* New York: Alfred A. Knopf, 1977.
Noble, John, John Banta, and John Rosenberg. *Groping through the Maze.* Washington, DC: Conservation Foundation, 1977.

O'Brien, Raymond. *American Sublime: Landscape and Scenery of the Lower Hudson Valley.* New York: Columbia University Press, 1981.
O'Connor, James. *The Fiscal Crisis of the State.* New York: St. Martin's Press, 1973.
————. *Accumulation Crisis.* New York: Basil Blackwell, 1984.
Olwig, Kenneth. *Nature's Ideological Landscape.* London: George Allen & Unwin, 1984.
Olwig, Karen, and Kenneth Olwig. "Underdevelopment and the Development of 'Natural' Park Ideology." *Antipode* 11, no. 2 (1979):16-25.
Oreskes, Michael. "State Aid Urged in Cuomo Plan for Nine Mile 2." New York *Times*, May 8, 1984, p. B1.
Overton, James. "A Critical Examination of the Establishment of National Parks and Tourism in Underdeveloped Areas: Gros Morne National Park in Newfoundland." *Antipode* 11, no. 2 (1979):34-47.

Parsons, Howard. *Marx and Engels on Ecology.* Westport, CT: Greenwood Press, 1977.
Petrich, Carl. "Aesthetic Impact of a Proposed Power Plant on an Historic Wilderness Landscape." Paper presented at the National Conference on Applied Techniques for Analysis and Management of the Visual Resource, April 23-25, 1979, in Incline Village, NV. Reprinted in *Our National Landscape,* pp. 477-84. Berkeley, CA: Pacific Southwest Forest and Range Experiment Station, 1979.
Phillips, Carl. "The Effect on Employment in Schoharie County of the Projects of the State Power Authority of New York." Study done for Assemblyman Charles Cook (105th District, New York) by the class of Industrial and Labor Relations 368 conducted by Professor Clark Hamilton, School of Industrial and Labor Relations, Cornell University, 1977.
Platt, Rutherford. *Land Use Control: Interface of Law and Geography.* Resource Paper 75-1. Washington, DC: Association of American Geographers, 1976.
Plotkin, Sidney. *Keep Out: The Struggle for Land Use Control.* Berkeley and Los Angeles: University of California Press, 1986.
Popper, Frank. *The Politics of Land-Use Reform.* Madison: University of Wisconsin Press, 1981.

Port Authority of New York and New Jersey, Committee on the Future. *Regional Recovery—The Business of the Eighties.* New York: Port Authority of New York and New Jersey, 1979.

Poulantzas, Nicos. *Political Power and Social Classes.* London: New Left Books, 1973.

Power Authority of the State of New York. *Annual Report for 1937.* Albany: Power Authority of the State of New York, March 1938.

———. *Annual Report for 1953.* Albany: Power Authority of the State of New York, February 1954.

———. *Annual Report for 1962.* Albany: Power Authority of the State of New York, March 1963.

———. *Annual Report for 1978.* Albany: Power Authority of the State of New York, March 1979.

———. *Annual Report for 1981.* Albany: Power Authority of the State of New York, March 1982.

———. *Annual Report for 1984.* Albany: Power Authority of the State of New York, March 1985.

Power Authority of the State of New York et al. *Nuclear Power for the Empire State: A Position Paper in Support of Nuclear Power.* Prepared by the Power Authority and the state's major private utilities. New York: Power Authority of the State of New York, 1975.

Pratt, Mary. "Power Plant Decisions." *New York State Environmental News* (Atmospheric Sciences Research Center, State University of New York at Albany) 7, no. 7 (1980):4-5.

Pred, Allan. *City-Systems in Advanced Economies.* New York: John Wiley, 1977.

———. "Structuration and Place: On the Becoming of Sense of Place and Structure of Feeling." *Journal for the Theory of Social Behavior* 13 (1983):45-68.

President's Committee on Urban Housing. *A Decent Home.* Final Report of the President's Committee on Urban Housing. Washington, DC: Government Printing Office, 1968.

Preteceille, Edmond, and Jean-Pierre Terrail. *Capitalism, Consumption and Needs.* 1977. English ed., New York: Basil Blackwell, 1985.

Public Policy Institute of New York State. *Meeting the Challenges of Hazardous Waste in New York State.* Albany: Business Council of New York State, 1981.

Pushkarev, Boris, and Jeffrey Zupan. *Public Transportation and Land Use Policy.* Prepared for the Regional Plan Association of New York. Bloomington: Indiana University Press, 1977.

Quante, Wolfgang. *The Exodus of Corporate Headquarters from New York City.* New York: Praeger, 1976.

Ratner, Shanna, and Peter Ide. *Strategies for Community Economic Development through Natural Resource Use in Northern New York.* Economics Resource Paper 85-10. Ithaca, NY: Department of Agricultural Economics, Cornell University, 1985.

Raymond, Parish, Pine and Weiner Inc. *The Role of Local Government in New Community Development*. Prepared for the Office of Policy Research and Development, U.S. Department of Housing and Urban Development. Washington, DC: Department of Housing and Urban Development, 1978.

Real Estate Research Corporation. *The Costs of Sprawl*. Prepared for the Council on Environmental Quality, the Department of Housing and Urban Development, and the Environmental Protection Agency. 2 vols. Washington, DC: Government Printing Office, 1974.

Reed, John. *The Hudson River Valley*. New York: Clarkson N. Potter, 1960.

Regional Plan Association of New York. *A Closer Look at the Regional Plan of New York and Its Environs*. New York: Regional Plan Association of New York, 1929.

————. *Organized Support for Planning Develops throughout New York Region and Elsewhere*. Information Bulletin no. 9. New York: Regional Plan Association of New York, 1932.

————. *From Plan to Reality: Progress Report. Vol. 1*. New York: Regional Plan Association of New York, 1933. *Vol. 2*, 1938. *Vol. 3*, 1942.

————. *Metropolis 1985. Its Meaning to Business*. Report on the Arden House Conference, March 3, 1961, in Harriman, NY. Pamphlet. New York: Regional Plan Association of New York, 1961.

————. *Spread City*. Bulletin no. 100. New York: Regional Plan Association of New York, 1962.

————. *The Spreading Metropolis: A Burden to Business?* Report on the Arden House Conference, February 11-14, 1962, in Harriman, NY. Pamphlet. New York: Regional Plan Association of New York, 1962.

————. *Goals for the Region Project: Background Booklets nos. 1-5*. New York: Regional Plan Association of New York, 1963.

————. *The Lower Hudson*. Bulletin no. 104. New York: Regional Plan Association of New York, 1966.

————. *Progress Report on the Second Regional Plan*. New York: Regional Plan Association of New York, 1966.

————. *Carrying Forward the Second Regional Plan*. New York: Regional Plan Association of New York, 1967.

————. *The Region's Growth*. Bulletin no. 105. New York: Regional Plan Association of New York, 1967.

————. *The Second Regional Plan: A Draft for Discussion*. Bulletin no. 110. New York: Regional Plan Association of New York, 1968.

————. *Linking Skills, Jobs and Housing in the New York Urban Region*. New York: Regional Plan Association of New York, 1972.

————. *Implementing Regional Planning in the Tri-State New York Region: A Report to the Federal Regional Council and the Tri-State Regional Planning Commission*. New York: Regional Plan Association of New York, 1975.

————. *Financing Public Transportation*. *Regional Plan News*, no. 98 (1976).

————. *The Region's Money Flows. Vol. 1. The Government Accounts*. New York: Regional Plan Association of New York, 1977.

————. *The State of the Region, 1977*. *Regional Plan News*, no. 101 (1977).

————. "Catskill Resources Management Commission Being Debated by New York Legislature." *The Region's Agenda* 6 (June 1977):1-2.

————. *A Fiftieth Year Review.* Annual Report for 1978-79. *Regional Plan News,* no. 106 (1979).

————. *News Release No. 1356: Regional Plan Association Celebrates Fiftieth Anniversary.* New York: Regional Plan Association of New York, 1979.

————. *The Region's Money Flows. Vol. 2. Business Accounts.* New York: Regional Plan Association of New York, 1979.

————. *Regional Accounts: Structure and Performance of the New York Region's Economy in the Seventies.* Bloomington: Indiana University Press, 1980.

————. *Financing the Metropolitan Transportation Authority. The Region's Agenda* 10 (May 1981).

————. *Annual Report for 1981-1982. Regional Plan News,* no. 112 (1982).

————. *Annual Report for 1983-1984. Regional Plan News,* no. 118 (1984).

Reilly, William, ed. *The Use of Land: A Citizen's Policy Guide to Urban Growth.* Report by the Task Force on Land Use and Urban Growth, sponsored by the Rockefeller Brothers Fund. New York: Thomas Y. Crowell, 1973.

Reilly, William, and S. J. Schulman. "The Urban Development Corporation: New York's Innovation." *The Urban Lawyer* 1, no. 2 (1969):129-46.

Reps, John. "Requiem for Zoning." In *Taming Megalopolis,* edited by H. W. Eldredge, pp. 746-60. Garden City, NY: Anchor Books, 1967.

Richardson, Ralph, Jr., and Gilbert Tauber, eds. *The Hudson Basin: Environmental Problems and Institutional Response.* Report sponsored by the Rockefeller Foundation. 2 vols. New York: Academic Press, 1979.

Rimer, Sara. "In Dutchess, Fear of the Future." New York *Times,* October 17, 1986, pp. B1, 5.

————. "Long-Abused Hudson Thrives Again." New York *Times,* November 6, 1986, pp. B1, 9.

————. "Power Line for City Stirs Rural Anger." New York *Times,* December 30, 1986, pp. B1, 3.

Roberts, Sam. "Battle of Westway: Bitter 10-Year Saga of a Vision on Hold." New York *Times,* June 4, 1984, pp. B1, 4.

Rochlin, Gene, Marjorie Held, Barbara Kaplan, and Lewis Kruger. "West Valley: Remnant of the AEC." *Bulletin of the Atomic Scientists* 34, no. 1 (1978):17-26.

Rockefeller, Nelson. *Our Environment Can Be Saved.* Garden City, NY: Doubleday, 1970.

Rockefeller Brothers Fund. *The Challenge to America: Its Economic and Social Aspects.* Special Studies Project Report 4. America at Mid-century Series. Garden City, NY: Doubleday, 1958.

Rogers, David. *Can Business Management Save the Cities? The Case of New York.* New York: Free Press, 1978.

Rogers, William. *Rockefeller's Follies: An Unauthorized View of Nelson A. Rockefeller.* New York: Stein and Day, 1966.

Rondinelli, Dennis. "The Structure of Planning in the New York Metropolitan Region." Department of City and Regional Planning, Cornell University, Ithaca, NY, 1966. Mimeographed.

Ruchelman, Leonard. *The World Trade Center: Politics and Policies of Skyscraper Development.* Syracuse, NY: Syracuse University Press, 1977.

Samuels, Marwyn. "The Biography of Landscape." In *The Interpretation of Ordinary Landscapes*, edited by D. Meinig, pp. 51-88. New York: Oxford University Press, 1979.

Sandler, Ross. "Settlement on the Hudson." *The AMICUS Journal* 3 (Spring 1981): 42-45.

Saunders, Peter. *Social Theory and the Urban Question.* New York: Holmes & Meier, 1981.

———. "Why Study Central-Local Relations?" *Local Government Studies* 82 (March-April 1982):55-66.

Sax, Joseph. *Defending the Environment: A Strategy for Citizen Action.* New York: Alfred A. Knopf, 1971.

Sayer, Andrew. "Epistemology and Conceptions of People and Nature in Geography." *Geoforum* 10, no. 1 (1979):19-43.

Sayre, Wallace, and Herbert Kaufman. *Governing New York City.* New York: Russell Sage Foundation, 1960.

Scardino, Albert. "Big Battery Park City Dreams." New York *Times,* December 1, 1986, pp. D1, 10.

Scenic Hudson Preservation Conference. *Scenic Hudson News.* New York: Scenic Hudson Preservation Conference, 1974.

Schanberg, Sidney. "Rockefeller Shifts Stand on Control of Atomic Power." New York *Times,* May 5, 1968, pp. A1, 57.

———. "Westway's Sleaze Factor." New York *Times*, October 9, 1984, p. A33.

Schiesl, Martin. *The Politics of Efficiency: Municipal Administration and Reform in America 1800-1920.* Berkeley and Los Angeles: University of California Press, 1977.

Schmalz, Jeffrey. "New York City Reaches Agreement on Housing." New York *Times*, December 27, 1987, Section 1, p. 6.

Schmidt, Alfred. *The Concept of Nature in Marx.* London: New Left Books, 1971.

Schoharie County Cooperative Extension Service. *People and Power: An Impact Study of Power Projects in Schoharie County.* Cobleskill, NY: Schoharie County Cooperative Extension Service, 1972.

Scott, Allan, and Shoukry Roweis. "Urban Planning in Theory and Practice." Paper delivered at the Seventeenth European Conference of the Regional Planning Association, August 1977, in Krakow, Poland. Toronto: Department of Geography, University of Toronto, 1977.

Scott, Mel. *American City Planning since 1890.* Berkeley and Los Angeles: University of California Press, 1971.

Scott, Randall, ed. *Management and Control of Growth.* 3 vols. Washington, DC: Urban Land Institute, 1975.

Segal, Martin. *Wages in the Metropolis.* Cambridge, MA: Harvard University Press, 1960.

Semerad, Ralph. "Article XIV." In *The Future of the Adirondacks,* pp. 5-21. *Private and Public Land*, Technical Report 1B. Albany: Temporary Study Commission on the Future of the Adirondacks, 1970. Reissued in 2 vols., Blue Mountain Lake, NY: Adirondack Museum, 1971.

Shabecoff, Philip. "Ruling May Stall Efforts to Block Toxic Dumps." New York *Times,* November 6, 1985, p. A16.

Sherry, Andrew. "The Low-Profile N-Plant." Syracuse *Herald American*, July 28, 1985, pp. E1, 4.

Smith, Randall. "Rockefeller Center May Refinance or Sell a Part-Interest in the Original Buildings." *Wall Street Journal*, February 4, 1982, p. 44.

Spieler, Cliff. "A Philosophy of Power." *The Catskills* (Spring 1973):41-44.

Stalley, Marshall. "Environmental Planning and the Defunct Hudson River Valley Commission." *Landscape Architecture* 62 (July-August 1972):327-30, 348.

Stashenko, Joel. "Rocky's 'Edifice Complex.'" Syracuse *Herald American*, October 6, 1985, pp. B1, 2.

Sterngold, James. "New Rivals Aside, Wall St. Still Calls the Tune." New York *Times*, October 9, 1986, pp. D1, 8.

Strong, Ann. *Private Property and the Public Interest: The Brandywine Experience.* Baltimore: Johns Hopkins University Press, 1975.

Sussman, Carl, ed. *Planning the Fourth Migration: The Neglected Vision of the Regional Planning Association of America.* Cambridge, MA: MIT Press, 1976.

Tabb, William. "The New York City Fiscal Crisis." In *Marxism and the Metropolis*, edited by W. Tabb and L. Sawers, pp. 241-66. New York: Oxford University Press, 1978.

Talbot, Allan. *Power along the Hudson.* New York: E. P. Dutton, 1972.

Temporary Study Commission on the Future of the Adirondacks. *The Future of the Adirondack Park.* Albany: Temporary Study Commission on the Future of the Adirondacks, 1970. Reissued in 2 vols., Blue Mountain Lake, NY: Adirondack Museum, 1971.

————. "Private Land Inventory." In *The Future of the Adirondacks,* pp. 44-61. *Private and Public Land.* Technical Report 1A. Albany, 1970. Reissued in 2 vols. by Adirondack Museum, Blue Mountain Lake, NY, 1971.

Terrie, Philip. *Forever Wild: Environmental Aesthetics and the Adirondack Forest Preserve.* Philadelphia: Temple University Press, 1985.

Thompkins, Kenneth. "Radisson: Honoring the Plan." Syracuse *Post-Standard*, November 16, 1984, pp. A1, 2.

Thompson, Ben, Roger Thompson, and Conrad Wirth. *A Report on a Proposed Adirondack Mountains National Park.* Issued by Laurance Rockefeller. New York: Rockefeller Center, 1967.

Toll, Seymour. *Zoned America.* New York: Grossman, 1969.

Tuan, Yi-Fu. "Our Treatment of the Environment in Ideal and Actuality." *American Scientist* 58 (May-June 1970):244-49.

Tucker, William. "Environmentalism and the Leisure Class." *Harper's* 255 (December 1977):49-56, 73-80.

————. *Progress and Privilege: America in the Age of Environmentalism.* Garden City, NY: Anchor Press, 1982.

Tuemmler, Fred. "Zoning for the Planned Community." *Urban Land* 13, no. 4 (1954): 3-8.

Tug Hill Commission Newsletter (Watertown, NY). "Tug Hill Issues Multiply." (June 1987):1, 3-4.

Underwood, James, and William Daniels. *Governor Rockefeller in New York: The Apex of Pragmatic Liberalism in the United States.* Westport, CT: Greenwood Press, 1982.

U.S., Bureau of the Census. *1977 Census of Governments.* Governmental Organizations, vol. 1 of 7, no. 1. Washington, DC: Government Printing Office, 1978.

U.S., Congress, House. Committee on Merchant Marine and Fisheries. Subcommittee on Fisheries and Wildlife Conservation. *Hearings on: The Impact of the Hudson River Expressway Proposal on Fish and Wildlife Resources of the Hudson River and Atlantic Coastal Fisheries,* 91st Cong., 1st sess., June 24-25, 1969. Series no. 91-10. Washington, DC: Government Printing Office, 1969.

U.S., Congress, House. Congressional Information Service. *Analysis of the Philosophy and Public Record of Nelson A. Rockefeller, Nominee for Vice-President of the United States.* Prepared for Committee on the Judiciary. 93d Cong., 2d sess. Washington, DC: Government Printing Office, 1974.

U.S., Council on Environmental Quality. *Environmental Quality: The Tenth Annual Report of the Council on Environmental Quality: 1979.* Washington, DC: Government Printing Office, January 1980.

U.S., Department of the Interior, Bureau of Outdoor Recreation. *Focus on the Hudson.* Washington, DC: Government Printing Office, 1966.

Urban Land Institute. *New Approaches to Residential Land Development.* Technical Bulletin no. 10. Washington, DC: Urban Land Institute, 1961.

———. *Large-Scale Development: Benefits, Constraints, and State and Local Policy Incentives.* Washington, DC: Urban Land Institute, 1977.

Vance, James E., Jr. *This Scene of Man.* New York: Harper's College Press, 1977.

———. *Capturing the Horizon: The Historical Geography of Transportation.* New York: Harper & Row, 1986.

Van Valkenburgh, Norman. "The Creation of the Forest Preserve." *The Conservationist* 39 (May-June 1985):10-15.

Van Zandt, Roland. *The Catskill Mountain House.* New Brunswick, NJ: Rutgers University Press, 1966.

———. *Chronicles of the Hudson: Three Centuries of Travelers' Accounts.* New Brunswick, NJ: Rutgers University Press, 1971.

Veblen, Thorstein. *The Theory of the Leisure Class: An Economic Study of Institutions.* New York: Charles Scribner's Sons, 1899.

Verner, William. "Wilderness and the Adirondacks—An Historical View." *The Living Wilderness* 33 (Winter 1969):27-46.

Vernon, Raymond. *Metropolis 1985.* Cambridge, MA: Harvard University Press, 1960.

Walker, Jack. "The Diffusion of Innovation among American States." *American Political Science Review* 63 (September 1969):880-99.

Walker, Richard. "The Transformation of Urban Structure in the 19th Century United States and the Beginnings of Suburbanization." In *Urbanization and Conflict in Market Societies,* edited by K. Cox, pp. 165-213. Chicago: Maaroufa Press, 1978.

———. "Editor's Introduction." *Antipode* (Special Issue on Natural Resources and the Environment) 11, no. 2 (1979):1-16.

———. "A Theory of Suburbanization: Capitalism and the Construction of Urban Space in the United States." In *Urbanization and Urban Planning in Capitalist Society*, edited by M. Dear and A. Scott, pp. 383-429. New York: Methuen, 1981.

Walker, Richard, and Douglas Greenberg. "Post-Industrialism and Political Reform in the City: A Critique." *Antipode* 14, no. 1 (1982):17-32.

Walker, Richard, and Michael Heiman. "Quiet Revolution for Whom?" *Annals of the Association of American Geographers* 71 (March 1981):67-83.

Walsh, Annmarie. *The Public's Business: The Politics and Practices of Government Corporations.* Cambridge, MA: MIT Press, 1978.

Walsh, Annmarie, and James Leigland. "The Only Planning Game in Town." *Empire State Report* 9 (May 1983):6-12.

———. "The Authorities: $24 Billion in Debt and Still Growing." *Empire State Report* 9 (July 1983):33-38.

Warren, Kenneth. *The American Steel Industry 1850-1970: A Geographic Interpretation.* Oxford, UK: Clarendon Press, 1973.

Weber, Max. "Class, Status, Party." In *From Max Weber: Essays in Sociology*, edited by H. H. Gerth and C. Wright Mills, pp. 180-95. New York: Oxford University Press, 1946.

———. *Economy and Society.* 3 vols. New York: Bedminster Press, 1968.

Weinstein, James. *The Corporate Ideal in the Liberal State: 1900-1918.* Boston: Beacon Press, 1968.

Weiss, Marc. "The Origins and Legacy of Urban Renewal." In *Urban and Regional Planning in an Age of Austerity*, edited by P. Clavel, J. Forester, and W. Goldsmith, pp. 53-80. New York: Pergamon Press, 1980.

White, Lucia, and Morton White. *The Intellectual versus the City.* Cambridge, MA: Harvard University Press, 1962.

White, Lynn, Jr. "The Historical Roots of Our Ecological Crisis." *Science* 155 (March 10, 1967):1203-7.

White, William Chapman. *Adirondack Country.* New York: Duell, Sloan and Pearce; Boston: Little, Brown, 1954.

Whyte, William H. *The Last Landscape.* Garden City, NY: Doubleday, 1968.

Wilkerson, Isabel. "Dean Witter Agrees to Lease 24 Floors of the Trade Center." New *York Times*, July 9, 1985, pp. B1, 4.

Williams, Raymond. *The Country and the City.* New York: Oxford University Press, 1973.

Wilson, William. "Moles and Skylarks." In *Introduction to Planning History in the United States*, edited by D. Krueckeberg, pp. 88-121. New Brunswick, NJ: Center for Urban Policy Research, Rutgers University, 1983.

Winerip, Michael. "One Man's Efforts Conserve Catskills Valley." New York *Times,* February 19, 1984, pp. A1, 2.

———. "Cheap Land in Catskills Not Always a Bargain." New York *Times,* September 7, 1984, pp. A1, B4.

Wood, Robert. *1400 Governments: The Political Economy of the New York Metropolitan Region.* Cambridge, MA: Harvard University Press, 1961.

Woodside, William. "Why Westway Is Right." New York *Times*, August 1, 1983, p. A15.

World (Journal of Peat, Marwick, Mitchell and Co.). "The City that Came Back." No. 4 (1981):18-22.

Worthley, John, and Richard Torkelson. "Intergovernmental and Public-Private Relations in Hazardous Waste Management: The New York Example." In *The Politics of Hazardous Waste Management*, edited by J. Lester and A. Bowman, pp. 102-11. Durham, NC: Duke University Press, 1983.

Wrigley, Robert L., Jr. "The Plan of Chicago." In *Introduction to Planning History in the United States*, edited by D. Krueckeberg, pp. 58-72. New Brunswick, NJ: Center for Urban Policy Research, Rutgers University, 1983.

Zeitlin, Maurice. "Corporate Ownership and Control: The Large Corporations and the Capitalist Class." *American Journal of Sociology* 79 (March 1974):1073-1119.

Zinser, Charles. *The Economic Impact of the Adirondack Park Private Land Use and Development Plan.* Albany: State University of New York Press, 1980.

Index

Labor (*continued*)
  representation on RPA, 47, 72
  residence of, 33, 41, 47, 49, 57–59, 66, 266, 267 (*see also* Housing)
  transportation for, 41, 55, 56, 67, 90n65, 107, 109
  See also Social movements
Lake George, NY, 194, 210
Lake Placid, NY, 194, 195
Lake Placid Club, 195
Lake Tahoe Basin:
  land use regulation in, 201, 205, 206, 207, 234n77
Land:
  condemnation of, 148, 151, 165 (*see also* Eminent domain, power of)
  development, 32, 201; and capital accumulation, 7, 60, 119; and social relations, 12; and state intervention, 187 (*see also* Property development)
  supply for industry, 32
  value of, 27n16, 31, 58
  See also Land use planning/reform/regulation
Landscape:
  influence of capitalism on perception of, 189–90
  planning and reconstruction of the urban, 36, 41, 48, 50, 61, 108
  use and exchange values in, 11, 33, 111, 188, 255
  See also Consumption; Nature; Preservation; Production
Land use planning:
  and capital accumulation, 20, 31, 118–19
  county, 62–63
  local and urban, 31, 38–39, 109; and RPA support, 45, 62–63
  regional: in Chicago, 35–36; in New York metropolitan area, 20, 35, 39–42, 44–45, 70, 72–73, 81 (*see also* DLMA; MHP, RPA); in New York State, 18, 35, 63; and the public interest, 20, 49, 191, 206; purpose of, 39–46, 67, 98, 110, 119, 206, 248; support for, 19, 34–36, 46–48, 62, 67, 82, 84n9, 86n19, 98, 107, 108, 111, 153, 206; *see also* Municipal reform movement; Planning reform, regional
  and the State, 6, 31, 248
  state-level, 63, 205
  and transportation policy, 59–60, 74–77, 89n64, 90n65
  See also Adirondack Park, Land Use and Development Plan; Business-sponsored planning organizations; HRVC; Land use regulation; Planning reform;

Temporary State Commission to Study the Catskills; Temporary State Commission on Tug Hill
Land use reform:
  balancing production and consumption, 17, 30, 170, 187–88, 252–53, 263, 260
  liberal, 3–4, 25n5, 31–32, 41, 265, 267
  literature, 1–2, 3, 24n3, 24n4, 265
  in states other than New York, 16–17, 209
  progressive, 267–69 (*see also* Democratic processes)
  support for, 3–4, 19, 41, 98, 125, 266
  See also Land use planning; Planning reform
Land use regulation:
  accommodating large-scale projects, 9, 19, 21, 31, 125, 166
  and capital accumulation, 3–4, 8, 9, 12, 14, 15, 30, 110–11, 256, 266
  centralization of, 2, 3, 4, 14–15, 18, 30, 31, 110–11, 264, 265–66, 267, 269
  enabling legislation, 1, 25n7, 62, 63, 119, 125
  local and suburban, 1, 8–9, 21, 30, 55, 69–70, 94n116, 125–26, 128, 168, 266
  in the New York metropolitan area, 37–39, 45, 62
  in New York State, 17–19, 119, 256, 265 (*see also specific regulated regions*)
  and planning, 37, 39, 62
  state-level, 4, 16–18, 22, 265; federal preemption of, 28n28, 166, 170
  state preemption of local, 1, 143, 166–67, 169–71, 187, 209, 211, 223–24, 264; analysis of, 2, 15, 22; by public authorities, 21, 107, 126, 148–49; 152, 161, 163 (*see also specific authorities*); support for, 31, 58, 82, 218, 226
  See also Land use planning; Land use reform; *specific regulations*
Lawrence, Richard, Jr., 203, 204
Lease-purchase agreements, 139
Lefebvre, Henri, 194–95
Legislation. *See* Environmental quality review legislation; Facility Siting Legislation; Land use regulation, enabling legislation; New York State
Lehman, Herbert, 92n90, 155, 180n96
Leisure class, 118, 253–54 (*see also* Class; Lefebvre, Henri; Social movements; Structuration; Veblen, Thorstein)
Leisure space. *See* Consumption, space; Recreation space
Lewis, Harold M., 63